TROPICAL COWB(

"Vue d'un quartier de Kinshasa," by Lama, 1993. Author's collection.

TROPICAL COWBOYS

Westerns, Violence, and Masculinity in Kinshasa

Ch. Didier Gondola

To Ron

Thank you for coming to my talk

Best wishes

Didier Gondola

2/18/2017

Indiana University Press

Bloomington and Indianapolis

This book is a publication of

Indiana University Press
Office of Scholarly Publishing
Herman B Wells Library 350
1320 East 10th Street
Bloomington, Indiana 47405 USA

iupress.indiana.edu

Manufactured in the United States of America

Library of Congress Cataloging-in-Publication Data

Names: Gondola, Ch. Didier, 1966- author.
Title: Tropical cowboys : Westerns, violence, and masculinity in Kinshasa / Ch. Didier Gondola.
Other titles: African expressive cultures.
Description: Bloomington : Indiana University Press, 2016. | Series: African expressive cultures | Includes bibliographical references and index.
Identifiers: LCCN 2015043496 | ISBN 9780253020666 (cloth : alk. paper) | ISBN 9780253020772 (pbk. : alk. paper) | ISBN 9780253020802 (ebook)
Subjects: LCSH: Gangs—Congo (Democratic Republic)—Kinshasa. | Young men—Congo (Democratic Republic)—Kinshasa—Social conditions—19th century. | Masculinity—Social aspects—Congo (Democratic Republic)—Kinshasa. | Youth and violence—Social aspects—Congo (Democratic Republic)—Kinshasa. | Kinshasa (Congo)—Social conditions—19th century.
Classification: LCC HV6439.C752 G66 2016 | DDC 302.3409675112—dc23
LC record available at http://lccn.loc.gov/2015043496

1 2 3 4 5 21 20 19 18 17 16

To my son Noah (aka 高诺亚), a Bill in his own right

Contents

Acknowledgments   *xi*

Introduction   *1*

Part I. Falling Men

1   "Big Men"   *17*

2   A Colonial Cronos   *31*

3   Missionary Interventions   *47*

Part II. Man Up!

4   Tropical Cowboys   *71*

5   Performing Masculinities   *94*

6   Protectors and Predators   *116*

Part III. Metamorphoses

7   Père Buffalo   *149*

8   Avatars   *179*

Glossary   *203*

Notes   *205*

Bibliography   *233*

Index   *245*

Acknowledgments

L<small>ONG IN COMING</small> and the fruit of toils and many a sleepless night, this book would have never seen the light of day had it not been for a number of persons and institutions that I would like to acknowledge and thank. When it was still in gestation, this research project benefited from two generous grants, a New Frontiers in the Arts and Humanities grant from the Indiana University Office of the Vice President for Research and a U.S. State Department Fulbright Fellowship that allowed me to spend time in the archives in Brussels and conduct fieldwork in Kinshasa in 2008–2009. Dean William Blomquist's generous leave package helped me afford spending two academic years in Kinshasa and Nantes, respectively, and maintaining a home in Indianapolis.

I am grateful to Charles Ambler, Phyllis Martin, and Carolyn Brown for reading the earliest draft chapter and providing insightful feedback and encouragement when a book manuscript on the "Tropical Cowboys" was still a long, long shot. A number of colleagues and former colleagues at IUPUI, including Annie Coleman, now a faculty at Notre Dame, Danna Kostroun, Nancy Robertson, Marianne Wokeck, Robert Rebein, and William Jackson, read portions of this manuscript at various stages in its development. Their thoughtful criticism and valuable comments were most helpful.

The bulk of the book manuscript took shape in 2011–2012 at the Institut des Études Avancées in Nantes, France, where I resided as a Eurias fellow. The idyllic location of the IEA Nantes, nestled within the confluence of the Erdre and the Loire rivers, where writing could flow uninterrupted, and the welcoming and stimulating intellectual company it keeps gave the manuscript its cohesion. I thank the entire 2011–2012 cohort of fellows and the IEA staff for making my stay in Nantes both pleasurable and productive.

In addition to the IEA Nantes, I had the privilege to present my research on the Tropical Cowboys at other venues in Europe and North America. I am indebted to Véronique Giroud, Karin Barber, Susanne Gehrmann, Dominic Thomas, Michael Barrett, Amandine Lauro, John Clark, and John Cinnamon for inviting me to share my project with their faculty and students.

I owe no small debt of gratitude to Susann Baller, Dianne Stewart, Maria Eriksson-Baaz, Heike Raphael-Hernandez, Sarah Demart, Kristien Geenen, Charles Tshimanga, and Filip De Boeck without whose friendship and encouragement this project would still be on the drawing board. While writing this book, I faced several informational and conceptual hurdles that threatened to impede its progress. A number of scholars that I solicited, including Guido Convents, Wyatt MacGaffey, Jan Vansina, Enika Ngongo, and Fu-Kiau Busenki, helped me sail through them. I would be remiss not to thank Katrien Pype, Beverly Stoeltje, Peter Bloom, Stephan Miescher, and Jennifer Cole, whose keen eye and theoretical command sharpened the dull edges of some of my narratives. Needless to say, I bear full responsibility for whatever flaws and failings that remain in this book.

Many of the materials used in this book were located with the help of a number of librarians and archivists. Constance Cournède, a gem for IEA fellows, left no stone unturned in her search for materials I ordered through the IEA interlibrary loan network. I also would like to thank the staff of the African Archives and the Bibliothèque Ministérielle in Brussels for their assistance and diligence.

The late Père Buffalo (aka Jeff de Laet) and many other informants (some of whom have since also passed) have shared a wealth of oral and written materials with me. I am grateful for their generosity and hope this book did not betray their expectations. Friends and relatives who assisted me with this research, each in his or her own way, are too numerous to list. My dear friend Raymond Mututala went above and beyond in helping me during my fieldwork in Kinshasa. I also thank Timothy Gondola, Nina Gondola, Alain Ngulungu, Placide Gondola, and José Lusende for their moral support.

Special thanks are due to Victoria Scott, whose corrections and queries have improved the text significantly, and to my editor, Dee Mortensen, and her assistant, Sarah Jacobi. Dee is everything an author would want in an editor. Her meticulous approach and soft touch have profoundly impacted my book in countless ways.

Last but not least, my son Noah (aka 高诺亚) gave me the strength and urgency to finish this book. One colleague at the IEA nicknamed Noah "atomic boy" for his fearless and explosive personality. A Bill in his own right, Noah kept me busy and relentlessly forced me back to toe the line when I tarried in a well-deserved respite. Colleagues and friends at the IEA often asked me how I got through this tedious project with my three-year-old son in tow. I never quite knew how to respond. At long last, I found the parade to this recurring question: "I can't imagine being productive without children. How do you manage to achieve anything without having to care for children?" became my favorite riposte. This book is dedicated to him.

TROPICAL COWBOYS

Introduction

WHEN VIEUX DEGAZIN welcomed me to his family compound at l'Avenue de la Victoire, in the Kauka township of Kinshasa, just a stone's throw away from the stadium where in 1974 Ali and Foreman faced off in the so-called rumble in the jungle, he tried to make sure that his children and grandchildren would not listen in on our conversation. But his small, dimly lit dispensary was too stuffy and lacked air conditioning so it was not sealed off completely from the outside. The small, dusty desk fan could barely circulate the stale and moist air that sent streaks of sweat running down my arms and spine. Besides, the sight of even a makeshift filming crew, a jeans-clad researcher flanked by a local assistant, was too exciting for the children. They could not be kept at bay. We talked for about an hour with the one window wide open to keep the warm air of the afternoon flowing into the room and invite natural light. The bespectacled seventy-two-year-old spoke in monotonous, at times muffled voice, using Lingala, Kinshasa's main vernacular, and only rarely, rather hesitantly, ventured into French.

It was hard to imagine that the old man sitting in front of me, a quiet and revered father and grandfather of many, had been in his youth a feared and fearless *Bill* (or *Yankee*) who wielded sway over Quartier Saint-Jean (today Lingwala), one of colonial Kinshasa's seediest townships. The interview confirmed the glimpses I had gleaned from other informants. In the heyday of Billism, Degazin was not just the sharpest barb on the hot wire of Kinshasa's gangland; he was an avuncular figure, a *sheriff*, who refrained from flexing his muscles by using his legendary *kamô* (magical protection)[1] to deter potential rivals. Many Bills went to him to seek powerful kamô to best their rivals in street fights. After he hung up his spurs, Degazin converted his kamô practice into a thriving traditional healing business in his private compound in Kauka. Patients who suffered from infertility, insomnia, chronic migraines, and mental illness, some of which were believed to be the result of nefarious spells, came in droves attracted by the hand-painted sign above the compound's tall steel gate that read "Établissement de soins de médecine traditionnelle de l'Union Nationale des Guérisseurs du Congo [Center for Traditional Medicine of the National Union of Congo's Traditional Healers]."

Before wrapping up the interview,[2] I asked Degazin to give me his take on how the Bill movement petered out in the early 1960s. His answer came as a surprise to me. The movement, he contended, never died out. "There are still some Bills around in Kinshasa, even today," he went on. "What do you mean?" I asked.

"Are you referring to people from your generation?" "Well no, the movement has continued with the *Shegue,* and other young people. The only difference is that we did not steal. We were not dealing in petty crime." He later added, to further drive his point home, that even the contemporary youth gangs, commonly called *Kuluna,* could be considered today's Bills. "Yes," he insisted, "the Kuluna are the Bills' heirs" (héritiers ya ba Bills).

After the interview concluded, I exited the small room and stepped into the compound to find a small crowd clearing out from beneath the window where the inquisitive assembly had gathered all along to eavesdrop on the conversation. A few children resumed their marble game in the dirt while older ones nonchalantly returned to their toils. Degazin's daughter, along with a couple of her relatives who had heard part of the interview, followed me to my car parked on the sidewalk. At the behest of her family, she begged me to make the videotape available to her family so that they could keep their father's memory alive. Then she asked pointedly whether Degazin had disclosed that his own son (her brother) was a notorious Kuluna gang leader in Kauka. "Did he mention that? Did he tell you that?" she probed insistently, betraying an uncanny mélange of scorn and pride. "Like father, like son," she bemoaned as we parted.

My recollection of this post-interview encounter with Degazin's daughter lay buried in my field notes until I discovered Richard White's (1981) article on postbellum American outlaw gangs. Drawing on Eric Hobsbawm's (1959) notion of the "social bandit," White discusses the ambiguity that surrounded social banditry on the American Middle Border. What I had first considered a mere coda, the tail end of an otherwise productive interview, gained a newfound importance when I read White's piece. The animated, albeit brief conversation with Degazin's daughter yielded more than I had initially realized. It turned out to be the key that put Degazin's impromptu confession in line with what would later become a major theme of my work.

This book focuses on youth, masculinity, and performative violence. In 1950s Kinshasa, Degazin was one among many young "tropical cowboys" who formed gangs of Bills (a moniker drawn from their eponymous hero, Buffalo Bill Cody), infused their quest for masculinity with deeds of derring-do and esoteric street slang, and relied on martial arts, *kintulu* (bodybuilding), as well as kamô to get the upper hand in fights over nicknames, turf, and girls. Therefore, this study addresses the manner in which a certain idea of the "West" engendered among Kinshasa's youth standards of masculinity and manhood that rested on the construction of a new vernacular of violence. The argument pays close attention not only to the ways in which state violence was meted out both as a form of social control and exclusion but also to the Bills' shifting sentiments about the role of urban violence as a catalyst of modernity and masculinity.[3] By locating masculinity at the center of the social and cultural changes that took place in colonial Kinshasa, this study takes a rather unorthodox view of popular cultures, exploring the grayish areas, those hard-to-reach places, the in-between zones where culture meets crime, dream meets drama, and resistance becomes a double-edge sword that liberates as much as it oppresses, where the freedom to perform one's body, the male body, comes at the expense of others' bodies, namely female bodies.

Emerging from this study is the Janus-facedness of Kinois youths, their proclivity to act as both "protectors" and "predators," to police the boundaries of gender within their townships and shield the hymen of "their" township girls while preying on out-of-township girls. As they challenged colonial strictures, dealing the last blow to Belgian colonial complacency, as discussed in chapter 7, they also drifted further away from both the trappings of modernity Belgian colonization had ushered in and the "traditional" ethos their elders sought to safeguard in the townships. In this regard, this study argues that the dereliction of large segments of youth in colonial Kinshasa gave way to a culture of liminality, whereby young people occupied and coped with the blind spots and interstices created by colonial neglect. They attempted to rearrange their urban space and channeled popular violence through its smallest corners and recesses in the performative process of *détournement,* a concept that harkens back to Henri Lefebvre and Guy Debord's avant-gardist Situationist International movement. The use of détournement here is perhaps not as Debord had intended it to be borrowed. For Debord, détournement is not meant to empower those who dare engage in it, nor is it merely subversive, aiming to destroy bourgeois order. Rather, it intends to obliterate the original and reduce it to oblivion through the rendering of a subliminal copy or parody of the original (Debord and Wolman 1956). Debord's teleological insistence that détournement, because it is a revolutionary act, must be premeditated, staged, and orchestrated overlooks a whole range of unintentional, spontaneous, almost unconscious détournement. I view détournement as one thread in a multilayered tapestry that crosses over genre, time, and space.

Degazin's claim that the Bills, through their long string of avatars, have continued to roam the streets of Kinshasa long after the original Bills had all but disappeared from the urban scene suggests at least three points. First, there exists a continuum in the ebb and flow of interstitial youth groups in Kinshasa since at least the late 1940s when the Bills and their immediate predecessors transformed Kinshasa into a tropical Far West. The Bills created a behavioral lexicon drawn from local lore and global flows—most notably from the Hollywood rendition of the American Far West—which they bequeathed to the interstitial youth groups that rode on their coattails. The rugged individualism and insouciance of the mythical cowboy, the larger-than-life celluloid characters that ran the entire gamut from the swashbuckler archetype to the imperturbable and laconic gunslinger, their walk, their ribald repartees, but also their silence and look, were as many scripts that Kinshasa's youth adopted in order to look the part and to be good at being men (Herzfeld 1985: 16). Second, the Bills did not just pave the way for Kinshasa's youths to act as "real men" and to perform a newfound, if complex, masculinity. Insofar as becoming a man in an oppressive colonial milieu remained a precarious proposition, fraught with painful setbacks and bereft of clear signposts, the road to manhood involved more than just testosterone-laden antics and bravado. Bills also supplied Kinshasa's youth culture with a legendary "art de la débrouille" (the art of making do) to cope with their position at the bottom rung of society. First honed within the oppressive urban milieu of colonial Kinshasa, survival strategies adopted by young people reached new heights of ingenuity and adaptiveness during the long reign of Mobutu, at a time when quotidian life in Congo (then Zaire) turned into a Sisyphean task (Biaya 2000; De Villers, Jewsiewicki, and Monnier 2002; Trefon 2004). Third, the Bills imparted their rebellious ethos to their heirs, including their latest avatar, the Kuluna, inspiring an age group that struggled to walk the line between compliance and defiance.

In February 2009, when my interview with Degazin took place, the "Phé-nomène Kuluna" had gained such momentum in Kinshasa that the government vowed to "eradicate" the "scourge" (*fléau*) of "urban banditry," as it called it.[4] Yet, at a time similar to what White (1981) describes in the postbellum American West when confusion reigned over who was on the side of the law, who was preserving order, and who was creating disorder, social bandits often endear themselves to the public while the powers-that-be are held in utter distrust and contempt. Finally, as White further notes, because social bandits are by definition Janus-faced agents, they owe their very existence to a support network that also involves people who may chafe under their wayward actions but who will nonetheless tolerate and even aid them because they too have some axes to grind against the authorities.

Infrapolitics

It is primarily within these seeming contrapuntal confluences and this maze of dissonant and tangled threads that this study is most concerned. When colonial officials, missionaries, and urban ethnographers first encountered interstitial youths in Kinshasa in the late 1940s, they readily applied to them several categories that befitted the mindset of the time. They framed their bodies and performances following a one-dimensional trope that later studies never quite jettisoned. Accordingly, young people appeared in colonial sources as a "social problem" and the most common and recurrent epithet that saddled them was "offender" (*délinquant*). Colonial reports and other studies from this period give some sense of the slant and vision that shaped colonial attitudes and policies vis-à-vis African youth. Hence one rarely sifts through these colonial sources

without inevitably encountering the cliché of "les problèmes de la jeunesse délinquante" (the problems of juvenile delinquency). Any study of male youths in
colonial Africa, I argue, must first and foremost restore the complexities of their
labile bodies and identities and explore their versatile performativity and agency.
Only then can we begin to understand the ways in which the drama of masculinity shaped the "colonial situation," as defined by such postcolonial scholars as
Samir Amin, Georges Balandier, Frantz Fanon, and Immanuel Wallerstein.

In 1989, when I came across Billism while a doctoral student in Paris, I may
have fallen into that colonial trap myself. Nowhere was this more clearly apparent
than in my neglect to pay closer attention to youth subcultures in my exploration
of Kinshasa and Brazzaville's cultural nexus (Gondola 1997a). Nor did I pause in
my analysis to recognize the extent to which a quest for masculinity[5] was at play
in the popular cultures that enabled young people in the streets of 1950s Kinshasa
to forge hybrid urban identities and to carve out spaces of infrapolitics, to borrow a notion that James C. Scott originally theorized in his evocation of peasant
resistance to quotidian oppression (Scott 1990). Scott's work gave rise to a crop
of social studies that laid new claims to Antonio Gramsci's notion of counterhegemony while putting issues of subalternity and agency front and center (Kelley
1994; Chin 1998).

Scott's theoretical breakthrough, premised on George Eliot's musing in her
social satire *Daniel Deronda* that "no action is really possible without a little acting" (Scott 1990: 1), compelled me to revisit the Bills. The result is a book that not
only lays to rest, once and for all, the hackneyed notion that young people act
under the influence of hormonal urges and that their behaviors have an inherent
proclivity for violence, but also explores the role of performativity in shaping
youth masculinity and identity. Along with the now-established idea that youth
violence remains by and large reactive, a response to its marginalization from
local and state power structures, violence as a performative, staged, and even
choreographed act which main function is to produce youth identity and a cultural configuration in which both modernity and masculinity figure prominently
is explored. By the same token, the argument is made that youth cultures are
not just youth cultures, confined to a peripatetic age group, ephemeral cultures
that recede and vanish as young people shed their precarious selves to become
men. Rather, young people create and perform scripts that outlive their time. In
Kinshasa, not only did the Bills' cult of the cowboy usher in new manly scripts
that later youth generations would recycle in a palimpsestic process, albeit with
only some partial erasures, but they also left behind a behavioral lexicon that
came to embody the spirit of Kinshasa (*kinicité*). They may have been attuned to
the global zeitgeist triggered by the Hollywood cowboy genre and they certainly
challenged colonial strictures in their steadfast resolve to thwart the colonial
project to emasculate the Congolese man, yet my study suggests that they left in

their trail cultural debris (Hunt 2008; Stoler 2013) that have become coterminous with kinicité, which is the essence of being *Kinois* (Kinshasan). Popular culture, I argue here (more emphatically than in my previous work), is a protean beast that can present variations in degrees of ambiguity that run the entire gamut from contestation to complicity and from containment to contingency. As shown elsewhere (Gondola 1999b), it can also be a site of hedonistic pursuit without losing its bite. Yet, no matter how it presents itself, it remains subversive at the core and has to be taken seriously.

Aufheben

Some of the questions this study endeavors to tease out deal with the ways in which the Bills left a permanent footprint on Kinshasa's urbanscape. What elements in the Bills' emblematic subculture ended up capturing the imagination of Kinois? How have Kinois, several generations removed from the Bills, come to identify themselves with these colonial *enfants terribles?* Bills, to be sure, brought several changes, not least of which were the tactics they developed to cope with the urban juggernaut, tactics that Kinois continue to use to this day. But, more to the point, to what extent does the versatile silhouette of the cowboy, which cast such a long shadow on the Bills' quest for manhood in the 1950s, continue to loom large in the way Kinois today, regardless of their walk of life and age, perform masculinity? One key that may help us address these questions lies with one man, the most Kinois of Kinois, General Donat Mahele, who lost his life on May 16, 1997, in a foolhardy attempt to disarm army mutineers when many of his fellow officers stayed put and waited for the volatile situation to abate. His showdown with Mobutu's diehard loyalists and untimely death would go down in local history as a folly. Yet many Kinois see it also as a gambit which, they claim, may have saved their city from a bloodbath (see chapter 8).

To understand why a Congolese army general would so brazenly risk his life rather than let the situation play itself out (which would have been a perfectly reasonable course of action at the time), a look at the Congolese army ethos is of little assistance. After all, Mobutu's ill-equipped, ill-disciplined, ill-fed, and ill-paid army often needed external help to defend its territory and win wars. It routinely flexed its muscles against unarmed civilians but recoiled before rebel militias and invading foreign troops. FAZ (Forces Armées Zaïroises) soldiers and their FARDC (Forces Armées de la République Démocratique du Congo) successors have even been known to wear civilian clothes under their uniforms so that when retreating they can quickly part with their weapons and uniform and melt into the civilian population as they did on November 19, 2012, when M23 rebels, backed by the Rwandan army, captured the city of Goma in eastern Congo.

What, then, does account for Mahele's remarkable journey and for the kind of pluck and mettle he displayed until his demise? Why was he so recklessly bold and daring? Like many Kinois who came of age in Kinshasa's townships in the 1950s and 1960s, Mahele had embraced the Bills' masculine ethos that diverted and reassembled a number of disparate elements, from American Far West lore (as projected through Hollywood lenses) to traditional Congolese badges of manliness. Mahele was a Bill through and through. He lived an ideal of *sans peur et sans reproche* (fearless and blameless) derived from the cult and culture of performative violence that stood as one version of hegemonic masculinity in colonial Kinshasa's townships.

Mahele's rise and fall followed a trajectory that mirrored the Parkour-like course that had become obligatory for many Bills in the 1950s. It exemplifies the central argument in this study that masculinity and the quest for manhood often operate, within the same group of youths, according to a pendulum process in which the construction of the body alternates with its annihilation. Indeed, the tension between preserving and abolishing youth, following Hegel's notion of *Aufheben* (sublation), was precisely the tipping point in the Bills' quest for manhood, the make-or-break moment in which manhood could be gained or lost, the vortex where one could forge a name for himself and be declared a Yankee (tough guy) or lose face and be downgraded to the unmanly status of *Yuma* (wimp, sissy, or half-wit).

Thus this book addresses the construction of masculinities through performative rituals (oftentimes involving violence) among Kinshasa's "tropical cowboys." Of particular interest is in teasing out the vexing issue of resistance through performativity and expressive culture, paying attention to how youths produce and enact their identity through discourse and mise-en-scène and looking specifically at the role sexual violence played in the construction of a masculine ethos in colonial Kinshasa, a form of violence with which African historians have yet to come to grips.

Masculinity, Manhood, and Manliness

Since this book makes copious use of the triptych masculinity, manhood, and manliness, as this introduction shows, it is worth noting here that each term refers to a discrete configuration of "being good at being a man." Masculinity is considered a construct intended to distance boys and men from femininity. In other words, it is relational (i.e., relevant only when defined vis-à-vis femininity). Yet, it is not examined through a "sex role" lens for reasons that scholars have abundantly discussed, namely because gender relations and roles are neither fixed nor entirely biological but socially and historically constructed. Manhood, on the other hand, should not be treated primarily as a gendered category. Rather, it should be viewed as a stage where boys become men and can finally perform with confidence manly roles ascribed to them by society. Boys find themselves on shaky ground once they reach the threshold where society expects them to jettison the last social, physiological, and psychological remnants of boyhood. Crossing this threshold is all the more precarious and perilous because manhood remains a moving target which, as Kimmel (1996: 5) notes, "means different things, at different times, to different people."

As they strive to become men, by repudiating female attributes and by shedding vestiges of boyhood, men adopt several manly scripts. Thus, manliness is the playbook of "high-scoring men," men who ooze confidence under duress and laugh in the face of danger. Yet, as Mansfield (2006: 17) observes in his exploration of manliness, within the same manly individual dwell conflicting impulses: the desire to maintain a high degree of independence, on one hand, and the ability and ambition to command, on the other. But here is the twist that complicates the attempt to deconstruct the triptych that started this discussion: to epitomize manliness, Mansfield starts his narrative by extolling not the manly virtues of John Wayne (who first appears only on page 17 of his book) but those of the "mightiest woman of our time," British prime minister Margaret Thatcher (2006: ix). The conclusion we are supposed to draw seems rather pedestrian: Because manliness is inherently performative and exhibits traits that are not unique to men, we need to acknowledge that women too have a stake in the game.

The exploration of this triptych led to a body of scholarship that provided the theoretical scaffolding for this work, starting with R. W. Connell's (1995) seminal scholarship on masculinities. Seldom has a study been more acutely relevant to parlaying the discussion of an old issue (in this case, masculinity) into a new field (i.e., men's studies). In fact, what we know about masculinity has progressed by leaps and bounds since Connell's *Masculinities,* whose major contribution was first to remind us how heterogeneous men are and how some of them tend to create a type of masculinity, which he labeled "hegemonic masculinity," or—in the discourse of sociologist Erwin Goffman—the "unblushing male." Though several masculinities can coexist, Connell explains that one particular heteronormative version, that is, "hegemonic masculinity," will hold sway and allow men who collectively claim it as their own to accumulate a "patriarchal dividend." For both Goffman and Connell any male who fails to make the cut is "likely to view himself—during moments at least—as unworthy, incomplete, and inferior" (quoted in Kimmel 1996: 5). In keeping with Gramsci's notion of hegemony, Connell sees little connection between hegemonic masculinity and violence. Although, hegemonic masculinity "could be supported by force; it meant ascendancy achieved through culture, institutions, and persuasion" (Connell and Messerschmidt 2005: 832).

Hegemonic Masculinities

Discussing masculinity no longer as a homogeneous category but in its plurality has enabled scholars to turn their attention to other types of masculinities and focus on homosociality rather than only on gender relations, as had been the case in the 1970s and 1980s. Sociologist Demetrakis Demetriou's work is especially useful in that it provides another way to look at hegemonic masculinity. Building on, yet complicating Connell's notion of heterogeneous or plural masculinities, Demetriou (2001: 345) rejects Connell's "elitist" and rigid model that in his eyes fails to account for the effect that subordinate and marginalized masculinities have had on the construction of hegemonic masculinity. Instead, combining Gramsci's idea of "historic bloc" with Homi Bhabha's notion of hybridity, Demetriou argues that hegemonic masculinity is constructed only through a transactional dialectic of appropriation and marginalization: "The masculinity that occupies the hegemonic position at a given historical moment is a hybrid bloc that incorporates diverse and apparently oppositional elements" (349).

The critique here rests on the assumption that historical configurations, such as social and political dynamics, can affect the way hegemonic masculinity deploys its arsenal of discursive practices. Hegemonic masculinity is seen as a useful theoretical scaffolding that enables scholars to explore, in their particular historical and relational settings, the ways in which masculinity constitutes an ongoing "makeshift process" (to borrow a term made popular by Ray Raphael 1988) in which performativity plays a critical role. There is no doubt that Connell's taxonomy shows some limitations within the African colonial context where gay men went largely unnoticed both individually and collectively,[6] where white males hardly constituted a homogenized group, and where entrenched forms of local hegemonic masculinities held sway in the interstices of colonial society.

Indeed, like Demetriou and other Connell critics (Cornwall and Lindisfarne 1994; Whitehead 2002; Hearn 2004; Howson 2006), this study takes issue with Connell's implied definition of power as hierarchical in favor of the Foucauldian model of power as circulatory, not hierarchical. Using the example of Kinshasa's gangs of Bills, I argue that the moment scholars attempt to naturalize hegemonic masculinity as a catchall category, it ceases to potentiate the rendering of power and gender inequalities in human societies. In other words, when hegemonic masculinity is treated as a commodity or is equated with successful masculinity while other categories (e.g., subordinated masculinity and complicit masculinity) fall under deficient masculinity, the concept indeed verges on obsolescence. Instead, we must recognize that in some settings multiple and competing hegemonic masculinities may coexist and tend to produce distinct subordinate variants.

Following this perspective, at least two types of hegemonic masculinities are at play in colonial Kinshasa, each one entangled in a maze of relationships that engendered multiple subordinate masculinities. Let us call the first one *European*, for lack of a better term, and its main subordinate variant *évolué*. The postwar period in the Belgian Congo was unique, in that it witnessed growing colonial anxieties over culture rather than over politics, as in other colonies. Having tightened its grip on the political and economic spheres, the Belgian colonial state projected a vision of imperial masculinity as a way to extend its hegemony to the soft spots of culture. The irony, as discussed in chapter 3, is that the task of making Africans into men by rescuing them from the clutches of savagery and granting them the rudiments of European civilization fell to a group of white men whom Africans regarded as effeminate, unmanly, and ungendered. Yankees had a name for them. They called them *mwasi-mandefu* (bearded women), an expression that highlighted their perceived androgynous gender identity. Under the tutelage of bearded, robe-wearing white missionaries, évolués embraced a kind of masculinity that Connell would probably deem "subordinate," a transient masculinity (as the name évolués itself implies) that led them to reject most local elements of masculinity for the idealized European male archetype.

The second hegemonic masculinity brand was embodied by the Yankees and would probably have qualified as subordinate as well had it not been for the density of the Yankees' discursive practices within the African townships. Insofar as access to the politicoeconomic capital of the colonial state was concerned (we may add here the obligatory Weberian state's monopoly on the use of legitimate violence), Yankees probably suffered the same emasculating fate as évolués. Yet when we reduce the scale and shift our focus from the state to the township, it becomes obvious that Yankees asserted their masculinity on their own terms. They became the "street elite," a term coined by sociologist Jack Katz that Eric Schneider (1999: 25) borrows to discuss how, in postwar New York, Puerto Rican youth gangs circumvented marginalization to construct their own version of (hegemonic) masculinity. The same reproduction of patriarchy, the same gender hierarchy, the same subordination of women and of substandard masculinities that define European hegemonic masculinity were exhibited by the Yankees as well. For Yankees, as discussed in chapter 5, the figure of the Yuma represented a "subordinate variant," the anti-Yankee par excellence. But évolués, too—who gravitated closer to the dominant (European) masculinity than any other Congolese group and who certainly assumed airs of superiority because they ranked higher than Yankees in the Belgian pecking order—lacked proper masculine pedigree as far as Yankees were concerned.[7]

African Embodied Masculinities

This contribution also builds on the recent scholarship on "African masculinities" to understand how youths have capitalized on becoming and being men within a colonial context where their maleness was constantly devalued and dehumanized.[8] They did this on their own terms, carving out their own spaces, establishing their own standards, and setting up their own stages where they could perform their scripts "outside the intimidating gaze of power" (Scott 1990: 18). Indeed, "gender performativity," or what Judith Butler, following such precursors as J. L. Austin and John Searle, has posited as "the power of discourse to enact what it names" (Butler 1993: 187), is always shaped by larger socioeconomic, religious, cultural, and political transformations (Lindsay and Miescher 2003). This is what Connell and Messerschmidt (2005) have theorized as "social embodiment" by emphasizing the body as "a participant in generating social practice" (2005: 51). Beyond the gladiator-esque jousting, packaged for popular consumption from sports to action-packed thriller movies, other less gory but equally manly examples—from tanning to tailgating grilling—also illustrate the role society has assigned to male bodies. Following their suggestion, masculinities are explored as embodied performances entangled in a maze of social contexts and as exhibiting bodies that are both objects of and agents engaged in social practice. Yet I also recognize that embodied masculinities remain fluid and versatile over time and space as they intersect with changing cultural and political dynamics. Finally, in analyzing gender performativity it is important to highlight individual agency, creativity, subjectivities, and experiences. The reason these aspects must be explored is that masculinity rarely manifests itself as homogeneous and uniform. Even within a close-knit homosocial group that constructs its masculinity largely in response to alterity, no two men are identical, nor do they represent and perform their masculine identities in the same manner.

Just as the emergence of women's studies did in the 1970s, focusing on men, albeit belatedly, triggered seismic changes in African studies. It has enabled Africanists working on the colonial period to disentangle male agency from the inchoate, generic, "gender-neutral" category of the "natives" or the "colonial subjects." In essence, men's studies, one of the newest additions to African studies, allows us to complicate our narratives and compels us to rethink some of our paradigms about agency and power, while adding theoretical layers to our broader understanding of how gender operates within African contexts. In this regard, this book has been thoroughly influenced by the literature in history, anthropology, and cultural studies that posit masculinities as a protean, plural, performative process that is as much a homosocial enactment as it is opposed to femininity. In turn, this book contributes to the growing literature in African studies (e.g., Morrell 2001; Waetjen 2004; Miescher 2005; Ouzgane and Morrell 2005; Uchendu 2008; Ivaska 2011) that engages with these different theoretical frameworks, looking at how "being good at being a man" in colonial Kinshasa can shed light on how African masculinities have developed not just as a site of resistance but also as a locus of urban modernity.

Drawing on cultural studies' notion that youth delinquency and social transgressions should be viewed as cultural practices through which youths display agency (Hall and Jefferson 1993; Bucholtz 2002), an attempt is made to show that Kinshasa's postwar masculinity was mediated through the interplay of two phenomena, the Bills' tropicalization of the "Wild West" (as seen through Hollywood's lenses) on one hand and their ritualization of colonial and post-colonial violence on the other. It is also argued that these street urchins appropriated the aesthetic of cowboy movies' violence to enact tactics against the colonial system, while creating the elements of a new masculinity that clashed with not only colonial but also "traditional" norms.

Although this book is first and foremost a study of youth and masculinities in colonial Kinshasa, it brings to bear other issues as well. Yet, it deals only obliquely with issues of viewership or with the dialogic relation between Holly-wood's romanticized "Wild West" and its détournement by Kinshasa's juveniles. It also makes only peripheral mention of the ways in which cowboy movies served as cultural reservoirs for these youths to tap into as they vied to create new sartorial and linguistic subcultures in their townships.

Book Overview

The narrative starts by following the threads of masculinities and violence back in time—to when Kinshasa displayed different geographic and social configurations—and draws some parallels with the changes that would occur later, during colonization. One of the goals of this work is to expose the multifarious veins that these youths tapped into to forge their masculine identities. One important vein, yet the hardest to discern and excavate, has to do with local sediments of masculinity that predated the colonial encounters and which no doubt informed the ways in which these young people performed their masculine selves, used violence, and interacted with women. Part 1 is organized around three chapters that set the background for the emergence of the Bills. The first chapter takes up the challenge of understanding how patterns of masculinities displayed by Congolese men in the late nineteenth century may have reemerged during the 1950s as the Bills took center stage in Kinshasa. In fact, evidence suggests that in precolonial Congo men asserted their masculinities through a web of discursive practices. The ability to display and deploy oratory skills in a cryptic and tangential way, using esoteric proverbs, conferred manly status. Socioeconomic mobility also figured prominently. Communities of men involved in trading, hunting, and fishing were considered manlier than their agricultural counterparts or those who were engaged in crafts, such as ivory carving or pottery making. Men also had a gendered exclusive access to mystical power (known as *nkisi*) that they used to enhance physical strength and to ward off or clash with rivals.

Chapter 2 looks at how Belgian colonization recycled Hegelian "Dark Continent" tropes about Africa and essentialized the Congolese man as a "big child" (*grand enfant*). Belgian colonial ideology tended to view the gap between colonizers and colonized through the prism of social and civilizational Darwinism. Congolese who aspired to ascend the colonial ladder were dubbed in colonial parlance évolués ("civilized" natives) and had to abide by numerous strictures (including vying for employment within the colonial economy, embracing the Catholic faith, offering proof of monogamy, being proficient in the French language, and following the European dress code and body and home hygiene). Yet these men served as mere cogs in the colonial economy. They continued to grovel at the bottom of a paternalistic pyramid both in the workplace and in the townships. A large section of youngsters in the townships rebelled against what they perceived as the emasculation of the Congolese man.

Chapter 3 is devoted to the group of Belgian colonists entrusted with the task of redeeming the natives. A particular area where Belgian Catholic missionaries proved extremely active, namely film, is examined. There were two broad categories of films: the missionaries' homemade educational films and imported films such as Charlie Chaplin silent shows, Tarzan movies, and Hollywood Westerns, which they introduced to the youth audience. These Westerns, full of cowboy heroes and Indian zeroes, too many and anonymous to be counted, captivated the imagination of township youths so much so that they became the mainstay in several makeshift, private theaters that sprouted across town. It was no accident that the missionaries favored the character of Buffalo Bill.[9] Having come of age in Belgium, where reenactments of Buffalo Bill Wild West shows were widely popular, the cassock-clad missionaries may have metonymically conflated the liminal figure of Buffalo Bill with that of their sovereign Leopold II, the Builder King. The two messianic figures of Buffalo Bill and Leopold thus came to embody the civilizational virtues of manliness, patriotism, and courage that extended civilization almost simultaneously in two imaginary places of obdurate savagery: America's Wild West frontier, on the one hand, and Africa's Heart of Darkness, on the other. Young African viewers were never duped by these missionary interventions. This chapter relies on the work of Guy Debord, especially his notion of détournement, as part and parcel of a larger set of discursive practices and performances (that included appropriation, rejection, and transgression), to discuss their viewing experiences.

The next three chapters, which form the core of my work in part 2, deal more precisely with the ways in which gangs of Bills in Kinshasa harnessed images from the Hollywood rendition of the American Far West to construct their own masculinities. Chapter 4 looks at the genealogy of youth interstitiality in Kinshasa from the 1920s, when Belgian Father Raphaël de la Kethulle made daily incursions into Kinshasa's townships to apprehend delinquent youth and hand them over to the police, to the late 1940s, when the city teetered on the precipice of a youth and masculinity crisis. And before exploring the Bills' genealogy in later chapters, chapter 4 also examines their eponymous hero, the "steel-thewed and iron-nerved" figure of Buffalo Bill, and how the young Bills came to identify with him.

Chapter 5 seeks to accomplish two intertwined goals. The first is to illuminate the context in which sexual predation ceased to be enacted as a discrete, idiosyncratic phenomenon—the sordid business of a handful of faux Bills—to become an integral and systemic part of Billism. (This context serves as a segue into chapter 6, which discusses sexual predation and the Bills' Janus-faced behavior as both protector and predator.) The second goal is to explicate how the quest for masculinity and manhood lay at the center of the rituals that Bills performed, rituals such as kamô, in which the body becomes a site of corporeal agency and identity.

The importance of the Bills cannot be overstated, for good reason. Not only did their culture of violence mobilize and channel "the social forces from the margin" by contributing to "the establishment of one of the most powerful forms of expression in Kinshasa's flamboyant popular culture" (De Boeck and Plissart 2005: 38), it also acted as a wedge that opened Kinshasa's townships to the possibility of insurrection, thus accelerating the decolonization process.

Part 3 is devoted to the end of the Bill movement, in the mid-1960s, following Mobutu's rise to power. As Mobutu's dystopian dictatorship deployed its tentacles to bring all cultural activities into the fold, many Grands Bills (older Bills) easily succumbed to the regime's hubris. In addition to this development, chapter 7 also examines the figure of Père Buffalo (aka Jozef de Laet), a maverick Belgian missionary who arrived in Kinshasa in 1957, when the Bill movement was in full swing. He befriended some of the Bills, learned their slang, mused about translating the Bible into the Bills' argot, and even smoked marijuana with them. As a result, Père Buffalo was able to bring many Bills to the Catholic fold.

The last and concluding chapter surveys the scene after the last tropical cowboy had sauntered off into the sun. It examines the Bills' avatars, the many interstitial youth groups that jockeyed for control of Kinshasa's townships from the 1960s onward, with emphasis on the Kuluna, which continues to wreak havoc in the streets of Kinshasa today. For the first time in this genealogy of youth gangs, young people are resorting to weaponized violence: the use of machetes and firearms in random and brutal attacks on residents even in their homes. This development is largely shaped by the current political environment, especially the war that has devastated Congo since 1996, a war some scholars have dubbed "Africa's first world war." It also speaks volumes about a "crisis of masculinity" that stands as one of the legacies of Belgian colonization in Congo.

PART I

FALLING MEN

1 "Big Men"

In every age, not just our own, manhood was something that had to be won.

Leonard Kriegel (cited by Gilmore 1990: 19)

The purpose of this chapter is to follow the threads of manhood and violence back in time—to when Kinshasa, and more generally the area around the lake-like expansion of the Congo River now known as Malebo Pool, displayed different geographic and social configurations—and to draw some parallels with the changes that would occur later, during colonization. The fact that manhood has been a constant quest in all human societies, if a difficult and precarious one, is something that is now well established. In all societies, boys are meant to become men, yet the meaning of becoming and being men varies considerably from one society to another. Thus, to borrow from Michael Kimmel (1996: 5), "manhood means different things at different times to different people." Even within the same society, the ways in which manhood and masculinity are constructed tend to vary as social, cultural, and economic changes unfold. Yet those differences and variations should not obfuscate the fact that some patterns remain the same.

In other words, it is quite conceivable that similar cultural notions may inform constructions of manhood over several generations. That is to say that young men may keep fragments from past experiences in each generation to reorder the puzzle that they have inherited from their immediate forebears. Indeed, using cipher, puzzle, and enigma as metaphors for unresolved gender identity (see Gilmore 1990: 5) is an astute way to capture its vexing and labile nature. It tells us something that we have known for some time: that we know little about how men and women form their gender identity, how they pick up pieces from a variety of sources so as to arrange and rearrange an unresolved puzzle. Before showing in coming chapters how young people in Kinshasa harnessed global images, most notably from Hollywood renditions of the American Far West, to construct both manhood and masculinity, here and in the next chapter, local sources, fragments, and experiences will be examined.

When the so-called Bills (named after Buffalo Bill, aka William Frederick Cody, the Bills' eponymous hero) or Yankees emerged in Kinshasa's townships in the late 1940s, various standards of masculinity competed for their attention. They did not have to look far, however, to figure out how manly society expected them to behave. Colonization in the Belgian Congo had morphed from a brutal venture based mostly on economic predation into a regimented and engineered process of social Darwinism. Like their fathers, most of whom were rural natives who had moved (or moved back) to Kinshasa following the end of the Great Depression and the beginning of World War II, the Bills chafed under a system in which manhood indeed had to be won. How daunting it must have been for these youths to become men in a colonial context and against a colonial ideology that essentialized Congolese man as a child or, worse, as the infamous Hegelian animal-man. Unless they accepted European tutelage, with all its paternalism and racism, African males could meet humiliating and emasculating treatment in the workplace and elsewhere in the colonial city. This may explain why Congolese youths eschewed the Belgian version of the Victorian male that missionaries, among others, tried to enforce in the townships and why some attributes of manhood that had been dominant in precolonial Malebo Pool beckoned so forcefully in the ways in which they constructed their manhood in 1950s Kinshasa.

Most works to date that explore precolonial societies in the Congo Basin rarely discuss manhood and masculinity as epistemological categories. Men loom so large and the focus on men is so sharp in these works that manhood and masculinity tend to disappear or, when they do appear, to seem like a collection of ungendered categories. Even later studies (Vansina 1973; Obenga 1976; Harms 1981) only make tangential references to these central issues and hardly concern themselves with the quintessential question of what it meant then to be a man. We know, for instance, that men monopolized social, political, and economic resources in precolonial Congo and that gravitation toward wealth and power (which were essentially one and the same) constituted the sure path from boyhood to manhood and drew a clear line between maleness and its gendered opposite. We also know that the ability to deploy and display oratory skills, using sometimes esoteric proverbs, qualified one for manhood. What these studies never discuss, however, is how much of this was constructed, negotiated, and privately and publicly performed; how the archetypal precolonial male at once revealed and obscured other forms of manliness; and, finally, how manhood perpetuated itself through rituals, enactment, and performances. It is, of course, beyond the scope of this work to redress this. Yet there exists a filiation between (1) manhood performances that can be surmised from works published on precolonial Congo and (2) patterns of manhood and masculinity that Kinshasa's youth exhibited in the late colonial period. This filiation, or line of descent, will become much clearer in later chapters.

The "Great Congo Commerce"

The area where Kinshasa sprawled in the 1930s was first settled by Tio (or Teke) traders, who had such a ruthless grip over regional trade that, according to French explorer Léon Guiral (1889: 254), their partners came to resent them as Congo ruffians (*écumeurs du Congo*). Sporadically, Bobangi traders and ivory carvers would also settle there. When Henry Morton Stanley arrived in February 1877, he did not fail to describe in his travelogues (1879: 327) the hustle and bustle of Nshasa[1] (Kinshasa), Nkounda, and Ntamo (Kintambo). Under Tio lords and big men, all three settlements witnessed the traffic of Zombo and Kongo traders, who came as far as the Loango coast to trade salt, cloth, secondhand European clothes, pottery, glassware, copper, guns, and gunpowder in exchange for ivory and slaves, which according to Jan Vansina (1990: 200) were not traded in Malebo Pool until the Portuguese appeared on the Kongo coast. Following Guiral's apt characterization, Vansina (1973: 248) has convincingly argued that the magnitude of the trade the Tio and their partners carried out in Malebo Pool warrants the term "Great Congo Commerce." Many fishing villages along the Congo River became trading centers, as people of the central Congo Basin sought to "benefit indirectly from international trade by using it to promote regional trade" (Harms 1981: 5).

Prior to the arrival of Stanley, a few important changes had occurred in Tio society which increasingly reinforced trade as the main activity in the area. For example, the Tio, like many other groups in Equatorial Africa, had abandoned the cultivation of maize for manioc, a New World plant that the Portuguese had introduced in the sixteenth century. According to Vansina, they also had foregone iron smelting, pottery making, and raffia-cloth weaving and depended mostly on imports from the coast (Vansina 1965: 81; see also Dupré 1982).

Kinshasa's central and convenient location had much to do with its importance as a nodal center of trade. This is where the powerful Congo River stretches into Malebo Pool—its last navigable expanse, which covers nearly 300 square miles, with 14-mile-long Mbamu Island in the middle—before rushing to the sea in a succession of thirty-two cataracts and several falls and rapids. From this point on, any travel to the coast had to be managed by human porters, both because animals in this tropical area were prone to trypanosomiasis and because transporting canoes overland, to bypass the cataracts, was a titanic task. The presence of this chokepoint forced traders coming from the upper Congo area to make a stop in Malebo Pool and trade. It also transformed the Pool into an important demographic hub that sustained at least 30,000 people on the south bank alone, according to Léon de Saint-Moulin's (1976: 464) estimate.[2] In addition to Tio permanent residents, the area saw temporary settlements of Bayanzi, Bobangi, Aban-Ho, and Bafourou, settlements that waxed and waned following periods of trading boom and bust.

It did not take long for Stanley to realize that if Leopold II of Belgium were to take control of the Congo Basin, the center of his colonial domain would have to be Malebo Pool (which Stanley originally named Stanley Pool, after himself). To make space for the new European settlement, the first colonial authority adopted a repressive policy that systematically drove the Tio residents out of their hubs in the Pool. In 1891, the Teke chief Ngaliema—whom Camille-Aimé Coquilhat (1888: 61) sardonically referred to as an "intruder" into a space that Europeans claimed the exclusive right to occupy—also had to make room for the newcomers and seek refuge across the Pool, in French-occupied Congo, after his village of Ntamo (or Kintamo/Kintambo) was ransacked and looted by colonial troops. A few years earlier, in 1888, the village of Lemba, which belonged to the Bahumbu, had been set on fire after its inhabitants refused to allow African laborers to cut down trees on their communal land for the construction of the new European post.

A similar fate met the village of Nshasa (or Kinshasa), which was perhaps the largest precolonial settlement on the south bank of the Pool (Gondola 1997a: 53). Its Bateke residents were forced to resettle farther upriver, near another Bateke village, Kingabwa, which in turn had to relocate toward Ndolo. By 1911, when the European settlement was permanently established where the village of Kinshasa had once stood, all the African villages either had been pushed farther up the Congo River or had moved across the Pool to the French-occupied Brazzaville area.

Lords and Big Men

The colonial onslaught upset a system that revolved around social endowment accumulated by lords and big men who held sway in the villages that dotted both banks of the Pool. There is no doubt that Ngaliema, who asserted his authority in Kintambo, acted as a power broker when Stanley set foot in the area. But he was by no means the only lord in this vast and coveted area, where the economic stakes were simply too high for a single man to cash in on the lucrative commercial flows that washed ashore of the Pool. In fact, Malebo Pool enjoyed a polycephalous political system, with several chiefs positioned at key economic nexuses, asserting their authority thanks to a combination of military might and mystical power. This was certainly the situation when the first European visitors arrived in the area.

Each village had its hereditary lord who acted on behalf of the community and represented its best interests in an environment rife with feuds and conflicts over land, trade, and prestige. The lord was assisted by several big men whom he might use as a collective body, a council, and a sounding board for important decision making affecting the village or simply as right-hand men and trusted advisers. These were usually kinsmen whom the lord would dispatch to other villages to negotiate deals and report back to him. When the matter required the presence of the lord himself, he was always accompanied by a retinue of big men.

At one such meeting, when Ngaliema paid a visit to Stanley to greet him on his second trip to the Pool, he was "accompanied by several chiefs of Ntamo; such as Makabi, Mubi, old Ngako, and four others" (Stanley 1885: 306). As in any feudal structure, in exchange for their services and loyalty, the lord provided protection to his chiefs and big men and administered justice in his entire realm. We should let Stanley describe a few of them:

> Old Ngako is garrulous and amusing, and requires but little prompting to spin out tales of adventure and war. The ancient fifer of Ngalyema [Ngaliema], who lives recluse-like in his lone hamlet halfway between Léopoldville and Kintamo, is a chatty, agreeable old man, and is by no means churlishly inclined. Makabi is a character also deserving closer study; he is an acute fellow, neat in person, fully possessed of the authority of a chief, and lord over a large number of pretty wives and bright-eyed children. Even Ngalyema himself at home is a better man than Ngalyema abroad; he has a miscellaneous treasure which he has no objection to show; he will tell you with equanimity of what will happen when he is dead; how he will be swathed in cottons and woollens and silks and satins, and, after many days of continued fusilading, will be buried in an honoured grave. (Stanley 1885: 391)

Stanley had initially misread the power dynamics in Malebo Pool after learning that Makoko, lord of Mbé, had ceded a huge territory to his French rival Savorgnan de Brazza. After inquiring of Gamankono, one of the rare big men who won his praise, Stanley was told by him:

> There is no great king anywhere. We are all kings—each a king over his own village and land. Makoko is chief of Mbé; I am chief of Malima; Ingya is chief of Mfwa; Ganchu is chief over his land. On the other side, Gambiele is chief of Kimpoko; Nchuvila is the great chief of Kinshassa. But no one has authority over another chief. Each of us owns his own lands. Makoko is an old chief; he is richer than any of us; he has more men and guns, but his country is Mbé. (Stanley 1885: 298)

Thus although Makoko seemed able to keep all the chiefs and big men in check on the north bank of Malebo Pool, in a huge area strongly secured by the central position of Mbe, the capital of his fiefdom, on the south bank of the Pool it was indeed Ngaliema who, according to Stanley, acted as "the umpire and referee in all disputes among minor chiefs between Kinsendé Ferry and Kintamo" (323). Stanley even called him "the supreme lord of Ntamo" (307).

Ngaliema's prestige rested on the wealth he had accumulated as a shrewd trader who used both flair and the threat of war to get what he wanted. Ngaliema and other Teke chiefs basked in such lucre, surfeited as they were with so much fine cloth and other imported goods, wrote W. Holman Bentley (1900, 2:19), that they could afford to keep their wives in laziness. From being a slave, Ngaliema had risen to considerable status and wealth. His compound in Kintambo was rumored to boast the largest collection of elephant tusks at the Pool, with some individual tusks weighing nearly 100 pounds, according to both Stanley and Coquilhat. He also had "piles of silk, velvet, rugs, bales of blanket cloth, glass ware, crockery, gunpowder, and stacks of brass rods, etc." (Stanley 1885: 311).

Lords and big men flaunted their wealth on certain occasions when a level of decorum and pomp was expected. Here is Stanley describing a precursor of the sartorial ostentation that was to become the hallmark of all youth movements on both sides of the Pool since at least the 1920s:[3]

> Ngalyema and his chiefs were dressed splendidly this day. It was probably a visit of state. Each chief was dressed with a flowing silk robe, under-vest of silk, cotton underclothes, with an outer dress of silk; yellow, blue and crimson seemed to be the favourite colours. Ngalyema's arms were almost completely covered with polished brass rings, over which were heavy brass wristlets and armlets. His ankles were adorned with red copper rings, which must have weighed 10 lbs. each. Makabi was similarly dressed, for he seemed to be a rival in dress and equipments. The other chiefs exhibited their individual tastes. (Stanley 1885: 364)

In a social environment where land ownership did not exist, men acquired status through personal qualities such as bravery, eloquence, and seniority, yet nothing could top the acquisition of goods, wives, and slaves. Lords and chiefs such as Makoko and Ngaliema distinguished themselves by the possession of staggering numbers of slaves and wives and the latest and fanciest wares from Europe that came from the coast during the dry season in the caravans of Kongo and Zombo traders. They lived in a cluster of houses that formed a courtyard built inside a palisade, so as to accommodate the wives, slaves, and clients who easily integrated into their extended families (Vansina 1973: 73).

Lords and big men also had exclusive access to stockpiles of imported guns and gunpowder that they used primarily as a deterrent to potential challengers, including Europeans. On his second journey to the Pool, in 1881, after four years of absence, Stanley had to curry favor with chiefs who were better armed than his party, rather than live up to his infamous nickname of Bula Matari (Breaker of Rocks):

> Ngalyema has about 150 guns; all the rest put together have perhaps 300 more. Makoko of Lema has almost as many as Kintamo; Kimbangu and Mikunga have about 200 each; while Kinshassa and Kindolo cannot muster 300 guns. You see that Ngalyema, when going to war, can bring over a thousand guns easily. It is this that has made Ngalyema's head big. . . . We know we cannot

fight him that way, but we have our own way of fighting, which is just as good. (Stanley 1885: 349–50)

Added together, the Bateke could muster firepower from at least 1,000 guns (Coquilhat 1888: 59)—more than enough to deal a blow to European early encroachment, had they offered a united front against the invaders. In addition, imported European firepower allowed the lords to carve out, each within his domain, a "monopoly of legitimate use of physical force" in order to enforce justice and rein in centrifugal tendencies. Yet the legitimate basis of their authority had more to do with their ability to harness mystical power than with the possession of material wealth, the display of military might, or the control of an extended kinship. To protect their respective domains and their power, lords and big men relied on the *nkira* spirit of the domain, whose objects, jealously consigned to a small crate (*nkobi*), were kept in a little house at the entrance of their compound (Vansina 1973: 315). One Teke scholar describes the nkira as pervading Teke's spiritual life as an invisible and invincible force to which influence people attribute all life events, good and bad, as well as all retributions (Ebiatsa 2010: 24).

Other nkisi (power objects) were placed inside men's personal huts, with the chiefs boasting the largest collections. Guiral (1889: 178) even described men's huts as the main depository of fetishes, "lion teeth, that protect from wild beasts; punctured grains that could ward off illnesses. [Teke] remove the teeth, claws and skin of dead animals and the person who wears them has nothing to fear from living animals of the same species." British anthropologist Robert Hottot, who visited the Teke country on two occasions in 1906, noted the absence of these powerful "fetishes" in the women's huts, where each woman lived with her children apart from her husband. Hottot also mentioned the use of "magical substances" that called for ingredients that were also widely used by Kinshasa's Bills half a century later, including "various parts of a snake" and "certain parts of certain other personal totem animals." For medicine intended to provide a speedy and robust recovery, Teke healers would use leopards' and other felines' claws, whiskers, and liver, combined with parts of birds and antelopes, "on account of their speed" (Hottot and Willett 1956: 30).

Clash of the Lords

As African chiefs jockeyed for increased access to resources, networks, clients, and commodities, conflicts were bound to arise. When they did, these chiefs relied not only on traditional sources of power but also on weapons brought to the area, starting in the heyday of the slave trade. Stanley, who was thoroughly invested in local politics, never failed to recount in his travelogues rivalries that he sometimes fueled in order to plant a wedge between different villages and pave the way for colonial takeover. Some of the conflicts erupted after men had drunk their fill of palm wine and other hard liquors[4] and become unhinged and can-tankerous. One such incident, which Stanley recounts at length, resulted in the death of one of Ngaliema's brothers at the hands of a man from Kinshasa, which was then headed by Chief Nchuvila. Several months later, at another gathering where a fair share of palm wine and banana beer had been consumed, another of Ngaliema's brothers avenged the death of their brother by shooting a Kinshasa man after a verbal altercation. Stanley describes the showdown that ensued:

> The murderer, though once a slave, being a person of importance, could not be captured, and a war was declared by Nchuvila against him. Ngalyema and his brother defended themselves for some time with varying success, but in one of the many fights that took place the brother was killed. The survivor, Ngalyema, took to flight that night, and escaped to Mfwa. There he resided for some time in peace, but trade was not so good at Mfwa as at Kinshassa, and much jealousy was caused by his presence; whereupon, to avoid further complica-tions, he fled to Ngako, a brother (by a different mother) of Nchuvila, chief of Kinshassa. Ngako's village of Kintamo was then an unimportant place, the ground of which had been obtained from the Wambundu. Ngalyema was then known as Itsi. Before however he could avail himself of Ngako's village as a place of residence, he had to acknowledge the territorial rights of the Wam-bundu, the chiefs of whom, Makoko, Ngamberengi, and Kimpalampala pro-ceeded to Kintamo to demand his authority for residing there. Ngalyema then related a most pitiful story of wars and troubles, and begged them to grant a place to build a village in Issi, the Wambundu country, debasing himself, as is the Mbama custom when pleading, by rubbing his face in the dust. He said that he only needed a small place to be safe from Nchuvila, who sought to kill him. He made each of the chiefs a present of a small tusk of ivory, and the permission was granted.
> "Since which time," said Ngamberengi, "he has grown great by trade. He is now a rich man." He married a daughter of Makoko of Lema, and another daughter of the chief of Kimbangu (about five miles above Kinshassa), and by his alliances he has put a ring round Kinshassa, so that old Nchuvila has been obliged to make peace with him. Ngako, who ought to succeed Nchu-vila as king of Kinshassa when the latter dies, is now old and foolish; and Itsi [Ngalyema], taking the power into his own hand, is the great chief of Kintamo. Several other Bateke chiefs have joined him, such as Makabi and Mubi. There are altogether nine chiefs at Kintamo, who have made it a much larger place than Kinshassa. (Stanley 1885: 349–50)

This seemingly rocambolesque tale of feud, murder, and revenge in the tropics is actually a factual account of the meteoric rise of Ngaliema from humble, even ser-vile beginnings to the status of chief and consummate power-broker in the Pool. At the same time, Stanley's story could hardly bear a more striking resemblance not only to the violence that Bills would perform seventy years later in Kinshasa but also to dime-novel and celluloid depictions of the American Far West.

Ngaliema's story, of course, serves as a meditation on manhood, for the rise from slavery to freedom can also be construed as successfully accessing manhood in a society where slaves, by virtue of their alien origin, "did not grow up in the interstices of the social and economic networks which situate a man with respect to others" (Émile Benveniste, quoted in Meillassoux 1992: 23). As in many societies, slaves in the Congo Basin, because of how they were acquired, were perceived as lacking some of the attributes of manhood that free men possessed. War certainly produced the bulk of the slaves, since war captives could be easily sold and enslaved. And being captured at war meant not only bad luck but a dearth of the masculine qualities needed to remain free. Commoners convicted of adultery, and who lacked the wherewithal to pay the required fee, also ended up being enslaved.[5] Others fell prey to small gangs of raiders who roamed the land and tricked their victims. One such tactic involved small-scale bands of raiders disguised as traders. They would target particular villages and pretend to be looking for items to buy. Then they would provoke a quarrel, capture as many people as they could during the melee that ensued, and abscond with their spoils (Harms 1981: 36). Other traders arrived in canoes laden with European goods, lured children into their canoes while adults were absent or busy, and then made off as fast as they could. It was also very common for two or three men, or sometimes just a single man, to lurk in hidden places and ambush isolated villagers—a woman returning to her community after toiling in the fields, a child coming back from an errand to a nearby village, or a man going about his business outside his village.

Because children and women made up the largest contingent of slaves traded in the Congo Basin, an enslaved man found himself in the company of people whom many communities had defined as weak and vulnerable, needing men to provide for them, and unable to defend themselves. In some instances, as an example from Robert Harms's remarkable study suggests, the term "slave" could be saddled with the most undesirable of connotations: among the Tio, he writes, the term *moboma,* originally used to designate slaves (because so many Boma people were sold to the Tio), came to mean a "stupid person" (Harms 1981: 32).

Ngaliema had gained power through courage and ruse; he had weathered adversity and knew, when in a position of weakness and when it mattered the most, how to cajole more powerful big men in order to obtain their protection. As a result, he became a big man himself in a society that rewarded courage and craftiness. After carving out an enviable position as chief of Kintambo, Ngaliema understood that constant fighting could be detrimental to trade and sought to diminish the level of violence among the rival villages in the Pool. Gun battles, or what Stanley would call "musket shots" (Stanley 1885: 375), somehow abated, though rivalry between the villages of Kinshasa and Kintambo continued to poison relations between the two groups.

The reasons for conflict in the Pool were no different from those that have been observed wherever a lack of central power has led people to create segmentary societies. Headmen fought over turf, territory, markets, resources, slaves, and women (the latter being, when the situation dictated it, likened to resources). Accusations of witchcraft provoked feuds that would sometimes drive a permanent wedge between two villages or kinships over several generations, preventing intermarriage, trade, and dealings of any sort between the two rival communities.[6] Such feuds would almost always escalate into killings, retaliation, lingering animosities, and, worst of all, all-out war. Yet it would be a gross mistake to view precolonial Pool as a lawless frontier, replete with ruffians and drenched in violence, for the display of magical paraphernalia and the likelihood that one would summon mystical forces to ward off one's potential enemies and increase one's power were enough to avert many a conflict that threatened to spiral into feuding.

In addition to internecine feuds, people in Kinshasa had to contend with the encroachment of their northern trading partners, the Bobangi. Initially, as trade picked up, Tio restricted access to the Pool. Bobangi traders coming from the upper Congo area, especially in and around their main hub of Bolobo, had to stop at Mbe, the capital of the Tio kingdom. From there, commodities intended for the coast would be hauled in overland caravans to their destination (Harms 1981: 127). Bobangi traders fought several battles throughout the first half of the nineteenth century to gain a foothold in the Pool. Despite swelling the numbers of their forces through alliances with non-Bobangi villages, however, all they gained was control of the narrows at Tchumbiri, a good 200 kilometers shy of the Pool (140), and a tenuous presence in the Pool itself, where a few of them built temporary compounds on the shore (Bentley 1900, 2:16). Conflicts between the two groups also arose because of the absence of strict rules of credit among Congo Basin trading partners. Every so often, Tio traders in Malebo Pool would accept a load of ivory or foodstuffs on credit from their Bobangi suppliers and then renege on repaying them as agreed.[7] In retaliation, Bobangi traders would assemble a fleet of canoes and launch raids targeting Tio villages in the Pool, with the objective of capturing Tio subjects and using them as bargaining chips to get their goods back and some sort of indemnity (Harms 1981: 83; see also Guiral 1889: 245).

Bobangi certainly had no monopoly over such a simple yet cunning tactic of collecting debts, which became a favored scripted trick in the Pool's punitive playbook. Sometime in 1882, for example, Ngaliema gathered a posse of thirty men armed with long knives and marched toward Leopoldville to abduct the sons of Kimpe, a lord who owed him a debt large enough to require such an action. They swooped down quickly on the small European-controlled settlement. The alarm rang out as soon as they arrived, and they found themselves quickly surrounded by the Zanzibari garrison who guarded the small European station.

A long palaver ensued that averted what could have escalated into a messy clash (Coquilhat 1888: 63).

Despite the will of powerful lords such as Ngaliema, who understood that trade and prosperity depended on peace and trust between trading partners, the fact that the area lacked a centralized power meant that smaller potentates could have a disproportionately harmful impact on the trade by looting or tricking their trading partners rather than abiding by the oral codes of conduct.

Belonging

By the time Stanley set foot in Malebo Pool, the sociopolitical model that dominated the land came from Bobangi traders. They had created a huge trading network that linked several nodal points in the Congo Basin, and many of these points were strategically located on the banks of the Congo River and its tributaries. With increasing trade input came some political reorganization. The Bobangi inaugurated new forms of segmentary schism that have served as models to account for recent phenomena in seemingly unrelated areas.[8] In the nineteenth century, as trading in slaves and ivory along the Congo and its tributaries peaked, some sons or trusted slaves of a powerful village chief would vie for power and move out of the common village to establish a new settlement. Such strategies, which were not opportunistic schisms per se, could be likened to the apprenticeship system in European medieval society, in which an apprentice would leave his master to establish his own independent practice and thus expand and reinforce a common network.

To return to the Bobangi: market and competition fueled the growth of these new settlements, and as they grew in size and started to attract considerable trade volume or became important hubs for other economic activities, such as ivory carving, they came to be known as *mboka* (villages). As Vansina (1973: 75) has observed among the Tio, upon the death of the founder, and especially if the village had not attracted enough economic activities, its residents would simply disband and abandon the settlement for a more prosperous one. In the late nineteenth century, the growth of some of these villages called for further subdivisions into wards,[9] with the head of the entire village retaining the title of *mokonzi* (chief; plural *bakonzi*), while those appointed to each different ward claimed the title of *nkonwa* (derived, like *mokonzi*, from *konza*, a Bobangi term that conjures up images of wealth and prosperity; Harms 1981: 143).

The Bobangi were not the only group affected by the expansion of trade, nor were they the only ones who started to think about new ways to refashion their political structures to match economic growth. One of their archrivals in Bolobo, the Moye, also adopted a new title for the head of their fishing village. He was known as *mpombe e mboka* (the village elder). Both terms, *mpombe* (or *mpomba*) and *mboka,* have been recycled into the cultural lexicon of Kinshasa's youth up to the present day.[10] In these youths' parlance, however, mpomba no longer refers to the village sage who settles disputes and safeguards the cohesiveness of the community owing to wisdom acquired through years of experience. Instead, these youths used mpomba to mean a hard-boiled "tough guy" who defends his township by using his body as a rampart. Hence mpomba no longer connotes right but might; it no longer celebrates the brainy but the brawny; and it no longer harkens back to a bygone era when manliness could be performed publicly through the command of rhetorical prowess but defines a time when a new grammar of physical violence allows young people to express and perform the self.

Along with the political title of mokonzi and the sociogeographical notion of mboka, borrowed from the Moye, the Bobangi added yet another element to their careful management of an increasingly complex society brought about by the increasing mobility of people and commodities: they started to view their social organization as being composed not only of *libota* (family) but also of a new structure they called *lingomba* (plural *mangomba*), which Harms (1981: 147) defines as "a collection of people not necessarily related through blood ties who were unified into a corporate group." People belonging to this "corporate group" considered one another *ndeko* (a relative; plural *bandeko*) as long as the ties that bound them together remained secure. Lingomba should not be confused with the usual "extended family" that organized so many societies across the African continent. Rather, it was a socioeconomic group that revolved around a mokonzi and that was deployed beyond a single mboka, a group that waxed and waned according to the fortune of its headman.

The lingomba incorporated the rich trader's children, wives, and close and distant relatives as well as his clients who benefitted from his largesse and protection. Slaves, too, were brought within the lingomba, oftentimes from distant places. Removed from their kinsmen, slaves quickly learned the Bobangi language and felt connected enough to the people who owned them to identify themselves as members of a Bobangi lingomba. The desire to quickly assimilate, though continuing to bear the stigma of bondage, can be explained by the fact that Congo Basin people lived in societies where belonging to a group rather than asserting one's individual autonomy provided one with identity, protection, and purpose. Belonging, indeed, became even more critical as the Bobangi created new institutions that further set apart strangers from bandeko. This is how Harms (1981: 148) expresses the danger of being a poor stranger within Bobangi villages: "If he got into debt, there was nobody to lend him money. If somebody wronged him, there was nobody to plead for him in court. If he got sick, there was nobody to take care of him." Given the dreadful alternative, belonging to a lingomba made sense because one could easily tap into the network of wealth and bandeko to bail oneself out and to avail oneself of opportunities.

What are we to make of these political changes that altered the social land-scape in the late nineteenth-century Pool? To what degree can we discern new patterns of masculinity and manhood, and how portentous might they have been in shaping existing notions of manliness for generations to come? One way to answer these questions is to look at how "ethnicity" became a yardstick for mea-suring manliness in the Congo Basin. The abundance of slaves, the rhizomatic growth of new settlements, and the unprecedented mobility of both people and goods added new layers to people's perception of ethnicity, which began to mean more than simply a social shelter. Just as race stood in so many historical contexts as a marker and badge of manhood,[11] so, too, did ethnicity, for it allowed men in the Congo Basin to protect what they considered to be even more precious than territory, family, or wealth: manhood. Being a man meant evoking and embody-ing a large set of attributes and images intended to underline differences not only between men and women and men and boys but also between men and slaves. If one belonged to a group that was engaged in trade (which, it will be recalled, also involved capturing and moving people, including men), then one's ethnic-ity became almost synonymous with manliness. For such men, slaves—and also other men who engaged in socioeconomic activities they deemed beneath manly standards—could be no better than women.[12] Real men bonded in mangomba (corporate groups) and held one another as bandeko.

In a social environment rife with potential conflicts, where men could come to blows over the slightest argument and the outcome of war could directly affect economic prosperity because it usually produced slaves, dominant standards of masculinity tended to be set according to several criteria, including but not lim-ited to (1) freedom, (2) mobility (e.g., traders vs. agriculturists), (3) aggressiveness (feuds vs. palavers), (4) possession (and use) of firearms, (5) reliance on magical rituals, and (6) solidarity based on collective interests. Subject to change as it may have been, belonging to a lingomba (corporate group) was therefore not unlike membership in one of the gangs that would proliferate decades later in colonial Kinshasa as a site where young men could hone their skills and perform a hyper-active version of masculinity. Indeed, nineteenth-century Pool ushered in new forms of hypermasculinity that appealed particularly to young men—and that displaced and stymied types of masculinity that recoiled from the performance of violence. One could not be a man if one could not fight. Thus the ability to deliver devastating head-butts (*bilayi*) and win fistfights, by breaching an op-ponent's guard and violating his bodily integrity, served as a fitting metaphor for crossing borders and encroaching on other people's territory.

Winning a fight was not left to chance, however, nor was it always a muscle contest. Young men looked to magical devices to get the upper hand over their opponents. Young Tio men, for example, resorted to a charm known as *inkooru* to win fistfights (Vansina 1973: 355). More generally, men who flexed their muscles, clenched their fists, and resorted to violence to settle disputes, rather than those who used their rhetorical skills to appeal to reason, became the standard bearers of masculinity and manhood in societies fraught with increasing political fragmentation. They also occasionally smoked hemp, which the Bangala called *mungulu* (Weeks 1909: 123), to build self-confidence and gain fortitude.

After the Belgians had secured the Congo as their sole and most valuable colony, they methodically moved from wanton exploitation of the so-called natives to social-Darwinist policies that were intended to refashion existing standards of masculinity and reshape the fabric of African societies. Despite their intention to gradually remake the Congolese "primitive man" into a modern, Victorian man—a euphemism that cloaked their project to create loyal colonial subjects—precolonial standards of masculinity resurfaced where Belgian authorities least expected them: in the heart of what was designed to showcase colonial modernity, the colonial city.

2   A Colonial Cronos

Le rêve de ma vie est d'élever les populations dont j'ai la charge. J'ai supprimé les guerres entre tribus, arrêté les invasions, expulsé les trafiquants de chair humaine, mis fin à la traite, empêché l'alcool d'empoisonner le coeur de l'Afrique, fait la guerre à l'anthropophagie, aux poisons d'épreuve, à toutes les coutumes qui déshonorent l'humanité. Maintenant que la pacification est terminée, et que les difficultés du début sont vaincues, je voudrais chercher à relever mes noirs, à les élever peu à peu à la hauteur de notre civilisation, si possible.[1]

Leopold II of Belgium (quoted in Mille 1913: vii)

In 1922, a year before Kinshasa became capital of the colony, Belgian journalist Pierre Daye visited the city to fulfill an assignment he had received from the Belgian newspaper *Le Soir* to report on the progress of Belgian colonialism in Congo. Daye, a globe-trotting reporter who may have inspired Hergé's *Tintin au Congo*,[2] marveled at the hustle and bustle of the Belgian tropical Klondike in a way that could not be more revealing. His was a tale of two cities, since his encounter with Kinshasa's mirror city, Brazzaville, on the other side of Malebo Pool, had left him utterly unimpressed. "My feeling upon arriving in Kinshasa," he rhapsodized, "could be best described as '*une impression d'américanisme*'" (Daye 1923: 159)—a hyperbolic trope that Kinshasa's youths would appropriate in the 1950s to re-create their own version of the Hollywoodized American Far West. "People live [here] with intensity," Daye marveled, "They are Americans." Then, he continued:

> J'avoue tout net que Kinshasa est ma plus grande stupéfaction au Congo. Je savais bien, par ce que l'on m'en avait dit, qu'un essor curieux avait fait lever du sol une ville nouvelle. Mais je ne m'attendais point à trouver ce que j'ai vu. (Daye 1923: 159, quoted in Gondola 1997a: 79)

> I must confess that Kinshasa is my greatest shock in Congo. I knew, because people told me, that a strange growth had raised from the ground up a new city. But I was not expecting to encounter what I saw.

There is, of course, a dash of nationalistic pride in Daye's unstinting praise for what his little Belgium had accomplished in the heart of the tropics. Indeed, the meteoric growth of Kinshasa in the 1920s was unrivaled in Central Africa, perhaps with the exception of Luanda in Angola, where an unparalleled postslavery boom had transformed the city beyond recognition and set it apart from the rest of colonial cities in sub-Saharan Africa. Yet the expanding colonial economy in Kinshasa, because it rested heavily on labor exploitation, transformed African workers into mere cogs in a system that benefitted the handful of European companies and colonists who controlled all large-scale economic activity. For African workers, most of whom had recently migrated from their villages in search for job opportunities, the initial feeling of awe upon witnessing the march of progress and colonial modernity (the African version of Daye's *impression d'américanisme*) quickly gave way to a sense of alienation and hopelessness.

Frontier War in the Malebo Pool

To be sure, urbanization in the Belgian Congo and elsewhere in colonial Africa occurred against the backdrop of a cultural tug of war between Victorian modernity and African tradition, to put it mildly. In the Belgian Congo, both Africans and Europeans were well aware of what was at stake, though their responses to urbanization varied considerably. For the Belgians, Kinshasa was a beachhead on the shores where African savagery and European civilization had met. It was—as portrayed ad nauseam in colonial literature—an instrument of colonization, the only real place in the colony that could turn an African savage into a civilized subject. Perhaps until the eve of World War II, Kinshasa stood as the city par excellence where Europe's lopsided frontier battle against Africa played out through violence, labor disputes, and infrapolitics (daily confrontations)—and hence as a mirage of modernity. A spatial battle at first, its favorable outcome for the Belgians depended on how quickly they could evict the local Teke communities. Time and again, the Bateke were painted in the crudest of brush strokes by zealous European explorers and scholars because of their refusal to go along with the colonial project. For instance, a 1931 colonial report, after describing them as "lazy," "good for nothing," and "living in utter abjection," explained that "all they want is to live in peace, hidden in the bush, at arm's length from the white man who [in their minds] has invented work," before lamentingly concluding: "Their inertia is a weapon against which we are powerless" (quoted in Gondola 1997a: 51).

Hence the Belgians felt they had no choice but to brutally displace the Bateke from their settlements in the Pool. The large precolonial village, Nshasa (Kinshasa), was gradually pushed upstream to make room for a European settlement and the industrial complex of CITAS (Compagnie Industrielle et de Transports au Stanley Pool), which was later to give its name to the most notorious township in Kinshasa. And although the gradual eviction of Bateke residents encountered little resistance in the village of Kinshasa and did not require military intervention, in other villages deliberate use of force led to wanton destruction. Such was the case in Lemba, which colonial forces razed to the ground after its residents had refused to let colonial workers cut down trees there for the construction of the new European administrative post. Ntamo (Kintambo) suffered a similar fate in 1891, forcing the legendary chief Ngaliema to seek refuge across the river in the French colonial territory.

Land grabs aside, the frontier war in the Pool also pitted competing economic interests against each other. The newcomers coveted control of the "Great Congo Commerce," which, as seen in chapter 1, had brought a large measure of wealth to the Tio (Teke) people and led to social and political innovations in the nineteenth-century Pool. Very early on, Belgians made no secret of their determination to undercut the Tio's lucrative ivory business. In the late 1880s, while some Tio "big men" still enjoyed enormous profits from the sale of ivory, European companies' insatiable appetite for ivory exports was set to grow. In 1887, ivory exports from Congo Free State represented nearly 30 percent of the value of all exports, more than those of the infamous "red rubber" that came to epitomize Leopold II's hellish rule in Congo. Congo Free State was then responsible for half of Africa's ivory exports.[3] By the 1920s, several decrees had been passed forcing Africans out of the ivory business, in both hunting and trading, and defining for the first time the notion of poaching, unknown to Africans before colonization. By then, Tio lords and big men had lost not only their lucrative business but also their position in the Pool, thus making the maintenance and even the survival of their political institutions nearly impossible. Ironically, the Bateke's erstwhile trading partners—namely, Bangala from the Upper Congo River and Lower-Congo Bakongo, whom they had successfully kept at bay—now secured a foothold in the Pool. In later decades, the Bangala would even lay claim to being the original inhabitants of the area, with all that this implied in terms of land ownership, the politics of place, and, most importantly, the notion of local citizenship, or what some recent commentators have labeled kinicité (the essence of being a Kinois),[4] a notion discussed in later chapters.

The Capital City

Although Stanley had recognized the importance of Malebo Pool as a commanding site from which the entire Congo Basin could be more easily controlled and despite the fact that all African demographic structures had been eviscerated, the Belgian administration that followed in his footsteps initially ignored Kinshasa. Instead, it chose Vivi as the site of the first capital (1884–1886) of the Congo Free State, and later Boma (1886–1923), which Stanley (1885: 91) had described in August 1879 as the "principal emporium of trade on the Congo." The same story was unfolding all over Africa. Europeans were dotting the Atlantic coastline, from Dakar to Luanda, with colonial capitals, sometimes establishing cities ex nihilo, to be able to connect more quickly with their respective metropolises. The coast was considered just a ship away from Europe and civilization—indeed, a door to Europe free of the encumbrances of an impenetrable jungle and spear-wielding savages, two stereotypical images that carried over from the early 1850s exploration forays into Central Africa.

Located in the Congo Estuary, Boma had just recently shed its inglorious past as a slave "factory," one of the last stops on the equatorial coast before the Middle Passage.[5] Locating the capital of the new colony there was not without its challenges and perils. With a bustling European population, including English, Dutch, French, Portuguese, and Belgian residents who had set up several factories and trading establishments, Boma was indeed a thriving coastal center. It also boasted a flourishing Catholic mission that competed for the souls of the natives against various Protestant societies, including the Baptist Missionary Society (British), the Swedish Missionary Society, and the American Baptist Foreign Missionary Society.

Yet it proved difficult to maintain the capital at Boma for reasons of climate and location. British naturalist and explorer Sir Harry Hamilton Johnston, who visited the city in the 1890s, scathingly depicted it as "perhaps, the most unhealthy place on the Congo." The heat was excessive, he complained, "and behind the European houses lie great swamps and fetid marshes, which not only give rise to much fever, but breed the most terrible mosquitoes for size and bloodthirstiness that I have ever known" (Johnston 1895: 31). As the colonial administration, now under direct Belgian authority (since 1908), extended its authority to the vast Congo Basin, Boma's location became a liability. The idea of moving the capital away from Boma because of its peripheral position was certainly not new. Already in 1889, Belgian administrator A. J. Wauters promoted the idea that Boma's status as capital of the colony could only be short-lived and the transfer of the central colonial administration to Kinshasa was but ineluctable (Ndaywel è Nziem 1998: 319).

Another Belgian official, Georges Moulaert, who would play an important role in the expansion of Kinshasa, also pleaded with colonial authorities for the capital to be relocated to Kinshasa. Location aside, Kinshasa held some obvious advantages that colonial authorities could not overlook for long. It was linked to the port of Matadi, located 80 miles up the estuary of the Congo River, by an uninterrupted railroad, the Chemin de Fer Matadi–Léopoldville (CFML), completed in 1898 after claiming the lives of almost two thousand African workers. This link gave Kinshasa all the advantages of a coastal city without the inconvenience of being peripheral. And while the CFML connected Kinshasa to the coast, the Congo River and its tributaries formed a major transportation network that converged on Kinshasa from all corners of the Congo Basin.

Yet another factor must also have weighed in the colonial authorities' decision to use the location to administer a colony that dwarfed the Kingdom of Belgium by nearly eighty times: across the Pool from Kinshasa, on the north bank of the Congo River, the French had decided early on to locate the capital and the most important agglomeration of French Equatorial Africa. Brazzaville, named after French-Italian explorer Savorgnan de Brazza, who in 1880 had tricked Tio King Makoko into relinquishing a large territory on the north bank of Malebo Pool, never put Belgian interests in great danger. While Kinshasa pulsated with intense economic energy, "Brazzaville la verte" (Brazzaville the Green City), as it was fondly dubbed, lay dormant under an immense canopy of vegetation by the Congo River, as though its administrative function had stymied any other activity. No one has put this contrast better than the Belgian journalist Pierre Daye (1923: 166), mentioned at the outset of this chapter, upon traveling to both cities in 1922:

> When the ferry takes one, after only a twenty-minute ride, from the Belgian city of Kinshasa [to Brazzaville], one is utterly surprised. One leaves a bustling, developed city to stroll in a vast park, very quiet, covered with majestic trees, gardens with bloomed hibiscus, flamboyant flowers and roses, and laid out into nice, shaded alleys.[6]

Yet for a number of decades Brazzaville would serve the Congolese of Kinshasa as a mirror in which to contrast the lack of political progress under Belgian paternalism with the fast pace of French reform. In 1908, Brazzaville had become the seat of the Gouvernement Général du Congo Français and, in 1910, the capital of French Equatorial Africa. In 1923, just two years after the French had decided to build their own railroad to link Brazzaville with Pointe-Noire, on the coast, the Belgians officially moved the capital of the colony to Kinshasa. Now, on each side of the Pool stood a capital city—the two closest capitals the world had ever known, astride of one of the most powerful rivers in the world—two mirror cities that took different paths and yet influenced each other.

As remarkable as these developments may have seemed, they accurately reflected precolonial demographic patterns and occupation of space. Belgian colonial propaganda never relented in vilifying African cultures and presenting the colonial occupation as a project that fashioned civilization ex nihilo and displaced antiquated barbarism. The case of Malebo Pool reveals a striking continuum from precolonial to colonial times, mainly because the needs of the newcomers remained the same as those of the indigenous denizens they displaced.

A Tropical Klondike

Between 1923 and 1929, when the colonial administration effectively moved from Boma to Kinshasa, the new capital underwent a construction boom that required even further removal of indigenous settlements. The development of the industrial complex of CITAS alone, between the main train station (La Gare) and the port, attracted not only a growing number of European colonists but also thousands of young workers who flocked to this tropical Klondike from the Lower Congo, the Upper Congo areas, and other parts of the colony. Most came alone. A few brought their families with them, lured by the promises of a new colonial dispensation in which, for many Africans, living in an urban center was seen as synonymous with progress and social mobility. Until World War II, these African migrants were referred to, in Belgian colonial parlance, as *détribalisés* (detribalized).

By the 1920s, in addition to Kinshasa, another European station, Leopoldville, had developed on the south bank of Malebo Pool. This station had been christened after the "munificent and royal Founder of the Association Internationale du Congo" (Stanley 1885: 386) on April 9, 1882, and stood west of Kinshasa, in the former village of Kintambo, Chief Ngaliema's stronghold. In fact, it was in Leopoldville that Stanley had established the first European settlement, after forcibly removing the Teke residents from the village they knew as Ntamo. In selecting Kintambo as a settlement for the first European colonists, Stanley acted according to a simple colonial paradigm that came to pervade all areas of life: by virtue of their superiority, Europeans had to grab not only the most attractive sites but also sites that allowed them to dominate the natives. In Kintambo, Stanley specifically chose Mount Khonzo Ikulu, which was later renamed Mount Leopold, not only because it was relatively mosquito free but also because it gave the Europeans a vantage point and commanding position vis-à-vis the native settlements below. Its spectacular view of the Kinsuka rapids and the lakelike expansion of the Congo River into Malebo Pool only added to the aura of power and progress that Europeans sought to project.[7]

As the two settlements grew separately, it became important for the Europeans to bridge the gap and enable faster communication between them. Before the two were connected by a short segment added to the CFML, which went from La Gare, in Kinshasa, to a makeshift train stop in Leopoldville, the 8 kilometers between the settlements could be safely managed only by smaller steamers due to the rapids downstream, toward Kinsuka. Traveling by land through the luxuriant flora that ran wild along the tumultuous Congo River took almost a whole day, and because human portage had been discontinued in the Belgian Congo, not much could be hauled overland from one area to the other.

In 1922, the two areas merged into a single urban district (*district urbain*) that bore the name of Leopoldville. Yet Kinshasa (now known as Leo I) remained indisputably the more bustling and thriving of the two. In keeping with the Leopoldian policy of opening the Congo Basin to international commerce, Leo I attracted Belgian colonists as well as French, British, Portuguese, Italian, and

Greek entrepreneurs and adventurers. From only a dozen European inhabitants in 1914, the European population of Leo I had swelled to a thousand by 1923 and to 2,327 by the end of 1929, more than five times that of Leo II (Kintambo).

Many of these Europeans owned small-scale family businesses that scarcely managed to absorb the growing contingents that made up the African labor force. The big firms in Kinshasa, however—those that were responsible for both the spatial growth of the city and the enormous demographic tide that brought in thousands of migrants every year—employed the bulk of the workforce. The largest private and most prosperous company among them, Huileries du Congo Belge (HCB), commanded such respect that Daye, who visited its industrial facilities in 1922, called it a "city within a city" (Daye 1923: 237). An overseas extension of the Lever Brothers, HCB employed thousands of African workers, including in its subsidiaries SEDEC (Société d'Entreprises Commerciales au Congo), originally specializing in acquiring palm oil, and SAVCO (Société Anonyme des Savonneries Congolaises), a maker of low-quality soap for local consumption (Fieldhouse 1978: 380). Two other companies, TEXAF (Société de Textile Africaine) and BRALIMA (Brasseries Limonaderies Malteries), which catered to the local market for textiles and beverages, provided employment for large contingents of African migrants. In addition, Kinshasa's newly built cargo port considerably expanded the activities of CITAS, which merged with SONATRA (Société Nationale des Transports Fluviaux au Congo) in 1925, within a larger state-owned company known as UNATRA (Union Nationale des Transporteurs Fluviaux). In 1929, UNATRA operated on the Congo River and its tributaries a large fleet that could handle cargo totaling over 30,000 tons as well as passengers (Gondola 1997a: 80).

The Roaring Twenties witnessed an unparalleled economic growth in Kinshasa. But this first growth did more than just attract businesses and provide work for the plethora of African migrants. It defined the city for many decades to come, not least by the unprecedented demographic boom it created. From 1924 to 1929, the population nearly doubled, soaring from 23,730 to 46,088 (Pain 1984: 19). Yet from the start, housing for the African migrants lagged behind housing for the European population. This was compounded by the Europeans' policies of enforcing a strict color bar, intended to keep at bay what Europeans thought were the unbecoming traits that characterized Africans: their lubricity and proclivity toward violent outbursts, the smells that emanated from their dwellings, and the noises that expressed their perpetually childlike temperament.

Residential segregation in a sprawling city where the great majority of the population comprised young, single male African workers was further motivated by colonial concerns to protect white females against the black man's purported sexual overdrive. Indeed, as Ann Laura Stoler (2002: 42) reminds us, colonial hegemony operated under two false yet powerful assumptions: first, that Europeans in the colonies "made up an easily identifiable and discrete biological and social entity" and, second, that "the boundaries separating colonizer from colonized were thus self-evident and easily drawn." Of course, colonial realities never quietly abided by these two principles, prompting a constant effort to maintain the fiction of strict separation and to police boundaries, especially the sexual boundaries that both Europeans and Africans deliberately flouted.

Stoler (2002: 45) is also right in pointing out that sexual control was more than just a convenient metaphor for colonial domination. It was an essential colonial process that facilitated the creation of a colonial order in which bodies as much as minds, in their racialized and gendered asymmetrical contrasts, served as linchpins. The arrival of European women, intended to curb prostitution and the practice of using African *ménagères* (maids) as concubines, with its unintended consequence of producing mixed-race children, actually led to the exclusion of African male workers from residential spaces occupied by Europeans (Lauro 2005: 145). This de facto segregation, or what several colonial propagandists called the "color bar," became an integral part of the urban experience for most Europeans and Africans beginning in the early 1930s. This prompted Belgian jurist Antoine Rubbens to write in 1949, "It appears as though the most ferocious Anglo-Saxon 'color bar' never produced so many discriminatory laws, never passed so many draconian segregation rules as our Belgian guardianship did" (quoted in Tshimanga 2001: 142).

No Green Pastures

As scores of young male migrants flocked to these settlements, which until the early 1930s were prohibited to African female migrants,[8] colonial authorities grew increasingly alarmed at the presence of so many young men in such appalling conditions. Visiting Kinshasa in 1924, the Belgian priest Father Van Wing (quoted in Saint-Moulin 1976: 468) could not help but denounce the situation in his diary:

> I found a loud assortment of peoples living in anarchy. I traveled the length and breadth of the immense black township where live, only God knows how under such despicable moral conditions, nearly 20,000 Negroes. . . . It's a camp; it's not a village. There is no greenery, virtually no children . . . even fewer mothers and little joy. Along the entire way I saw only two children.

At the time of Van Wing's visit, Kinshasa's economic boom had no parallel in the entire colony. The city had just replaced Boma as the colonial capital the year before. In addition to the administrative apparatus that expanded there, economic growth took place overnight. The European population nearly tripled between 1923 and 1929, while the number of European companies increased tenfold between 1920 and 1928 (Gondola 1997a: 79–80). Father Van Wing was obviously interested in the human tragedy that had unfurled in the city. Underlying his scathing description was the conviction that thriving colonial capitalism had dealt a blow to Belgium's civilizing mission. Instead of fulfilling its intrinsic mission as the locus and showcase of European modernity, the colonial city had mutated into a capitalist behemoth where African workers found themselves at the bottom of the social ladder. Although there was no shortage of work, jobs did not necessarily enable workers to make ends meet. Instead, the workplace became a place of exploitation and humiliation, a place where African men lost their dignity and experienced daily attacks on their manhood.

Coming on the heels of the Roaring Twenties, the Great Depression foreshadowed a wider gender shift that would deeply affect manhood in Kinshasa. A watershed with respect to gender relations, the 1930s also witnessed shifting colonial thought about the nature of the colonial city. Before the Depression, Kinshasa had represented in the colonial discourse not just the frontier, where civilization triumphed and savagery retreated, but, as on any frontier in history, a place unfit for women. Moreover, the notion that African workers were "strangers to the city," that they were rural folk by virtue of their culture and merely temporary urban migrants, militated against a steady influx of female migrants. Until at least the early 1930s, areas populated by African workers in Kinshasa remained as Father Van Wing had seen them ten years earlier—bereft of any signs of urbaneness, with the majority of workers living in overcrowded, poorly built housing, without an adequate supply of clean water, and wearied by long, arduous hours of labor under the supervision of paternalist white employers[9] who were given to racist sermonizing. After toiling from dawn to dusk, workers came home to residential areas that were segregated according to their *race* (tribal affiliation)[10] and policed by a native *capita* (head) who could always count on the assistance of a cohort of Force Publique (Public Force) agents when needed.[11]

The Depression changed things in Kinshasa to an extent that warrants the term "urban revolution." Its first obvious impact had to do with the massive layoffs of African workers from the big European firms that bore the brunt of the economic downturn. Faced with scores of young unemployed men living at close quarters without adequate means of subsistence and roaming the streets in search for odd jobs, Belgian municipal authorities resorted to massive deportations between 1929 and 1933, to the extent that the city lost more than 40 percent of its population.[12] To avoid deportation, an increasing number of young men went to the Bourse du Travail Indigène (Labor Exchange for Natives) to seek placement in European homes as launderers, gardeners, and cooks, jobs that traditionally devolved to women and that no man in previous generations would have filled. Wages came at the price of gender and racial demotion. One has only to think of Buchi Emecheta's 1979 novel, *The Joys of Motherhood,* in which Nnaife, the main female character's second husband, takes a job as a launderer in the Meers household and ends up washing Mrs. Meers's underwear, to understand the predicament many African men faced. In Emecheta's novel, Nnaife evolves into a tragic, ineffectual figure unable to retain fragments of his Ibo traditional manhood and gradually falls into the pitfalls of alcoholism to cope with his emasculation. Emecheta set her novel in 1930s Lagos, when that city, like Kinshasa, was in the throes of sweeping economic and demographic change. Her fictional account, although steeped in the ideals of incipient 1970s African feminism, reverberates with echoes of the gender struggle that transformed Africa's urbanscape starting in the 1930s.

With many male residents forcefully sent back to their villages, municipal authorities converted areas previously occupied by Africans into a "cordon sanitaire," a sort of buffer zone insulating the European quarter (*la ville européenne*) from the African workers' camps. Running along the entire length of the African camps,[13] this no-man's land fulfilled several prophylactic and securitarian functions, as indicated by the presence there of greeneries and military camps. In some areas, it was large enough to shield the European quarter from all the supposed nuisances and miasmas that oozed out of the African slums.[14]

Perhaps one the most striking differences between the two urban areas, and one that reinforced the colonial gap, was seen in the street names. While the streets of the *cité indigène* (native quarters) bore the names of Congolese *lieux-dits* (localities), those in the ville européenne were emblazoned with the names of a pantheon of colonial heroes (all white, of course), from Avenue Maurice Lippens and Boulevard Gouverneur Général Tilkens, which laced through Pointe Kalina (named after an Austrian officer), along the Congo River, to Boulevards Albert Ier and Léopold II; Avenues Princesse Astrid, Stanley, Frère Gillet, Colonel Vangele, and Ministre Godding; and the emblematic thoroughfare Prince Baudoin, which served as the main connector between the two areas. Given the importance of naming in Congolese precolonial and colonial societies alike (see Likaka 2009), this had serious implications for urban and colonial imaginaries, for it cast a pall over the African settlements, implying that they were mere extensions of village life, while singularizing the European quarter as the active shaper of history. It certainly added to the aura of historicity and invincibility that were the hallmarks of Belgian colonialism.

Returning to the critical juncture of the 1930s Depression and its impact on African agency: to weather the economic downturn, a few of Kinshasa's unemployed men joined the ranks of women who took advantage of the opportunity to transform the cordon sanitaire into a thriving gardening business that supplied the city with vegetables (including cassava) and fruit. This was a female arena where women controlled the whole supply chain, from production to sales,[15] and accumulated enough money either to sustain their household as breadwinners or, for those who were single, to afford the tax imposed upon single urban women.

Not surprisingly, the recession also led to the proliferation of clandestine *buvettes* (beer halls) in the African townships' blind alleys and other recesses. That such places, within an oppressive colonial context, serve as a *parlement du peuple*[16] is a view that pervades the literature. In the context of 1930s Kinshasa, these buvettes loomed as loci of homosociality, where men rubbed elbows and, in the words of James Baldwin, were "forced each day to snatch [their] manhood, [their] identity, out of the fire of human cruelty that rages to destroy it" (quoted in Kimmel 1996: 271).

Yet the buvettes were also, above all, the bellwether of the gender struggle that would emerge in the late colonial period. There, for the first time in a Central African context, women lorded it over men and used both their femininity and sexuality to upset "traditional" gender strictures that had stacked the decks against their economic and social freedom. In the 1930s, many if not most of these beer halls were owned and operated by white adventurers of dubious pedigree— Portuguese, Greek, Italian, and Syro-Lebanese wage-earners and small-shop operators who had lost their jobs and who, rather than return home, "went native." They used their proximity to African women, which several reports vilified for contributing to the increase in the number of mixed-race children in Kinshasa,[17] to woo male patrons to their buvettes.[18] To say that the emasculation of African male workers took place in these locales would be a gross oversimplification, for we cannot ignore the daily indignities meted out to African workers. At a time when the Belgians had yet to set standards of masculinity for the natives, other than their ability to serve as beasts of burden in the burgeoning colonial economy, African men found it exceedingly wrenching, and increasingly impossible, to adhere to the "tribal" traditional masculinity norms. Their emasculation in the buvettes, at the hands of what in colonial parlance were coyly referred to as *filles publiques* (literally, "public girls"),[19] must be contextualized within a broader pattern of gender oppression that unfolded in the city.

A Colonial Cronos

To understand how living conditions in 1930s Kinshasa irreversibly altered manliness norms for the majority of the African men who formed its urban backbone, perhaps we should start with Mongo Beti's harrowing depiction of the fictional character Tanga in *Ville cruelle*. Written in 1954, *Ville cruelle* takes its readers back to the 1930s, when the first wave of city-dwellers was swept up and crushed in the urban vortex. The city Beti describes affords African workers few if any opportunities to earn decent wages and lead dignified lives. Not only does it loom as the epitome of colonial alienation, but it also acts as a ubiquitous colonial Cronos, devouring those young workers who find themselves ensnared in its tentacles.[20]

"A colonial Cronos" is indeed a fitting way to describe Kinshasa in the 1930s, when the growth of African labor became a concern for the colonial municipal authorities. Although the colonial city undoubtedly empowered some women, enabling them to gain economic freedom and assert control over their sexuality,[21] for African men it turned out to be a social and economic context for emasculation. Much of this emasculation took place in the workplace, where it was customary for European overseers and managers to yell at their workers and call them *macaques* (monkeys). For the slightest mistake, workers would be routinely stripped of their clothes and forced to lie on the floor. The white overseer would then proceed to flog them with the infamous *chicote* (whip),[22] in front of timorous and resigned co-workers. Before the Depression, the lack of collective consciousness among workers made walkouts rare, although not unprecedented, as demonstrated by the wave of strikes that hit Kinshasa in 1920 and 1921 (Gondola 1997a: 113). More often than not, workers adopted individual strategies to escape these abusive conditions, finding solace in sabotaging machinery, stealing tools, and faking illness. Yet at a time when dreadful living conditions in the city could not but elicit nostalgia for the simple and often idealized rural life, workers would also simply abandon their jobs and return to their villages.[23]

Of course, rural life, with the harsh demands exacted by the colonial economy and the stifling authority exercised by abusive elders, was hardly the vaunted idyll workers tended to imagine it to be. But the urban slums did not provide the kind of outlet workers needed after their toils—at least until after World War II, when Kinshasa's townships became home to some of the most festive and subversive nightspots in urban Africa. And even when the hardship of their daily toil vanished behind the tall malebo trees[24] that crowded the cordon sanitaire, African workers could never escape colonial strictures.

Perhaps the most blatant sign that colonial authorities would not relent in their intent to further infantilize the African workforce came as night fell on the townships. A strictly enforced curfew, which ran from dusk to dawn, as elsewhere in colonial Africa, had a double aim: to curtail Africans' mobility within the townships and, most importantly, to ensure that no African ventured across the cordon sanitaire into the European quarter unless he or she was on duty. However, the Belgian curfew in colonial Kinshasa went one step farther. Holding hurricane lamps and armed with sticks or chicotes, Force Publique agents routinely patrolled the streets shouting "Tolala! Tolala!" (Go to sleep! Go to sleep!), a tocsin of apathy that echoed in all sections of the ghostly townships, a sort of hypnotizing incantation intended to rock the natives into quiescence and political inertia.[25] This was also a crude way to infantilize African men, to sear and saturate their sensory experience of colonization with sounds, images, smells, and tastes of domination. One évolué (a "civilized" native)[26] spoke for many when he expressed the colonial relationship in the stark terms of father and child:

Le Noir est le pupille du Blanc civilisateur qui, par consequent, le traite en bon tuteur, étant, sous ce régime, jusqu'au jour de son émancipation.[27]

The Black man is the White civilizer's pupil who, as a result, treats him the way a good tutor would. He should remain under this regime until the day of his emancipation.

Until independence finally loomed on the near horizon in the 1950s, this arsenal of oppression, emasculation, and infantilization remained fully intact, to the dismay, among others, of several writers who lifted their voices to defy what the prolific Belgian novelist, essayist, and pamphleteer Oscar-Paul Gilbert correctly identified as *l'empire du silence*.[28] For example, Jean Labrique, who served as press secretary to Governor General Pétillon in the late 1950s, took some pains to expose the mechanisms of Belgian paternalism and its triune essence, which united the colonial state, its Catholic missionary arm, and private companies in the common project of controlling the "native" from cradle to grave. His account, although cluttered with minutiae, is quoted here at length because it reveals the holistic nature of Belgian paternalism vis-à-vis the Congolese:

> On le distrait sagement. L'employeur verse d'office une partie de sa paie à la Caisse d'épargne. . . . Son repos est assuré par le couvre-feu des cités dans lesquelles il vit et où la présence de l'Européen n'est pas tolérée pendant la nuit. La formule de son bonheur est étudiée par des hommes de science, appliquée par des hommes d'affaires avertis qui s'emploient à lui éviter les erreurs de conduite. Dernièrement encore, il lui était interdit de détenir, et à plus forte raison de consommer, du vin ou de l'alcool. . . . Il ne peut se déplacer d'une région à l'autre sans autorisation de l'administration. . . . Quant à l'Européen qui débarque au Congo belge, il se sent, se croit, s'arroge d'office une action éducatrice. Quelle que soit sa profession, quel que soit son travail. Un libraire ouvre-t-il boutique ? Il censure la lecture des clients noirs. Le commerçant, l'épicier, le boucher, font l'éducation de leur clientèle noire à des guichets particuliers. . . . Le paternalisme est intégral.[29]

He is wisely entertained. His employer deposits in his behalf a portion of his pay into a savings account. . . . His rest is protected by the curfews enforced in the townships where he lives and where the presence of Europeans is not allowed at night. The formula for his happiness is studied by men of science, implemented by savvy businessmen who make sure that he does not stumble. Until very recently, he was not allowed to possess, let alone consume, wine or alcohol. . . . He cannot move from one area to another without an authorization issued by the administration. . . . Europeans who arrive freshly in the Belgian Congo feel, believe, claim for themselves the role of tutor, whatever their profession or their line of work. A bookseller opens a bookshop: he censures what black customers should and should not read. [European] merchants, grocers, and butchers all participate in educating their black clientele at designated checkout counters.[30] . . . Paternalism is integral.

Following World War II, the Belgians instituted what historian Jean Stengers (2007: 250) reminds us were dubbed *brevets de civilisation* (certificates of civilization), a twofold status awarded to Congolese évolués who had repudiated "tribal" customs to emulate the European lifestyle with respect to social mores (they were not to be polygamist), education and training, professional qualification, and good citizenship (no convicted felons could apply). First came the Carte du Mérite Civique, which, starting in July 1948, gave Congolese recipients the right to be tried in nonnative courts, to move about the city at night, to access stores and venues reserved for Europeans only, and to own land and other properties. Yet even those Belgian administrators who favored a special status for Congolese évolués and actively lobbied for it viewed Congolese through Hegelian paternalistic lenses. One such administrator appealed to the minister of colonies as the debate raged:

> To deny this group the outward sign that they demand, that is, a special identity card, gives them the impression that we are not consistent with our *oeuvres,* that somehow *we have disowned our own children,* the product of our education, of our teachings, of our evangelization.[31] (emphasis added)

Second, in 1952, the Belgian revamped the *immatriculation* (registration) status—a status that went back to the creation of Congo Free State and had originally rewarded African chiefs and notables who sided with the Leopoldian state. When Governor General Jungers condescendingly trotted out the idea at the 1951 meeting of the colonial Governing Council, there was every reason to believe not only that the status would be doled out in drops to deserving évolués but also that those few who did become *immatriculés* (registered) would always bear the stigmata of their erstwhile native status:

> Reconnaître par l'octroi d'un statut legal d'assimilation, les efforts tenaces grâce auxquels certains Congolais, dont le nombre certes est encore très restreint, atteignent en fait un stade de civilisation égal à celui de leurs *tuteurs* [européens] (quoted in Ndaywel è Nziem 1998: 461; emphasis added).

> Acknowledge by granting a legal status of assimilation the tenacious efforts made by some Congolese, although very few in number, to reach the same level of civilization as their [European] *tutors.* (emphasis added)

In 1957, out of nearly 13 million Congolese, only 50,000 were deemed évolués,[32] only 10,000 more than the estimate Father Van Wing had provided for 1948 (Markowitz 1973: 104), and among these, only 1,557 held a Carte du Mérite Civique. In keeping with Belgian "No elite, no problem" policy, no more than 227 men were immatriculés (Schrevel 1970: 152). Évolués who had suffered great humiliations[33] to obtain the immatriculation status were in for a rude awakening. Largely ignored by the majority of Europeans, who continued to treat immatriculés as Untermenschen,[34] these reforms failed simply because they ran counter an entrenched if not visceral colonial ideology that had both infantilized and emasculated Congolese men and long opposed the emergence of a Congolese elite.

Perhaps the most poignant denunciation of immatriculation came when it no longer mattered. Speaking for many disillusioned évolués, Prime Minister Patrice Lumumba declared in his impromptu independence address on June 30, 1960:

> We have known ironies, insults, blows that we endured morning, noon and evening, because we are Negroes. Who will forget that to a Black one said "*tu*," certainly not as to a friend, but because the more honorable "*vous*" was reserved for whites alone?

Lumumba, who had acquired his immatriculation card in September 1954, a rare privilege for a provincial évolué, moved from Stanleyville to Leopoldville in 1957. It was there that his political trajectory would take a radical turn after he experienced Belgian racism and paternalism at their worst. One incident left such an indelible mark on him that it would resurface in his independence address.[35] Shortly after arriving in Leopoldville, Lumumba inadvertently bumped into a white woman in the street. Before he could apologize, she upbraided him and blurted out, "Sale macaque!" (Filthy monkey!).[36]

Already in 1941, one of the most prominent and longest-serving prelates in the Belgian Congo, Monsignor Roelens, had warned of the potential threat of the évolués. He certainly voiced the opinion of many colonists, including a growing number of missionaries, who during the war felt threatened by *l'éveil des évolués* (the rise of the évolués) and deplored one of the unforeseen impacts of the war, the quickening pace of Belgian prewar gradualism:

> These half-scholars (*demi-savants*), who like to boast about the meager intellectual baggage their feeble brain contains, are tempted to consider themselves equal to whites and capable of replacing them. These poor rascals, unhappy that their purported merit goes unacknowledged, are likely to become exposed to subversive ideas of foreign origin that infiltrate the country. If we do not pay enough attention, they might even become troublemakers.[37]

The large body of literature dealing with the postwar social and political reforms directed at the évolués tends to view the late 1940s and early 1950s either as an incubation period for the perfect political storm of the late 1950s (Lemarchand 1964; Young 1965; Mutamba Makombo Kitatshima 1998; Stengers 2007) or as a decade vitiated by incrementalist politics that hardly matched the fast-paced growth of the colonial economy (Slade 1960; Merlier 1962; Anstey 1966). Yet these years did witness the most serious attempt yet to reshape manliness norms for the growing number of urban youth, against a backdrop of deep-rooted ideas about African humanity, culture, and manhood.

Leopold II's dream of redeeming African savages by bringing them up to the level of their civilized European tutors did indeed find echoes in the Belgian postwar social discourse that culminated, before imploding, in policies such as immatriculation and the Belgo-Congolese community. At the same time, however, growing, inchoate groups of young Kinois recoiled at the idea that their masculinities could be defined only along the sliding scale that the Belgians had devised for the évolués, where savagery and civilization, tradition and modernity, "tribal" customs and European lifestyle constituted repulsive poles. They chose instead to harness images and elements from a variety of sources, including the Hollywoodized American Far West, in their attempts to complete their manhood puzzle. Chapter 3 focuses on the birth of a tropical Far West in Kinshasa where, starting in the early postwar period, unlikely bedfellows begot one of the most original and emblematic youth cultures in colonial Africa.

3 Missionary Interventions

L'image, la presse et le cinéma sont trois agents directement criminogènes. Surtout le cinéma.

Image, press, and cinema are three direct criminogenic agents. Especially cinema.

Bissot (1958: 52)

In postwar Kinshasa, missionary interventions loomed large within the vortex that reshaped manliness norms and standards for the majority of Kinois youth. Ever since Leopold II had set his sights on the Congo Basin, Catholic missionaries, and especially Belgian missionaries, had taken charge of the education and training of the youth there with the unwavering blessing of the colonial government. Both Leopold and Belgian authorities did everything they could to ensure that Congo remained the exclusive field of Belgian Catholic missionaries.[1] Suspicion of foreign missionaries existed even before the so-called Congo Reform Movement, in which Scandinavian, British, and African American Protestant missionaries[2] played a crucial role in setting in motion an international campaign to force Leopold II to relinquish his private domain to the Belgian government. Even after the demise of the Leopoldian state, these events continued to cast a pall over the relationship between the Belgian authorities and Protestant missions. The new authorities never departed from a policy that one of its architects, Edmond Van Eetvelde, enunciated as one of "active and intense sympathy" toward Belgian Catholic missionaries (Tshimanga 2001: 82). Indeed, as Markowitz (1973: 10) has noted, "The Leopoldian regime had sown the seeds of collaboration between the Catholic missions and the state. These were to germinate and flourish in the colonial atmosphere of the Belgian Congo."

Thus while they held Protestant missionaries in mortal suspicion, never allowing them to fully carry out their activities, and kept tabs on foreign Catholic missions, Belgian authorities doted Belgian Catholic missionaries, providing them with the indispensable resources and purview to fulfill a single mission: to turn the Congolese natives into "fidèles et loyaux sujets de la Belgique" (faithful and loyal Belgian subjects).[3] Such quid pro quo between Belgian missionaries and the colonial authorities allowed the former to maintain a quasi-monopoly over the youth, a group that nourished seemingly contrapuntal colonial visions, as recipients of racial redemption and fodder for the emerging colonial economy.

We start this chapter with the Catholic missionary project, which, as we shall see, did not always abide by the blueprint developed by the colonial authorities but strayed at times in order to fulfill its own agenda. Together with the colonial government and private companies, the Catholic missions constituted what, following Young (1965), scholars have dubbed the "colonial trinity." But, as Masandi (1982) has shown, all three institutions pursued their separate, distinct goals, which were not always in accord with the overarching mission of the colony's *mise en valeur* (development) vaunted by colonial propagandists.[4]

Redeeming the Savage

As economic activity picked up steam following World War II, it became obvious that capitalistic expansion in Leopoldville had its drawbacks. The city's demographic surge, mainly due to migration, soon outstripped its economic growth, forcing municipal authorities to deal not only with a volatile population of young male wage earners but also with an increasing mass of young unemployed, some of whom gathered together in bands starting in the early 1920s.

One of the first Europeans to report on this situation was Scheutist missionary Raphaël de la Kethulle,[5] who headed one of Leopoldville's parishes:

> These urchins spend their time wandering in the streets of the European district and the African quarters and everywhere their presence is feared by people who know all too well their propensity for marauding. . . . These juvenile thieves operate in small, independent bands well known to one another and to the natives. . . . The two main leaders of one of these bands have spent time in jail in Leopoldville and Brazzaville. . . . They all are without work; many of them without parents and a permanent home. They live sometimes in the open, sometimes in abandoned slums. (de la Kethulle 1922: 727–29)

One would think that these lines were written today, for street children have become a permanent fixture in Kinshasa's landscape and have developed an entrenched street culture. Yet de la Kethulle's account harkens back to a time when Kinshasa's youth population remained transient (in terms of both generation and geography) and had yet to develop an exclusive urban identity. As quickly as they formed, these bands could also rapidly dissolve, not so much because of the repression that one can surmise from de la Kethulle's account, or because the old guard joined the colonial workforce, but merely due to frequent returns to village life.

As a member of the colonial state's religious arm in Kinshasa, Raphaël de la Kethulle had a vested interest in bringing these juveniles back into the colonial fold. Moreover, just as colonial employers strove not only to discipline the bodies of their African workers but also to redeem their minds, so missionaries such as de la Kethulle, who were entrusted with their religious instruction, sometimes seemed even more preoccupied with their physical fitness. In other words, employers, educators, army officers, missionaries, and government officials alike all adhered to the holistic credo, *Mens sana in corpore sano* (A sound mind in a healthy body).

Going beyond the simple idea of imperialism, V. Y. Mudimbe (1994: 119) has posited Belgian colonization in the Congo as an attempt at domestication, which he defines as "the conversion of the African space and the African minds," through a panoply of schemes and programs that worked only because of the steadfast alliance between the church and the colonial state. Conversion to the West, which underpinned the postwar reforms that gave rise to the évolués and immatriculation, was coterminous with conversion to Catholicism, argues Mudimbe. The two programs of conversion, to use Mudimbe's terminology, sought to buttress the fundamental idea of the right to colonize, an idea loudly echoed in Governor Pierre Ryckmans's paternalistic mantra of "Dominer pour servir" (Dominate in order to serve), the Belgian colonizers' self-imposed mandate to rule the natives in order to bring them to conversion and redemption. Colonization, both as theory and praxis, was propounded not only as the overarching relational mode between colonizers and colonized but as an unquestionable one, the only relation possible between Belgians and their African subjects. Opposing the right to colonize with non-Catholic ideas and non-Western ideologies, rituals, and performances was tantamount to denying scientific truth (Mudimbe 1994: 118).

The domestication of the African space, body, and mind permeated Belgian colonial ideology in Congo, even though evidence suggests that greater emphasis was placed on taming the body[6] than on redeeming a mind that most considered essentially irredeemable. Not surprisingly, de la Kethulle's response to this youth crisis followed the same pattern. Most of Kinshasa's sports and leisure facilities, including its two main stadiums, were developed under his aegis, as were Boy Scout groups and school musical bands, though all these benefitted from government subsidies (Tshimanga 2001: 110).

Taming and redeeming indeed stood at the two ends of the colonial spectrum and informed much of the missionary doctrines and ideology vis-à-vis the natives. At times, the balance seemed to be tipping toward redemption, as when, for example, de la Kethulle broke ranks with the colonial authorities and decided to open the way for Thomas Kanza to become the first Congolese layperson to attend graduate school in Belgium. Yet until 1960 the idea of taming the savages seemed to lurk behind even the most progressive-seeming reforms, such as immatriculation. Belgian reluctance to grant the colony independence, despite sweeping changes taking place throughout colonial Africa, especially in French neighboring Congo, stemmed from the same notion, even though economic calculations likely played a major role as well.

By 1959, a year before Congo's emancipation—when Belgians still contemplated independence not as a foregone conclusion, as in the rest of Africa, but as an eschatological event—the white missionary presence was 6,000 strong. Assisted by 500 African priests, 1,200 European religious personnel, and 25,000 catechists in nearly 700 missions throughout the Belgian colony (Masandi 1982: 38), these missionaries had come in droves, starting with the first Scheutist Congregatio Immaculati Cordis Mariae (CICM) mission of 1888[7] and then the Sisters of Charity from Ghent in 1892, Jesuits in 1893, Trappists of Westmalle and the "White Sisters" in 1895, Franciscan Missionaries of Mary in 1896, Fathers of the Sacred Heart in 1897, Norbertines from Tangerloo in 1898, Redemptorists in 1899, and so on.[8] As Mudimbe (1994: 107) describes it, this massive presence of the Belgian "holy army" in the Congo sprang from an orchestrated combination of the Catholic faith and a nationalist call to enlist young Belgian men and women and convince them that they "could engineer a historical rupture in the consciousness and the space of Africans." Thus, from early on, Belgian colonization in the Congo rested not just on the imperial project's relentless drive to exploit Africa's economic resources or on the assimilationist fiction that triumphed in the French imperial discourse but also on the entrenched notion that colonization was first and foremost a salvific mission the goal of which, it turned out, remained eschatological by definition.

This explains why Belgian colonization attracted not only philanthropists, doctors, teachers, and merchants but also, above all, missionaries, imbued as they were with the idea, expressed early on by Monsignor Victor Roelens, Congo's first Belgian bishop, that

> only Christian Catholic religion, based on authority, [was] capable of changing the native's mindset, of imbuing our blacks with a clear and intimate consciousness of their duties, of instilling in them respect for the authorities and the spirit of loyalty toward Belgium. (Masandi 1982: 40)

Defined as benighted, Africans could not be rescued from atavistic savagery simply by letting the progress of modernity run its course and by eradicating superstition, fetishism, and ignorance. Progress and freedom from superstition (and all the other "native evils") could be accomplished only through the selfless work of benevolent Catholic missionaries.[9]

The symbiotic relationships among the triumvirate of the missionaries, the state, and large companies led to the missions' monopoly on education, training, and health care for the natives. Catholic missionaries would, for instance, provide training in specific areas at the request of employers. Employers would in turn hire trainees who came out of Catholic schools over those trained in Protestant (i.e., foreign) schools.[10] Both the state and public and private employers also depended on the missionaries to boost the workers' morale and productivity and instill in their pupils discipline, loyalty, honesty—in short, a staunch work ethic.

Yet, the missionaries' most significant contribution to the colonial oeuvre, and one that only they could effectively carry out, had to do with the notion that colonization's main goal was to bring about a "Congo ya Sika" (new Congo) free of the local, "traditional" customs that hindered the mission to civilize the Congolese man. Through schooling and evangelization, missionaries endeavored to remake the Congolese man and abolish the local initiation rituals, dances, sexual initiation rites, and facial scarifications that marked the passage from boyhood to manhood (Masandi 1982: 54). Controlling this process was essential, so missionaries resorted to several activities, rituals, and media to introduce young Congolese to new masculinities and new ways of being a man.

"Le Noir est-il intelligent?"

In their mandate to offer young Africans a new path to manhood through evangelization, education, training, and labor, Catholic missionaries wrestled with the psychology of the black man much in the same way that their nineteenth-century predecessors had contended with what Philip Curtin (1964) euphemistically termed "Africans' 'place in nature'"—namely, their humanity. Under the spurious heading of "The Psychology of the Black Man," the main question that kept cropping up—and that *fin d'empire* never really settled—had to do with the intelligence of the black man.

Because colonization presented itself as an othering process, contrasting Christianity with heathenism, civilization with barbarism, and whiteness with blackness, and produced itself as a masculine, virile act, the black woman could easily be essentialized as the "absolute other." Her gender and race made her a prime subject for colonial neglect. We will thus not be preoccupied with her in this chapter but only mention that, just like the Congolese man, her purported sexual overdrive contributed to colonial lack of interest in promoting her social status. Besides, according to one missionary, black women could not be trusted to grasp the civilizational change that colonization had introduced and should therefore be excluded from the outset on account of their lack of will (Mudimbe 1994: 125). One author even blamed the black woman for the general *abrutissement* (impairment) of African children because she failed to fulfill her role as the "first educator" (Maistriaux 1957: 191).

Reduced to its essentials, this debate, according to Masandi (1982: 95), harkened back to the eighteenth-century trope that the Negro was no better than a *grand enfant* (a big child) and his continent "the land of childhood" (Hegel

1902: 148) for two centuries of slave trading and plantation slavery seem to have convinced Euro-Americans of this.[11] Belgian anthropologists and psychologists, in particular, devoted a fair amount of time and effort to the vexing question of the black man's intelligence.[12] For example, French psychologist André Ombredane, who did fieldwork in the Congo on behalf of the CEMUBAC (Centre Scientifique et Médical de l'Université Libre de Bruxelles), laid out his findings in a piece published in 1949, when postwar waves of change were giving rise to the évolués. Without denying the basic assumption that blackness accounted for lack of intelligence, his conclusions reminded his European audience that the stultifying social and environmental milieu of the Congolese could well be a factor. Yet, before arriving at such conclusions, Ombredane (1949: 522) highlighted the common recurring opinion found in the Belgian Congo about the intelligence of black people. Its first iteration came from a high-ranking magistrate who contended that, when blacks are young, they are as bright (*éveillés*) if not brighter than white children. When they reach puberty, however, they become dull (*s'abrutissent*), and as they enter adulthood they display an innate inability to think and act as adults.

To what should this mental and intellectual sclerosis be attributed? Not surprisingly, to the blacks' so-called sexual excesses, caused by an inordinate sexual drive that only proper education and an adequate social environment can curb and restrain. This being the case, Ombredane (1949: 525) postulates, "The attitudes and capabilities of Blacks can only be defined in relation to a set of physical, socio-economic, political, cultural, and technical conditions." As these conditions undergo change, progress, and refinement, presumably through the benevolent tutelage of white educators and administrators, so do blacks' capabilities and behaviors.

More damning still is Robert Maistriaux's 1957 study. Whereas Ombredane tended to attribute the innate *sous-évolution* of the Congolese man to his environment, Maistriaux saw a correlation between physiology and psychology. In keeping with post-Darwinian ideas on the primitive mind developed by such scholars as Franz Boas, Lucien Lévy-Bruhl, and Jean Piaget, Maistriaux devised a battery of cognitive tests he administered to three groups of natives: bush population (*population de la brousse*), long-time urban dwellers (*population des centres extra-coutumiers*), and évolués. Bush people and some urban residents, whom he labeled *sous-évolués* (underevolved), scored the same as European phrenasthenic subjects, leading him to emphasize that, "taken as a whole, Central African Blacks show marked inferiority in all exercises requiring abstract intelligence" (Maistriaux 1957: 167). As for "intuitive intelligence," most illiterate people tested in nonurban centers never reached beyond Stage 2, which European children between the ages of four and seven go through gradually (173). Even Congolese évolués lagged behind European children who would complete tests faster than the former. Although they did score higher than their "underevolved" counterparts, évolués only achieved such scores through a considerable amount of effort, whereas European children took similar tests effortlessly (111).

Maistriaux's conclusions? The influence of the milieu only partially explained the relative lack of intelligence of the Congolese. Their "emotivity" and "proverbial" idleness accounted also for their intellectual atrophy vis-à-vis whites. Maistriaux's conclusions had a practical objective as well, for they brought home to European employers the futility of treating African laborers as anything other than children: "If white employers understood that, perhaps they would be more patient with their black workers and strive to make them understand what is expected of them, even if that means spending more time painstakingly and thoroughly explaining instructions to them" (Maistriaux 1957: 177).

Ombredane and Maistriaux's hortatory theory, contending that "conversion" of the natives, to use Mudimbe's apt notion, could be engineered through a wise formula of societal changes, appealed to missionaries and emboldened their resolve to refashion a new "Congolese man" through their youth educational programs. They projected on the Congolese youth images of a "Congo ya Sika" (new Congo) peopled by hardworking monogamists and devoted Catholics who had been successfully lulled into complacency by the colonial oeuvre, rendered impervious to foreign propaganda that painted Belgian colonization in any less-than-exemplary light, and above all made politically amorphous and acquiescent to the pace of political reforms and the eschatological narratives of Belgian colonialism. Congolese youth, then, became the future of Congolese man, the colonial laboratory where missionaries strove to re-create Congolese man in their own image—or, at least, in the image of the triumphant West.

Darkest Hollywood

The Catholic missionaries' salvific interventions were, of course, deployed primarily within the education system that they alone controlled until the late 1940s, when two important reforms broke their monopoly by creating a secular school system (1946) and providing public subsidies to Protestant schools (1948), which until then had to make do without state support (Tshimanga 2001: 161). Yet Catholic missionaries did not rely on homilizing and schooling alone in their attempts to educate Congolese youth and instill in them new manly values. They also tapped into sports, boy scouting, and films, the last still being considered a new medium in the prewar period.[13]

Initially, film projections in the Belgian Congo represented an antidote for homesick Europeans who never quite anticipated the rigors and boredom of colonial life in the tropics (Goerg 2015: 49). As early as 1911, films produced in France and in the United States were shown to small European audiences in

Elisabethville and Leopoldville and, as intended, provided a vital link to and vicarious window onto "civilization" (Ramirez and Rolot 1985: 20). But very quickly European missionaries realized that cinema could easily appeal to Africans and reach wider audiences and thereby spread the educational schemes that had until then been limited to religious, school, and training programs.[14]

A distinction must be made at the outset between (1) the homegrown missionary film production in the Congo,[15] which was promoted by a handful of Belgian missionaries, including Abbé André Cornil,[16] and (2) the foreign film projection, most notably of Hollywood feature films, that became the mainstay in most movie houses across the colony. What strikes anyone remotely familiar with Belgian colonial society is the fact that, under the guise of producing films that somewhat reflected the society around them, missionary filmmaking neophytes reproduced the contradictions of Belgian colonialism, which touted its transformative prowess yet harbored an immutable view of Africans. Thus films produced in the postwar era give some sense of this view—and of the moralizing tone that many whites continued to use—even as the figure of the modern évolué became emblematic of the whole era.

In the late 1940s and early 1950s, colonial filmmakers produced educational films on the trot aimed at imparting to rural as well as urban African audiences some rudiments of civilization, as though no significant changes had transformed their social and cultural landscape. Films such as *L'Heure* (1947, to teach the natives punctuality), *L'Utilité de la couverture*[17] (1947, on how to use a blanket), *La Propreté du corps* (1947, on bodily hygiene), *La Brouette* (1948, about the wheelbarrow), *La Propreté de la maison* (1950, on how to keep the house clean), and countless other documentaries and feature films subjected their African audience to vexing sermonizing. Time and again, missionary movies recycled the demeaning off-screen tropes that defined Congolese as childish and apelike.

An example is Abbé Cornil's foray into feature-length film, which in 1951 resulted in *Sikitu, le boy au coeur pur,* which Belgian critic André Bondroit derided as a "native Western," a paltry effort that demonstrated missionary film production's infantilization of the Congolese adult public (Convents 2006: 99). Sikitu, the main character, is a loyal houseboy who bravely confronts thieves trying to break into his white masters' house while they are away, foiling their plans. Yet Cornil uses this valiant character in the crudest way possible: to summon and prop up the primitive figure of the African as the Belgians saw it. Sikitu is given a pair of binoculars by his employer's young son but never quite manages to look through the right end of them, even when shown how to do so by the child. He finally gives up and climbs atop a pole to contemplate the beautiful horizons without the aid of the white man's strange contraption, trusting only his sharp vision (Ramirez and Rolot 1985: 348). The symbolism is too obvious to warrant further analysis here. Suffice it to say that these racist images proved so entrenched and acquired such a scientific imprimatur that they could migrate seamlessly from one context to another, from one medium to another, from table talk to the big screen without being challenged by the évolués and indigènes who flocked to watch these movies.

When, in the postwar period, colonial filmmakers portrayed African workers as intelligent and capable of performing complex tasks at the helm of sophisticated industrial machines, they sought above all to woo investors and showcase the Belgian Congo as a bustling colonial frontier where large profits could be made thanks to a docile and skilled workforce. This was perhaps one of the first visual attempts to cast the Congolese native workforce as human capital, adding to the lucrative credo of the Belgian colony as a natural resource bonanza.

Another stereotype that was recycled ad nauseam in missionary narratives has to do with the use of Congolese actors and actresses in colonial films. It is beyond the scope of this work to explore how African actors may have choreographed their performance in films, as Christraud Geary (2002) has observed in the realm of colonial photography, to alter the "image world" that colonial filmmakers sought to project about Africa. Colonial filmmakers essentialized African man as innately predisposed to acting, owing to "his total lack of timidity and gaucherie" ("son manque complet de timidité et de gaucherie"). "His acting is completely natural and his sense of humor highly developed," noted L. Van Bever, who was appointed to the helm of the Colonial Cinematographic Office instituted by the general government. In contrast, the African woman underwhelmed these colonial filmmakers as "awkward, timid, and self-conscious." Because "it will never be possible to count on her," Van Bever prescribed omitting female characters from educational films and, when they had to appear, using "an African woman who has already been affected by European influence" ("une Africaine qui a déjà subi l'influence européenne"; Ramirez and Rolot 1985: 38).

As for the growing African audience that these films aimed to reach, missionary filmmakers took it upon themselves to shape their viewing experience through several devices, including censorship. Films for the native, most filmmakers agreed, had to be extremely simple,[18] since, in a widely quoted statement by Van Bever,

> High, low, and oblique panoramic sequences and tracking shots befuddle him. He does not understand that it is the camera that moves. He sees trees moving on the screen, buildings moving up and down. . . . He does not understand it! Oftentimes he thinks he is being fooled and throws rocks at the screen.[19] (Ramirez and Rolot 1985: 137)

Dialogue had to be kept to a minimum and appear in French subtitles on the screen. Depending on the locations where movies were projected, missionaries made sure that a speaker was on hand to read aloud, through a microphone, a prepared translation in the local language[20] (Van Bever 1950: 59; see also Mosley 2001: 93). Hence, in their effort to transform Congolese into "fidèles et loyaux sujets de la Belgique," missionary cinematic enterprise focused not only on indoctrinating their African audience with propaedeutic images but also, in the words of Van Bever, on teaching them "how to view images" (Ramirez and Rolot 1985: 138). Whether they knew it or not, missionary filmmakers thus initiated a confrontation with the African audience—a confrontation in which the images unreeling on screen symbolized just one of the battlefields.

Another way colonial authorities sought to shape Africans' viewing experience came in the form of surveys that spectators were asked to fill out after seeing a film. One such leaflet that has survived comes from a 1946 film shown to Leopoldville's évolués. True to form, the leaflet, laden with *tu* (rather than *vous*), departs little from the condescending tone and paternalistic tenor that évolués came to resent:[21]

> Spectator, this leaflet is for you. The Service de l'Information du Congo Belge wants to help you (*te rendre service*). It has organized this cinema showing for you (*pour toi*), Congolese évolué. We will organize more showings. To plan for future showings, answer the following questions:
>
> 1. Did you like this cinema showing? Why or why not?
> 2. What movies did you like this evening?
> 3. Was the 5-franc admission fee right for you? Why not?
> 4. What movies would you like to see at future showings?
> 5. Do you have other ideas to offer? Which ones?
>
> Answer those five questions. Send your answers to the "Service de l'Information du Congo Belge" in Leopoldville. Don't send us a long letter, only precise information. We want to give you good entertainment and allow you to continue your training. It's up to you to earn the authorities' trust. (Ramirez and Rolot 1985: 182)

Clearly not intended to grant ownership of their viewing experience to the African audience, the leaflet blatantly exposes colonial cinema's overarching mission, which was to parlay colonial dichotomies into film. Both off and on screen, the white paternal figure was invariably juxtaposed and contrasted with the infantilized, feral black figure of the indigène and with the image of his colonial avatar, the évolué.

On- and Off-Screen Schemes

As Philip Mosley (2001: 93) has pointed out, missionary filmmakers, unlike their secular counterparts, "had an excellent grasp of the importance of narration, tale, and palaver in the local culture, and they proceeded to use these elements to great effect in their films," thus attempting to control what images African audience viewed, how they viewed them, and how these images affected their attitudes and behaviors vis-à-vis the colonial situation. For instance, several missionaries' films follow traditional local versions of the *mythe du héros* and deftly exploit their educational and entertaining value. As Cornil explained in a 1952 interview, keeping and transposing these traditional myths into a modern medium enabled him to capture the audience's attention and build viewer loyalty. "They should help us make [natives into] men (*faire des hommes*)" (Ramirez and Rolot 1985: 271), Cornil contended. There is, of course, a certain irony in missionaries recycling African traditional myths into a new medium that, for all intents and purposes, aimed to radically reshape the African ethos in the likeness of European culture. Whether it dawned on them that they were doing so matters little here; what matters, as we will examine later, is how some viewers in the audience reacted, deciding to reject missionary films altogether and instead claim attributes of masculinity from an unlikely source—American Western movies.[22]

When films were projected outdoors to several thousand African spectators, crowded next to each other at close quarters,[23] the presence of whites watching them view the films—especially homemade propaganda films—often served to keep African viewers from expressing spontaneous negative responses.[24] Cornil, for example, categorized his African audience into four groups: those who lived in the jungle and had no exposure whatsoever to cinema; village dwellers for whom showings amounted to big events because films were few and far between; township residents who became moviegoers; and évolués, the only group that could grasp cinematographic subtleties as Europeans did. He explained his strategy as follows:

Regularly I would show in Leopoldville's townships films about the life of our Lord. Those films closely follow the Gospel. . . . Dialogue, if not well commentated, risk ruining the projection. The spectator does not understand it, becomes distracted because of lack of action, and loses interest in the movie. What method did I adopt? Since these movies are American, I would first proceed to screen them in private and translate them. . . . Then, I would give the transcript to my commentator who would read them several times. I would schedule a private showing for him with the adequate explanations, always insisting on the passages that mattered the most, and would give him further explanations. During the first public showings, I paid attention to the crowd's reaction and watched for scenes that left the audience unfocused. Following the showing, with transcripts in hand, I would make additional remarks to the commentator to gear him up for future showings. This was undoubtedly a long and tedious process, yet it enabled me to draw a crowd of seven to eight thousand spectators who would watch a religious film in the utmost silence. (quoted in Ramirez and Rolot 1985: 275)

What is striking in Cornil's admission is his determination not to give his African audience any opportunity to display agency. Thus missionaries did not rely on films alone (even films they themselves made) but also employed off-screen ancillaries and schemes that framed viewers' moviegoing experiences.

In addition to their own productions, missionaries exposed the African audience to foreign films that the colonial Censorship Commission (Commission de Contrôle des Films Cinématographiques) deemed suitable for the natives. Although censorship did not exist in Belgium, as Convents (2006: 19) and others (Biltereyst et al. 2012: 187) have made clear,[25] colonial authorities did agonize over the issue in light of the fact that, until May 1936, movie houses in the main cities were not yet segregated. Even when some movies deemed suitable only for the European public were screened, Africans who worked in the facilities as bartenders, doorkeepers, and janitors could always take a peek at them. This seems to have been a concern very early on, for in July 1917 the colonial government issued an ordinance regulating film projections for the natives (Convents 2006: 31). The government knew, however, that barring Africans from watching films reserved for European eyes was as futile as preventing them from moving to town.

The introduction of segregated theaters in 1936 solved the problem only partially because private film distributors could not afford to cater only to the limited European market. Profitability could not always go hand in hand with indoctrination but also had to court entertainment. For that reason, private film entrepreneurs tended to focus on wide distribution of movies, and hence on their entertainment value, rather than on following the edicts of the colonial government.[26] Each movie had to be viewed by the Censorship Commission, which deemed it suitable or unsuitable[27] to the African audience. After clearing the Commission, the film would then be issued a *carte de contrôle* (control card), a copy of which was attached to the reel box, to be exhibited to the authorities upon request wherever the film premiered. Although a January 12, 1945, ordinance prohibited showing any movie *in the presence of natives* that had not gone through the Commission, an investigation confirmed that many private entrepreneurs and foreign missionaries flouted this rule. Hundreds of imported films that circulated throughout had never gone through the Commission.[28]

Some movies that missionaries initially used with great success as tools of evangelization met a surprising reception when they were shown to youth audience in Leopoldville after World War II. Most of these movies, such as Julien Duvivier's *Golgotha* (released in 1935) and Cecil B. DeMille's *The King of Kings* (1927), include a Passion of the Christ scene. Until that scene appeared, young people would be watching the movie quietly. Then when a Roman soldier started to flog Jesus with a lead-tipped whip, the young audience would erupt and start to shout "makasi! makasi!" (harder! harder!) to the missionaries' horror. Movies such as those mentioned above never went through the Censorship Commission since they were rejected by the missionaries themselves.[29]

Immatriculés pushed hard and obtained, thanks to the July 5, 1955, ordinance, the right to mingle with Europeans in their movie theaters, such as Leopoldville's Ciné-Palace, and watch movies that censorship still prohibited to the rest of the Congolese.[30] Other cinephiles would simply cross the river to Brazzaville to binge on films and wine, which, true to form, the French never denied their colonial subjects.[31] Segregated movie theaters hit such a nerve that they figure prominently in the litany of oppression and humiliation excoriated in Patrice Lumumba's impromptu June 30, 1960 independence speech.[32]

Policing Cinema

No one knows exactly when the first intramural movie theater opened its doors in Leopoldville's cité indigène (native quarters).[33] According to Rik Otten (1984: 19) and Philip Mosley (2001: 92), in 1937 Father Alexander Van den Heuvel, a Scheutist missionary, had the first movie theater built in the cité indigène. Guido Convents's (2006: 47–48) richly documented study broaches the topic only tangentially, alluding to 1950 as a watershed in the proliferation of indoor theaters in the African townships, some even owned and operated by Congolese. Francis Ramirez and Christian Rolot (1985) examine colonial film production more than its reception by African audiences. A little-known thesis by Henri Daubresse (1955: 46) on the cité indigène provides some numbers for these open-air theaters at a time when they could still be counted on one hand: only two in 1950, their number jumped to four in 1952, and six the following year. Colonial administrator Emmanuel Capelle (1947: 80) identified only one private indoor theater under construction in the cité indigène in the late 1940s.

At any rate, the advent of World War II proved to be a boon for film production and projections in Leopoldville and elsewhere in the Belgian Congo, as film became an indispensable weapon on the home front to counter enemy propaganda in kind. In 1942, Father Van den Heuvel, who ministered to the Force Publique, started mobile projections in Leopoldville Province, targeting not only the Force Publique troops but also civilians (Gondola 1997a: 310). By the late 1940s, cinema had become part of an established genre in Leopoldville's African areas in terms of film selection and projection, audience participation, and venues (see table 3.1). Africans from all walks of life were exposed to film. In their *cercles d'études* and *cercles de loisirs* (social clubs), usually organized under missionary and government patronage, évolués entertained themselves with private film projections.[34] For a membership fee of 50 francs, they could also join any of the film clubs (*cinéforums*) that multiplied in Leopoldville starting in late 1953.[35] Ordinary Congolese (or indigènes) attended outdoor projections sponsored by the

Table 3.1 Fixed and mobile film projectors in the Leopoldville Province

Year	Fixed	Percent	Mobile	Percent
1949	9 (n/a)	50[1]	2 (n/a)	17[1]
1950	41 (31%)[2]	50	17 (59%)[2]	21
1951	42 (36)	39	23 (61)	26
1952	50 (36)	43	24 (63)	22
1953	57 (35)	36	33 (56)	22
1954	68 (31)	39	39 (59)	24
1955[3]	80 (26)	34	49 (57)	29
1956	83 (30)	29	54 (50)	30
1957	94 (28)	32	52 (50)	21
1958	95 (23)	27	58 (50)	23

Source: *Rapport sur l'administration de la colonie du Congo belge* (1949–1958).
[1]Percentage of total projectors operating in the Belgian Congo.
[2]Percentage owned by missionaries.
[3]According to Babillon (1957: 120), a total of only 14 projectors operated in the cité indigène of Leopoldville by the end of 1955.

missionaries and the Service de l'Information du Congo Belge. Increasingly, they patronized privately owned theaters because these venues tended to offer the best and most recent commercial film selections.[36] Indeed, by the early 1950s, there appears to have been no shortage of venues in Leopoldville where cinephiles could enjoy a vast array of film genres.

Before exploring the cinematic culture that the African audience created in an attempt to assert its agency, let us look at how Congolese were finally granted access to a cinematic world from which they had hitherto been banned. When Belgian missionaries exposed African audiences to Hollywood feature-length films for the first time, the Tarzan movies were almost the only cinematic diet they all agreed could be spoon-fed to domesticated évolués.[37] Cornil, who promoted Tarzan films more than any other missionary, felt compelled to explain their "success" in a 1953 article:

> C'est facilement compréhensible, ces films se passent dans la jungle . . . et les animaux y ayant souvent un rôle important, le Noir, même évolué, est encore si près de tout cela. (Convents 2006: 49)

> It's easily understandable. These movies are cast in the jungle . . . and due to the important role animals have in them, Blacks, even évolués, are still so close to all that.

Beyond Tarzan, every other movie genre had to present itself in the best possible light in order to clear censorship, even if that meant losing a few scenes here and there at the hands of overzealous colonial censors. For instance, although Charlie Chaplin's silent films seemed innocuous and appealed widely to African audiences, missionaries worried that Chaplin's hijinks could damage the immaculate image of the white man they had so painstakingly composed. What else could an immature and benighted black audience conclude when they saw "Charlot," as Chaplin was fondly nicknamed, flouting table manners or thrashing a policeman (and other white characters stone drunk, picking their noses, butt kicking, or otherwise behaving unbecomingly), if not that all whites in Europe must be unmannerly?

When it came to Westerns (or "cowboy films," as they were locally referred to), colonial suspicion was kept at bay until African audiences started to copycat Hollywood's epic gunslingers in their townships. In 1953, for example, a colonial report lamented the "real danger" that Western movies posed to immature and emotionally feeble minds.[38] "In centers such as Elisabethville [Lubumbashi] and Jadotville [Likasi]," the report continued, "the provincial governor bemoans [the fact] that organized 'cowboy' bands are attacking residents at night, leading to complaints being filed in court."[39] Another colonial source deplored the "bad influence" of Western movies on Congolese youth (Daubresse 1955: 46).

Western films continued to elicit disapproval because of their link with off-screen antics. According to one Congolese évolué, the outbreaks of youth banditry in Leopoldville could be explained largely by youth exposure to Westerns:

> Upon leaving the theater after watching such a film, one could hear these kids, the future of the nation, yell: "I am a cowboy" (*Je suis cow-boy*) or "I'll do you cowboy" (*Je vais te faire cow-boy*) or "Let's try cowboy on this man" (*Essayons le cow-boy sur un tel monsieur*).[40]

In 1958, Jadotville authorities apprehended a group of youngsters who had attempted to derail a train. Brought before the court, a local newspaper reported, the culprits confessed their misdeed of derring-do and candidly attributed it to wanting to reenact a Far West scene they had seen on the big screen (Ramirez and Rolot 1985: 274)—a pattern that seemed common everywhere cowboy films reached African audiences.[41] For that reason, the Censorship Commission scrutinized Western films. It banned some, like Budd Boetticher's *Seminole* (*L'Expédition du Fort King*, 1953) and Jerry Hopper's 1953 *Pony Express* (*Le Triomphe de Buffalo Bill*), starring Charlton Heston in the role of Buffalo Bill (see figure 3.1), but allowed others, such as Randolph Scott's movies (except for *Le Relais de l'or maudit* [*Hangman's Knot*], 1952). Other movies that made the cut included *Les Desperados* (*The Desperadoes*, 1943), *La Vallée maudite* (*Gunfighters*, 1947), *Retour des sans loi* (*Return of the Bad Men*, 1948), *La Charge héroïque* (*She Wore a Yellow Ribbon*, 1949), and countless B Western movies, especially one that would have a lasting impact on Kinois youth: *The Lone Ranger*.

Figure 3.1 "Le Triomphe de Buffalo Bill." Advertisement for the French version of Jerry Hopper's *Pony Express.*

Invariably, informants cite *The Lone Ranger*—or, rather, its dubbed French versions, *Les Justiciers du Farwest* and *Le Dernier des fédérés*—as the quintessential Western film that influenced them the most. *The Lone Ranger* first appeared as a radio series in 1933 and was later (1949–1957) adapted to a television series that starred Clayton Moore as the masked Texas Ranger who rides along with his faithful, laconic Indian sidekick, Tonto, to enforce law and order and set up cliffhanger shootout and fistfight denouements. The visual version, which is what the Bills were exposed to, supplied an inexplicable mystic that reached deep into their psyche. The masked man with his native-born sidekick continues to fascinate contemporary audiences as exemplified by the new Disney remake in which actor Johnny Depp attempts to rescue Tonto from the clutches of racism.[42] For the Bills, Tonto had no place in their imagination. He was what he was meant to be, a shadow, who not unlike Zorro's mute confidant and acolyte, Bernardo, softens the rough edges of the hero's steel-thewed persona, yet is conveniently placed to enhance the hero's masculinity. The masked man, and him alone, captivated the Bills. He had all the lore and allure: his silver stallion and his silver bullets, his backstory—coming back from a near-death experience—his righteousness and his strengths. He commanded the right weapon, the right vehicle, the right skills, and the right helper. He cut a striking heroic figure with panache and clout, strangely attractive, and able to summon skills to get himself out of danger and save the day.[43]

Attributing youth interstitiality to the influence of foreign films—especially films that originated from an Anglo-Saxon, Protestant source, viewed with deep distrust in the history of the Belgian Congo—no doubt deflected attention from the pernicious nature of Belgian colonization itself. Blaming foreign films for youth delinquency conveniently downplayed an endogenously generated phenomenon in a way that denied township youth any cultural and social agency. It also added to the "specterization" of global cultural flows. Finally, it enabled the creation of a united censorship front that ran the gamut from missionaries to évolués. Thus the quixotic battle to forestall any foreign influence that might resonate within the Belgian *empire du silence* actually reflected Belgian anxieties and rearguard actions in a postwar world where even undesirable cultural flows could no longer be kept at bay.

In the mid-1950s, Leopoldville's Censorship Commission broadened its membership to include Congolese évolués. Joseph Kasa-Vubu, former seminarian and freshly elected president of the Abako (Alliance des Bakongo), joined the Commission. So did Alphonse Sita, who worked at the public prosecution office in the Kikwit district. It is hard to say what impact the presence of these Congolese really had on the Commission's work. However, where white censors squarely focused on banning movies deemed inappropriate to the African audience, Congolese members insisted on drawing a line between viewer categories.

Sita, perhaps its most active Congolese member, lobbied the Commission not to concentrate only on film selection. The Commission, he argued, should strictly enforce admission policy and effectively ban children from seeing adult movies.[44] Apparently, lax and profit-driven theater owners turned a blind eye to the Commission's loose admission policy and indiscriminately admitted children and adults to films labeled "enfants non admis" (no children allowed).

Sita's indefatigable campaign found a triad of sympathetic allies in journalists Philippe Kanza (*L'Avenir du Congo*), Michel Colin (*La Voix du Congolais*), and Paul Kalambaye (*Courrier d'Afrique*). They attended several film projections and used their respective outlets to voice their concerns. After watching a Western film projection at Cornil's theater at Stade Reine Astrid, amidst a raucous juvenile audience, Colin wrote a scathing indictment:

> What was shown, if not fistfights, killing, and looting? . . . Every blow, every stab wound in the neck, every act of brigandage was greeted with applause. Is this the education designed for the masses and, above all, for school children?"[45]

"Le grand mal est dans les salles de cinéma" (Great evil is in the movie theaters), he continued, in his relentless crusade against cowboy films and cowboy gear sold in Leopoldville (Convents 2006: 176).

The fact that policing the cinema became a cause célèbre for Congolese évolués meant several things, of course—and chiefly that the colonial authorities had lost the censorship battle.[46] The reason did not involve film viewing per se, but when, where, and how African audiences watched movies.

(E)motion and Commotion

In a piece devoted to orality and film reception and drawing on multiple examples from the Belgian Congo, Vincent Bouchard addresses the critical issue of film viewing and how, according to prevalent convention, members of the audience are expected not to engage the film and fellow moviegoers but to keep silent throughout the projection. This is because, as Marks (2000: xiii) argues, "optical visuality has been accorded a unique supremacy" in the modern Euro-American film-viewing tradition. It has been defined as an idiosyncratic experience, unlike other forms of popular entertainment, such as sports and popular music concerts, that usually involve communal experience and expression. Bouchard argues:

> Other viewing practices, however, are possible. In the popular forms of film projections, the brouhaha and various audience activities modify the reception of the film shown. At times, the interaction between the spectators and the film allows for appropriation. (Bouchard 2010: 95)

Instances of seemingly unruly and boisterous audiences at Western film shows abound. The rambunctious scenes he witnessed in West African movie theaters, with some in the audience screaming frantically, prompted French ethnologist and filmmaker Jean Rouch to remark that dialogues and music played no role in the way African audiences viewed movies (Goerg 2015: 165). Writing about 1950s southern Rhodesia, American anthropologist Hortense Powdermaker notes, "During the film men, women, and children rose to their feet in excitement, bending forward and flexing their muscles with each blow the cowboys gave." The commotion and pandemonium, she insists, "could be heard several miles away" (quoted in Burns 2002a: 116). Participation at the movies elicited greater excitement and emotional investment from the African audiences than Sunday afternoon tribal dances, Powdermaker contends (Burns 2006: 69). In Kinshasa, the experience of going to movies elicited the same degree of elation that drove throngs of soccer fans to stadiums:

> Going to the movies was worse than going to a soccer game. Those who saw the movie [the previous week] came back as [self-appointed] commentators. We could see the same movie two or three weeks in a row. We couldn't even follow dialogue. We were more interested in the action. It was worse than a stadium. It was impossible to ask people to keep quiet.[47]

> As soon as projection starts, the crowd gets spun into a frenzy. At the first appearance of the cowboy, a deluge of applause and an explosion of deafening voices and whistles fill the room. The film dialogues are drowned out by the screams of vociferous spectators jumping to their feet, asking for more violent action. Some climb on top of their seats, clench their fists, and lash out at imaginary opponents. (Kolonga Molei 1977: 28)

Richard Wright witnessed similar scenes on the Gold Coast and penned his tortured experience in *Black Power: A Record of Reactions in a Land of Pathos* with detachment and distance, subjecting "the African" to the type of psychoanalytical treatment only prejudiced white colonists would:

> Indeed, the laughter, the lewd comments, and the sudden shouts rose to such a pitch that I could not hear the shadowy characters say their lines. I could not follow the story amid such hubbub and came to the conclusion they could not either; it soon became clear that the story was of minor interest to them. . . . When a cowboy galloped across the scrubby plains, they shouted in chorus: "go, go, go, go, go . . . !"
> During stretches of dialogue, they chatted among themselves about the last explosion of drama, waiting for the action to begin again. It was clear that the African was convinced that movies ought to move. . . . A fist fight took place and each blow that landed brought: "swish-um! Swish-um!"

> Throughout the film the audience commented like a Greek chorus, and when the heroine was trapped I was sure that they wanted the villain to violate her. (Wright 1954: 173–74)

The fact that many of these movie houses operated right next to or shared the same compound with a buvette or a beer hall added fuel to the volatile mix. After all, these were places where masculinities came under attack as courtesans plied their trade in a sort of Rabelaisian saturnalia and men absorbed alcohol[48] in an attempt to regain control over their bruised manhood (Gondola 1996). After watching a Western movie at Astra (an open-air theater that could seat up to 1,500 spectators), Siluvangu, MacCaulay (which belonged to a Nigerian entrepreneur), or Mingiedi, spectators, including youngsters, would pour into the adjacent buvettes to drink and emulate their favorite Western heroes.

Indeed, as James Burns argues (2006: 69), the performativity of African audiences reflected local ways of engaging with actions on screen that contrasted with audience reception in Europe and the West in general. In other words, what colonial officials and some évolués derided as disorderly conduct and cinematic illiteracy can instead be viewed as détournement (diversion), appropriation, and attempts by these audiences to create a cinematic culture of their own.

There also seems to be a deeper logic at work here, and these young viewers may have actually shown a better grasp of the Western genre than they are given credit for. After all, if it were not for action, the Western would have probably not existed. The Western's concomitant commitment to both action and silence, as Lee Clark Mitchell and Jane Tompkins have demonstrated, is what sustained its appeal. "When heroes talk, it *is* action," writes Tompkins, and by that she means a nonverbal language that conveys self-containment, self-restraint, and the physicality of masculine control over emotion (Tompkins 1992: 51, 56). "Valuing action over words, marking silence as the most vivid of actions, the cowboy hero throws us back onto the male physique, shifting attention from ear to eye in the drama of masculinity," echoes Mitchell (1996: 165). If silence and action make the man, they also create rhythm and movement that draw the viewer to the film.

Young people, especially, parlayed their vision of the Far West from the screen into the street, creating in the process a unique hybrid blend that conflated the Hollywood version of the drifting cowboy with local elements of manhood and fashioned township gangs after frontier posses. Kinshasa was hardly the only milieu in colonial Africa where this cultural détournement played out, both on and off screen. For example, Sébastien Le Pajolec's work on the *blousons noirs* and cinema lays bare the conflicting perceptions over the influence of cinema on youth violence. Bursting onto the Parisian scene in 1959, the blousons noirs, as French historian Françoise Tétard nicely put it, "ont rendu la société bavarde" (turned society into a chatterbox) (quoted in Le Pajolec 2007: 61). Narratives that purported to explain the appearance of the blousons noirs uniformly and stereo-typically indicted cinema as "une école du crime" (63).[49] Yet as Le Pajolec argued, cinema crystallized public fears about shifting cultural patterns and family values in the postwar period, fears that were then projected onto a large segment of youth. Yet for young people, American cinema merely served as a way to reinforce group identity.

Another example comes from Rob Nixon's (1994: 32) discussion of Sophiatown's notorious *tsotsis*—"frontiersfolk who survived by staying not within the law but just beyond its grasp"—with an emphasis on their agentive power. For Nixon, tsotsis created a subculture that is eminently and indisputably indigenous and authentic, and this is in no way precluded by the conspicuous appropriation of the American bioscopic lexicon deriving from both cowboy and gangster movies. Paralleling Nixon's analysis of Hollywood movies as iconic beacons that helped Sophiatowners harness their idea of urbanness and modernity is Charles Ambler's (2001) discussion of the reception of Westerns in northern Rhodesia. Copperbelt moviegoers not only unyoked Hollywood's disjointed images from their original contexts, whatever those might be,[50] but also turned these bioscopic experiences into forums. By engaging with film narratives as they unreeled on the big screen, segregated African audiences were creating a cinematic literacy with which to combat incipient charges leveled at them by whites and members of the African "elite" who scoffed at their inability to "get it." Hollywood cowboys—the epitome of American lore, heroism, and exceptionalism—were tropicalized into "Copperbelt cowboys" who roamed the streets in the African townships (Ambler 2001).

However nowhere but in Kinshasa did Hollywood's romanticization of the cowboy generate a cultural détournement that came to embody the urban experience itself and to define urbanness for decades to come.

PART II

MAN UP!

4 Tropical Cowboys

Je viens!

I am coming!

Buffalo Bill (on a French Wild West show poster)[1]

IN HER STUDY of the American West in film, Scottish literary historian Jenni Calder (1974: 197) tells us that John Wayne's father advised him, "Don't go around looking for trouble. But if you ever get in a fight, make sure you win it." How this "Western" admonition got translated in Kinshasa's tropical West—if indeed it did so—into the proverbial "Mama alobaki, soki moninga abeti yo, yo pe obeti ye" (Mother said, if a schoolmate hits you, you must hit them back) provides a point of entry into this chapter on "tropical cowboys." When a boy in Kinshasa was trounced in the schoolyard and came home mortified, someone in his household was sure to remind him, "Mother said, if a schoolmate hits you, you must hit them back." Usually, an older relative or the mother herself would then proceed to administer another beating to the pugilist.

That the admonition switched from the paternal figure (John Wayne's father) to the Congolese mother (who, as seen in chapter 3, had been utterly neglected in the redemptive schemes of colonial administrators and missionaries) provides yet another twist to this seeming détournement. How can we tell with certainty that *Mama alobaki* originated, even remotely, in Western lore and its Hollywood lure? Might it not instead be linked to the "traditional" ethos, which "evolving" men and évolués in 1950s Kinshasa eschewed, leaving women (who were considered *sous-évoluées,* or "underdeveloped") to become its most ardent guardians? Or perhaps the idea belongs to Kinshasa's postwar culture itself and thus to a time when waves of new ethnic migrants were pouring into the urban crucible and had to sort each other out, compete for scarce resources, and find ways to navigate the changing urbanscape?

Whatever the case, the urban environment that witnessed the emergence of tropical cowboys registered several upheavals, in which the advent of Western movies figured, perhaps, as the eye of the vortex. Although juveniles' inherent fascination with violence may have served as backdrop to Kinshasa's gangs, it was the postwar colonial urban context, which could no longer hold global cultural flows at bay, that provided the impetus. Kinois youths did not respond to the appeal of American Westerns by simply reenacting some of their rambunctious scenes and appropriating their antics, sartorial elements, and ribald jokes, as other youths did elsewhere.[2] Rather, they also parlayed these movies' mystical paraphernalia into a hybrid culture, tropicalizing the Western in such a way that it became almost impossible to examine the long and tumultuous genealogy of interstitial juvenile gang movements in Kinshasa without reference to the Western matrix.

To understand this genealogy, how it has suffused Kinshasa's vernacular culture (kinicité), and how it has defined its landscape and shaped society as a whole, from music to politics, we must begin with the figure of the Yankee or the Bill. Building on part 1, devoted to precolonial patterns of masculinities and film reception in postwar Kinshasa, this chapter focuses on the 1950s, when young people who had fallen through the cracks of the colonial strictures commandeered the urbanscape and performed their own tropical version of Hollywood's Far West. We begin with the figure of Buffalo Bill, the Bills' eponymous hero, a contested figure whom Catholic missionaries ushered in on celluloid and who immediately caught the attention of young audiences. By tracing the unlikely trajectory of the famed plainsman from the American frontier to the African tropics, this chapter shows how Buffalo Bill's "fiction on the frontier" contributed to the emergence of new standards of masculinity in Kinshasa.

Buffalo Bill: The Man and the Legend

After leaving office, Theodore Roosevelt (known as the "cowboy president") accepted the honorary vice presidency of the Buffalo Bill Memorial Association in memory of a man whom he regarded, in his own words, as "the most renowned of those men, steel-thewed and iron-nerved, whose daring opened the West to settlement and civilization . . . and American of Americans. . . . He embodied those traits of courage, strength and self-reliant hardihood which are vital to the well-being of the nation" (quoted in Carter 2000: 2). American journalist Gene Fowler, who had met William Frederick "Buffalo Bill" Cody (1846–1917) in person and conducted several interviews with him, had earlier penned his own eulogy of the plainsman in much the same dithyrambic vein:

> Remember the time when your cheeks were hot
> From the Indian raids on the vacant lot?
> Remember the rush of the boyhood thrill
> When the kids next door called you "Buffalo Bill"?
> . . .
> And now you've grown to the world of men,
> But you long for your boyhood days again.

And today the lips of the scout are still—
For God has taken your Buffalo Bill.
                    (quoted in Carter 2000: 3–4)

"American of Americans," America's quintessential cowboy, the roughest of all riders that the frontier begat, Pahaska (Long Hair, his Indian name—"Jesus, he was a handsome man," as the poet E. E. Cummings so emphatically immortalized him), or a "secular messiah," as Jane Tompkins (1992: 199) puts it, tongue-in-cheek—Cody was all this and more. Perhaps what set him apart was his ability to always drink upstream from the herd. Before Cody appeared on the scene as Buffalo Bill, Jenni Calder (1974: 191) writes, the cowboy roamed the West as a lonely, "unshaven, smelly, and sweat-stained" saddle tramp.[3] One press article published just after the Civil War echoed this century-old trope about cowboys, describing them, "in the quaint parlance of the time," Carter quips, as

> foulmouthed, blasphemous, drunken, lecherous, utterly corrupt. Usually harmless on the plains when sober, they are dreaded in towns, for then liquor has the ascendancy over them. . . . Employed as cow-boys only six months in the year—from May till November—their earnings are soon squandered in dissoluteness, and then they hunt to get odd jobs to support themselves until another cattle season begins. (Carter 2000: 261)

As the Civil War wound down, leaving behind a ravaged country and acrimonious feelings on all sides, men spilled over the vanishing frontier and, unlike Hollywood rendition, "they remained broke and broken, and drifted through the Western territories with just sufficient hope on the horizon to keep them moving" (Calder 1974: 32). Then Buffalo Bill rode, not just into town but right up on stage (and on screen as well), and singlehandedly transformed the image of the cowboy from hellion to a gun-toting centaur—"America's contribution to the world's stock of mythic heroes" (Kimmel 1996: 148)—at a time when, ironically, the West and the frontier that had created the cowboy had been long domesticated and seemed about to disappear (White 1994: 49). This was all the more impressive when one considers that Cody was not even himself a cowboy but spent a large part of his career out West as a plainsman, a scout, and above all a buffalo hunter who lent a hand to the killing of over fifty million American bison that roamed the plains.

How did Cody achieve this feat? Among the many answers historians have suggested, one seems to best the others. Cody's fame and legacy sprang not so much from his actions on the frontier, where there were many who outdid him, as from his ability to parlay his frontier exploits into stage acts in a performative quest for authenticity that blurred the already murky line between fact and fiction.[4] In fact, as Calder (1974: ix) has rightly noted, "Indians in showy costumes performed in New York and London while others fought their last battles in the deserts and mountains, or others starved on the reservations." Cody straddled seamlessly all three scenes of frontier, stage, and screen. From 1883 to his death in 1917, he brought the West to avid audiences in the United States and Europe, earned rave reviews from critics, performed before Queen Victoria and French president Sadi Carnot, entertained Pope Leo XIII in Rome, inspired Baden Powell to create the Boy Scout movement, and, last but not least, supplied the Western movie with his own iconic image, portrayed by actors in at least twenty-seven films, complete with the boots, hat, gloves, guns, and other accoutrements of a properly mythic cowboy-frontiersman hero.[5]

When the cowboy appeared in the first Western novel in 1887, writers sought to portray him as the "noble descendent of chivalric knights and crusaders" (Kimmel 1996: 152), according to one of those propagandists. Turning the lawless cowboy into a folk hero took place at a time when Americans craved new standards in the face of their own "crisis" of masculinity. And as Kimmel suggests, "nowhere could American men find a better exemplar of rugged outdoor masculinity than out west with the cowboy, that noble denizen of the untamed frontier" (148). The outdoors became an antidote to the overcivilization that, following Theodore Roosevelt, many came to regard as effete.[6] It promised, in the words of Tompkins (1992: 4), "a translation of the self into something purer and more authentic, more intense, more real." Among those who led the way to this incipient masculinity that reconnected man with nature was the larger-than-life figure of Buffalo Bill. Following an established tradition, one historian rightly credits Buffalo Bill's Wild West as "the point of origin for the premier Western character, the cowboy" (McVeigh 2007: 33).

Most Cody biographers attribute the creation of the Wild West show to Cody's patriotism one summer in North Platte, Cody's hideaway in Nebraska where he later purchased a 4,000-acre ranch. As the story goes, in 1882, despite the general apathy of North Platte residents, Cody decided to commemorate the Fourth of July in a most memorable fashion, by showing folks how to "rope and run and tend cattle." Then, he continued, "I'll stage an imitation buffalo hunt and show them how I used to hunt and shoot buffalo" (Carter 2000: 239). Patriotically inspired, the Wild West show would tap into this inexhaustible vein at home[7] as well as abroad, where it became a shorthand reenactment of the Manifest Destiny of the indomitable American spirit. "The Star Spangled Banner" (played by a cowboy band) figured prominently on the program, a solemn routine that Cody insisted must open each show.[8] Cody's shows were also billed as mixing entertainment with education, for Cody claimed to be not just a showman and a storyteller but, above all, an educator.[9] For instance, he wrote in the program of one of the shows: "The bullet is a kind of pioneer of civilization. Although its mission is often deadly, it is useful and necessary. Without the bullet, America would not be a great, free, united, and powerful country" (Rydell and Kroes 2005: 114).

As the frontier was disappearing, Cody placed himself both in the West, which according to Theodore Roosevelt he had opened to settlement and civilization on behalf of the great American nation, and in the representations of the West, where he endeavored to show on stage, to both American and European audiences, how, in line with the Turnerian frontier thesis,[10] the West shaped American identity. Richard White brings an incisive perspective to this well-orchestrated narrative by showing how this patriotic plot could only be achieved by reversing roles, with the conquerors becoming victims and the Indians being turned into murderous foes attacking valiant whites (White 1994: 29). Cody's Wild West show, with its authentic Indians circling wagons and racing around the arena on horseback in full tribal gear, certainly did not reenact the stereotypes of Indians as dirty cowards and the like. But it did evince and reinforce popular perception of Indians as "a whooping savage, a race of wild men" (McVeigh 2007: 33), especially because the highlight of the show was the reenactment of Custer's last stand, an Indian triumph.

Even when confined to battling enemies on stage in front of a captivated audience, Cody never truly hung up his spurs. When Congress declared war against Spain in 1898, after the American battleship *Maine* had been destroyed in Havana harbor, Cody offered to lead a company of cavalry scouts, even though his show was still running in New York. Fifty-two years old, addicted to alcohol, hardly the intrepid scout of his early days, Cody was willing to jeopardize his very profitable business to "stand by America."[11] Cody's services were never requested in the Spanish-American War. Until the end, however, he stood by America. In 1916, a year before his death, when another war beckoned America, Cody went on a lecture tour, promoting his Western films and calling for America's "preparedness" for the conflict that had already engulfed most of Europe (Carter 2000: 439).

Buffalo Bill's Wild West ultimately contributed, according to Joy Kasson (2000: 243–44), to postbellum American nationalism, by "giving audiences in North and South a common experience of patriotism and uniting former enemies against a symbolic common enemy. In Buffalo Bill's Wild West, Civil War memories were evoked and transformed in the service of an emerging nationalism."

Pausing her narrative, Kasson (2000: 45) ponders why Buffalo Bill had become a "singular, world-recognized celebrity" while his contemporaries and rivals "stayed in the ranks of struggling showmen." Some of these rival entertainers outlived Cody; others displayed the same avidity and egomania he did when it came to money and fame; and still others were better sharpshooters and even better performers than Cody. Yet their stage careers never took off. No one seemed able to replicate the "magic formula" (50) that Buffalo Bill had so easily concocted to bring audiences to their feet. According to Kasson, the elements that made Buffalo Bill so successful and inimitable were his ability to define his performances as "fictions of the frontier," his "sense of theatricality," and his partnership with savvy publicists and men with strong business acumen (51). Together these made Buffalo Bill a "commercial property" (54) of the men who built his career and from whom he eventually parted with bitterness and lingering ill will.

Cody's genius was his talent for blurring the difference between Cody the man and Buffalo Bill the hero and for performing as his own alter ego, both on the frontier and on stage. He thus came to embody what it meant to be a "real man," a "true man," at a time in American history when men tended to reduce masculinity to physicality, or when, to quote Kimmel (1996: 127), "the body did not *contain* the man, expressing the man within; now, that body *was* the man" (emphasis in the original).

Buffalo Bill in Leopoldville

As the West began to recede into the realm of memory following the closure of the frontier, several American adventurers, including former American president Theodore Roosevelt and celebrated author and humorist Mark Twain, ventured to Africa. Their forays into the "Dark Continent," as McCarthy noted, were in fact a vicarious journey back to the mythical West. And as they encountered Africa, these American travelers began "thinking of Africa in terms of America" (McCarthy 1977: 192). One such traveler, drawn to Africa by the prospect of hunting big herds of large mammals and wild beasts, thought of himself as the "Buffalo Bill of an extemporized African Wild West" (193). Upon touching African soil, another exclaimed, "This is not Africa; this is the American West!"[12]

Of course, there are many topographic similarities between the highland areas of the Rift Valley and the rugged portions of Wyoming and Colorado where the frontier once stood. But the likeness between these two mythicized places, the Dark Continent and the American West, consists of far more than what meets the eye. In eastern and southern Africa, the removal of native peoples from their land to make room for white settlers bears a startling resemblance to the ways in which the West was won.

Although these topographic and demographic similarities hardly applied to the rest of the continent, especially to the Central African basin, one could argue that a European version of Manifest Destiny—likening the American conquest of the West to the European colonization of the tropics, on the one hand, and American frontier pioneering to European bush soldiering, on the other—floated in the back of many a European official, missionary, and colonist's mind. The two colonial expansions certainly had one thing in common: their ostensible justification as a battle between civilization and savagery. Difficult to document but equally difficult to refute, it remains possible that at least some of the missionaries who introduced the character of Buffalo Bill to Congolese youth had been exposed to the famed scout's Wild West shows as they themselves came of age in their native Belgium. In fact, in their study of the worldwide expansion of American mass culture, Robert W. Rydell and Rob Kroes note the continued fascination with Buffalo Bill in Europe. After Cody and his motley crew of roughriders, sharpshooters, acrobats, and Sioux warriors pitched their tents and tepees in Paris, young children reenacted the Wild West's reenactment of the West in the Bois de Boulogne, just as other children did in so many other European cities (Rydell and Kroes 2005: 109). In 1958, at the World's Fair in Brussels, the Denver-based "American Wild West Show and Rodeo" (including 71 cowboys and cowgirls, 59 Indian performers, and 200 head livestock) staged a rerun of Buffalo Bill's Wild West. Its main act revived Buffalo Bill and Annie Oakley in a spectacular buffalo chase, complete with Indians on the warpath circling and attacking covered wagons.[13] Even today, the famed scout remains popular in Europe; his signature performance is still reenacted at a Wild West theme park on the outskirts of Munich that has more than a million visitors a year, and "a dozen other wild west attractions stretch from Spain to Scandinavia" (117).

Congo itself, perhaps, exemplified the universal appeal of Buffalo Bill more than any other locale. There, Buffalo Bill captured the imagination of both the downtrodden African youth and the white colonial elite. Whereas the former had only their imaginations to rely on when reenacting their hero's exploits in their shabby townships, European residents attended elaborate Buffalo Bill Wild West shows in the Cercle Hippique de Léopoldville (Leopoldville Equestrian Circle), complete with horses, bonfires, a replica of a saloon, and performers in full cowboy gear (Convents 2006: 170).

Why did Catholic missionaries expose Congolese youth to the legend of Buffalo Bill in the first place? Missionary films provide some clues to the popularity of Buffalo Bill, especially those that lionize colonial cities as an equivalent of the American frontier, where the battle between civilization and savagery is being played out. One such film, *Le Rêve d'un grand roi: Léopoldville capitale du Congo belge* (The dream of a great king: Leopoldville, capital of the Belgian Congo), released in 1951, describes Kinshasa much as American historians depict the frontier: as a spectacular crossroads of two civilizations, one modern and "nordic" (*sic*), the other "savage" and tropical (Ramirez and Rolot 1985: 207). The "grand roi" in the title is, of course, a hagiographic reference to Leopold II, de Koning-Bouwer (the Builder King) who, just as Buffalo Bill, was mythologized for supposedly bringing civilization to *terra nullius*.

The two empire builders probably never met, although it is safe to assume that they knew of and admired each other's civilizing work. In the eyes of Catholic missionaries, the two may have had more in common than just their resplendent white beards and august demeanors. Perhaps the missionaries even viewed Leopold and Buffalo Bill (consciously or unconsciously) as kindred spirits who had simultaneously tamed the "wild" and advanced Western civilization in a "waste space"[14] of obdurate savagery. Yet unlike Buffalo Bill, who muddied his boots wrestling with the Far West both on the frontier and on stage, Leopold II never set foot in his tropical fiefdom, nor could he have imagined that the place named after him would mushroom into an African megalopolis. Nevertheless, in keeping with Belgian historical tradition, missionary film narratives rhapsodized about Congo's founder in terms that evoke a sort of tropical Buffalo Bill—namely, as the embodiment of colonial masculinity, selflessly opening terra nullius to civilization, erecting symbols of modernity where stultified tribes had once languished, and showering the wretched natives with Europe's cultural largesse. Although the king's actions were spurred more by greed and egomania than by patriotism, as recent historiography has pointed out, missionary films glossed this over, establishing a fictitious filiation between Belgian Congo and Congo Free State.

Falling through the Cracks of Colonial Strictures

Although Catholic missionaries were ubiquitous in Kinshasa's townships as priests, teachers, headmasters, filmmakers, and occasionally caregivers and family counselors, they found themselves at odds with segments of Kinshasa youth who eschewed their ministries and never accepted the idea of white-bearded priests in white cassocks as male role models. Father Raphaël de la Kethulle, for example (see chapter 3), clashed with these youths starting in the late 1910s, when the first juvenile bands emerged in the cité indigène (native quarters). Described in confidential memos by his superiors as blunt, rude, severe, and even dictatorial and martial toward blacks,[15] de la Kethulle acted more like a sheriff than a shepherd.[16] His daily incursion into the cité was enough to strike fear into the hotheads, for he would immediately hand over to the police anyone he had caught prowling there. Never pausing to consider the social problems that led young people to drift away from the fold, de la Kethulle overemphasized the securitarian order, calling on the police to impose longer prison sentences. Borrowing from the eugenics lexicon of the 1920s, he suggested ridding the cité of "degenerate" elements by creating "farming colonies," reminding his audience that "we are dealing with Blacks in Congo" (on a affaire à des Noirs au Congo), who should be treated with the most draconian measures. Hence, de la Kethulle incorporated his arguments about youth unemployment and petty crime into the larger, Manichean narrative of civilization versus savagery, the city being here the frontier where law and order constantly battled the last bastions of primitive anomie.

Nevertheless, his early account provides useful information about the first youth bands of colonial Kinshasa. According to de la Kethulle's observations, roughly one hundred youngsters gathered in bands around one or two leaders, usually the oldest members, to engage in marauding, pickpocketing, and shoplifting (*vol à la tire*), using all kinds of schemes to evade the law. They would target anything that could be lifted—furniture, clothes, livestock, foodstuffs, and money. Most of the time the leader would carry out the most daring misdeeds while younger members acted as lookouts and others distracted potential victims.

In 1920, two bands hooked up under the leadership of a thirteen-year-old ringleader named Michel Fataki for a holdup that befuddled the city's residents: under cover of darkness, they broke into a freight car packed with cans of sardines and made off with most of its cargo. Undeterred by jail time, since they had become expert jailbreakers, they operated in Leopoldville and Brazzaville in small groups that cut across ethnicities. Bakongo and Bangala youths formed the nucleus of most bands, with Balari youths from Brazzaville and boys from Angola, Senegal, and other West African colonies making up the rest of this motley crew of *gavroches*.[17] They all hustled in Kinshasa—jobless, homeless, relying only on their wits and friends to stave off hunger (de la Kethulle 1922).[18] These were the earliest groups in a long line of *enfants de rue* (street children) who have come and gone in Kinshasa while leaving their marks on its urbanscape.

One vein that runs from the 1920s all the way to the present, gaining strength with each passing decade, can be described in statistical form. In the early 1920s, out of 3,000 "children" residing in Leopoldville, only 220 attended school. The vast majority had come to the city to work for as long as they could find employment but could also return to their villages at the end of their contracts or when they had accumulated enough "urban" commodities.[19] Still others eked out a living hustling and marauding in the townships. In the 1930s, missionary schools in Leopoldville turned away children who arrived in town just as they entered early adolescence. Too old to be enrolled in primary school, yet too young and with no training or skills to join the colonial workforce, they spent most of their time loitering with their peers on the street.[20] We learn from a letter written by Emmanuel Capelle, head of the Service de la Population Noire in Leopoldville, that in January 1949 about 500 boys had been "eliminated" from the city's Catholic schools, either because they were too old or because they were considered poorly equipped (*peu doués*) for being schooled.

Ironically, some schools also did away with entire grades and sections for lack of qualified teachers. Missionary education, which in theory was meant to cast a wide net, had turned into a fine-meshed filter that removed more and more undesirable elements, thus establishing a two-tiered colonial society of évolués and indigènes. Capelle's letter expresses the conundrum the colonial authorities thus faced, caught between their unwillingness to spend more on black youth and their fear of juvenile delinquency:

Des centaines de jeunes gens se trouvent actuellement dans la Cité, évidemment très peu désireux d'assurer un travail de manoeuvres, trop jeunes et trop mal formés pour se voir acceptés pour un autre travail. Il y a là pour eux et pour la communauté un réél danger de les voir, pour leur oisiveté forcée et leur manque de ressources, devenir des éléments de trouble et de graine de bandits.[21]

Hundreds of young people live today in the townships. They are unwilling to take on low-skilled jobs and are too young and unqualified to be hired in other jobs. There is a real danger for them and for the community since their idleness and lack of resources could lead them to become troublemakers and petty thieves.

The situation had worsened by the end of the colonial period, with at least one-third of the school-age population falling through the cracks. In 1952, *La Voix du Congolais* estimated that, of 45,000 school-age children, fewer than half attended school.[22] On January 1, 1956, with the city facing a chronic shortage of school facilities and seat space, out of 70,000 school-age children nearly 25,000 (10,000 boys and 15,000 girls) could not attend school (Lafontaine 1957: 60). As Jean La Fontaine (1969: 196), a Cambridge-trained anthropologist who arrived in Leopoldville in 1957 and did research there until 1963, noted, "schools occupy only a small proportion of children. In 1960–1961 there were 50,867 boys and 36,567 girls in school out of a total juvenile population of school age of about 140,000." As a corollary to this, Paul Raymaekers (2010: 36) identified a proliferation of *écoles pamba* (nonaccredited substandard schools) where unscrupulous individuals pretended to offer primary education to desperate students in exchange for hefty fees.

Kompani Kitunga

Around 1950 a change occurred that could not go unnoticed and unnamed: youth bands in Leopoldville no longer confined their unlawful activities to the African townships, nor did they operate only under cover of darkness. They loitered in markets, train stations, and buvettes and wandered into shops, even in some sections of the ville européenne. Bedeviled local shopkeepers braced for their tricks, for if things went awry, these youths resorted to violence to get what they wanted. The apparent apathy of the municipal police force, which the press did not fail to note,[23] emboldened them. They came to be known as Compagnie Kitunga, or Kompani Kitunga,[24] and were referred to by the dreaded initials "KK."[25]

Although the lore of the American Far West does not seem to have significantly shaped the way KK youths structured their bands and performed their rituals of violence and masculinity, evidence does suggest that these bands foreshadowed the Bill movement of the late 1950s. There is also every reason to believe that because the two movements overlapped in the mid-1950s, many KK youths simply morphed into Bills, transferring to the new movement some of their rambunctious antics and tricks. Like the Bills, KK members went about in groups and operated in groups. Yet safety lay not only in numbers but also in the boys' individual abilities to strike blows, for KK youths were not ones to shrink from a good fistfight. At night, they would manhandle and mug passersby in dark corners, at a time when only the newest African township of Renkin (now Matongé), inhabited mostly by évolués, was lit at night.

KK members possessed what they dubbed "magic wallet" (*portefeuille magique*), which they claimed had the power to surreptitiously and mystically attract money they had spotted in somebody else's wallet. Many crossed the river to neighboring Brazzaville to receive training on how to steal without arousing the suspicion of either their intended victim or the police. There, *nganga nkisi* (healers or magicians)[26] would instruct them on how to use charms and magical formulas[27] to conceal their misdeeds, how to avoid getting caught—in short, how to break the law with impunity.

Nganga nkisi also introduced KK youths to the art of stealing what mattered to these youths even more than money: love. Through a charm known as *moselebende*, which became an essential ancillary in the seductive paraphernalia of many Kinshasa male youths, KK young men courted even "hard-to-get" township girls. Cocksure about their seductive power, they each claimed a bevy of girlfriends in different townships, including in Brazzaville, upon whom they lavished gifts, money, and beer. These girls served also as lookouts, while their places made for safe hideouts during episodic police raids and roundups that hardly made a dent in the gangs' lucrative activities. The youths' network of girlfriends allowed them to easily slip away to another township and as far as Pointe-Noire, where they would lie low and wait out the threat.

Writing in the évolué journal *La Voix du Congolais*, Joseph Davier decried the KK movement as *la gangrène*[28] while Eugène N'Djoku labeled it "a scourge" and called for its eradication. Antoine-Roger Bolamba, the editor-in-chief of *La Voix du Congolais*, chimed in with an editor's note enjoining the urban population to remain vigilant. Although Bolamba sounded less concerned than N'Djoku and cautioned against exaggerating the scope of the KK phenomenon, he, too, urged the people to denounce the culprits and the threat they posed to law and order (N'Djoku 1953).[29]

KK youths and the Bills who emerged hot on their heels ran the gamut from what Bolamba, N'Djoku, and others likened to the mob (*la pègre*) to a model of sociality that united disenfranchised youths and furnished them with a behavioral repertoire for coping with life in colonial Kinshasa. A colonial source listed quite a variety of activities that KK youths would pursue, day in and day out, in their respective *quartiers*:[30]

1. Mug passersby at night.
2. Play soccer.
3. Fight between quartiers.
4. Deny youths from other quartiers access to their quartier at night.
5. Flirt with girls.
6. Learn to fight like cowboys.
7. Learn fencing.
8. Look for fetishes (*fétiches*) to help in fighting and get love charms.
9. Ride bicycles without brakes.
10. Beat girls who behave too properly.
11. Learn how to play the guitar and dance the swing.
12. Rub the bodies of passersby with a mixture to provoke itching.
13. Learn English boxing.
14. Learn to smoke cigarettes and marijuana.

It would be a mistake to read into this list only what its compilers wanted it to convey. Although some évolués appropriated the colonial narrative and indicted the KK movement for what it represented in their eyes—namely, a threat to the Belgian paternalistic order—others must have resented on a visceral level these young men's subversion of a traditional order that granted elders privileges that these youths simply usurped.

The KK youths' independence vis-à-vis colonial strictures, their ability to amass large sums of money (hence enhancing their gift-giving capacity in the Maussian sense),[31] and their access to multiple sexual partners did not sit well with évolués who had opted instead for the promise of civilization and the eventual end of empire (*fin d'empire*). Yet even N'Djoku himself, perhaps unconsciously, acknowledged the extent to which KK members considered each of their violent forays to be a performance and an "adventure," for he described in detail a ritual that followed each KK adventure. Members would converge on a secret hideout, each showing off his spoils and celebrating his exploits. They would bask in schadenfreude at the expense of their victims, one of the trappings affected by dominated groups according to Scott (1990: 41), heap praise on each other, chastise some for being weak minded and advise others on how best to use their bag of tricks, and scatter only after their next foray had been planned (N'Djoku 1953: 721).

KK youths did not just rob people: They enjoyed robbing people—robbing them in style, that is. They took both pleasure and pride in the sense of camaraderie that membership in bands fostered. They increasingly thought of their actions as performances, rather than just acts of social banditry. In that sense, they foreshadowed and set the stage for their avatars, the Bills of the late 1950s, who would take the ritualization and stylization of violence to new levels.

Tropical Cowboys versus Other Cowboys

KK youths did not part company but gradually merged, for the most part, into a more colorful and complex movement that cropped up in the mid- to late 1950s. One of the earliest accounts of the Bills, when it was still too early for them to be known by that name, comes to us from an anonymous source. Writing under the initials G. L., a correspondent for Katanga's main daily newspaper, *L'Essor du Congo,* attested to the changing of the guard. While noting that the KK's presence had largely ebbed away, he warned of a new, more dangerous and vicious wave of youth delinquency, which he claimed had rolled into the city like the mob. "These youths," he bemoaned, "have an agenda that will offend the moral standards of honest people." Bound by a code of honor and silence (*omertà*), they used an esoteric language (Indoubill[32]) to conceal their activities and subjected their new recruits to secret rituals and trials. What is more, they claimed to be abiding by some inchoate ideal that G. L. dismissingly attributed to their spiritual and material dereliction.[33]

According to another source, perhaps more reliable and certainly more exhaustive (Babillon 1957: 114), bands of Bills emerged in Kinshasa as early as 1950, when the KK movement still held sway in most quarters. One of these bands, "Les Cowboys du Farwest," coalesced under the leadership of a youngster named Bulu, who went by the cowboy moniker of Windy.[34] The group hung out at Windy's place, in between occasional "adventures" in the cité. What made them pop up on the authorities' radar screen, however, was not marauding, for that was what all delinquent juvenile groups did in Kinshasa; rather, Les Cowboys du Farwest smuggled adolescent girls across the river, from Brazzaville, in small pirogues. And they did it at night to avoid being caught.

What could these joyrides be, if not the prelude to some sinister proposition? The idea that girls could in no way adhere to the same rebellious ethos that drove boys into the streets was a basic tenet of colonial attitudes toward juvenile delinquency. Interstitial juvenile groups could only be male, so if girls appeared among them it could only be the result of coercion and for purposes that colonial officials and missionaries coyly referred to as "debauchery" (Babillon 1957: 119). That township girls belonged to the category of (consensual) victims and were ancillaries of male agency and masculinity is part of the discussion of rape and sexual violence in chapter 6.

Before further narrating the emergence of the Bills, we should briefly discuss one main feature of late 1950s Kinshasa that provided a crucial background to the kind of gang culture the city witnessed during that period. As Kinshasa expanded, adding new townships in far-flung areas, so did its increasing fragmentation. With no public transportation to link the different quarters and no singular urban identity, parochial, insular township mentalities developed that shielded these quarters from the rest of the city. Thus the opposition of the ville européenne versus the cité indigène (soon to become the *cité africaine*) was only one of the many divides that enabled the rise of a "cowboy" culture. To be sure, the cité itself never constituted a monolithic entity but loomed large as an urban archipelago teeming with insular infracultures and gaping fault lines. Before assuming an urban identity, Kinshasa's youths first acknowledged their township identity and sense of place. Loyalty to school, soccer teams, and gangs only deepened this insularity.

Nothing more clearly accounted for this insularity than the 1957 municipal reforms that jettisoned the quarters and replaced them with communes, using thoroughfares, military camps, rivers, and swampland as administrative boundaries that further insulated townships from one another. This was done in response to intense pressure from évolués, who demanded self-rule at the municipal level until the colonial authorities finally relented and agreed to devolve some municipal power to elected African *bourgmestres* (burgomasters). Under this new top-down urban redistricting, the original cité indigène became four communes (Kintambo, Barumbu, Kinshasa, and Saint-Jean), while the newer additions made up six distinct communes (Kalamu, Dendale, Ngiri-Ngiri, Bandalungwa, Matété, and Ndjili). The European city for its part included the three communes of Leopoldville, Ngaliema, and Limété (see maps 4.1 and 4.2).

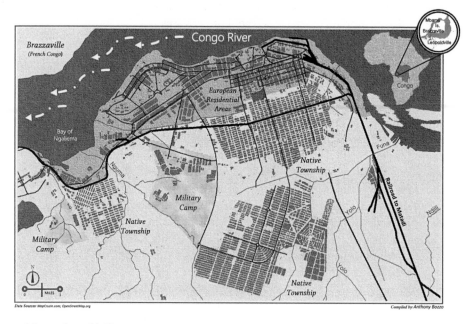

Map 4.1 Leopoldville, 1954.

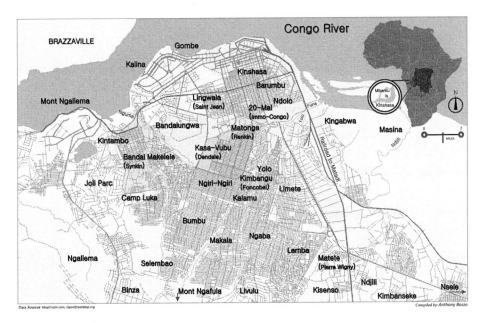

Map 4.2 Kinshasa, 1960.

By replacing porous boundaries between quartiers with rigid demarcations between communes, this new division of the city not only exacerbated brewing tensions among youth bands over territories and girls but also opened the floodgates to many residents of the original and saturated townships (namely, Barumbu and Kinshasa) to pour into the newly created housing subdivisions (Kolonga Molei 1979: 213). For example, Ngiri-Ngiri, one of the newest additions, which Kinois continue to refer to as *mboka sika* (new city), became the fulcrum and flagship of the Bill movement. There, in the late 1950s, older Bills (Grands Bills) such as Néron, Ross Samson, and Billy would revamp the movement and add new layers of meaning to it, so that even its critics had to admit that it consisted of more than youthful rebelliousness and disorderly conduct. It was also in Ngiri-Ngiri that Bills contemplated a path beyond Billism, after befriending the Belgian priest Jozef de Laet (aka Père Buffalo; see chapter 7).

The emergence of the Bill movement in early 1950s Kinshasa was not unlike patterns of youth rebellion and violence seen in other places where Western films provided a new grammar of violence. Kinshasa was by no means the only place in Congo to witness cowboy activities. Colonial reports signal "groups of cowboys" in Jadotville and Elisabethville as early as 1953.[35] In the postwar period, the cowboy fad cropped up in several other African locales as well. It has been documented in Lamu (Kenya), where, in his study of Beni dance, T. O. Ranger (1975:

78) mentions a "squad of young and boisterous men dressed as cowboys." They would line up in dance processions decked out in "black trousers, red shirts, and khaki hats, like cowboys" (146). In 1950s Dar es Salaam, colonial administrator J. A. K. Leslie (1963: 112) noticed a "cult of the cowboy" involving young migrants who unabashedly adopted the "idioms of tough speech, the slouch, the walk of the 'dangerous man' of the films; the ever-popular Western films teach [them] in detail the items of clothes that go with the part."[36] This was not an innocuous sartorial fad but a subversive infraculture that challenged administrative authority, defied the police, and dodged taxation in all its forms. This explains Leslie's offhanded and over-the-top analysis when he wrote:

> The cult of the cowboy clothes is a safety-valve of the dangerous mob element which is likely always to be part of Dar es Salaam. They are unformed *Hitlerjugend,* as yet, their uniform jeans and wide hat, their march gun-on-hip cowboy slouch, waiting for a *Fuehrer* to give respectability to their longing to be admired, to be feared, to have a place in the sun. (Leslie 1963: 113)

This preposterous comparison between fin d'empire in Tanzania and the rise of the Third Reich epitomizes colonial fears about power devolving to the Tanganyika African National Union (TANU), even though TANU leaders controlled the country's youths just as their colonial predecessors had done, for example, by removing many unemployed males from the capital (Burton 2001: 215).

"Cowboys" were musical in colonial eastern Nigeria, where P. E. H. Hair (2001) found them in successive waves, from Lagos (in 1930), Kano, and Enugu down to the small village of Ebe, where a group calling itself "The Courageous Company of Cowboys" appeared in 1948, gathering youths who had had no prior exposure to Western films. Although composed mainly of Igbo youths, The Courageous Company mastered Yoruba songs that they would perform at town festivals, private parties, including Christmas and New Year's gatherings, and bars. In exchange for their performance, patrons would present the Cowboys with small gifts of food, drink, and money. Unlike other cowboy-clad youths discussed above, their uniforms and field maneuvers bore a striking resemblance to the Boy Scouts' activities. Like the Boy Scouts, they also carried a "flag," and when battles broke out between two companies, as they often did, capturing the enemy's flag would generally seal the outcome, proving one group's mettle over the other (Hair 2001: 85).

One of the earliest groups of cowboys in Africa was sighted in Johannesburg as early as the 1910s when cowboy movies, including Buffalo Bill's "quick-firing expeditions," trickled down from European settlers to African audiences. In the streets of Johannesburg, young toughs and drifters, as well as a number of young miners, "began sporting Western fashion: a colorful handkerchief around the neck, cowboy hat perched on the head, and pants tied below the knee to imitate breeches" (Reynolds 2015: 116). Several elements, Reynolds contends, that begat the most famous denizen of the American Wild West after the Civil War also pervaded turn-of-the-century southern Africa, from the open plains landscape, to the gold rushes and boomtowns (with their indispensable railroad stations), to the sense of belonging cowboy movies provided, and to the cowboy drama itself that paralleled the "return of the hero" myth found in Africa's oral tradition. Together, they allowed what Reynolds (126 and 129) calls, following Hortense Powdermaker, the "Africanization of the American frontier myth."

Kinshasa's tropical cowboys did share some features with their counterparts elsewhere. Some, but not all, went to town to look the part, adopting (as Leslie so vividly put it) the air of a "dangerous man," or at least of a hard-boiled tough guy. They all were notorious for their antics and raw tempers that could flare up at the drop of a hat, especially in the face of a perceived slight. The least peccadillo could make their blood boil and send them "from zero to rage" in a heartbeat. They also staged ritualized violence in their respective quartiers in an attempt to establish and monitor the borders that defined youth, gender, and masculinity. Music and sports (mainly soccer) were integral to how they constructed their masculinities, though unlike Lamu and Ebe's Courageous Company of Cowboys, their performances remained cryptic and therefore outside of public consumption. Whereas Ebe's "Cowboys" embedded their performances within a gift economy (music for beer) that kept them connected with the local communities, Kinshasa's tropical cowboys' versatility as "protectors" and "predators" (see chapter 6) elicited ambivalent sentiments from the township communities, ranging from unstinting praise to utter vilification.

Yankee versus Bill: The Battle That Was Never Fought

In this pursuit of the elusive tropical cowboys, we would do well to pause to disentangle two terms that tended to be intertwined in the memories of many of my informants. Seldom have people offered such a wide range of opinions on attitudes and experiences they have shared and time they have spent together.

Several informants acknowledged differences between the Yankee and the Bill, but what these differences might entail is precisely where the contention begins. For Père Buffalo (see chapter 7), the term "Yankee" harkens back to World War II, when Congolese youths got their first glimpse of American servicemen. Eleven American Dakota airplanes landed in Leopoldville in 1942[37] as part of President Franklin Delano Roosevelt's plan to ferry and supply troops via Congo. At least 1,500 white American troops garrisoned in the city until 1943, when the American military command moved its operations to Morocco. Kinois instantly fell under the Yanks' spell and started to pepper Lingala with "you come," "please," "mister," and other niceties. Young Kinois hovered around the American camp day and night, supplying the soldiers with whatever would entice them (mostly women). The lure of a hat, a pair of used overalls—anything that might connect them to the land of cowboys and Indians—prompted some young Kinois to go so far as to rummage daily through the American camp's garbage heap.[38] It was during this brief period of World War II, rather than due to the proliferation of Western films in the late 1940s,[39] that the term "Yankee" gained currency in Leopoldville. Kinois used it to denote American troops' swagger and supremacy in the face of both Belgian and French discomfiture.[40] According to Père Buffalo, young gang members opted for Yankee to define themselves but then jettisoned it for Bill once Western films became widely available.[41]

Another informant, Vieux Chege, who in his youth had swallowed a 9mm Mauser bullet during a kamô ritual (see chapter 5), may have confused the two terms when he insisted that Bills were nothing but assassins and gangsters, whereas Yankees were the "good guys," the township defenders who "would fight only if you enter their territory or township."[42] The dominant iteration of this difference, however, seems to be quite the opposite. For example, when I asked Vieux Zanga Zanga what it meant back then to be a Bill, he replied unblinkingly that Bills were:

> Un groupe d'intellectuels qui voulaient rassembler les amis pour les faire revenir à la raison. Les Yankees c'était des hommes du désordre, des fumeurs de chanvre, des voleurs de chikwangue.[43]

> A group of intellectuals who wanted to gather friends to make them come to their senses. Yankees were men of disorder who smoked marijuana and stole cassava bread.

Vieux Fantomas echoed the same determination to separate the wheat from the chaff, explaining that Yankees were only good at sowing the seeds of disorder: "They were the real troublemakers, but Bills were smarter. Yankees were *éboulementaires*.[44] But *we* never did those things. We were the defenders [of our quartiers]."[45]

Of all the informants who attempted to contrast Yankees and Bills and heap scorn on the Yankees, perhaps none was more forceful and convincing than Vieux Néron, whom I interviewed along with one of his former minions, Petit Moloch,[46] in Quartier Mofewana (Farwest) in 2005. Néron had earned accolades from other Bills, and not just because he had emerged in Mofewana as the sharpest barb on the wire. In the early 1960s, Néron contributed to Bill culture with his musical gift, jazzing up their gatherings with several compositions he would play on his guitar. Around that time he composed *Zambele Kingo,* a song many still regard as the Bills' anthem and manifesto, with lyrics that celebrate marijuana consumption, fistfighting, and the affirmation of manliness through sexual bravado. Using a lexical potpourri that blended Christian allegory and a reference to the heroes of September 11, 2001, Néron depicted Bills as "good Samaritans." Yankees, in contrast, acted as terrorists (*terroristes*) hell-bent on spreading chaos and fear in the quartiers. "They committed robberies, rapes, sometimes even murders," Néron added. Petit Moloch chimed in:

> Yes. Yankees were délinquants. . . . Bills didn't want the Yankees to run the show. You see, there is a difference between Bills and Yankees. Bills were stronger and would give Yankees a run for their money and even repel them [from their quartier].[47]

Then came Caïman, unceremoniously throwing a monkey wrench into this convenient Manichean narrative. "Yankees and Bills walked together," he claimed. They were two sides of the same coin.[48] Paul Kabaidi, who reappears later in these pages, agreed with him. Responding to my question, he opined unequivocally, "Yankee et Bill c'est la même chose" (Yankee and Bill were one and the same).[49] A few other informants agreed with this narrative.[50] Using the two terms interchangeably, Burlan (short for Burt Lancaster), for instance, downplayed any difference between Bills and Yankees and instead distinguished *Yankees civilisés* from *Yankees criminels*.[51]

The most verbose supporter of this opinion was Roitelet (Kinglet), an iconic musician and a Bill in his own right, like so many second-generation Congolese musicians, including artists such as Franco (François Luambo Makiadi) and Simarro Lutumba. His answer to my standard question addressed sexuality, politics, and culture, issues that are discussed in detail in the following chapters:

> Un Yankee c'est un éducateur et un justicier. Quelqu'un qui fait des troubles est un faux Yankee. Il y avait des vrais et des faux Bills. Bill azali mutu ya normal. Alingaka mosala na ye. Les filles nous suivaient parce qu'on allait à l'école et qu'on jouait à la guitare. Les faux Yankees venaient nous attaquer parce qu'ils n'arrivaient pas à avoir des filles. Les Yankees allaient à l'école, comme Vieux Kabaidi, un vrai Yankee qui est allé à l'école et à l'université. Les Bills on les retrouvait dans tous les secteurs. Il y a des universitaires, des non universitaires, des veilleurs de nuit. . . . Les Bills étaient des patriotes, des gens qui aiment le développement de leur pays. Les faux sont arrivés pour salir notre idéologie. C'est une idéologie de travailleurs, de gens qui aiment leur pays et leur prochain. Tu viens et tu trouves ton ami en train de manger? Il prend son manioc et le partage avec toi. Tu ne peux pas laisser ton ami crever de faim. Nous étions pour la solidarité. A l'école on partageait notre nourriture avec les plus petits.[52]

A Yankee is an educator and an avenger. A troublemaker is a fake Yankee. There were true Bills and fake Bills. The Bill is a normal person who loves his work. Girls followed us around because we went to school and played the guitar. Fake Yankees came to attack us because they couldn't have girls. Yankees went to school, like Elder Kabaidi, a true Yankee who attended school and college. Bills could be found in all areas: college graduates, non-college graduates, watchmen. . . . Bills were patriots, people who want their country to advance. The fake ones came to tarnish our ideology. It's an ideology of workers, people who love their country and their neighbor. You drop by your friend's place and you find him eating? He takes his cassava bread and shares it with you. You can't let your friend go hungry. We promoted solidarity. At school we shared our lunch with the little ones.

This interpretation has found its way in the work of N'sial Sesep, the author of a remarkable sociolinguistic study of Indoubill, the Bills' argot. He provides no clear definition of the Yankee but uses the term interchangeably with what appears in his narrative to be its synonym, the term "Bill." Bills or Yankees came in three types, according to Sesep's (1990: 22) analysis, which can be summarized as follows:

1. Notorious for championing the rape of out-of-township girls as a badge of manhood, *éboulementaires* walked a tightrope between delinquency and criminal activity, even within a context (as we will show in chapters 5 and 6) where rape hardly fell within the scope of the law.
2. Next came the *gang,* an individual who may have occasionally participated in rape but who really cultivated the frontier myth of the "toughest of the tough" (*dur des durs*) in trying to get the upper hand against his rivals. A gang could earn the coveted epithet of sheriff or *Goza* (or *Godias*)[53] if he had demonstrated preternatural spirit and sangfroid.
3. Last came the sheriff who, just like his Far West counterpart, appeared on the scene with all the inevitability of a deus ex machina, at the most climatic instant, to restore order and justice. Rarely involved in fighting, the sheriff, unlike the gang, was feared not because he exhibited his might willy-nilly, at the drop of a hat, but because he used it only at the last resort. His was a steady hand on the rudder to steer township youths away from the pitfalls of retaliatory violence, whereas the gang's wayward and cantankerous behavior only fueled and escalated conflict. Oftentimes, the sheriff's appearance was enough to cool down hotheads and force them into submission.

This gamut of opinion about Yankees and Bills would not be complete without two other iterations that add threads to the already thick semantic web that crisscrosses this section. I tracked down Jean-François Muteba Kalombo to Quartier Lemba, after his name came up a couple of times during interviews. He agreed to speak with me and brought along a friend, Jean-Christian Matabul (a former Bill who went by the name Poison). They immediately warmed up to me after Poison discovered that he and my late father had been buddies in the same Boy Scout troop in Brazzaville. In preparation for our meeting, Muteba Kalombo had photocopied a chapter of his unpublished manuscript, "Mémoires de Léopoldville," devoted to Billism and Yankeeism (or *kiyankee* in Indoubill). His manuscript and interview contrast Yankees and Bills in a unique way that conflates age and agility:

> Younger boys we called Bills or Indianas, older ones we called Yankees. Yankees protected Bills. That's why all the young people could not escape from Billism. When Bills fought, they were merely practicing. We aspired to become like Yankees.

Muteba Kalombo and his friend Poison described the organization of gangs of Bills along much the same feudal lines that had allowed Tio and related groups to hold sway over large territories in precolonial Malebo Pool (see chapter 1). Similarly, Yankees acted in their respective territories as "big men," demanded loyalty from the Bills, and imposed upon them a whole range of assignments, from providing food and money (a covert form of racketeering) to riskier missions such as carrying a missive to an out-of-township girl or supplying Yankees with dope. In exchange for these "obligations," Yankees remained avuncular and domineering in their daily interactions with their younger protégés. They provided much-needed protection that sometimes extended out of township, since the division of the cité into territories held by competing gangs meant that trespassing on a rival territory (or in some cases going to school there) could trigger attacks.

This was the most plausible and commonsensical interpretation of the Yankee-versus-Bill conundrum that I had encountered thus far, and one that went beyond Caïman, Kabaidi, Roitelet, and Sesep's rather plain synonymy. I was inclined to accept it until I stumbled over yet another iteration. Its author, Emmanuel Kandolo, graces the blogosphere with some very astute and erudite Lingala commentaries but remains elusive in person. His generational take on the question hints at how shifting patterns of masculinities, as projected in 1960s Western films, may have shaped the experiences of generations of postcolonial tropical cowboys in different ways:

> Ba Yankees bango babotamaki na ba années 1963. Bango bazali ba leki ya ba Bills. Ba acteurs na bango mpe ba héros na bango bazali: Lee Van Cleef, Clint Eastwood, Charles Bronson, John Charles Carter "Charlton Heston," etc. Na ba films lokola: *Pas de pitié pour les salopards, Django, Pour une poignée de dollars, Et pour quelques dollars de plus, Les Douze salopards, Le Seigneur de la guerre,* etc. (Kandolo 2009)

> Yankees came about around 1963. They came after the Bills. Their actors and heroes were: Lee Van Cleef, Clint Eastwood, Charles Bronson, John Charles Carter "Charlton Heston," etc. They starred in such films as *Beyond the Law*

[1968], *Django* [1966], *For a Fistful of Dollars* [1964], *For a Few More Dollars* [1965], *The Dirty Dozen* [1967], *The War Lord* [1965], etc.

Kandolo's sequencing is not without problems. First, films that he regards as foundational to the changeover from Bills to Yankees did not even come out in U.S. theaters until 1964. Second, from the early 1960s onward, tropical cowboys bore the brunt of the upheavals that had ushered in independence in 1960. The new grammar of international violence that flared up in Congo during the Cold War heightened a sense of dereliction and impinged upon the Bills' overall culture. Although tropical cowboys continued to patronize movie theaters and to identify with Far West heroes, the movement tended to enact Cold War violence as Bills morphed from tropical cowboys into Cold War warriors. Belgian sociologist Paul Raymaekers, who surveyed the urban scene in the early 1960s, noted a discrete name shift in some quartiers, where gangs dropped Far West references to fully embrace the Cold War lexicon. Names such as Ambassade des Juifs, AJC (Association des Jeunes Capteurs de Filles), AJAM (Association des Jeunes Amoureux), ONU, and URSS pervaded the Bills' underworld. Not surprisingly, gang leaders and members adopted sobriquets that suited the new zeitgeist. For instance, ONU's gang leader went by the moniker of Dag Hammarskjoeld, while other gang leaders styled themselves Billy Kroutchev and Staline (Raymaekers 1963: 343).

It is important to reiterate just how befuddling this gamut of opinions is, given that Billism and kiyankee, to borrow Muteba Kalombo's terms, have suffused Kinshasa's culture and continue to be relevant even today, when myriad other cultural forms, both global and local, vie for Kinois' attention. My own tentative conclusion is that the term "Yankee" probably predated the Bill movement and had secured its place in the juvenile lexicon by the time the first cowboy movies became widely popular in Kinshasa after World War II. As social anthropologist Michael Herzfeld has noted, speaking of Greek men of the Cretan village of Glendi, the term "Yankee" denoted *"performative excellence,* the ability to foreground manhood by means of deeds that strikingly 'speak for themselves.'" The focus here is not so much on "being a good man" as on "being *good at* being a man" (Herzfeld 1985: 16; see also Gondola 2013: 173).

The script, the swagger, the silence[54] of the true man—in short, "performative excellence"—pervaded Kinshasa's townships already in the early 1950s. Coming on the scene in the mid- to late 1950s, the Bills first rode on the Yankees' coattails before the visual grammar of Western films gave their movement its unique sartorial, linguistic, organizational, and performative features. More so than the Yankee, the Bill became transfixed and enamored by the Western image of a peripatetic hero, the itinerant crusader of the Far West who rides far and wide to enforce justice in a lawless land.

The term "Yankee" still continued to generically convey toughness—a Congolese version of the "macho man" that Cornwall and Lindisfarne (1994: 13) describe as the epitome of heterosexual virility—and, indeed, one could be a Yankee without being a Bill, but to be a true Bill one had better be a Yankee.

One final note: sometime in 1964, Père Buffalo (see chapter 7) gathered the Bills of Ngiri-Ngiri at the headquarters of the JOC (Jeunesse Ouvrière Chrétienne), dubbed "Château JOC," for a pep talk. He began by rhetorically asking his *masta* (buddies) who they thought the foremost Yankee was: "Vrai premier Yankee, nani?" Père Buffalo shot again at his nonplussed pupils. The answer moved his young audience:

> Vrai premier Yankée [sic], ye moko Yezu Kristu, zambi ye alobaki mateya ma ye manso vis-à-vis, abangaki misu ma batu te. Atalaki mpasi eloko pamba. Vrai mobali wana. Vrai grand-bill, na marque eleki oyo ya biso.[55]

> The foremost Yankee, Jesus Christ himself, who being God preached in the open and was not afraid to look people in the eye. He was not concerned with pain. He was a real man, a real Grand Bill, far superior to us.

Using Jesus as a foil to bring the Bills back to the Catholic fold completes a bifurcated trajectory that started back in the 1940s, when Belgian missionaries exposed Congolese youth to the peripatetic figure of the cowboy but denied them entry into manhood. With Père Buffalo, Jesus became a mirror image of Buffalo Bill, bereft his wayward excesses. Idealized as the quintessential male and as the yardstick Bills could measure themselves against, the image of the manly Jesus shone down upon the Bills as they sought entry not only into manhood but also into the mainstream. Yet, as we shall see in the next chapter, the Bills' path to manhood was by no means a seamless one but one fraught with tensions and contradictions.

5 Performing Masculinities

If a man is not a man, then what is he?

Rotundo (1993: 20)

THIS CHAPTER SEEKS to accomplish two intertwined goals. The first is to illuminate the context in which sexual predation ceased to be enacted as a discrete, idiosyncratic phenomenon—the sordid business of a handful of faux Yankees—and became an integral and systemic part of Billism (as addressed in detail in chapter 6). The second is to discuss the extent to which the quest for masculinity and manhood lay at the center of the rituals that Bills performed.

Perhaps we should begin with a theoretical discussion of masculinity: not only how it stood at the nexus of global cultural flows (namely, films) and local practices, but also how it remained intrinsically relational, contextual, reactive, and above all protean and performative. Adolescents, as Mary Bucholtz (2002: 529) reminds us, perform ritual activities that often dramatize and seek to abolish the liminality of youth—that transitional space of invisibility, ambiguity, and possibility, as Victor Turner (1967: 95) defined it, a space that is neither here nor there but betwixt and between. Because youths are rendered "inactive" by adult society, confined as it were to a "standby" status until they undergo the proper rites of passage, they seize on the immanence of the possible to display agency. Though not inherently transgressive and delinquent, the activities that adolescents engage in to display their agency and prove their valor to their peers, to adults, and to girls tend to be violent and narcissistic. The reason for this ties in with the Oedipal complex: violent behaviors are more likely to register, to be noticed, and to challenge the authority of the father figure than are nonviolent ones, especially within a society divided by social and/or racial fault lines.

This chapter argues that youth violence is never gratuitous but a means to an end. The analysis rests on the assumption that violence among boys is experiential rather than innate and has to be learned, rehearsed, and enacted in order to become part and parcel of their behavioral repertoire. As Gary Barker (2005: 63) contends, the more boys learn and perform violence, the more they tend to resort to violence as an effective means to acquire income, power, respect, and prestige and to attract girls. Following the proverbial vicious circle, violence begets violence, especially when young people join gangs and are caught in cycles of retaliatory violence. Barker devotes a good deal of his study, *Dying to Be Men,* to the inner life of adolescent gangs in Brazil and the Caribbean, describing how youths embrace gangs and resort to violence to fulfill what in their minds amounts to manhood entitlement, a trifecta that includes money, status, and girls. They succumb to gang culture and become inured to its reliance on violence as a way to resolve conflicts and settle disputes. This happens precisely because young people lose trust in their families' and other social institutions' ability to ease their transition into manhood and adulthood (65). The thought of an emasculated future looming on their horizon is enough to cause trepidation and anxiety and, in the worst case, give way to entrenched nihilism.

In other words, "Il faut que jeunesse se passe," and "Boys will be boys," but boys must not linger in the liminal twilight zone that boyhood can sometimes represent, for "being boys" is only a transition to "becoming men." Just as societies have prevented the dead from returning to haunt the living by providing them with proper funeral and burial rites, so have they instituted other "rites of passage." Anthropologist Arnold van Gennep, who coined this term in the early twentieth century, uncovered the role of such rites in mitigating both social conflicts and the threat posed to the stability of society as a whole by transition, transiency, and liminality. In some preindustrial societies, for instance, a boy undergoes circumcision at puberty, and his foreskin, the appendage of boyhood, is buried in a symbolic and metonymic ritual in which the boy sheds his boyness to emerge a man. "They endured physical hardship, hunger, and derision as their parents and siblings worked to toughen them for the circumcision that would mark their transition to adulthood," Hodgson (2001: 111) wrote of the Maasai, while among the Zulu these rituals culminated with "an early morning bath to wash away the ways and habits of childhood and assume manhood" (Uchendu 2008: 7). Thus a "man child" (or *grand enfant,* to recycle the blanket colonial term discussed in chapter 3) elicits the same anxiety and fright that a zombie would provoke. It is precisely when boys are left to their own devices to figure out what it means to be a man, without the intervention of social institutions and rites, that they pose the greatest threat to social stability and order.

"We Yankees Were Good Samaritans"

Speaking today with people who engaged in gang violence in their youth, some of whom were notorious for their masculine gests, can make many a researcher seek the solace of familiar and cozy metropolitan archives. Although not all Yankees were sexual predators, the recent "zero-tolerance" policy[1] toward sexual violence taking place in eastern Congo, its connection to the ongoing war, and the renewed international media coverage[2] it has received (Eriksson Baaz and Stern

2010) may account for former gang members' reluctance to discuss the topic. Some interviewees utterly denied their own or their buddies' involvement in predatory rape. When they conceded that rape had taken place,[3] they were quick to describe it as a discrete phenomenon. As they strove to dismiss rape, informants often cast themselves in a positive light. According to one of them, Bills or Yankees, as they dubbed themselves, were "gentlemen" who were out there policing their quartiers, protecting the chastity of their teenage girls against strangers and deterring truancy among schoolchildren. Only bad apples—or faux Bills, as one informant referred to them—had participated in the abominable business of rape.[4] One informant, Roitelet, added this unexpected quip as he attempted to defend Yankees: "We Yankees were good Samaritans."[5] This should be taken neither as an ad hoc image born of the interview context nor as a rationale that Yankees actually used in their day. Rather, it should be viewed as a trope that harks back to the time when many Yankees joined the JOC (Jeunesse Ouvrière Chrétienne) and were exposed to Father Jozef de Laet's redemptive ministry. When Paul Kabaidi, the former mayor of Kinshasa and a Bill in his own right, was asked to provide a definition of the Bill, he, too, plucked at the same chord and provided this paean to the battered figure of the Bill:

> Être Bill c'est quand vous demandez à quelqu'un d'être un homme. C'est être un homme. Moi je suis un Bill et fier de l'être. C'est l'homme droit, qui défend les justes causes, qui ne recule pas devant un danger, qui sait défendre les faibles, qui s'investit. On ne peut pas prendre ce mot dans le sens péjoratif qu'on lui a donné.[6]

> To be a Bill is when you ask someone to be a man. It's to be a man. I am a Bill and proud of it. It is an upright man who defends just causes, who never balks at danger, who knows how to defend the weak, who commits himself. We should not take this term in the pejorative sense people have given it.

Bills, it turns out, were not just the defenders of their quartiers, nor were they simply taking cues from Western movies by playfully reenacting some of their most rambunctious scenes. To be fair, the Yankees or Bills did provide a sense of belonging to the growing number of youngsters who made up the bulk of the townships' population in the middle of the twentieth century. They offered the most colorful and close-knit urban culture available to African youths in 1950s Kinshasa, by bringing their members together in a single community that knew none of the ethnic and language barriers that doomed Patrice Lumumba's (1925–1961) vision of a united postcolonial Congo. In 1950s Kinshasa, it should be remembered, there was widespread aspiration for the end of colonial rule. Concerns arose about the role that ethnicities were to play in an independent country rid of Belgian paternalism. Because of its political role as the capital city,

Kinshasa experienced heightened ethnic sentiments that were to coalesce into ethnopolitical tensions with the creation in 1950 of the ABAKO (Association des Bakongo), the first major urban ethnic association. Yankees, for their part, stayed above the ethnic fray. Their use of the common argot known as Indoubill further distanced them from the ethnic essentialization that simultaneously mired the road to independence and paved the way for the rise of Mobutu's authenticity project.

Although Yankees greatly contributed to the creation of a township culture and life that ran counter to the prevailing ethnonationalism and often played an avuncular role in the lives of younger residents, both boys and girls, some of them also actively engaged in fiendish sexual behavior. The desire to enhance one's status as a gang leader or inflate one's reputation as the "toughest of the tough" (*dur des durs*) also led Yankees to engage in practices that might be considered ancillaries to sexual violence. These are discussed below, before examining rape and sexual violence in the following chapter.

Kintulu (Bodybuilding)

One such ancillary practice was called kintulu, and Bills who faithfully pursued it were known as *Apollons*. In the late 1950s, young Apollons flexing their muscles in their hangout spots drew huge crowds of onlookers, some sitting atop walls, others perched in trees for a better view of these formidable scenes (see figure 5.1). Many in the crowd were girls who, like the younger boys, were attracted by the bulging torsos and raucous atmosphere that these sessions of kintulu exhibited.

Representations of Apollons provide a glimpse into this demimonde, revealing the tight connection between kintulu and masculinity, especially as it intersected with notions of courtship, seduction, and sex appeal. Sketches published in the Bills' makeshift magazines provide hints of how they represented themselves. Bills depicted themselves much in the way superheroes are portrayed in comic books and cartoons, with brawny torsos, overinflated muscles, and egos to match. In one of those renditions, used to illustrate an article that appeared in the first issue of *Esprit de la Jeunesse*,[7] a young Bill stands tall, his hands behind his back, proudly displaying his bulging pectorals, big biceps, and slim waist.

Bills also appeared in several photographs taken by Jean Depara in the early 1960s[8] (see figures 5.2 and 5.3). In one of them, taken at Quartier Citas (or Casamar) in 1963, a young Apollon stands in typical bodybuilding pose with a young woman on each side (see figure 5.4). The gender dichotomy is all too apparent. The two women wear conventional *pagnes* (wraparound skirts) that conceal the shape of their bodies and enhance their femininity.[9] They shyly regard the Apollon, succumbing to his commanding gaze, with unfeigned admiration and meek demeanor, as though he has cast a spell on them. In comparison, the Apollon

Figure 5.1 Group of Apollons taking part in a contest at their hangout in Quartier Mofewana before an avid crowd of onlookers ca. 1958. © Photo Jozef de Laet collection.

looks larger than life, his naked upper body flexed to the extreme. This juxtaposition certainly enhances the young Apollon's masculinity, and Depara's composition recycles many familiar themes. Yet there is no doubt that Depara, himself a former Bill turned photographer, intended, perhaps unconsciously, to portray the Apollon in his best role: as a protector of female chastity and a rampart against intruding predators. It is precisely for this reason that his two female companions are not lusting after his body but looking up into his eyes with gratitude.

There nevertheless seems to be a deeper and more sinister logic at work in this seemingly innocuous composition as well, especially when one looks more closely at the Apollon's interaction with his two female companions. He is protectively holding the hand of one while staring suggestively at the other, hinting at troubling sexual innuendos. It is this ambivalence (of protector *and* predator) that complicates how we are to make sense of the Janus-faced Yankee.

The Kamô Ritual

In addition to kintulu, Yankees partook in a magical ritual known as kamô.[10] Although physical strength and stamina naturally played a role in one's ability to

Figure 5.2 Apollon enjoying a beer break. © Photo Jean Depara, Kinshasa ca. 1950–65. Courtesy of Revue Noire.

get the upper hand in *billing* (Indoubill for "fights") between rival gang members, it was kamô that was thought to determine the outcome. For a little less than 5 francs (what one would have paid for a loaf of bread in 1950), Bills would go to older Bills (Grands Bills), such as Degazin, Debarron, Eboma, Moruma (known as "Le Roi du Kamô"), and Verre Cassé (Broken Glass), in search of "traditional" medicine to increase their physical abilities. Many would cross the Congo River to Brazzaville not only to indulge in drinking sprees[11] but also to have the potent medicine of kamô applied to their wrists, ankles, chest, or temples. Thus Fantômas, who turned twenty-two in 1950, occasionally went to see a certain Makoubounzou in Brazzaville to receive powerful kamô for just 1 CFA franc,[12] while Jean Christian Matabul, who was nicknamed "Poison" because of his merciless rages, only trusted a certain Aimant (Magnet) for strong kamô and serious training.[13] Many in Quartier Mofewana also made regular trips to Brazzaville to receive kamô.

The kamô ritual involved two distinct procedures. First, minor incisions (*nzoloko*) would be made on the aforementioned parts of the body. For example,

Figure 5.3 Aspiring Apollons. © Photo Jean Depara, Kinshasa ca. 1950–65. Courtesy of Revue Noire.

two or three (rarely more) parallel incisions measuring half an inch each could be made on one's wrist, resulting in small bloodletting. Then, depending on who cut the kamô or the type of strength one badly wanted, a particular mixture of burnt powder (nkisi) would be applied to the open wound. Degazin invariably used a speck of leopard fur, lion's nails, gorilla pelt, the bone of a river fish known in Lingala as *mina,* and some tree bark. When a customer requested, for instance, the ability to strike devastating bilayi (head-butts), Degazin would also throw in razor blades, nails, and needles and cook the whole thing in a small cast-iron skillet until most of the ingredients had been reduced to ashes. Others mixed in the bone of a snake's head. After the hot mixture had cooled down, the ashes would be applied to the nzoloko.

Figure 5.4 Apollon in Quartier Citas. © Photo Jean Depara, Kinshasa ca. 1950–65. Courtesy of Revue Noire.

Degazin, who has been at the head of Congo's organization of tradi-practitioners since the late 1980s, learned the trade as a child and perfected it as he watched Eboma (whom he affectionately called "Vieux Ebo") cut kamô in Mofewana. Once Degazin (see figure 5.5) began his own profitable business, his followers grew at such a rate that he quickly eclipsed his old master.[14] To Eboma's bag of tricks, Degazin added his own personal touch. He always kept a catalogue of formulas handy, so that clients could choose from a list of 27 different mixtures the type of kamô they wanted and could afford.

Singing before or after administering kamô also became Degazin's trademark. The same song he would use before billing was often recycled at the kamô

Figure 5.5 Vieux Degazin in Quartier Kauka, March 2009. Photo by the author.

ritual, especially when "treating" people such as Paurret (see chapter 6), the toughest Yankee in Kintambo:

> Degazin simba nzenga, kelele
> Mama simbila mwana, simba nzenga, kelele
> Hê, tata simba nzenga, kelele[15]

> Degazin, hold and cut
> Mother, hold the child, hold and cut
> Father, hold and cut

Degazin and some of the people who flocked to him to receive kamô, including Nimy Mayidika (a former Bill and President Mobutu's chief of staff), glorified kamô as the quintessential masculine brand. All young men—even the "brainy" ones, such as Jean-Jacques Kande,[16] Bomina Nsoni,[17] Paul Kabaidi,[18] and Nimy Mayidika himself—resorted to kamô. "We all cut kamô,"[19] recalls Bomina Nsoni, and "we all believed in its power."[20]

The power of kamô was both mystical and physical, for it shielded the masculine body.[21] If we are to believe stories that surround kamô and not dismiss them as tall tales, then kamô compels us to look at masculinity as an ongoing construct fraught with tensions between self-destruction and self-preservation. Through a sort of embodied dialectic akin to the Hegelian notion of Aufheben,[22] the body verged on a quandary as it negotiated the tightrope that stretched between the abyss of nihilism and the peaks of performance. Immediately after administering kamô, Degazin would break a bottle over the head of his client, who had by then already entered a trance. He would then have him swallow broken glass. Some clients would bring packs of brand-new Gillette razor blades, which they would crush with their teeth, chew, and swallow, sometimes in front of bewildered crowds.

Of all the encounters I have had with Bills, the one with Chege yielded the most candid descriptions of kamô. When I first met him, Chege was working as a janitor at the Grand Hôtel of Kinshasa. He struck me as a small, shy, unpretentious Muyaka man who knew his place, not only in the cutthroat hierarchy of Kinshasa's most exclusive hotel but in Congolese society. I had my doubts about learning anything from him until he told me that he would feel more comfortable if we did the interview after work, at his home in Kintambo-Chicago. Scenes of dire poverty and the village-like layout of Kintambo-Chicago belied what I had once heard about this quartier—namely, that it had been christened after America's third largest metropolis because of its newness and urban cachet.

Born Baudoin Makenge in Bandundu in 1939, Chege moved to Kinshasa with his uncle at age twelve. They first resided in Saint-Jean (now Lingwala). The family later moved to a new settlement, Camp Renkin (now Matongé), before relocating permanently in Kintambo, which was known then as Léo II. Chege's claims about kamô seemed outlandish and hardly fit his unprepossessing demeanor. Sometimes, he recalled, rather than cut nzoloko, the practitioner would insert several needles under the skin of his arm in preparation for an upcoming billing (fight). At another visit to a nkisi specialist, Chege said, he was instructed to swallow an 8mm Mauser bullet. Chege complied only after he was given a small cup of palm oil to ease the painful transit. Immediately following the ritual, "I would try my [newfound] strength on a tree and give it a serious head-butt. The tree would then catch on fire, as though it had been hit by thunder."[23] (Another story, taking place in Saint-Jean sometime in the early 1950s, recounts that an unhinged Vieux Eboma, a Grand Bill and kamô master, head-butted a tree, causing it to immediately shrivel.)[24]

Kamô invariably entailed a set of *bikila* (taboos and prohibitions; the plural of *ekila*) that one had to follow scrupulously lest one lose one's mind. These included: not looking back if someone calls you as you walk down the street; if you are in the toilet and someone calls your name, responding not verbally but by clapping your hands; if it rains, not running, walking instead; and so forth. The list also included a variety of sexual taboos that Bills had to observe to guarantee that their kamô would remain potent and "act up" during fights.

Ingesting nails, needles, bullets, razor blades, broken glass, and other sharp objects most likely has its counterpart in local initiation rituals. For the Bills, internal absorption of sharp objects was also intended as an act of defiance and magical fortitude that mirrored external cutting (nzoloko). Furthermore, it embodied a vision of manliness which, as Harvey Mansfield (2006: 18) reminds us, evokes the Greek word ανδρεία, a term the Greeks used also for "courage, the virtue concerned with controlling fear."[25] We also find the same notion, *wandnat*, among the Amharas, in Ethiopia, where it similarly "involves aggressiveness, stamina, and bold 'courageous action' in the face of danger" (Gilmore 1990: 13). Indeed, Yankees cared nothing about pain, hurt, or injury, laughing at the sight of their own blood, like so many men Gilmore encountered in his study (Gilmore 1990: 67).

Kamô was less about physical invincibility than it was about taming one's inner vulnerability by daring to do the unthinkable. This is how an informant (born in 1932) recounted his experience with this extreme form of kamô:

> I swallowed nine needles three times: that's 27 needles! I brought my own needles that I had bought. It was my friend Marteau [Hammer] who got me into that business. He wrapped the needles with some thread and told me to swallow them with water before cutting kamô. Today I wouldn't be able to do that. I wonder where these needles ended up in my body. It was in Brazza[ville]. I did that over three sessions.[26]

Another informant, Sylvain Eboma, who was born to a Congolese mother and an affluent Portuguese businessman, came of age in Casamar (or Citas), one of Kinshasa's early settlements for African workers. In the late 1950s, Casamar boasted some of the toughest Bills in Kinshasa. Dangwa emerged there in the late 1940s as Grand Bill with his posse of myrmidons—men such as Tamba, Elo Jazz, and Zapata, who would make names for themselves in the early 1960s. Because his mother was friends with Wendo Kolossoy, Congo's first popular musician, young Dangwa developed a liking for Congolese rumba and could be seen regularly with his makeshift band at Mokomboso Bar, entertaining customers. But what made Dangwa the most feared Yankee in Casamar was his indomitable strength, much of which came from his faith in kamô. Sylvain Eboma witnessed Dangwa trouncing his opponents with a single head-butt that sent some eating grass on the ground (*aliakisi bango matiti*). As a prelude to each of his billings, Dangwa would crush glass bottles with his bare feet. If that were not enough to intimidate opponents, he would thump his chest with his knuckles and produce a raw, metallic sound that struck fear into the hearts of even the bravest contenders.

Cutting kamô was such a lucrative business, Sylvain Eboma recalled, that many charlatans had set up shops to woo customers. He only trusted a certain Valère, who cut kamô in his parents' compound on Mbomu Avenue (in Quartier Ruwet). On one rare occasion, after the kamô ritual had been completed, Valère had the young Sylvain swallow a 2-franc hexagonal coin with a homemade potion. A bewildered Sylvain then saw the coin move through his arm, under the skin, all the way to his closed fist. When he finally opened his fist, there appeared the coin, in the palm of his hand![27]

From these disparate accounts emerge the outlines of a coherent view of hypermasculinity. It expresses not just what these young people lassoed from the Hollywood rendition of the American Far West but also local and traditional constructions of masculinity as well, in which mystical resources played a role as important as physical strength. Yet rather than taking these jarring accounts as spurious claims or prima facie evidence, what is proposed here is to view them as narratives intended to make sense of the hubris that came to define the Bills' attitude toward sexuality and violence. Underlying this analysis is the notion that hypermasculinity (Peck 1981: 96) among the Bills functioned as an extreme reaction to colonial anxieties and the emasculation of the African male. As illustrated by kintulu and kamô rituals, hypermasculinity in the townships enabled Yankees to regain in their townships the control they had lost within the colonial society. This explains why most of the interviewees who had cut kamô insisted that it not only increased their physical strength and dulled any sense of pain, fear, and guilt but also made them invincible and incontrollable.[28]

Zoumbel (Marijuana)

Indeed, kamô provided many Yankees with the same exhilarating sensations that marijuana did—and perhaps with a justification for some of their most wayward behavior. Cutting kamô and smoking marijuana became two sides of the same coin, two compulsory rites of passage within Kinshasa's gangs.

Narcotic use among Kinshasa youths slipped under the radar until, alarmed by high unemployment and the rise in youth delinquency, the colonial administration decided to launch an investigation. The official entrusted with it, Louis Bissot, worked in the Unemployment Section (Problèmes de Chômage) of the Service de la Population Noire (Black Population Bureau). Young, meticulous, and keenly interested in local cultures, Bissot spared no effort to carry out his mission. His report appeared in 1958, under the title *Étude qualitative sur la dé-linquance juvénile à Léopoldville*. This document (hereafter the Bissot Report) was immediately swept under the rug and did not reappear for decades,[29] even in colonial archives.[30] One has to wonder why. What prompted the Belgian colonial administration to bury a report that filled a gap in its knowledge of juvenile problems in Kinshasa? After all, it was widely known in colonial circles that a growing number of unschooled and unemployed youths in the cité indigène lacked adult supervision and were fending for themselves. The simplest answer, and one reflected in sociopolitical studies dealing with the Belgian Congo, is the sense of complacency and denial that prevailed until the January 1959 insurrection.[31] To this we can add the fact that "black-on-black" violence, in the Belgian Congo as in other segregated contexts, never registered as a threat to social order until, as in the example of South Africa, the walls of segregation came tumbling down. A larger explanation is provided in chapter 7.

Most postwar colonial studies devoted to juvenile delinquency and criminality downplay the issue of drug use in several ways. For some, like the crown procurator in Leopoldville, there was no cause for concern (*rien d'inquiétant;* Lafontaine 1957: 53). Others sought to allay fears over the presence of alleged legions of black "parasites" grinding their axes in the cité indigène by minimizing the numbers of stowaways, parasites, and unemployed (Capelle 1947: 35–36). Finally, there were those who stressed Kinshasa's soft and almost anecdotal criminality compared to that in the crime-plagued cities of the developed world—New York, of course, being one of them (Sohier 1958: 236). Such was the colonial mindset when the Bissot Report came out, giving European officials a frightening glimpse into the dregs of colonial society.

The Bissot Report delineated much of what the Bills stood for, with an emphasis on drug trafficking, drug consumption, and sexual debauchery. One of the main gangs Bissot investigated, "Les Cowboys du Farwest," combined teenage boys who had fallen through the cracks of the colonial regimen and adolescent girls, many smuggled by pirogue from Brazzaville (as mentioned in chapter 4). This gang had formed in the early 1950s on Kinshasa's west side, initially as a bunch of rebellious youngsters led by Paurret (Bissot 2009 [1958]: 18). Many of these tropical cowboys had been reduced to eking out a living via illicit activities. Long hours spent watching cowboy movies and reading comic books fostered among them a camaraderie and collective fascination with violence. As the band grew in size, so did its illicit activities, which included smoking marijuana, intergang feuding, and stealing. Gang members met regularly at the squat of Paurret's acolyte, an older teenager named Bulu who styled himself "Windy" (Babillon 1957: 119). Following a practice that became widespread in most gangs in the late

1950s, Les Cowboys du Farwest subjected its new recruits to hazing and initiation rites involving oath taking and smoking marijuana.[32]

Yet smoking marijuana (zoumbel in Indoubill),[33] because it remained a recurrent concealed activity beyond the law, provided an even stronger bond among Yankees than the sporadic hazing of new recruits. After the initiatory rite, every subsequent collective puff of zoumbel renewed an acute sense of identity with and belonging to the group, and Yankees partook of zoumbel frequently. When former ambassador Bomina Nsoni was asked why older Yankees in his quartier had coaxed him to smoke his first joint, he said that they had resented his intellectual airs and wanted him to be like them. "The focal point [of the movement]," he added, "was marijuana. The true Bill was in marijuana (Le vrai Bill était dans le chanvre)." Even Father Jozef de Laet (Père Buffalo, profiled in chapter 7), the white Belgian missionary who befriended the Bills and tried to steer them away from interstitial nihilism and back into the Catholic fold, had to go through the zoumbel ritual in order to be accepted by them. And Jean-Jacques Kande, a Congolese journalist who conducted a thorough investigation in the Bill milieu for *Quinze,* broke some deontological rules in the process: he bought some marijuana to share with his informants, although he assured me, à la U.S. president Bill Clinton, that he did not inhale even once during the week he spent with the Bills of Citas.[34]

Zoumbel was an illegal yet readily available substance[35] that served to bond gangs of Bills. As with cutting kamô, it also allowed them to narcotize the pain that dereliction at the bottom rung of the urban ladder inflicted upon them. But Bills were not just at the receiving end of this social violence that wreaked havoc in Kinshasa's quartiers. They were, as Honwana and De Boeck (2005) have posited, "makers and breakers of society"—that is, in an ambivalent posture where they simultaneously acted as agents of change by shaping the ideological, social, and material world around them and bore the brunt of changes that affected their society. Especially in the 1950s context of apocalyptic fin d'empire, at a time when a new grammar of international violence ushered the Cold War into the Congo, Yankees felt little control over the direction their country was taking and therefore asserted their power over their townships.

Kintulu, kamô, and zoumbel provide evidence of universal attempts by juveniles to frame their bodies as "subversive sites" (Honwana and De Boeck 2005: 11). What is more, these bodies display an aesthetics of selfhood realization as much as they counter and subvert dominant paradigms about manhood, culture in general, and the contentious notion of body politics. There is no doubt that to examine the manifold use of the Bill's body is to disentangle the inextricable symbiosis of aesthetics and politics one thread at a time. It is to peel away layers of quiescence in order to uncover concealed patterns of subversion and defiance.

Naming and Billing

In *Naming Colonialism,* a riveting study on memory and colonial anthroponyms, Congolese historian Osumaka Likaka explains the importance of naming in the Congolese village-world. Through rituals, people posited naming as a rebirth that called to existence and determined one's life and social trajectory. Naming rituals, Likaka argues, continued in the colonial period to encode the memories of village communities, registering the importance and the meanings that communities attached to specific events, patterns, and dynamics that would otherwise have been skewed and eclipsed by colonial narratives. Names were used, for example, to extol the masculine virtues of certain colonial officials, as in *mondele ngolo* (Lingala for "strong white man") or its Swahili equivalent, *Simba Bulaya* (Europe's lion). Yet these names could also conceal a duplicitous meaning, excoriating overbearing officials under the guise of praising them (Likaka 2009).

Through naming and names, the Bills also coincidentally reclaimed a tradition that harkened back to Buffalo Bill Cody himself. Rhetorical and performative jousts over monikers were a trait that connected the Bills to their eponymous hero, for Cody had had to contend with rival "Buffalo Bills" throughout his career. The name Buffalo Bill apparently had several claimants, including a certain William C. Mathewson, a frontiersman whose life was as adventurous and tumultuous as that of William Frederick Cody. In 1911, at the ripe age of 81, Mathewson renewed an old charge against Cody, a charge that had first surfaced in 1894, when Cody's fame had circled the globe and the name Buffalo Bill had long been copyrighted. Upon learning that Cody's Wild West show was coming to his city of Topeka, Kansas, Mathewson, never one to mince words, challenged Cody to a showdown no doubt aimed at derailing his profitable business:

> You have no right to call yourself "Buffalo Bill" and you know you haven't. . . . You know I am the original Buffalo Bill and was known by that name ten years before you ever worked for the Kansas Railroad. When I was post trader I was called Buffalo Bill because I killed buffaloes to supply meat for them that didn't have any meat or couldn't get it and I never charged them a cent for it. When you and your show come to Topeka I aim to tell you to your face that you are using a title that doesn't belong to you. (quoted in Carter 2000: 98)

To heap further scorn on his nemesis, Mathewson fired one last volley: "I was shooting buffalo when Cody was shooting jackrabbits" (quoted in Carter 2000: 98). As it turned out, the old plainsman had squandered his meager fortune and fallen heavily in debt. He had even been forced to suffer the worst indignity that could befall a buffalo hunter: pawning his most valuable rifle.

Cody, *en grand seigneur,* avoided the showdown. Weeks before the Wild West planted its tent in Topeka, he dispatched one of his lieutenants to retrieve

Mathewson's rifle from the pawnshop and return it to its rightful owner. He further diffused the potential showdown, and the bad publicity it could have created, by helping Mathewson financially. Finally, when the show opened in Topeka, Mathewson enjoyed one of the best seats in the house, courtesy of Buffalo Bill (Carter 2000: 98).

The most serious challenge, however, and one to which Cody devoted an entire chapter in his autobiography, came from William Comstock, who went by the nickname of Billy "Medicine Bill" Comstock and claimed to have wild Cheyenne blood running through his veins. Comstock challenged Cody, not over the name Buffalo Bill per se, but to a hunting match to prove that he was the better buffalo hunter. The showdown took place sometime in June or July 1868, shortly after the railroad had reached Sheridan, Kansas, the place where the two plainsmen dueled. Billy Comstock had apparently thrown down the gauntlet at the behest of some officers of Fort Hays who harbored old grudges against Cody. The contest pitted the two best scouts and buffalo hunters of the frontier against each other and subsequently found its place in the annals of the West, although some historians have dismissed the whole thing as apocryphal and simply another instance of Cody's wild imagination. Be that as it may, according to Cody the exciting scene drew a huge crowd of ladies and gentlemen who arrived by train to witness his feats. The rules were as follows:

> We were to hunt one day of eight hours, beginning at eight o'clock in the morning, and closing at four o'clock in the afternoon. The wager was five hundred dollars a side, and the man who should kill the greater number of buffaloes from on horseback was to be declared the winner. . . . The buffaloes were quite plenty, and it was agreed that we should go into the same herd at the same time and "make a run," as we called it, each one killing as many as possible. A referee was to follow each of us on horseback when we entered the herd, and count the buffaloes killed by each man. (Cody 1978: 171)

After the first two rounds, it became clear that the much-awaited contest had petered out into a mismatch. Sensing an opportunity to do what he did best, which was to blur the line between life and performance, Cody told the crowd he could ride his horse, Brigham, without saddle or bridle, so as, in his own words, to "give an extra exhibition of [his] skills" (Cody 1978: 173). Riding bareback and using his favorite buffalo-hunting rifle, which he had nicknamed "Lucretia Borgia," he killed nearly twice as many buffaloes as Comstock. The referees then declared Cody "the winner of the match, as well as the champion buffalo-hunter of the plains" (174).

Did the Bills learn through movies depicting their hero, Buffalo Bill, that he had had to defend not only his manhood but also his name? Probably not. More generally, did the Bills' own rivalry over names originate in Hollywood's rendition of Far West lore? Nothing is less certain. Yet it matters little whether or not they took their cue from the frontier fantasies of Western movies, in which fistfights and gun battles were rarely fought over names per se, but for honor, vengeance, money, and women. Evidence suggests that billings (fights) over names had to do with the very finite repertoire of popular cinematic monikers, on the one hand, and the geographic separation and inherent rivalry between gangs, on the other. Yankees were no weekend warriors but were always on the lookout for a good fight and fought every day, all day long. One way to provoke a fight with a rival gang was to "steal" the name of one of its members and then challenge the other group to a billing to determine who would keep the name, for there could not be two Yankees bearing the name Tarzan, Burt Lancaster, or Pecos Bill (see table 5.1). Often a new recruit would be given a name that belonged to a rival gang member of equal valor and then asked to go fight and defeat him in order to earn the right to keep the moniker. Such duels could easily expand into an all-out billing between two gangs if a Grand Bill decided to enter the fray and bail out his struggling protégé.

Monikers encapsulated one's claim to manhood and Bill identity. In fact, they played such an important role in providing a sense of self-identification and belonging to a gang that Bills became known exclusively by their nicknames.[36] Even parents and other relatives who may have frowned on their street activities referred to them by their Bill names. Particular monikers meant to elicit fear and command respect became a gang's coveted asset. As if a bold nickname were not explicit enough, some had epithets attached to them, such as "Néron, le Prêtre de la Puissance" (Nero, the Priest of Might) and "Vieux Ross, le Grand Maître de la Force Physique" (Elder Ross, the Grand Master of Physical Strength). Dangwa,

Table 5.1 Names of legendary gang members by quartier

Farwest Dima (Kintambo/Mangembo): Paurret (aka Monganga), Esoot Law (Esukuma), Buffle, John Likangwa, Teketeke, Tex Bill, Bingema, Cassidy, Opalon [Hopalong], Pecos Bill, Zanga Zanga, Bicros Bill, Santos, Windy

Citas/Casamar, Ruwet, Santa Feu (Barumbu): William Booth, André Ndoba, Dembegar, DeSoto, Dangwa, Debaron, Tamba, Elo Jazz, Zapata, Mwana Ngando, Gonga François, Cassans, Ringo, Frank Sinatra, Monstre

Cowboys (Citas): Andrada, Roy* (aka Thérèse Muyaka and Thérèse Longo), Meta,* Lilima,* Kunguniko brothers (Johnny, Hubert, and Simon)

Singa Kwanga (Saint-Jean/Lingwala): Jimmy l'Hawaïenne, Moruma, Eboma, Degazin, Moins le Quart, Jeune Cowboy, Caïman, Buffalo Bill, Simaro, Rex

Mofewana (Ngiri-Ngiri): (1) Tarzan, Marregon, Sheriff, Dewayon, 6600 Volts, Windy, John, Contrôleur, Gary Cooper, Franco (aka Luambo Makiadi), Johnny

Table 5.1 (*continued*)

(aka Johnny Bokelo), Cyprien, Bungalow; (2) Néron, Rossy Ross, Mivais John
(aka John Wayne), Samy, Lang Liz, Carol, Fantôme, Muanda Ngara, Ebende,
Roy, Bayard, Elo, Mobarona, Payine Niama na Etumba, Accident, Cooper, Vitos,
Dereck, Marie Kapote*; (3) Djamuskete, Zabara (aka Moloch), Biceps, Sidos, Elan,
Meurtre, Athos, Commando, Diabolo, Marguero, Sodome, Mpakasa, Sheriff,
Dereck, Mozande Zapata, Satan, Lambrane; (4) Burlan (Burt Lancaster), Zinga,
Bazigard, Moguagol, Kijos, Mofe, Rodo (aka Petit Moloch), Onu, Apache,[1] Bill
Hadock, Walo, John Dereck, Bruno Walker, Kroutchev

Sans Loi (Ngiri-Ngiri): Jane Russell,* Jane Kelly,* Maria Montez* (sources do not
provide names of male gang members)

Dynamique (Ngiri-Ngiri): (1) Bikunda, Eboma, Samy Kula, Derrick, Hercule, Cail-
lou, Hopalong, Châtelet, Kondolo Mpangi, Buffle, Langliza, Kelou Billy, Assassin,
Amoureux Magique, Bémol, Sam Castadet, Comet, Amateur, Talisman, Miss
Crocker,* Rita Hayworth,* Jeanne Dechaud,* Doudou, Marina Kiss*; (2) En-
gwanzos, Le Noir, Zapata, Billy, Théophile, Tshombé, Zuluwe, Matunga,
Ouragan, Napoleon

Bandal: Maître Degoum, Bungalow

Bois Vert, Bois Dur, Dakar (Dendale/Kasa-Vubu): Arraignée Pierre, Welo, Tex,
Viking, Demoyen, Verre Cassé sans Réparation (Broken Glass beyond Repair),
Devis, Le Rosé, Rossignol d'Amour, Thomas d'Aquin, Damas, Zorro Sauveur

Balawatha (Dendale/Kasa-Vubu): Willysmer Indoubill, Crosby, Satan, Mofuta,
Gangster, Rossignol, Texas Bill, Indien, Bandit, Elégance

Matété: Godzilla, Lupatem, Buffalo Bill, Wagon, Océan, Raph, Zorro, Libre

Ndjili: Magon, Mivais John, Marie Cowboy,* Ali Baba

Yolo: Carré, Chaplin, Arizona, Carlos

Sources: Bissot (2009 [1958]); Raymaekers (1963); Kolonga Molei (1977); Tchebwa (1996); and Paurret (aka Iyoma Bayaka Jacob), Bingema, Petit Moloch (aka Abraham Koko Yawadio), Burlan, and
Jean-François Muteba-Kalombo, personal interviews.

Note: * = Cowgirl, or Billesse; (1) = first generation, (2) = second generation, etc. See also chapter 4,
which describes the 1957 municipal reforms that jettisoned the quartiers and replaced them with
communes.

[1]Apache is about the only "Indian" name this author encountered among Kinshasa's Bills, another
indication that these young moviegoers conformed to what Hollywood Westerns attempted to
convey. They related to Indians with little sympathy, just as Hollywood expected of viewers. Indians, as Jenni Calder wrote, provided "so many faceless dead in Western carnage" precisely because
"everyone knew Indians had lost, and this could only encourage the squandering of Indian lives on
the screen" (Calder 1974: 42 and 47). For Bills, cowboys had cool names, whereas Indians (depicted
as a pathetic horde of anonymous feathered savages, hideously painted, and signing rather than
talking) had comical, primitive names connected to nature. Bills rooted for the cowboys and identified with them rather than with the Indians.

for his part, was also known as "L'Homme au Coup de Tête Mortel" (The Man with a Deadly Head-Butt). And Satan also went by "Satan, Zwa Ye!" (Satan, Take Him!), a phrase he would trumpet after knocking an opponent unconscious, thus indicating that he had sealed the deal and turned his rival over to hell. To earn such a name, braggadocio alone would not do; one had to show physical prowess during a billing. A gang member could also be demoted to his lackluster given name following a trouncing, in effect going from hero to zero.

Rivalries could build up over territories as well as over names. Ross, for example, had justly earned both his name and the title of *grand maître* during a legendary billing that pitted him against Mivais John.[37] To keep the rivalry between the two from festering, Vieux Néron decided to split Mofewana into two territories, Molokai and Farwest (or Fewe). Nestled between three thoroughfares (Assosa, Joséphine Charlotte, and Prince Baudoin Avenues), Mofewana had had one of the most fearless gangs in Ngiri-Ngiri. After taking over Molokai, Ross understood that a gang's longevity could not be left to chance, nor could it be safeguarded by swelling numbers alone, especially after Ngiri-Ngiri had become such a haunt of hoodlums, each of them eager to attract followers and be recognized as a sheriff. In the midst of such intense competition, Ross was determined to do more than always drink upstream from the herd. He created a *gouvernement* of *les durs des durs* (the toughest of the tough) that looked after younger gang members and defended the gang's reputation during billings. His Apollons, including hard-boiled guys such as Ebende (Iron) and Fantôme (Ghost), could be seen at their usual hangout, flexing their muscles before a crowd of enthusiastic Bills and female admirers.

Another example occurred in early 1964, when Camp Luka's main gang split into two rival factions as two of its sheriffs vied for leadership. The two rival gangs, Mottawana and Santa-Feu, engaged in vendettas, much to the dismay of Camp Luka's residents. Tension boiled over later that year, climaxing in a Western-style showdown at the "Montagne ya Yamaïque" (Mountain of Jamaica), where the two gangs converged after Bruno Walker decided to throw down the gauntlet. After bantering and hurling profanities at each other, the two gangs got down to the business of billing. So fierce was this joust that it left many injured, some with serious bone fractures. Bruno Walker, Mottawana's main leader, trounced his former buddies, Buck-Danny and Buck-John. The Indoubill expression that Buck-John used to describe his own discomfiture—"Buck-John le Grand ale matiti" (Buck-John the Great bit the dust)[38]—conveys the intensity of the brawl.

The self-deprecatory quality of this Indoubill quip also signals another meaning that Buck-John may have intended to convey, a meaning deeply rooted in the Bills' cult of violence. Gang fighting in the view of the Bills was a performance, a contest, a ritualistic outburst of violence that did not necessarily drive a wedge between two gangs. Its outcome could potentially be celebratory. Bruno

Walker had prevailed by exhibiting such mastery of fighting techniques and such superior, overwhelming strength as could only command respect, even from those he had just thrashed. Although he had been humiliated, Buck-John thus wryly applauded his nemesis and lauded him for his valor.

Yankee versus Yuma

In 1950s Kinshasa, the Yankee was defined primarily against the negative image of the Yuma. To be Yankee was first and foremost *not* to be Yuma,[39] a term that conjured up unmanly qualities such as cowardice, naiveté, and gaucherie. To avoid being labeled a Yuma (wimp or half-wit), a stigma that no one in his right mind dared contemplate, many embraced some or all of the attributes of the Yankee. This was one of the main reasons Durango and some of his *camarades* decided to join the movement in Kintambo-Assassin[40] in the late 1950s:

> If you weren't called Bill, then you are Yuma. There was a huge difference between a Yuma and a Bill. Yuma was someone who was gullible and who could be fobbed off easily. To be a Bill was to be sharp.[41]

Sharp and street smart were what every youngster growing up in Kinshasa's seediest quartiers aspired to be. Girls had no time for sissies who lacked swagger, flair, and a reputation for toughness. Because street life stood as the only space where one could assert one's manhood, it beckoned to Kinshasa's youth with such force that even studious youngsters who enjoyed a nurturing and stable family life flirted with the idea of joining a street gang. Back then, Sylvain Eboma reminisced:

> If your *modega* (collar) is not raised, then you could be mistaken for a Yuma. A girl wouldn't like you. She thinks you're a Yuma. You had to have your buckle on the side, change your gait by lowering your shoulder while strolling. Then nobody can mess with you because people know you're a Bill, someone who keeps his wits about him.[42]

Younger Yuma who tired of being bullied and who wanted to toughen up could learn the ropes under the tutelage of "tough guys," in exchange for money and unflinching loyalty. They would then be offered protection and rewards as long as the required booty was forthcoming and they faithfully carried out perilous missions, such as delivering a missive to an out-of-township girl.

The only alternative to either Billism or the embarrassment of being labeled a Yuma seems to have been schooling. Yet the shame of being publicly scorned as a Yuma—or, worse, as *embousou* and *ngotobobo* (or *ngorobo*), that is, retarded—led many studious kids to seek to be brawny as well as brainy. Two exceptions were Camille Mwissa-Camus and Jean-Jacques Kande, who both pursued remarkable careers in journalism, the latter even becoming minister of information in

Mobutu's first cabinet. They both scoffed at the notion that Bills could be anything but "thugs" (*voyous*). Although presumably the result of firsthand encounters with gangs of Bills in their respective townships, their vision of Billism seems also to have been refracted through the colonial prism. Bills flaunted all the rules that Mwissa-Camus and Kande held dear. Many Bills skipped school or never attended school but spent their time bullying and racketeering children on their way to school. They routinely catcalled at girls and sometimes harassed them as they returned home from school. Their attire was provocative, a far cry from the neatly starched school uniforms that Mwissa-Camus and Kande had to don daily. Following parental example, both these future journalists had religiously forsworn the use of Indoubill, the Bills' ribald idiom. And of course Bills smoked marijuana, something that Mwissa-Camus and Kande had learned to despise owing to the strict missionary education they received at Sainte-Anne.

One would think that soccer, that great equalizer, would have brought together all the kids of a given township, regardless of whether they were street or school smart. Yet even on the soccer fields, Yankees and Yumas never mingled. Bills had their own teams, with names that hardly concealed their proclivity toward bellicose competition, known sometimes as *bikumu*.[43] These were team names such as "Bombardier" (Bomber) and "Terreur" (Terror), a sharp contrast to "Renaissance," "Sporting," and the other elegant names that school teams adopted. On the rare occasions when Yankees played Yumas, braggadocio always marred the game. For instance, at a game that pitted Quartier Hirondelle's team against the Salvation Army team, the Roitelets (Kinglets), the referee called a Bill player on a blatant foul and awarded the Roitelets a well-deserved penalty kick, prompting the Bills to pull a fast one on their opponents: Hirondelle's goalkeeper, Mpia Romain, left the goal empty and simply stared at the kicker. Knowing all too well that scoring would lead to bikumu, the kicker intentionally missed the goal.[44]

At the end of the day, it did not matter what township, gang, or soccer team a Bill belonged to, whether or not he smoked marijuana, whether he was brainy or brawny, whether he was a ruthless *éboulementaire* (see chapter 6) or a suave charmer. What mattered above all was that he be a Bill. That was the only safe side to be on.

For all the differences between Yankees (or Bills)[45] and Yumas, there can be little question that there was mutual fascination as well. Yankees knew all too well that education was the yardstick that would measure one's success in a new Congo. Many of the Grands Bills often admonished township children who skipped school and reported them to the white missionaries. Many of these township children also found no insurmountable contradiction between their quasi-devotion to the missionaries who were in charge of their colonial education and their loyalty to the Grands Bills who held sway over their quartiers. So-called

Yumas, for their part, envied Yankees for their braggadocio and assertiveness in a society that had little tolerance for weakness. After all, both Yankees and Yumas grew up in townships where the standard of masculinity had less to do with school success than with street prowess. Foreign and violent though the outward forms of Yankees' manly standards were, they also drew on a pervasive culture of physical courage inculcated at home. This partly explains why even studious schoolchildren had to learn self-defense. This is how the former Bill Jean-François Muteba Kalombo (introduced in chapter 4) explained this self-defense ethos that most youngsters ended up embracing in 1950s Kinshasa:

> When we were growing up here in Kin, we had one philosophy: *"Mama alobi"* (Mother said). You go to school and get beaten, you come home and tell [your parents] you were hit at school: you get another beating because *"Mama alobaki soki moninga abeti yo, yo pe obeti"* (Mom said if someone hits you, you must hit back). This was the spirit of the time.[46]

It is this zeitgeist that explains why Yankees' manly norms were readily embraced by all juveniles and became the hegemonic brand of masculinity in the quartiers. And because the boundaries between Yankee and Yuma were so porous, this apparent dichotomy must actually be expanded into a trichotomy that includes not only Yankees and Yumas but *nzele* (girls) if we are to understand how masculinities operated in Kinshasa's quartiers. The following chapter deals with sexual violence, how it pivoted around the axis of masculinity, and how it was complicated by the Bills' ambivalent, Janus-faced relationship with *banzele* (the plural of nzele).

6 Protectors and Predators

It was very consensual. Most of the time girls were willing to lay.

Grand Bill Degazin (aka Jean Sumbuka Bigonda)

IN HER HISTORICAL ESSAY on rape, *Against Our Will,* feminist Susan Brownmiller maintains that "women are trained to be rape victims" (Brownmiller 1975: 309). By this she means that women are socialized in an acknowledgment of their status as potential victims of rape and sexual abuse. Through popular culture (she dutifully provides her own sexualized interpretation of *Red Riding Hood,* which she calls a "parable of rape"), she writes, girls "become indoctrinated into a victim mentality" (309). According to Brownmiller, in some societies the existence of rape as a word, concept, set of cautionary tales, or fate worse than death serves both as a way to further cleave gender roles and as one more patriarchal foil to keep females in line and teach them their (proper) place in society. Joanna Bourke takes the argument even farther by removing the "socializing" element and what Brownmiller sees as the indispensable role of culture. For Bourke, a woman is a potential rape victim simply by virtue of being female (Bourke 2007: 421). In asserting this, she seems to lend credit to a biological argument that became the cause célèbre of first-generation feminists, who tended to regard femininity as "victimhood" by nature and rape as the drop that makes the glass overflow.

Rape in Precolonial Africa

In many societies—and here African societies do stand out—rape scarcely existed as a social concept and thus did not register legally (as adultery did almost universally). The patrilocal Gusii of Kenya, an example that Brownmiller draws from the work of anthropologist Robert LeVine, used several euphemisms to qualify and discuss rape, referring to it as "to fight," "to stamp on," and to "spoil" (Brownmiller 1975: 287), the latter coming quite close to the way many non-African societies have conceived of rape. This is not to say that rape did not exist in precolonial African societies. What Brownmiller (376) characterizes as "sexual invasion of the body by force, an incursion into the private, personal inner space without consent—in short, an internal assault from one of several avenues and by one of several methods—constitut[ing] a deliberate violation of emotional, physical and rational integrity" of a female person did occur fairly often in Africa. To maintain otherwise would be a gross misconception of both rape and African societies.

Yet we must concede immediately that, rather than being exposed by moral and legal notions, as in other places, sexual violence in African societies was concealed by social practices that heightened the possibility of rape as defined above. In the case of an arranged marriage, for example, a would-be bride who resisted could face sexual violence and be forced into an abusive relationship. Women who infringed on certain community rituals could also be punished with rape. Running errands at night when masked spirits roamed the villages or trespassing on initiatory areas reserved for boys could constitute grounds for sexual violence.[1]

From positional succession (the equivalent of ancient Jews' Levirate and the codified Roman "universal succession," according to which a deceased man's name, spirit, status, title, and affinal relations, including his wives, were passed through inheritance to the next of kin) to the hospitality practice of wife sharing (which took on a life of its own with the arrival of the first European explorers), African social practices left little room for females to exercise sexual agency and volition. In some societies a not-yet-nubile girl who found herself betrothed to an older, polygamous man could be subjected to rape if her future husband decided to force himself on her and consummate the union before she reached her majority, which in many African societies was set around the age of thirteen. More generally, females who disrupted the patriarchal gender order could easily become the targets of violence. And as we know, when men inflict physical violence on women, the traumatic experience often extends to violating women's sexual integrity as well.

Since in many societies women owned no property but were themselves the property of men, they seemed to men to possess a sexual capital in their bodies. Violating these corporeal selves became the universal punitive and retributive method to use against women, a way for men to help themselves to women's sexual capital, since rape has long been legally constructed as much as an "acte de sexe" as an "acte de possession" (Vigarello 1998: 63). This was true in many societies, especially those in which marriage did not depend on female virginity and local customs tolerated, and in some cases encouraged, premarital sexual encounters.[2]

To sum up, in precolonial Central Africa rape was a way for men to police gender boundaries and reproduce patriarchy. Although premeditated, large-scale rape and rape during wartime (known as martial rape) likely came about only with colonial conquest, a variety of male hegemonic social practices, albeit accepted by the majority of women, exposed recalcitrant women to rape.

Contextualizing Rape

I agree with Brownmiller and other feminist authors (Bourke 2007, among others): rape should not be romanticized in any way, shape, or form but must be "placed where it truly belongs, within the context of modern criminal violence" (Brownmiller 1975: 377). Not all practices and behaviors within a given culture or subculture should be viewed as "cultural," and rape, even when it becomes systemic within a group, should by no means qualify as "culture." Nor should rape be subsumed under the fancy category of popular culture, even in cases where a permissive and misogynistic environment extols sexual violence and allows it to become a "way of life" for a segment of its youth.

At the same time, the context in which rape among Kinshasa's youth became a badge of honor for some gang members as well as an activity that owed much to the sinister banalization and minimization of violence against women in the history of Congo should be described (Lauro 2005: 34). This pattern of rape as an instrument to accomplish economic, social, or military objectives[3] echoes in repetitive tremors the convulsive eruption of sexual violence that presided over the creation of Congo itself (Hunt 2008). As Adam Hochschild (1998) so eloquently pointed out, in Leopold II of Belgium's so-called Congo Free State, rape and mutilation were used as the most effective terror weapons to coerce villagers into fulfilling compulsory quotas of wild rubber.

A brief digression on the Belgian colonial ideology shows how, by constructing and elevating the Promethean figure of the white man and promising civilization, progress, and modernity only to African men, Belgian colonizers contributed to the commodification of the Congolese woman's body. This female body could be used, misused, and abused at will precisely because the Congolese woman was defined as being impervious to the modernizing changes that the Belgians supposedly brought. She was a road map to the past, to "traditional Africa," whereas the Congolese man was evolving toward modernity with the help of his "benevolent" Belgian masters. She appeared as the embodiment of terra nullius within a colonial lexicon that eroticized both the colonial act (with terms such as exploration, conquest, erection, penetration, and possession) and the colonizer (whose virility colonial literature portrays as taming Africa's savagery).[4] The African male, in contrast, was busy laboring to erect the buildings, bridges, and railroads that came to represent colonial modernity.

In the early 1950s, the Belgians created a social category to reward the natives who successfully advanced toward civilization. As discussed in previous chapters, it was understood by all that only a few deserving African males could vie for it. Successful recipients who could show proof of monogamy and loyalty to the Catholic faith (among other criteria) received a *certificat d'immatriculation* (certificate of registration) and its upgraded version the Carte du Mérite Civique.

As the black woman was reduced to her reified and commodified body, rape and sexual violence tended to be framed within the discourse of males' sexual prerogative or as a male reaction to female lascivious and promiscuous proclivity (Lauro 2005: 35; Posel 2005: 240). Rape may also have been tolerated by colonial authorities as a safety valve, an outlet for delinquent juveniles lest they turn against the state itself and its patriarchal endowment. Finally, one cannot easily brush aside Brownmiller's militant yet pertinent argument that men have criminalized rape not as an act of sexual violence targeting a female's bodily integrity but "as a property crime of man against man. Woman of course was viewed as the property" (Brownmiller 1975: 18). This explains why Belgian authorities could look the other way when it came to sexual violence in the townships yet take umbrage at a black man wolf-whistling at a white woman.[5]

Within this context, not only was rape dismissed, marginalized, and concealed, but also it never presented a legal threat to society because it was rarely viewed as an assault on a woman's self and integrity. Even sexual violence against child brides, historian Amandine Lauro has discovered from colonial jurisprudence and archives,[6] hardly shocked colonial officials.[7] Firmly established in the colonial mindset, the idea that African females always consented to sex, no matter the age of the partner or nature of the sex act, may explain the trivialization of rape in colonial Congo (Lauro 2009: 304). The target of rape was the sexualized female body, not her mind or inner self. The pain inflicted was assumed to be physical, not emotional or social. Rape, then, quietly retreated to the margins of the legal system and away from collective consciousness. Only whispers and collective indifference (perhaps collective shame, too)[8] ensued after a case of rape was uncovered in colonial Kinshasa. Rape remained at once such a taboo and so concealed that in 1940s colonial Kinshasa a native who hit a white person was more likely to end up in jail than was a serial rapist of a black woman, and his affront was more likely to appear in the local media than was a gender-based violent crime.

Colonial ideology thus exposed and sexualized the black female body, treating it as site for fantasies and sexual hubris, a surface where European males could break with impunity all sexual taboos inherited from the bygone Victorian age. At the same time, it equally sexualized the white female body by protecting it from the natives' gaze. Indeed, the "colonial virgin," as the white female appeared in colonial mythologies, was as much part of the colonial hubris as were other devices intended to widen the civilizational gap between the colonizers and the colonized. A testimonial to this idealization of the white female body can be found in Congolese popular representations. It is shown elsewhere how in Congolese popular music the trope of the modern and "free" black woman was simply an ersatz version of the colonial virgin (Gondola 2003: 119). Others, especially Jewsiewicki (2003) and Fabian (1996: 198), have also noted that the iconic figure of the mermaid (*mamba mutu* in Swahili and *mami wata* in Lingala) so celebrated in Congolese popular painting camouflages the figure of the colonial virgin.

This dichotomy between the black female body (oversexualized because it was exposed) and the white female body (oversexualized because it was concealed) leads to further contextualizing rape in colonial Kinshasa. Once young viewers managed to have access to uncensored Westerns through the movie parlors that sprouted in the quartiers, they encountered "rape scripts"[9] that may have contributed to the sexually related performances discussed later in this chapter. The Great Plains, Walter Prescott Webb wrote, "repelled the women as they attracted the men" (quoted in Calder 1974: 159), for as Roach (1990: xviii) has remarked, everything conspired against women as they faced the perils of the treeless expanse of the Great Plains, leaving them exposed in more than one way. This being the case, women in the West became commodities, merely existing in a man's rugged world for his pleasure. A woman trapped in one of those forlorn frontier towns had no choice but to offer her services to the town's dance hall, saloon, or brothel; as Calder (1974: 166) so baldly puts it, "sultry flesh at easy rates" populated most frontier towns.

How did women make the leap from the Far West itself to Western movies? Since, for fear of "slipping into a version of romance rather than a version of outdoor action story" (Calder 1974: 182), Westerns had to present the cowboy as inclined to die rather than marry, we get two versions of women in these films: the woman of ill repute, and—when Westerns fancied the more desirable version of the female, as they often did in the 1950s—the "child-woman," beautiful and, above all, vulnerable (Brownmiller 1975: 334). Yankees, of course, grew familiar with the recurring formulaic, plot-based narrative of most of these Hollywood renditions, in which females appear only as hapless, clumsy characters to be rescued by heroic men who then ride off into the sunset.

Thus the victimization of the white woman character in cowboy films, coupled with the objectification of the black female body in colonial Congo, set the social stage for the Yankees' glorification of rape. Added to this was the fact that hegemonic masculinity, deployed through notions of territoriality, toughness, and invincibility, often relied on forms of sexual coercion targeting women (Asencio 1999: 108). Yet another factor also contributed to sexual violence in colonial Kinshasa: until the postwar years, this capital city of the Belgian Congo (and one of the fastest-growing cities in tropical Africa) remained a demographic oddity. Conceived as a place where African male workers were to cater to the needs of their colonial masters (Maximy 1984: 89), Kinshasa was predominantly young, black, and male until the March 26, 1947, decree, when the creation of communes gave African townships their urban identity.

If the average gender ratio saw the male population largely outnumbering its female counterpart, this demographic imbalance was even more acute within the

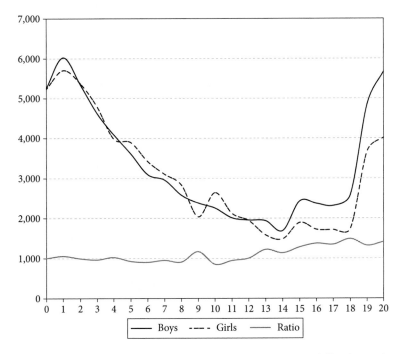

Figure 6.1 Leopoldville's 1955 African population (ages 0–20). Source: Babillon (1957: 47).

adolescent population. As figure 6.1 shows, between ages fourteen and eighteen, a crucial age in terms of sexual awareness, the sex-ratio gap widened considerably. At age eighteen, when a young woman attracted male suitors who were not confined to her own age group, there were just 1,734 girls for 2,583 young men. According to the 1955–1957 *Tableau Général de la Démographie Congolaise*, males outnumbered females in Kinshasa by almost 2 to 1 (Comhaire-Sylvain 1968: 69), a situation that seems to have heightened competition for township girls.

When former gang members, now well into their seventies and eighties, were asked to explain why violence, and especially gender-based violence, saturated their townships, they invariably cited the shortage of girls as the main contributing factor. Time and again, access to girls became such a problem that the defense of one's *territoire* (territory) amounted to preventing rival gang members from courting, dating, or preying upon the teenage girls of one's own quartier.

Éboulement

Yankeeism and most of what Yankees stood for revolved around the ability to have girls. A young man who had no success with girls became fodder for all sorts of putdowns and insults, including being branded with the opprobrious term "Yuma" (wimp or half-wit).[10] Therefore, the trichotomy of Yankees, Yumas, and nzele (girls) stood at the core of what was considered to be manly behavior in the townships. Girls, and expressions surrounding dealing with girls, seem to have mattered so much that no other activity, not even drug consumption, gave rise to a greater variety of cryptic and colorful vocabulary. The Yankee or Bills' street language known as Indoubill included almost eighty terms relating to girls (Raymaekers 1963: 310). *Nzele*, the most ecumenical and iconic one, a shorthand take on the French term *mam'zelle (mademoiselle)*, gained more currency than its cognate *nzazi* or its other synonyms, *momie*,[11] *munini, nzoukoul, gonzo, mifide*,[12] *popi*,[13] *terd, tétard, mord, pétale, ngulufwa, kimwana mwana*, and *petit mbongo*, some of which remained too parochial and quickly fell into disuse.

Yankeeism adopted some of its male chauvinistic and misogynic notions from an Afro-Victorian colonial society in which women rarely escaped subaltern status and chafed under a phallocentric vision of colonial modernity. Ironically, this is a rare instance where Victorian ideals, promoted by white missionaries and enforced through colonial policies, ultimately buttressed some African urban views of women. Most urban families encouraged boys to attend postprimary institutions, while girls were fortunate to be whisked away to training schools after completing their primary education. The main purpose of girls' education aimed to foster their role as "spouse and mother" (Comhaire-Sylvain 1968: 18). It was largely due to their marginalization in mainstream society that girls bore the brunt of gang violence in the quartiers.

Given their poor status and lower numbers respective to boys, it is not surprising that girls represented trophies for Yankees and were regarded as "territory bound." Boys frequently ventured outside of their quartier, even at the peril of trespassing on another gang's territory and incurring immediate retaliation. But girls found themselves confined to their townships. Even there they had to observe gender rules and comport themselves in public according to an Afro-Victorian ideology that hardly tolerated the visibility of women in the public space, except in their quotidian tasks as housewives and helpmeets, porters and petty-traders. One epithet that labeled girls who skirted these rules speaks volumes as to how gender operated in Kinshasa: the term *kolúka* (to wander)[14] emerged to characterize a nubile girl's "rebellious" and flirtatious behavior and to rationalize Yankees' requited riposte to such behavior—namely, sexual abuse (see figure 6.2). It follows that proper feminine behavior reinforced the invisibility of girls, while ubiquity in the public space became one of the most salient masculine traits across the quartiers.

Why did Yankees inflict sexual violence on girls? Taking up soldiers' narratives that locate sexual violence at the center of their construction of masculinity, Eriksson Baaz and Stern (2008: 67) have uncovered a behavioral arsenal

Figure 6.2 Nzele, in front of Afro Negro Night Club in Kinshasa, ca. 1962. © Photo Jean Depara, Kinshasa ca. 1950–65. Courtesy of Revue Noire.

that resonates with my own fieldwork. They posit martial rape in eastern Congo as an "effort to humiliate (and feminise) enemy men by sullying their women/ nation/homeland, and proving them to be inadequate protectors." Yet their analyses show that in war-torn Congo "rape tend[s] to be committed against any woman, regardless of political or ethnic affinity with the perpetrator" (Eriksson Baaz and Stern 2010: 14). The symbiotic identification of women with a particular locale or territory—which researchers have identified with respect to martial rape in Bosnia and Rwanda, for example—is less clear in Congo. Eriksson Baaz and Stern (2009, 2010) also show that it is only by combining discrete factors—such as lack of regular pay, low morale and self-esteem, breakdown of the chain of command, soldier's vagrancy, competition for resources among army units, hostile civil-military relations, widespread use of alcohol and drugs, and total impunity—that we can reach a full understanding of why soldiers rape.

Reducing Congo's martial rape to the weapon-of-war narrative (a conclusion that Eriksson Baaz and Stern steer clear of) negates and silences the pain that raped women experience as a consequence of rape, precisely because such a weapon-of-war narrative posits women not as the ultimate recipients of martial rape but as mere bodily representatives of their territory, community, or homeland.[15] Reducing the rape of women to a manifestation of man-on-man violence can ultimately operate only in a metonymic and symbolic way. By viewing rape as an act of symbolic violence that targets a community through the female territorialized body, rather than the female body itself or an individual woman, men who rape become even further desensitized than they do by the act of rape itself and sometimes proceed to inflict on their victims the most horrific acts imaginable, what Eriksson Baaz and Stern (2010: 31) call "evil rape."

If the weapon-of-war explanation fails to fully account for endemic martial rape in eastern Congo,[16] then the next logical explanatory model is, for Eriksson Baaz and Stern, one that percolates in various feminist studies on rape.[17] Calling for a "male erotics" to eradicate the scourge of rape, Bourke (2007: 436) first indicts rape as a "crisis of manliness" associated with "degraded masculinities." Similarly, Eriksson Baaz and Stern (2010: 49) ultimately attribute rape to "failed masculinity." In other words, Congolese soldiers rape women as "a way to perform and try to regain masculinity and power" they have lost on all fronts.

Yankees, however, resorted to sexual violence as a way to delineate their territory and encroach upon the territories of rival gangs. Perhaps the time has come to put to rest the notion that essentializes young men as slaves to hormonal urges, taken over by desires they cannot control and often unable to engage in sexual relations without resorting to violence. In Kinshasa's townships, rape and sexual violence were not spurred by an excess in hormonal secretion, which supposedly fuels young men's sexual overdrive. Rather, rape was a controlled, staged, and performative activity that young men used at least as much to wield power as to gain pleasure.

Access to the girls in one's own township being limited, to prove one's valor one had to date or prey on girls from other townships. Take Degazin, for example, who sometime around 1958 gathered his posse in Saint-Jean for a raid on Kintambo, where he hoped to corral a few girls and take them back to Saint-Jean. Starting in 1957, Kintambo had been under new management, after Paurret had been arrested and deported to the village of Monkoto, near Mbandaka. The new

Grand Bill in Kintambo, Tex Bill, sought to stamp his authority on the quartier by renaming it Kintambo-Mangembo. The day Degazin forayed into their quartier, Tex Bill and his gang were lifting weights at their usual hangout place. Degazin and his group were spotted near Synkin attempting to cross the Makelele River with their spoils. Tex Bill and his band, including tough guys like Bingema, Buffle, and Jeune Cowboy, caught up with them before they had a chance to cross the river and slip away.

What followed was a classic Yankee dustup—namely, a local reenactment of "the rescue of the maiden in distress by the gallant knight" (Calder 1974: 162) that Western movies themselves recycled so histrionically. Tex Bill threw down the gauntlet, but Degazin, despite being a kamô master (see chapter 5), balked and instead ordered one of his minions to fight Tex Bill. A few minutes into the billing, Tex Bill gained the upper hand with a devastating head-butt (bilayi) that sent his opponent to counting stars on the muddy ground. As the poor boy was attempting to get up, Jeune Cowboy dealt him another blow and broke his arm. Resigned to defeat and his ego bruised, Degazin handed the girls over to Tex Bill and retreated with his dispirited bunch.[18]

In this story, as in many accounts of outright abductions, Yankees intended to use their female victims as mere passive vehicles of retribution and retaliation "within a larger battle between two [gangs]," as Brownmiller pointedly argues about gang rape. The process by which Yankees captured and wooed girls was encapsulated in the term "éboulement" (for which there is no ready translation, but which was generally conceded to encompass elements of coercion and rape). Yet the mention of éboulement to informants was usually met with expressions of contrived ignorance or sheepish denial. Most informants arrived determined not to broach the topic of rape. Thus when I visited Degazin for the second time, to discuss this story with him, he denied it flat-out. Girls, he explained, were "willing to lay"; they came all the way from Brazzaville of their own volition to stay with him for weeks on end.[19] "I never conducted nor did I take part in *éboulement*," he insisted in his droning voice. But when, attempting to draw attention away from him, I asked the bespectacled seventy-two-year-old whether he had known of any éboulementaires back then, his eyes lit up behind his thick lenses and he unhesitatingly uttered the name that had come to haunt me ever since I began doing research on the Yankees. "Oh, yeah, William Booth [pronounce "bot"] was an *éboulementaire!*" Degazin exclaimed.

William Booth

Piecing together William Booth's life is a daunting task, given the paucity of information about this Robin Hood figure whom many consider to have been a kingpin in the heyday of the Bill movement and a paragon of manliness.

An ethnic Ngombe, young William Booth moved his fishing business to Kinshasa in the late 1940s, in search of a reliable market. He settled in Citas, a part of Kinshasa's oldest and most ethnically diverse settlement. Although William Booth never joined the Salvation Army, whose headquarters sat in one of the busiest sections of Citas, he enjoyed the dignified military uniform and enthralling fanfare of the Salvation Army band. He may have been exposed to the Army's propaganda long enough to identify himself with its founder, General William Booth. William Booth's real name remains a mystery because, as Sylvain Eboma explained when referring to Vieux Dangwa, "to call him by his customary name (*kombo ya mboka*) was to take him backwards. He didn't like that. He could beat you for that."[20]

Around 1952, after numerous odd jobs, William Booth finally found a niche as a brick maker for the growing number of projects sponsored by missionary groups, especially the building of schools and missions. A jocular figure, Booth established himself in the good graces of white missionaries who helped his thriving business. His blithe spirit and self-reliant lifestyle earned him the fondness of many a youngster who was drawn to his place.[21] Some skipped school to come help William Booth in his business in exchange for a few coins and a copious meal or merely for fun. Under a mango tree, Booth regaled his fan club with stories of derring-do on the Congo River and tales that captivated his young audience. With his trademark, a V-shaped hairdo ("V" standing for "Vieux," or Elder) and a fake bald spot, he cultivated an avuncular mystique that led many youngsters to flock to him.

For all his charisma and kind-hearted munificence toward his younger apprentices, William Booth engaged in appalling activities. Unbeknownst to many of his younger followers, he used his shelter, a nondescript abandoned house, to sequester and rape females. Some of his minions, such as Paurret (see below), who prided himself on having served as William Booth's lieutenant, may have learned under his tutelage some of the éboulement strategies they would later employ themselves. William Booth operated occasionally with the complicity of some corrupt police agents whose part it was to apprehend girls in the evening and bring them to Booth's den. After William Booth disappeared from the scene,[22] the term *prévenues* (defendants, or accused), which had originally stigmatized the victims, continued to be in usage even though police collusion was a thing of the past.

At Booth's squat, the prévenues would be stripped naked and their clothes confined to a bucket filled with water. They would then be forced to smoke marijuana and have sex on the dirt floor of William Booth's den: hence the term *te-terre* (on the ground) to describe these nonconsensual acts of sexual intercourse. Sometimes Booth would prolong the agony and release his prévenue only when she started her menstrual flow.

Éboulement involved a chain of schemes, from baiting and convoying girls to determining the "crime scene," posting lookouts, and finally proceeding to the actual act of raping (*te-terre*). The whole process involved cooperation and for that reason remained a collective project, a ritual of solidarity and a bacchic communion that reinforced the cohesion of the group. Performing one's nudity while raping the same girl (as others looked on, waiting their turn) no doubt further bonded the Yankees who participated in it. The very act in which men proved their virility was consumed collectively, as when Yankees collectively fought and smoked hemp. The fact that Booth used raping as an initiatic ritual to provide some of his young protégés with their first sexual experience further secured their loyalty and his avuncular status.

Booth's sexual hubris bears resemblance to a practice known as *ngobo* that involved young Bapende and Bambunda men from the Kwango District, a practice that came under intense colonial scrutiny in the 1930s. Its precolonial precursor was first recorded by Hungarian anthropologist Emil Torday, who visited the Kwango River Basin in 1910. Torday noted that before the harvest season a dozen or more young men would "hire" a *mobanda*, usually a prepubescent girl from a neighboring village, and confine her to a special hut whose outside walls they would adorn with white and red painted triangles. For two months, each young man would have sexual access to the girl ad libitum. The ritual, according to Torday, seemed to have taken place with the full acquiescence of the girl's mother, who regularly would bring her daughter food and palm wine and presumably also tend to her pain with an assortment of remedies. At the end of the ordeal the girl would be freed while the mother received fifty to sixty rolls of salt from each of her daughter's "captors." A girl would undergo this ritual only once in her lifetime without in any way jeopardizing her chance to become marriageable. In the event she were to die during the ordeal, the men would pay a much heftier price to her mother and her village.

Other such sexual practices that predated colonization may have included forms of social punishment whereby a woman who flouted social rules and remained unrepentant would be branded *ntambi* (public woman) by the village chief. She would then be "fair game" to any adult male member of the community. Anyone could have sex with her. Those that she spurned could sexually assault her. The punishment lasted for about a year until the village chief suspended her sentence. When that happened, the ntambi would then publicly name the men who had sex with her and expose each of them to a symbolic fine and some gifts they had to give to either her husband (in the case of a married woman) or her parents.[23]

When ngobo surfaced in the early 1930s, both the social function that had regulated similar sexual practices in the past and the social control village chiefs had often exercised over them had all but vanished. Here is the way colonial reports described ngobo: a loose-knit group of young Bapende and Bambuna men would persuade or coerce a young girl or, sometimes, a married woman to confess publicly that she had become ngobo (in order for them to avoid being charged with adultery and to have to pay the required fine). They would then take their victim to a hut, usually in a secluded area, away from the village, intoxicate her with palm wine, and force themselves on her as those who waited for their turn cheered. Sometimes, boys as young as six or seven would be admitted to the sex hut either as mere spectators or, for the daring ones, as active participants. Parents who went to claim their daughters suffered all sorts of indignities in the hands of their daughter's tormentors. By the late 1930s, colonial outrage against ngobo had reached a boiling point, leading to its eradication as a result of the collaboration between colonial authorities and Bapende village and clan chiefs.[24]

It is quite conceivable, given his rural roots and peripatetic lifestyle, that Booth came across and perhaps even participated himself in ngobo raping before he moved to Kinshasa in the late 1940s. Before he appeared on the scene éboulement and its arsenal of tricks and schemes were unheard of in the city. Indeed, according to several informants, William Booth was the first of Kinshasa's long line of éboulementaires.

Vieux Paurret

I met Paurret for the first time at La Voix de Dieu, the church of the late Sakombi Inongo in Bandal, where Paurret still works as a watchman. Sakombi had served in Mobutu's regime as minister of information and its chief propaganda mouth-piece. Accordingly, Kinois nicknamed him "Buka Lokuta" (Spewing Lies), a moniker that stuck with him even (and especially) after he had become a born-again Christian and pastor. In 1993, after Paurret's house had been irreparably damaged during one of those flash floods that regularly afflict Kinshasa's populace, Sakombi, whom he knew through Kabaidi, offered him the job. On my way from downtown Kinshasa to Binza-UPN, where I lived, I would occasionally stop in Bandal to visit Vieux Paurret and just see how he was doing. These visits usually came at the cost of a few 500-franc bills,[25] as my host would often find subtle ways to solicit financial assistance. On one such visit he greeted me with a broad smile and erupted with something to the effect of "I prayed this morning for your visit, and here you are!"

Paurret had learned to cut kamô (see chapter 5) under Vieux Eboma's tutelage; before acquiring the nickname "Paurret," everyone had known him as "Monganga" (Doctor).[26] Eboma taught him where to get ingredients (usually from Senegalese vendors at the central market), how to mix and cook them in a cast-iron skillet to produce powerful nkisi (burnt powder), and how to administer them to power-craving Yankees. Before long, Paurret was running his own kamô shop in Kintambo, collecting money from Bills. Sometimes, he recalled, he would try out his own kamô by inciting other township Bills to fight. Tripping someone (*croc-en-jambe*), shoving, or just spitting in someone's path was enough to start a fight and test out his own kamô.

In 1949, at age seventeen, Paurret fell under Booth's spell. He started to orbit around Booth, running errands for him, repairing his bike, until he was finally drawn closer, into Booth's inner circle of éboulementaires. The two remained friends and reunited briefly after independence in 1960, when they both came back to Kinshasa—Booth mellowed with age, broken by solitary confinement and with waning vision, and Paurret wiser and sober but still a rebel without a cause (see figure 6.3).

Figure 6.3 Vieux Paurret in Quartier Bandal, February 2009. Photo by the author.

Although Paurret crassly admitted to having been a notorious éboulemen-taire, he remained evasive about the modus operandi of his old business. "We did that," he confessed tersely. "Yes, we did that back then."[27] After encountering so many former Bills who flatly dismissed the topic—or pretended not to know what éboulement meant—Paurret's candid admission was unsettling. Yet in the next breath he would turn to a different topic in the same animated voice. Clearly, his business (and probably that of William Booth as well) had had a sinister side. Otherwise, why had both men been arrested? Why was William Booth incarcerated? Why was Paurret deported and kept under quasi–house arrest, to be released only when colonization ended?

To this last question, Paurret's reply was inchoate and general. By proclaiming himself the sheriff in Kintambo, he indicated, he had provoked colonial wrath and ended up in jail and then deported. Had this been all there was to it, it would stand to reason that other Grands Bills would have met the same fate. Yet Tex Bill, who replaced Paurret as Kintambo's kingpin, and other Grands Bills and inveterate éboulementaires in other townships never found themselves in the crosshairs of colonial repression. Why Paurret and not Andrada, a notorious éboulementaire and Ruwet's Robin Hood? Why not DeSoto, who lassoed and dragged girls like cattle?

The answers to these questions are buried in the Bissot Report, the controversial document written by the Belgian official Louis Bissot in 1957 after an extensive investigation into Kinshasa's gangland (see chapter 7). According to the report, "Vieux Porrect [*sic*], alias Mongànga," whom Bissot calls an *ignoble personnage,* collected under him a motley crew of young ruffians that he would dispatch across town to steal money. As Paurret himself put it:

> I was the "big man" in Kintambo. I gave orders and everybody obeyed. . . .
> Sometimes, I was sitting down and would give an order: "*Petits,* go get me some money!" They would go and pull a stunt somewhere and get money. Sometimes they would barge into a store, distract people, and steal money. . . .
> I would call a girl, "Come here!" and she would come without balking and I would take her inside the house. Back then, my father thought I was weird (*mystique*). He had given up on me. He told himself, "The child has lost it." We lorded it over (*kovunka*) our parents back then.[28]

And as Bissot described:

> [Paurret's] gang would swarm the market in the evening, yelling wildly, over-turning everything in their path, and stealing anything that could be carried away, even young girls who would be later subjected to male gang members' lustful drive. (Bissot 2009 [1958]: 18)

According to Bissot, Paurret used his gang of "Far West Dima" as a site of sexual exploitation of girls who were caught in his nets and as a playground where young township boys could experiment in anonymous, impersonal, unencumbered sex with doped-up out-of-township girls. Paurret collected admission fees of 50 francs or more to these pot-fueled sex romps known in Indoubill by the term *tournoi* (Bissot 2009 [1958]: 21). His pimping business became even more lucrative when, around 1956, he began to cater to Leopoldville's adult market. He teamed up with a certain Windy (the same Windy mentioned in chapter 5 and earlier), and together they abducted *petits mbongo* (minor girls) in Brazzaville, smuggled them back to Leopoldville by canoe, and pimped them out to the highest bidders. When the law finally caught up with Paurret, his victims, Bissot hints, numbered by the hundreds: "There's no gang leader [in Leopoldville] who was not schooled by this wicked individual (*infect individu*)" (Bissot 2009 [1958]: 19).

DeSoto

While William Booth operated in Citas and Paurret in Kintambo, DeSoto,[29] not to be undone, emerged as the most notorious éboulementaire in Ruwet, a quartier that many thought had an uncannily large concentration of "pretty girls." Kinshasa has always boasted at least one saturnalian hub that symbolized the heart of the city, and Matongé was for many years that heart. Before Matongé there was Ruwet.

Considered Kinshasa's trendiest and most festive quartier, Matongé functioned as a crucible for cultures. It registered the versatile moods of the city. Its streets and compounds pulsated with music, ambiance, and revelry. There, it seemed, the daytime hustle and bustle served only as a dress rehearsal for its effervescent nightlife. Today Bandal, with its famous "Bloc," has eclipsed Matongé.

Matongé and Bandal's predecessor, Ruwet, was located in the Kinshasa district, the oldest and most populous section of the capital. Ruwet boasted several cosmopolitan nightspots, including the Parc de Boeck,[30] which served as a venue for dance contests, beauty pageantry, music concerts (Tchebwa 1996: 106), and several bars, including the OK Bar (owned by Oscar Kashama), where Congo's most famous popular music band, OK Jazz, sprang up. Each of these bars attracted a bevy of young, voluptuous women, known as *bana* (children) or *numéros* (tickets), who organized themselves in several *sociétés d'élégance* with suggestive names such as La Beauté, La Mode, Diamants, La Violette, La Rose, and La Reconnaissance (Gondola 2003: 120).

With each of their sorties into one of Ruwet's boisterous bars, these bana were sure to make many a man's head spin. In addition to the colorful maputa or pagnes[31] that enhanced the shape of their bodies, the bana would don a *zikida* (string of pearls) around their waists to bewitch their suitors. They could purchase this necessary fashion item from a nearby market still known today as Somba Zikida. As they shopped for provisions in the market or strolled its busy streets, the bana would be relentlessly exhorted by zikida vendors to "somba zikida!" (Get your zikida!), a phrase that thus became the name of the market (Fumunzanza Muketa 2011: 109).

As Congo's iconic popular musician Franco has suggested in several of his compositions, Ruwet set the stage for the emasculation of the Congolese man. In a mid-1960s composition titled *Numéro ya Kinshasa*, Franco portrayed the gender permutation that first unfolded in Ruwet:

> Ngai mwasi na yebana numéro ya Kinshasa o
> Mobali aluka ngai, liboso abanga ngai
> Sala keba, tokoniata koniata
> Balingi ngai mingi, o
> Okoswana nde na bato
> Banga nde makambo
> Ya liboso na boya ba mbanda
> Po nde nayebana mingi, o
> . . .
> Na motema libala ya bo mbanda, soni na ngai
> Ngai numéro lokola ngai
> Na kobotola mibali ya bato
> Po nayebani, kitoko ya mwasi
> Ngai Lulu, o, na welaka te
> Mibali o, bakoya kobenga ngai
> na ba Vespa pe na ba VW
> Po balingi ngai, pe nayebani
>
> People know me in Kinshasa as a "ticket"
> Before dating me a man should first fear me
> Beware, we'll stamp our authority
> Men, they just adore me
> You'll make yourself a lot of enemies
> Beware of trouble
> For one thing, I hate to share my man with rivals
> Because I need to preserve my reputation
> . . .
> I loathe a relationship that involves rivals
> A "ticket" like me!
> I rob other women's husbands
> For I am well known and gorgeous
> Me, Lulu, I am picky
> Men are the ones that flock to me
> On their Vespas and VWs [Volkswagens]
> For they love me and I am well known
> (quoted in Gondola 2003: 120–21)

Such was the cultural and gender environment in which DeSoto earned for himself the dreaded title of éboulementaire. As a young boy, DeSoto had fallen from a mango tree and suffered a serious leg injury that left him with a severe limp for the rest of his life. He compensated by strengthening his upper body through a strenuous bodybuilding regimen (see figure 6.4). Anyone fighting DeSoto would always be careful to keep his distance, for his powerful grip could prove lethal. Victims were stalked and snatched with the same vicious grit that sealed the outcome of most of his fights, as Monstre (a moniker meant as an oxymoron), one of DeSoto's former myrmidons, explained:

> DeSoto snatched girls like a hunter would hunt down game in the forest. . . . It always took place at night, not in broad daylight. DeSoto had his own brigade. In his brigade I was part of a group called *Les Amoureux* (The Lovers), that is, the good-looking boys. When DeSoto spotted a pretty girl, he would send us to go get her.[32]

Les Amoureux would then deploy their seductive arsenal of smooth-talking and false promises to woo the so-called prévenue (defendant) and drive her within DeSoto's range, for him to grab and carry away to his lair. If they found the girl with a male escort, they would beat the man and carry the girl as they would a sack of cassava.[33] DeSoto's gang particularly preyed on évolués. Snatching a girlfriend or courtesan from évolués was not simply a thumbing of the nose at them but a way to emasculate them and expose their inability to protect their women.

Once a girl arrived at DeSoto's makeshift den, each man present would take turns forcing himself on her, in an ordeal by orgy that continued for days on end while she remained high on dope (zoumbel). Sharing the same girl, like passing a joint around, was a sort of bacchanalia that reinforced performatively a heightened sense of power and group masculinity (Brownmiller 1975: 194). The rape victim's body, Eric Schneider (1999: 133) observed among the youth gangs in postwar New York, "served as a sexual communion, joining the participants together, assuring them of their power, and providing an appropriately masculine alternative to heterosexual intimacy." *Tournoi* (or "line-ups," as New York youths dubbed gang rape) may also have fulfilled a desire to enjoy unencumbered and egotistical sex without having to bother with foreplay and romance. The fact that such sexual intercourse was partaken of communally, with the help of narcotic substances, no doubt mitigated postcoital awkwardness and guilt as well.

Much could be said about silence and sexuality as young men enter the world of sexual desire and learn sexual literacy. As Victor Seidler (2006: 31) has noted while surveying Latin American urban centers, young men "might have inherited cultural notions which suggest that speech serves to interrupt desire and so diminish passion, making it hard for them to learn that speech can also intensify

Figure 6.4 DeSoto (right) and an acolyte flexing muscles. © Photo Jean Depara, Kinshasa ca. 1950–65. Courtesy of Revue Noire.

desire and bring closeness as individuals risk expressing how they feel as sexual beings and they like being touched and how they can be aroused." The lack of sexual and emotional literacy, coupled with the sense of feeling trapped in their embodied selves and the strong desire to assert their masculinity, explains why young men in Kinshasa, as elsewhere, tended to relate to women through the language of the body, not through the language of (spoken) words. Therefore, "sex becomes a statement, a demonstration of virility and an assertion of male identity" (145).

For young people, sexual awkwardness occurs not only in the postcoital state but as soon as boys understand that courtship stands in the way of their desire to have girls on their own terms. It is thus perhaps not surprising that Bills usually referred to rape as *amour forcé* (forced love). By engaging in amour forcé they were able to bypass courtship, which many viewed as a cumbersome, convoluted, almost unmanly ritual that would lead only to anxiety and stress. The demographic imbalance between males and females in the townships increased competition for girls to such an extent that predatory behavior trumped dating. Preying on young women became a toxic and addictive substitute for dating, a quick fix not only for sex but also for how young men were to relate to and interact with young females. This explains why even Bills renowned for their magnetism and good looks—and who by all accounts ought to have had no need to resort to amour forcé—became notorious éboulementaires.

Andrada

Métis (biracial), handsome, and flamboyant, Andrada engaged in a very different kind of éboulement in Ruwet and Casamar in the late 1950s (see figure 6.5). Before his emergence, girls who orbited around the Bills had merely supporting and cheerleading roles. They cooked for William Booth, for example, or ran errands to the market for Paurret. As Clive Glaser uncovered in 1960s Soweto, they "were sometimes drawn peripherally into gangs as girlfriends, decoys and lookouts" (Glaser 1998: 722) or "acted as spies" and "concealed weapons for the boys" in postwar New York City (Schneider 1999: 130) because gang subculture remained so eminently male.[34]

Female gangs, which several authors uncovered in their respective areas (Campbell 1984; Rubi 2005; Madzou 2008; Diamond 2009), or even females *in* gangs, were unheard of in Kinshasa until Andrada appeared on the scene. On the "mean streets" of Chicago, for example, girls joined gangs as a way to secure a manly attribute: mobility and the right to travel about under the protection of their male buddies. To that end they created gangs that served as female branches to male gangs and could always count on the guys to bail them out in an urban environment fraught with perils, including rape. Hence the Vice Lords produced the Vice Ladies, the Rangers the Rangerettes, and the Cobras the Cobraettes (Diamond 2009: 191). The same went for the Parisian suburbs of the 1990s, where, according to former gang leader Lamence Madzou, female gangs formed as mere extensions of male gangs, the most notorious being the Amazons and the Fight Girls. These girls dressed like the boys, talked like them, and hung around with them. Some even fought. Yet once violence escalated to all-out gang battles and fighters wielded knives and guns, girls' participation tended to wane. During such fights, their role remained peripheral: they would carry bags containing weapons or be on the lookout for rival gang members (Madzou 2008: 52–53).

Figure 6.5 Andrada in full cowboy gear, with fake pistols. © Photo Jean Depara, Kinshasa ca. 1950–65. Courtesy of Revue Noire.

No such thing existed in Kinshasa. Then, lo and behold, came Andrada with his cohort of cowgirls, as it were. Thérèse Muyaka, whose tumultuous life would in itself make for a fascinating biopic, was Andrada's Bonnie Parker. Borrowing from what others have observed about the inclusion of women within the Congolese armed forces, such "feminization" of Andrada's posse led to the "masculinization" of these tropical cowgirls, or Billesses,[35] into "a particular idealized type of masculinity" (Eriksson Baaz and Stern 2008: 68).

Thérèse Muyaka is seen in one of the most iconic pictures of a cadre of Bills (see the book's cover). In this shot by photographer Jean Depara stand Andrada

Figure 6.6 Meta, in full cowboy gear, with a toy gun. © Photo Jean Depara, Kinshasa ca. 1950–65. Courtesy of Revue Noire.

and Hubert Kunguniko, decked out in full cowboy regalia, with large hats, spurs, and fake pistols. Crouched down in front of them, Thérèse (then sixteen) and Meta (see also figure 6.6) look as masculine as their male companions. One has to scrutinize their faces to discern traces of their gender. In fact, until one sees an enlarged print of Depara's picture, for example, at the home of Baudoin Bikoko, a Congolese photograph collector, it could just as well be of four tropical cowboys.

I met Thérèse Muyaka for the first time at her modest rented place in Limété (Première Rue) on the afternoon of June 29, 2009. At sixty-nine, Thérèse still cut a distinctive figure, with her neatly manicured hands and feet and a knack for matching colorful pagnes to her silk blouses. She had gone through her nine lives unscathed. She felt blessed, she confided to me, that after the reckless escapades of her youth and a slew of liaisons that produced seven children, each from a different genitor, she was now an adored grandmother and a devoted Christian at Mama Olangi's charismatic church. One of her daughters, who had followed in her mother's footsteps as a "hot dancer," with the strange scene name of Bête Sauvage, is also a born-again Christian. For this fact, Thérèse felt doubly grateful to God.

Thérèse, an only child, was orphaned at an early age and ended up in the custody of an aunt who moved with her husband to Kinshasa in the early 1940s. Very early on she started to "wander" (kolúka) and burst into the limelight of Kinshasa's whirlwind nightlife scene, just as Josephine Baker took Paris by storm, with her sexually suggestive *zebola* (traditional Mongo dance) moves in Alexis Tshibangu's traditional dance ensemble. She was celebrated in such songs as *Thérèse d'amour*, composed by one of her paramours, musician Rossignol (aka José-Philippe Lando), in 1956 when Thérèse was only sixteen:

Thérèse, nani abotaki yo?
Soki ata mibale bazala lokola yo

Kisasa mobimba naluki nalembi
Mwasi lokola yo na zwi te, oh

Thérèse, who gave birth to you?
I wish there was another girl like you

I looked all over Kinshasa, in vain
I couldn't find another girl like you

Like many other male onlookers Andrada fell under her spell, and he soon beseeched her to join his small gang of Yankees. As a new recruit, Thérèse (nicknamed Roy) participated in the same rituals as her male counterparts, rituals that involved kamô, zoumbel, and bilayi (see chapter 5). She would abscond from home for days on end and run to Andrada's hangout place with her cowboy outfit neatly tucked in a bag.[36] There she would shed her saucy dress for the cowboy duds that concealed her gender, especially as many of their nightly sorties took them to dance bars where gender rules were disrupted and subverted altogether (Gondola 1996: 254). Unlike DeSoto, or even William Booth, Andrada had charm, wit, and flair. He ingratiated himself with township girls by letting them sometimes ride for free in "his" *fula-fula*[37] but had incessant run-ins with the police for speeding and reckless driving.

Female recruits to Andrada's gang may have been treated like any other gang member—indeed, as stated above, membership in the gang tended to blur gender lines—yet their femininity never totally disappeared. It could be summoned and exploited to support the gang's sexual and financial needs in several critical ways. For example, Roy and Meta (see figure 6.7) were encouraged to start friendships with out-of-township girls. As the friendships developed they would lure the girls to Andrada's hangout, which he had christened "Palais Laeken," after the royal palace in Brussels from which Leopold II had orchestrated Congo's takeover and

Figure 6.7 Meta and Thérèse (aka Roy). © Photo Jean Depara, Kinshasa ca. 1950–65. Courtesy of Revue Noire.

abuses. Once there, the prévenues would be sexually assaulted. Andrada would also tap into Roy's magnetism to fleece male patrons who flocked to the townships' buvettes and nightclubs. Sometimes when the gang was strapped for cash, needed to replenish its wardrobe, or was simply feeling a sudden and collective adrenaline rush for bravado, Andrada would dispatch Roy and a few other gang members on a shoplifting spree: They would hide in a shop at closing time and spend the night stuffing their bags with clothes and cash. The next morning, Andrada would show up with his band and distract the store staff so that Roy and her accomplices could slip out unnoticed.

On a few occasions, Roy recalled, the gang would barge into one of Quartier Ruwet's trendy nightclubs, manhandle a few male patrons, and commandeer the whole place while two gang members stayed on the qui vive at the entrance of the establishment to prevent people from going in and out. Andrada and the rest of the gang would then pull up chairs and sit down cowboy style, leaning back with their dusty boots up on the table, an unmistakable cue that they expected to be served beer and bites galore on the house. While their male escorts steered clear of the dance floor, female patrons would be forced to drink beer and dance in couples with Andrada's posse. Eager to find out what role Roy played on the dance floor, I asked her if she, too, grabbed a female dance partner:

> "Did you also dance with a girl," I asked.
> "Of course, I did," she replied. "I was a Bill!"
> "I understand that, but you were a girl, why not dance with a man?" I countered.
> "Because I was just like one of them. I was a Bill," she insisted, looking at me in the eye and, perhaps, wondering why it was so hard for me to get it.

Girls no doubt joined gangs as full-fledged members for the same reasons as boys did: the desire to run away from a broken home, the solace that life in Kinshasa's gangland provided, and the thrill that one's swagger could command respect and elicit fear. Nonetheless, for most of these girls, including Roy, it was also a calculated way to protect and take control over their bodies and their sexuality in a social environment that reified female bodies and targeted them for sexual violence. Roy performed masculinity to the hilt and adopted manly scripts to conceal not just her gender but also her vulnerability, without, however, completely losing her femininity and her sexual orientation. In doing so she ended up embracing and buttressing a violent and symptomatic expression of masculinity.

The notion that Yankees served as guardian angels to their township girls, as seen in the confrontation between Tex Bill and Degazin in Kintambo (described toward the outset of this chapter), has some validity. But even Bills' own township girls had to conform to the gangs' gender codes if they were to enjoy the protection of Grands Bills. And in accord with these codes, Yankees were protecting their "sisters'" hymens as much as (or more than) they were policing sexual boundaries and behaviors. Once township girls started to "wander" (kolúka) and flout gender rules, Bills could swiftly turn against them.

Moreover, as convenient as kolúka claims may have been, they also served to conceal other sexual subtexts—subtexts that help explain the Bills' frequent about-face from protector to predator. Unrequited love, for example, or refusal to answer a love missive sent through one of their young minions, incensed Bills, resulting in éboulement. A township girl who carried herself improperly, appeared to be haughty, or displayed any other "precipitant behavior," to borrow a phrase from Brownmiller (1975: 354), could also become the target of éboulement. Indeed, as Bourke (2007: 74) so tellingly puts it, a female's "complicity in her own sexual abuse" pervades popular cultures in many places, and may even posit rape as a "well deserved" fate because some females supposedly invite peril by behaving flirtatiously. Kolúka, then, served essentially as a discursive and performative foil intended to enhance the Bills' masculinity at the expense of personal and sexual freedom for the majority of township girls.

Hegemonic Hypermasculinity

The Bills' versatile performances, as protectors and predators, compel us to take a closer look at hegemonic masculinity: how it functions through dominant discourse, how it claims multiple meanings (Connell and Messerschmidt 2005: 841), how it "restricts and suppresses alternative masculinities" (Magnuson 2007: 32), and ultimately how, in the Gramscian sense, it ends up being buttressed by those whom it oppresses—in this case, most women and some men who "fail" to live up to its standards. By the same token, it is important to note that hegemonic masculinity never goes unchallenged. It never deploys itself in a homogeneous sea of quiescence but must navigate an archipelago teeming with defiance, subversion, and counterhegemonic masculinities that constantly threaten to swamp it, or at least wash away some of its complacency and veneer.

While the Bills' hypermasculinity challenged colonial hegemonic masculinity by becoming the standard in the townships, it was itself both dodged and challenged through negotiation, selective appropriation, or outright rejection. The challenge came mostly from Yumas and "Je le connais" (smartasses) who valued schooling as an avenue to a different kind of masculinity, though they also embraced many of the Bills' masculine codes.

Unwilling tenants under the same roof, hegemonic and counterhegemonic masculinities can also be fostered by a common ideology, referred to above as Afro-Victorian, for lack of a better term. It is also worth recalling here that the Bills' infatuation with sexual violence took place within a permissive legal and social environment, in which sexual predation figured prominently as a quint-essential manly attribute that played out through gendered performativity. Whereas the male body underwent several performances, cutting kamô, kintulu (bodybuilding), and smoking zoumbel, which enhanced its virility, the female body became a playground of sorts for the construction of hegemonic masculin-ity. We find this echoed in the lyrics of what could be considered the Bills' cult song and anthem, Néron's *Zambele Kingo*. In the song Néron puts girls on notice with a blunt threat: "Petit Nzele na kosala yo mabe" (Baby, I'll hurt you good).

Describing DeSoto's predatory practices, one informant reminisced about sexual violence in a way that leaves no doubt about this asymmetrical construc-tion, in which the trivialization of sexual violence stands just one step away from impunity:

> DeSoto took girls by force. . . . It was a kind of abduction. Back then, the police did not do anything. It wasn't considered a crime. Parents were just scared to go claim their daughters, because [Bills] were brutal and tough. Yet they never killed those girls; they just kept them as long as they wanted for their own needs.[38]

Fear alone cannot explain parents' and other relatives' reluctance to go claim their daughters. Parents held ambivalent views about the business of rape. Some may have consciously or unconsciously espoused the Bills' kolúka narrative and have laid the blame at their daughters' wandering feet. If their girl had not strayed, parents reasoned, if only she had behaved like a "good girl," then certainly the Bills would not have targeted her. In the minds of many parents, rape was a de-served retribution and a corrective ordeal. They felt indebted to Grands Bills for the role they played in keeping township girls in line and deterring wandering (kolúka). In addition, starting in the early 1960s some parents had lost their grip on their children and leaned on Grands Bills to help prevent their offspring from becoming recidivist hooligans and shirking their responsibilities.

Paurret, for instance, took an interest in children in his township remaining in school. A notorious éboulementaire in Kintambo who, as already mentioned, had learned most of his tricks serving as William Booth's right-hand man, Paur-ret ended up caught in a police net. One day in 1957, a police patrol met him at the Chanic naval shipyard where he worked as a boilermaker. Paurret resisted and laid several policemen out before they finally managed to handcuff him and haul him away in a police truck. He spent a few months in the Ndolo prison before be-ing sent to Monkoto, a village near the town of Mbandaka, where he was placed under quasi–house arrest for almost four years.

Reminiscing, decades later, about his years as Kintambo's Grand Bill, Paur-ret rhapsodized about policing Kintambo and, as described earlier, admitted his éboulementaire past. His favorite movie, *Le Dernier des fédérés* (*The Lone*

Ranger), had provided a few scripts for rounding up truants in his territory. Yet to play Kemosabe (as the Lone Ranger's sidekick Tonto calls his friend the masked man) in Kintambo, Paurret needed a horse. *Pas de cheval, pas de cowboy!*[39] Fair enough. Paurret acquired a bicycle,[40] and young Bills in Kintambo who knew how fond he was of *The Lone Ranger* immediately christened it "Silver," after the Lone Ranger's famous white stallion. To give the two-wheeled frame an air of Kemosabe's trusty mount and mirror a thoroughbred's many gaits, Paurret jettisoned the brakes and lowered the seat. Indeed, the relationship between the Bills and their bicycles could be as breathtaking as the way cowboys mounted and handled their steeds on the Hollywood screen: speeding down the streets, Paurret would greet other Bills with a loud "Bill oyée!" while rearing up his bike as he had seen the Lone Ranger do with Silver. The Bills' formulaic reply: "Serumba!" Paurret recounted:

> As I rode my bike, I would often halt it as I get closer to a child and say reproachfully: "I know you skipped school today." I'd then take him to the Brothers [Belgian missionaries], where he'd usually get upbraided. They'd thank me and let me go. In the evening, I'd sit with them [the children] near the public water fountain where women washed their clothes to deliver a pep talk.[41]

In Mofewana, Grands Bills acted in a similarly avuncular fashion. Yet unlike Paurret, most of them attended school themselves. As Petit Moloch recalled:

> When it was time to go to school, they went. For example Vieux Zabara [aka Vieux Moloch] was educated and didn't want us to steal but to go to school. Vieux Tarzan too got his education and became director of the Forescom building. Vieux Kroutchev and Vieux Billy too had degrees. They would chase us down the street and drag us to school.[42]

Petit Moloch was born Abraham Koko Yawadio on February 17, 1955, in Mofewana. By the time little Abraham was toddling around the quartier, Vieux Tarzan had relinquished *biyalo* (authority) to Vieux Néron (aka Katshaya Kopombo Joseph, born 1942), who then held sway and served as the main rampart against Mofewana's rival gang in Quartier Dynamique.

In 1957, Mivais John (Bad John) had returned to Mofewana after spending several years at the Madimba juvenile detention ward for accidentally killing a white boy while stealing his bicycle. At first Vieux Néron, *en grand seigneur,* had taken him under his wing and even nicknamed him "John Wayne" after Mivais John knocked down Cyprien with a couple of blows. But Mivais John quickly got under everyone's skin by claiming to be Mofewana's *pomba* (strong man). A fierce billing erupted between him and Rossy Ross, so brutal that it tore Mofewana's close-knit gang apart at the seams. Néron, who had endeared himself to his bunch with his soft grip and guitar prowess, flew off the handle.

Mivais John was casting a long shadow in Mofewana, and despite his boiling anger Néron understood that only a Solomonic decision could contain the damage. Hence he divided Mofewana into two somewhat rival territories: Molokai (under Rossy Ross) and Farwest (or Fewe), which he let Mivais John rule, though not without keeping close tabs on his protégé. Soon enough, a spirit of rebellion against Mivais John's wayward leadership was brewing in Farwest—a godsend for Néron, since it enabled him to shake himself free of his enfant terrible. After Mivais John left town in disgrace and later hooked up with Marie Cowboy to rule Ndjili (see table 5.1), Néron replaced him with Zabara (who went also by the moniker of Moloch, aka Mpindi David) before finally reuniting the two split territories. Moloch, in turn, took a liking to little Abraham and decided to nickname him "Petit Moloch."

Like Néron, Zabara (aka Moloch) would be remembered as a sheriff whom people elevated to the level of a father figure. As Petit Moloch recalled:

> You don't go to school, you get flogged. Sometimes our mothers went to see Zabara and weepingly asked him why their child didn't get good grades. Zabara would follow us to school and ask our teachers what we were up to. If the teacher said we weren't working hard enough, Zabara would start beating us right there. If he found us in another quartier socializing with [ba]*fakwa* (thieves), he would beat us on the spot and say, "If you stray I am the one your mothers gonna blame." We would come back home crying. He could send us to run errands even twenty times a day and we couldn't balk or drag our feet. A bad child is the one that never gets sent to run an errand. He would tell us, "Go buy me some cigarettes." We would take off immediately, barefoot, even as far as Gambela [market]. To cross Assossa [main thoroughfare], to cross Assossa's sand barefoot was excruciatingly painful with the heat.[43]

A parallel could be drawn here between the Bills and what historian of the American West Richard White calls "social bandits," a take on Eric Hobsbawm's gallant Robin Hood figure, a figure that traverses many places and times. White contends that social bandits in the American West "needed popular support" and "could not undercut it by indiscriminately robbing the inhabitants of the regions in which they lived and operated" (White 1981: 393). Yet it was not just their Robin Hood redistributive justice that buoyed them. In the postbellum Far West, frontier denizens held Union sheriffs and deputy marshals in utter contempt and distrust for using their offices to "settle old scores from the war" and grab land for themselves and their proxies. American outlaws, White argues, embodied "certain culturally defined masculine virtues" and became cultural heroes and "symbols of masculinity . . . at a time when masculinity itself was being widely worried over and glorified" (397).

Despite their éboulement, Yankees are remembered today as township heroes. No other juvenile group out of the many that waxed and waned in Kinshasa, from Kompani Kitunga (chapters 4 and 8) to the Kuluna (chapter 8), managed to garner the kind of sympathy dividend that Yankees did. Kompani Kitunga never managed to shake off the label of petty thieves, nor have the Kuluna been able to shed their reputation as dangerous thugs. (Indeed, in the absence of government action, some local residents have become vigilantes to deal with the scourge that the Kuluna represent.) Although Yankees can hardly be portrayed as Robin Hoods of the tropics,[44] their performing hypermasculinity, the strict and clear gendered boundaries they drew in the townships, and their roles as big brothers and, at times, father figures gave solace to many township parents who had lost their footing in the face of the colonial Cronos. As a result, the Yankees' balance between being protectors and predators was easily seen as tipping toward protection by township residents.

Rape and Colonial Debris

The connection between éboulement and the martial rape taking place today in Congo's war-torn areas is hardly a discrete one. Rather, this connection is tied both to the permissive legal environment in Congo and to the ways in which sexual violence operates as an accepted pattern that ends up reinforcing gender norms and hierarchies. Thus a nonconsensual act (perhaps even an act of terrorism) is reframed as a sexual encounter in which there are no victims but only consensual partners. For this reason, too, we must dismiss the convenient persuasion that constructs rapists themselves as victims. Hypermasculinity, especially when it involves gender violence and rape, cannot be reduced to a form of "protest masculinity," which Connell (1995: 116) defines as a type of masculinity found among working-class men or ethnically marginalized men who vie for gender power but lack economic wherewithal and institutional authority.

This is, of course, just one side of the story. The other side concerns oblivion and "historical forgetting," a "missed opportunity to work with 'toxic imperial debris,'" Hunt (2008: 221) tells us. For Hunt, following such "bits of debris" that pervade the present landscape takes us to a vast ethnographic field littered with stubborn repetitive reincarnations, haunting photographic images that evoke humanity at its worst, but that can also distract us from voices that were never silenced and from silences that speak even more loudly than shocking photos or the cries exacted by the worst sadistic torture. The silence Hunt refers us to is that of Boali, a Congolese woman in the village of Ekolongo who froze like death and gave no "sign of life" while the man she refused to give herself to, after blasting a bullet through her body, proceeded to sever her foot with a sharp blade in order to steal the brass anklet she wore (225). Boali later spoke, as did 258 other Congolese, before King Leopold's Commission of Inquiry in 1905–1906. Her words of pain and sorrow, never to be silenced again, are the first testimony along the trail of ruination and debris that Hunt has beckoned to us to follow. Between 1903 and 1996, when the first accounts of rape surfaced from Congo's eastern border, Hunt notes, there have been multiple repetitions. "At the same time, much is new," she is quick to add.

PART III

METAMORPHOSES

7 Père Buffalo

He left a blank that's hard to fill
For there never will be another Bill.
Both black and white will mourn the day
That the "Biggest Boss" took Bill away.

Eulogy for Bill Pickett (1870–1932)[1]

In July 1964, Père Buffalo bid farewell to the Bills and Billesses with whom he had broken bread, sung, danced, and smoked marijuana. It had all begun one day in 1960, when he had befriended Billy in Quartier Dynamique, Quartier Mofewana's rival in the township of Ngiri-Ngiri. On April 3, 2006, when I walked into his office in Sint Pieters-Leeuw, a small town in the western part of Flanders, fairly close to Brussels, Père Buffalo greeted me with an ebullient smile. He had been waiting for a biographer, he later confided in me, and suggested I meet with the Parisian-based Angolan filmmaker who had been working on a biopic about his ministry in Congo.[2] Père Buffalo exuded an inexhaustible youthfulness and energy (see figure 7.1). I had little difficulty picturing him dealing with the brashest éboulementaires in Dynamique, Mofewana, or Citas back in the 1960s. When the topic of his smoking hemp came up during the interview, he flatly dismissed it.[3] Bills did continue to smoke even after they had joined his Christian youth ministry. "They were no saints," he quipped—nor was Père Buffalo the saint to deter them from partaking of their sweet indulgence.

That day in July 1964 provides a tantalizing glimpse of the last stage of the Bill movement, when several Grands Bills contemplated hanging up their spurs and leading a less tumultuous life in postcolonial Congo. Before taking his leave to return to Belgium, Père Buffalo summoned the Bills for a last pep rally. Speaking in colorful Indoubill, Père Buffalo began with the formulaic rallying cry, "Babill oyée, banzèles oyée!" (Vive the Bills, vive the girls!):[4]

Kala wana lamuka, ngai mbembe wa binu Buffalo, na wadié oh . . . Kasi liboso ngai nabendana, nalingi nasundela nainu babill na ngai vrai meeting . . .
KAMWA VE, LOTA VE, BABILLS.
Soki ngai nakei, nalingi babills ba ngai bazonga nsima te, BOTAMBOLA NA VRAI RYTHME YA BISU YA KIBILL ndenge tozalaki. Mbamba ba mivais témoins ba koseka bisu, bakoloba 'te: Ah, tala babills yango bazalaki kosala boye kaka

Figure 7.1 Père Buffalo with his stepmother, Gimbergen, Belgium, 2006. Photo by the author.

mpo na père BUFFALO. BOKEBA NA KIYUMA mpo mwa dimi kiyuma ezali na motema ya motu moko moko wa bisu, BOKEBA.

MASEKE MPE MABUTA!!!

Bomoni ba mivais témoins bazali yélé, mo na yango bampelas, bolamuka mpe bocapter, boyebi mosala ya mivais témoins? Ezali kokosa mpe kokebisa ba mista na ye . . . BO-AUGMENTER VOLUME YA KIBILL na binu na ba quartiers mosusu, bayuma bazali steck, na BA-FAKWA, na babill ya simple simple, na BA-BULAWAYO.

BOREVER BANGO!!!!

Bolamuka babill, Méthode ya KIYUMA SIMPLE, A BAS! Bisu babill tokoki kondima tokolanda bango te. Babills, banzèles, BOYOKANA BINU NA BINU! ALORS, Ngiri-Ngiri, Mangembo, Nzili [Ndjili], Yolo, Kinsasa . . . BOPESANA MABOKO!!

SINON TE: MIVAIS EZALI!

Ngai na binu, Grand Godias, Père Buffalo.[5]

It's time to wake up; I am your elder, Buffalo, I am gone oh . . . But before I take off, I'd like to give you my Bills a real pep talk.

DON'T BE CAUGHT OFF GUARD, DON'T BE TRIPPING, BILLS.

When I be out, I don't want my Bills to slacken; FOLLOW THE TRUE RHYTHM of Billism, just like we carried ourselves. Or else sneaks [false witnesses] will laugh at you; they'd say: "Ah, look at the Bills, they were acting that way because of Père BUFFALO." DON'T BE FOOLED! W'all can be a little soft-boiled, but BEWARE.

BE ON THE LOOKOUT!!!

Sneaks, as you know, are all over the place, foaming and plotting. Wake up and get their number. You know what they're up to? They go around lying and warning one another. TURN UP THE VOLUME OF BILLISM in other townships; too many soft-boiled guys there, too many HOODLUMS, even too many soft-boiled Bills and HOOKERS.

GET THEIR NUMBER!!!!

Wake up, Bills, DOWN WITH THE WAYS OF SOFT-BOILED DUDES! We're the Bills and we can't take after them. Bills, *Nzele,* GET ALONG WITH ONE AN-OTHER! SO THAT Ngiri-Ngiri, Mangembo, Ndjili, Yolo, Kinshasa . . . ALL WORK TOGETHER!!

OR ELSE TROUBLE WILL COME!

I am with you, Grand Godias,[6] Père Buffalo.

Père Buffalo's final exhortation, as recorded by one of the Bills who attended the rally, treads on familiar ground. The opposition between Yuma and Yankee (discussed in chapter 5) seems to be the leitmotif of his homily. By harping on uncompromising toughness as the true yardstick against which all Bills must be measured, Père Buffalo was sure to preach to the choir. But his sermon also touched on several changes that had altered Billism, especially in the wake of Kinshasa's January 1959 riots and the gaping ethnic fault-lines that had threatened to stall Congo's disorderly march to independence. By admonishing the Bills to "follow the true rhythm of Billism," Père Buffalo had in mind a version of Billism shorn of some of its disturbing features, namely, éboulement, billing, and idleness.

This new version of Billism was not simply a matter of proselytizing, or "turn[ing] up the volume of Billism in other townships," as Père Buffalo put it. In his mind, Bills could walk away from éboulement only by abolishing the gender division that had sustained this practice in the townships, a gender division that reified girls, reduced them to their bodies, and restricted their mobility. To the asymmetrical gender relationship that prevailed in the townships, Père Buffalo's Bills opposed a new gender dispensation which, though falling short of establishing gender symmetry between Bills and banzele, did afford girls with some opportunities to carve out agency.

Although this chapter is largely devoted to Père Buffalo's ministry to Kinshasa's Bills, it explores related issues as well, such as the Bills' connection to the January 1959 riots and how Congo's transformation into a battleground for the Cold War played out in the streets of Kinshasa. In the end, however, it was not Père Buffalo's tireless ministering that convinced the Bills to bury the hatchet and move on. The demise of the Bill movement coincided with Mobutu's rise to power and his determination to co-opt all political and cultural entities that might pose a threat to his incipient totalitarian rule.

Enter Père Buffalo (aka Jozef de Laet)

Jozef de Laet was born in 1931 in Vilvoorde, north of Brussels, to a small, pious Catholic family. His father, who owned a small farm in the Flemish Brabant area, worked hard to keep his family afloat during the Great Depression. In the late nineteenth century, the town of Vilvoorde had undergone impressive changes due to its role as one of the main industrial hubs in the Brabant area. In fact, when in 1835 the first railway on the European continent was built, it linked Brussels to Mechelen (Malines in French) through the bustling industrial complex of Vilvoorde. With this technological breakthrough came factories and canals, but also the kind of social inequalities that arise anywhere industrial wealth accumulates. Like most industrial cities, Vilvoorde had cozy, upscale neighborhoods, away from the miasmas generated by the factories. It also contained slums and working-class sections. Jozef came of age in one of the roughest neighborhoods of Vilvoorde, one that the Brabant bourgeois looked down upon as the *quartier des bandits* (hoodlum section).

At age ten, young Jozef spent hours on the street, rubbing elbows with Vilvoorde's "jeunes délaissés et pauvres" (impoverished and disenfranchised youth). However, as the only son even of a modest farmer, he had to acquire some education, not just what the street had to offer. His father sent him to the *petit séminaire* at Mechelen. There, for six years, young Jozef learned Latin and Greek and some rudiments of theology and rhetoric. After completing his *humanités* at Mechelen, he aspired to enter the army as an officer and even took the required qualifying exams. But the young firebrand had a sudden change of heart and decided to become a priest instead, much to the chagrin of his father, who, although pious, had envisioned a different future for his only son. He received training in theology at Scheut and Leuven before being ordained at Scheut's Congregatio Immaculati Cordis Mariae (CICM, Congregation of the Immaculate Heart of Mary) on August 5, 1956.

Before de Laet arrived in Kinshasa in late October 1957, he had never traveled outside of Belgium, and most of what he knew about Congo came from fellow missionaries who had returned from the colony (see figure 7.2). Like most Belgians, he had also seen popular images that circulated widely in Belgium and remained redolent of heart-of-darkness effluvia, especially as fin d'empire loomed on the horizon. But like many of his peers at the Scheut mission who were bound for the Congo, de Laet had also dutifully done his homework. He had learned Lingala even before setting foot in Congo and could read the Scheutist periodical *Kongo ya Sika,* which reported on missionary progress in the Belgian Congo through articles and commentaries penned by missionaries themselves.

His first appointment was in Matété, a far-flung *cité planifiée* (planned township) designed by the Office des Cités Africaines (OCA) in 1952 to decongest

Figure 7.2 Père Buffalo in Kinshasa, ca. 1957. © Photo Jozef de Laet collection.

Kinshasa's oldest townships and deal with the capital's dizzying demographic growth (figure 7.3). Since the church's building was still under construction, Père Joseph (as he was known before Ngiri-Ngiri youth nicknamed him Père Buffalo) and his parishioners celebrated mass in the nearby police station. Once the new church became operational, CICM decided to establish Saint-Alphonse School to cater to the growing number of youth in Matété and appointed Père Joseph its first schoolmaster.

In 1958, when Père Joseph took the helm of Saint-Alphonse and started his signature activity by enrolling Matété's youngsters into the JOC (Jeunesse Ouvrière Chrétienne), the Bill movement had yet to spill over into Kinshasa's satellite townships. Matété was the first OCA cité planifiée and the largest one by far, with 6,000 housing units built by 1956 (Gondola 1997a: 181); like most other planned townships, it initially welcomed those évolués who clamored for their first taste of homeownership. Access to housing credit (*fonds d'avance*) being limited to the few meritorious Africans who could not only demonstrate financial solvency but also supply proof of monogamy and Catholic faith, the system amounted to a form of social segregation. As a result, only with independence did the kind of gang violence that older quartiers had witnessed throughout the postwar period become a fixture on the social landscape of these new townships.

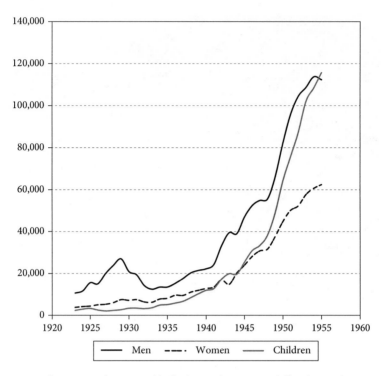

Figure 7.3 Population growth in Leopoldville (1923–55). Source: Babillon (1957: 23).

In early 1960, when Belgian colonial society was still reeling from the January 1959 riots, Père Joseph inherited the parish of Ngiri-Ngiri, which had recently established itself as one of the main hubs of gang-related activities in Kinshasa. The riots had revealed long-standing resentments and frustrations that no colonial institution, least of all the Catholic Church, could afford to brush aside. Young people especially boycotted missionary activities and no longer attended mass. The Church, to its credit, and in contrast to the colonial state, heeded the call for *aggiornamento* and acted swiftly to Africanize part of its cadre.[7] In Ngiri-Ngiri, Père Joseph found himself serving as *vicaire* (assistant parish priest) under Congolese Abbé Jean Loya, a close friend of Joseph Kasa-Vubu.[8] There he discovered the Bill movement at its peak, with Grands Bills holding sway in two main quartiers, Mofewana and Dynamique, and acting as the real sheriffs in a postriot climate where white missionaries had all but relinquished their control over township youth.

If Père Buffalo deserves any credit at all, it is not so much for helping some Bills shed their antics as they made the transition into adult professional life, which would probably have occurred in any case, as for bringing the Bills out from under the colonial radar. Père Buffalo drew attention to the Bills not to indict them as *jeunes délinquants* (young offenders), as the colonial discourse so conveniently did, but to underline how the Bill movement had resulted largely from colonial dereliction and how, under duress, the Bills had managed to create cultural spaces on their own terms. As mentioned in earlier chapters, not long before Père Buffalo entered the scene, a colonial official, Louis Bissot, undertook a wide and lengthy study of Billism, embedding himself in some of these interstitial groups, only to see his detailed report (Bissot 2009 [1958]) lambasted and censored by his superiors. The Bissot Report adds surprising layers to the already thick tapestry that Billism presents.

The Bissot Report

While working at the Service de la Population Noire (Black Population Office) in Leopoldville, Louis Bissot witnessed firsthand the high rate of unemployment among large segments of township youth and felt some qualms of conscience about it. He took it upon himself to investigate township youth for several months, especially the relationship between unemployment and delinquency.[9] His detailed, unsolicited report was released in 1958 under the innocuous title *Étude qualitative sur la délinquance juvénile à Léopoldville (ca. 1957).* Had Bissot adopted the criminalizing approach found in most colonial narratives since at least the 1920s, when Father de la Kethulle had singlehandedly rounded up young *malandrins* (thieves) in the cité indigène and handed them over to the police (see chapter 4), his report would have likely secured him a place in the colonial annals. But Bissot recoiled at such a notion. Instead, he chose to candidly "face the facts as they are" (voir les choses en face, telles qu'elles sont), even though, as he warned in the introduction to the report, "the truth is not always pretty."

Bissot found it necessary to mention the usual overt gang activities, which revolved around money, marijuana (see chapter 5), and girls, if only to treat them as the proverbial tip of the iceberg. At times, these activities burst into the public space, as when Bills were spotted passing around joints, lifting weights, making lewd remarks and catcalling to every passing girl, and picking pockets for fun and for funds with which to buy marijuana and dole out their girlfriends. Yet the patterns of the gangs' covert activities were even more disturbing. Pegging the fortune of his report to the notion that by laying out "the truth" about interstitial juvenile activities he could spur the colonial administration to seriously tackle youth unemployment, Bissot proceeded to expose some of the Bills' murkier activities.

These included a recurring pattern of homosexual behavior, which according to Bissot happened fairly often when older boys (sixteen to eighteen years old) took younger boys (seven to fourteen years) under their wings to toughen them up, teach them how to be a big guy (*gaillard*), and initiate them "into the mysteries of sex." When girls were not at hand (*à défaut de filles*), older boys would practice sodomy on younger boys. Bissot witnessed the most extreme behaviors in gangs that had a cohort of long-timers, to such an extent that older age seemed to correlate with anomalous, hard-core practices. This was the case in Quartier Bois Dur, located within a perimeter delimited by Gambela and Victoire Avenues, in what is today the commune of Kasa-Vubu (see chapter 4 and table 5.1). Bissot describes the Bois Dur posse's secret hangout place, which they called the "Château" (probably in imitation of Père Buffalo's hangout; see further below), as a "laboratory of vice and debauchery" (Bissot 2009 [1958]: 12) where, in the blind spot of society, gang members freely participated in homosexual relationships.[10] Notorious among gang members who engaged in "vice and debauchery" was of course Monganga (alias Paurret), whom as seen in the previous chapter was vilified in the Bissot Report as "le sinistre Vieux Pollet [*sic*]," "un personnage ignoble"), and "un individu infect." I was curious to find out what Paurret knew about Bissot and what he would make of his claims of homosexual sex among Kinshasa's Yankees. I had developed such a good rapport with him that I felt comfortable enough to discuss the topic with him.

I finally caught up with him again in July 2014 and made sure that our conversation, that time, would be carried out in the privacy of his watchman guerite at the church of La Voix de Dieu in Quartier Bandal. Vieux Paurret never once winced when I brought up the topic of homosexual sex, nor did he deny its existence in 1950s Kinshasa's gangland. He insisted, however, that he himself never engaged in it. This was the business of a handful of Yankees, he assured me. A handful of Yankees, he said, without using any excoriating epithet or without his voice and body betraying a hint of disapproval. In fact, one of his own friends, a certain Debosard (aka Abosa Philippe), and another Yankee who went by the moniker Mwana Ngando (Crocodile Cub), he told me, used to sleep "bango na bango" (with other males). When I asked him to tell me more about his friend Debosard, Paurret did not blink once and in the same breath described his friend as follows:

Azalaki castard. Alekaki kutu ngai na mbinga. Alingaki momie te. Nayebisi ye kutu na koki kozwela ye ba momie. Aboyi. Alingaki kaka adober ngai. Ngai naboyaki.

He was big and strong, much bigger than I. He didn't care for girls. I even offered him to get him some girls, but he refused. He just wanted to lay me. Of course, I didn't want that.

If indeed homosexual practices took place in the "Château" and elsewhere, as both Bissot and Paurret seem to suggest, they may have followed the pattern that Vale de Almeida has observed in the Portuguese village of Padrais where, in order to prove their masculinity, some men reduced other younger and more vulnerable men into symbolic girls. Indeed, competition among men, as Vale de Almeida (1996: 92) notes, is about feminizing other men, sometimes through jokes and gestures that turn the victim into a symbolic woman. Some men, without relinquishing their manhood, cross the line to engage in homosexual practices to vindicate their masculinity at the expense of other men. Several Bois Dur gang members, according to Bissot (2009 [1958]: 13), even celebrated a cult of homosexuality ("un veritable culte de l'union entre mâles") after several of their female members left the gang to settle down into married life and motherhood.

Bissot dwelt on other intimate practices as well, such as masturbation contests, which may have been initiated by a certain Thomas d'Aquin of Quartier Bois Vert. Other leaders, such as Paurret and Windy, took éboulement to new heights by pimping out prepubescent girls (*petit mbongo*) and collecting admission fees from young boys to watch sexual intercourse. How Bissot gained knowledge of such practices is never fully disclosed in the report but glossed over.[11] Yet the level of detail he provides does suggest a close proximity to and trust from some of the gangs he infiltrated.

To say that Bissot's exposé jarred missionaries and colonial officials who read it would be a gross understatement. Though remarkable for describing juvenile delinquency in unadulterated detail, what the report drew fire for was its candid and at times passionate narrative. Paul Raymaekers, from whom I obtained a reprinted copy of the report, remembered how shortly after Bissot shared it internally[12] the colonial administration scrambled to curtail its circulation. Raymaekers dodged the administration's monition to return the report and somehow managed to hold onto his personal copy.

At this point, I shall add my own coda to the reception of the Bissot Report and conclusion as to why it ultimately vanished from circulation. It does not take a thorough reading of it to get a sense of what may have unsettled colonial readers the most. It was not the discussion of sexual lubricity per se, nor the fact that large numbers of youths in the townships had drifted away from colonial strictures. Rather, Bissot enabled his readers to peer into the abyss of juvenile perdition, only to lay a moral onus on them to rescue these youths from the clutches of colonial oblivion. After surveying that abyss himself, Bissot's original disgust and discouragement had given way to feelings of sympathy, commiseration, and, finally, guilt.

Europeans living in the Belgian Congo had learned to ban the word *guilt* from their colonial lexicon. Guilt for the plight of township youths was the last thing that could overcome the colonizers' visceral notions about their civilizing mission and one of its major obstacles—namely, blacks' purported sexual immorality and overdrive. Insisting that the predicament of young people in the townships should be approached from a moral and social standpoint, not a criminal one, Bissot centered his plea for action on rehabilitation, whereas the pervading ideology tended to criminalize youth deviant behaviors. Bissot (2009 [1958]: 30), in contrast, saw it thus:

> Behind the dark veil one discovers the comforting landscape of amazing inno-
> cence, strong fascination with beauty, and unshakable hope: three indispens-
> able elements for the rehabilitation of this so-called delinquent youth, which
> in reality is unhappy youth (*jeunesse malheureuse*).

Bissot found this innocence and beauty in the eyes of "le petit Ernest," "la petite José," and "la grande Honorine," whose broken backgrounds and sordid stories he recounts with rare empathy.[13] Yet his affection for these disenfranchised youth nauseated his critics, perhaps because, in their eyes, Bissot's investigation reeked of betrayal and evoked insufferable images of the "white-man-gone-native," es-pecially coming, as it did, from a colonial official with no missionary vocation or affiliation.

The Perfect Storm: January 4, 1959

It was against this background of complacency and scotoma that the "unthink-able," a category Michel-Rolph Trouillot deftly uses to frame the Haitian Rev-olution,[14] unfolded in Kinshasa on January 4, 1959.[15] That morning, European residents awakened to a "perfect storm," the dawn of an *annus horribilis* for col-onization in Congo. Few had actually slept the night before as unprecedented bouts of violence wreaked havoc in the capital of the colony. Just how Kinshasa's first political riots started is a fitting testimonial to the power of infrapolitics. A botched political rally mushroomed into an insurrection of such magnitude that it prompted an about-face, shifting Belgian colonial policy from incrementalism to a hasty and precipitous colonial retreat.[16]

Although ignited by a volatile, politicized crowd and fueled by anticolonial sentiments that resonated deeply with large sections of Kinshasa's population, the protest would likely have fizzled out and never spread beyond the ethnic confines of the Abako[17] had it not been for the Bills, whom Congolese historian Antoine Lumenga Neso Kiobe calls the "third element" of the January 1959 insur-rection.[18] According to Lumenga Neso Kiobe, the Abako rank and file, an angry mob with axes to grind after their political rally had been canceled, provided the first element. Disgruntled soccer fans returning home after their much-favored home team, Vita Club, had been clobbered 3–0 by the underdog Mikado supplied the second. When the Bills, who were always on the qui vive, joined the urban jacquerie, the unrest escalated into a widespread insurrection that prompted the colonial authorities to carry out a military operation such as had never before been seen in the Belgian Congo. The entire city was sealed off, and several battalions, brought in from other garrisons, took up positions at key points within the African townships and the European district. They did not quell the insurrection until the early hours of January 7.

Fueled by anticolonial impetus, the uprisings were sustained by the "politics of masculinity" and the Far West culture of violence that the Bills, many of whom spearheaded the insurrectional forays, had developed since World War II. Owing to the Bills' ubiquitous mobility within the townships, their awareness of space and places, and their fascination with the ritualized, staged violence performed in cowboy movies, the anticolonial protest spilled over much of the city. Not surprisingly, the gangs of Bills steered the flow of demonstrators toward locales that symbolized both their oppression and their alienation, including the Portuguese-owned stores in Foncobel, which they looted and burned to the ground. Missionary schools seem to have also attracted much of the rioters' fury, as well as welfare homes (*foyers sociaux*) for women and other missionary buildings.[19]

The 1950s had witnessed an ever-increasing number of young *désoeuvrés* (idlers), mostly school-age children who had fallen through the cracks of the school system and other young unemployed persons. Most Bills were désoeuvrés, so during the riots they directed their wrath first toward school and missionary facilities. In the township of Ngiri-Ngiri, soon to be Père Buffalo's missionary ground, the disorder picked up steam on January 5 and continued for several days. There the Bills led the charge against the crown jewel of Belgian incrementalism, the Athénée Officiel Interracial, one of Kinshasa's first interracial public schools. After looting and ransacking the premises, the Bills covered the walls, doors, and blackboards with repetitions of a single word: "Indépendance." One particular gang, the Écumeurs du Texas (Texas Raiders)—which appear in the record only in connection with the riots—proudly couched this demand in unequivocal terms and signed with its gang name.

Scheut missionaries counted their losses after the storm and attributed the destruction to the vengeful frenzy of thousands of "adolescents désoeuvrés" who had supposedly acted at the instigation of religious sects (namely, the Kinbanguist Church and the Jehovah's Witnesses), Congolese politicians, and the left-leaning Belgian government's anticlericalism. They bemoaned the fact that the once-sacrosanct triarchy of the (Catholic) church, the state, and private companies could no longer implement its *programme de civilisation* in a social and political vacuum. Just across the river, they reckoned, Congolese in Brazzaville enjoyed political freedom, electing their own president and representatives, while the residents of Leopoldville could scarcely get an African mayor![20]

Further proof of the Bills' massive participation in the January insurrection is to be found in the list of those caught in the web of colonial repression. Twenty-seven of the 243 insurgents detained after the riots were minors between the ages of fourteen and eighteen, and all belonged to gangs of Bills.[21] Not only did the Bills' participation widen the insurrection in terms of ethnicity, space, and time, it also defined the movement and epitomized a new brand of mass protest unheard of until then in the Belgian Congo. Popular protests in colonial Congo had been both sporadic and limited in scope. Except for the Luluabourg Revolt of July 1895 and the rebellion of the Boma garrison in April 1900, most popular uprisings had taken place in the rural areas. They involved expropriated peasants or ethnic groups that felt victimized by colonial encroachments, and as in the Bapende Revolt of 1931, they could be imbued with profound mystical characteristics (Mulambu-Mvuluya 1971).

Urban protests did indeed occur in Congo before the 1950s, but they usually took the form of what James Scott (1990) has termed "hidden transcripts" or what, before him, Michel de Certeau (1990 [1980]: 51) referred to as *tactics* as opposed to *strategies*. This "undeclared ideological guerrilla," to borrow from Scott, rages within a political terrain demarcated by quiescence and revolt, occasionally bursting into open conflict. This happened fairly often in the Belgian Congo when, for instance, disgruntled workers took to the picket lines in Leopoldville (May 1920), Elizabethville (1944), and Matadi (November 1945) or when soldiers mutinied, as did the Luluabourg garrison on February 20, 1944. However, it would be a stretch to view these events as precursors to the January 1959 insurrection, with which they had so little in common. For example, they made no explicit public demand for independence and never entirely rejected the colonial programme de civilisation. They opposed the oppressive colonial system of taxation, corporal punishment, forced labor, pass laws, and the color bar but not colonization per se, which had also brought Western modernity, with its symbolic and commoditized arsenal of fashion, music, schooling, bicycles, football, and so forth. No one can deny that those earlier protests threatened the colonial status quo and did indeed, as T. O. Ranger (1968: 443) has suggested, "shatter the early European attitude of masterful complacency." Yet they lacked the anticolonial thrust that moved the January 1959 insurrection far beyond the confines of ethnic or labor disputes.

The January 1959 insurrection was unprecedented in that it departed from the pattern of hidden protest that had shaped mass resistance to colonization in Congo, and this no doubt owed much to the ritualized violence the Bills staged in Kinshasa's townships (see Gondola 1999a). It was the Bills' gang violence—to the public no different from other manifestations of urban violence and yet so unique—that commandeered the mass emotion of January 1959 and supplied it with its insurrectional spirit. Indeed, as Filip De Boeck has discerningly argued, the Bill, and behind him the peripatetic cowboy silhouette, emerged in these colonial times as an "emancipatory figure, representing the spirit of the coming independence" (De Boeck and Plissart 2005: 39). One sees clearly this spirit at work and suffusing even the political metanarrative of independence. Just as American sociologist Michael Kimmel (1996: 18–19) has called the U.S. Declaration of Independence a "declaration of manly adulthood," a rebellion of the sons (American revolutionists) against an abusive and emasculating father (England), so we could and should read the *Manifeste de Conscience Africaine* in the same vein. This foundational narrative, crafted by a group of Congolese évolués in response to A. J. Van Bilsen's Thirty-Year Plan for the Political Emancipation of Belgian Africa (Gondola 2002: 106), rebutted Belgian paternalism and the eschatological agony of a deferred emancipation.

Belgians, the authors of the *Manifeste* argued, "must change their attitude towards Congolese: depart from their attitude of contempt and racial segregation, avoid constant harassment and humiliation, stop being condescending. *We do not like to always be treated like children*" (emphasis added). In a way the *Manifeste* served as a palimpsest of and a placeholder for Patrice Lumumba's June 30, 1960 speech, which bore all the marks of a parricidal drama with its impetuosity, extemporaneousness, and comeuppance. In a moment of prophetic anger, Lumumba righted eighty years of "humiliating slavery," rescued the benighted Congolese child-figure from the clutches of Belgian paternalism, and restored its manhood. Lumumba's unfulfilled dream—"We are going to show the world what the black man can do when he works in freedom, and we are going to make of the Congo the center of the sun's radiance for all of Africa"—has haunted Congo ever since he proclaimed it on June 30, 1960.

Désoeuvrement

In the aftermaths of the January 1959 insurrection, while the political timetable quickly took shape, set in motion by both the internal and external push for independence, the pace of economic progress lagged behind. The much-touted Ten-Year Plan (1949–1959)—initially intended to endow the colony with infrastructures, a denser transport system, and industries, and therefore to boost employment—generated enormous returns that never trickled down to the population. Young people especially bore the brunt of colonial neglect. In Leopoldville, as their number swelled, overtaking the adult male population for the first time in 1955 (see figure 7.3), so did competition for jobs. At the very bottom rung of the social ladder, young désoeuvrés and délinquants struggled to find employment within the formal economy.

The initial response to youth participation in the insurrection proved as ineffectual as it was draconian. Thousands of young désoeuvrés who lived in Kinshasa without parental supervision were rounded up in the streets and deported back to their villages, even when they held a valid residence permit.[22] Inspired by various youth projects, including the Israeli youth villages and the pilot villages in French Africa, Belgian authorities created a series of seven *chantiers de jeu-nesse* (youth camps) in Leopoldville Province: Duale (270 boys), Mongata (130 boys), Bombo Nord (187 boys), Base Bombo (24 boys), Kivulu-Thysville (256 boys), Luozi (64 boys), and Kunzulu (60 boys), for a total of 987 boys.[23] Young people joined the chantiers on a voluntary basis, and those who had already acquainted themselves with jamborees, bivouacs, and other Boy Scout activities learned to cope with the duress of these camps.[24] But for the rest, the initial banter and frolic quickly wore off as hardship set in. Many came to the camps branded by adversity and determined to flaunt the quasi-military rules enforced by the adult overseers. Soon, reports surfaced of reconstituted gangs abusing villagers, smoking marijuana, and stealing whatever they could. Paul Raymaekers, who served as the head of the initial pilot project in Mikondo (30 kilometers southeast of Kinshasa), attributes the downfall of the experiment to the presence of what he calls "les incorrigibles" (Raymaekers 1993: 98).[25]

In addition to the failed chantiers de jeunesse, several child protection committees were set up to assist young désoeuvrés in finding employment as part of the December 6, 1950, decree on juvenile delinquency. Many of these young people had spent time in the Ndolo prison in Kinshasa and, starting in 1954, in the Madimba juvenile detention and reeducation center in the province of Leopoldville, the only center of its kind in the whole colony (see Ngongo 2012: 90).

Housed in a section of the Madimba prison, the juvenile center opened its doors on January 1, 1954, with an initial population of eighty-three minors (Lafontaine 1957: 62). Under strict regimen and monitoring,[26] these children received training as masons, mechanics, carpenters, tailors, and electricians, though minors under fourteen had no choice but to enroll in the agriculture program. The largest contingent of inmates came from Leopoldville, pursuant to the decree of December 6, 1950, which abrogated the practice of detaining children in adult prisons. Hence, starting in 1954, when the decree came into force, juvenile court judges in the three districts of Bas-Congo, Cataractes, and especially Leopoldville turned young offenders over to the Madimba center with sentences that commonly locked up these youths until they reached eighteen.[27] However, Madimba filled up quickly, reaching full capacity by 1957. Ndolo, Leopoldville's main penitentiary center, then resumed receiving young offenders in separate wards.

Leopoldville's child protection committee initially included a handful of European public servants and private business managers, but not a single missionary. In a blow to the so-called colonial trinity, Georges Six, the vicar apostolic of Leopoldville and the highest religious authority in the colony, demurred at the idea that priests and missionaries could serve on the committee.[28] Taking a cue from their hierarchy, missionaries not only declined the administration's solicitation to serve but turned down its request to have young délinquants and désoeuvrés placed in their institutions.[29] As for private companies, although many did accept the invitation to appoint a *délégué* (representative) to sit on the committee, only a few agreed to recruit delinquent minors under the vocational training contract regime. In 1954, only two big employers, Otraco and Petro-congo, agreed to take on a few of these minors as trainees.[30]

Only when the shortage of European délégués became a cause for concern in maintaining these committees as planned did the administration decide to turn to African évolués, cherry-picking representatives from the pool of Carte du Mérite Civique holders and those évolués who could demonstrate the acquisition of civic virtues and professional success.[31] Yet, like the chantiers de jeunesse, these committees failed abysmally to deliver on the job front and to mentor young désoeuvrés.

"Château" JOC

Although Père Buffalo's infiltration of Kinshasa's interstitial youth gangs may have marked a turning point in the Bill movement, it was hardly the first such foray. In 1957, the Routiers de la Croix du Sud, a Catholic Boy Scout group affiliated with the Saint-Pierre parish in Kinshasa, decided to infiltrate and rehabilitate several gangs in quartiers Bois Dur, Farwest, and Sans Loi. Although the experience fell short of expectations and resulted only in a big rally held in the Reine-Astrid Stadium (Babillon 1957: 128), the lesson that could be drawn from it seemed obvious to its promoters: these troubled youths could get back on the right track if given the opportunity. With characteristic myopia and cocksure conviction, the Belgian authorities also concluded that such a rehabilitating project could be established without necessarily committing substantial resources (Babillon 1957: 129). Hence, despite the postwar demographic upsurge that saw Kinshasa's youth population double every four years, Belgians implemented policies on the cheap to deal with the youth crisis. Not only did such projects as the chantiers de jeunesse and the Madimba juvenile detention and reeducation center never cast a wide net, but they also never addressed the root cause of youth delinquency in Leopoldville—namely, unemployment.

Going against the grain, Père Buffalo committed the structure and resources provided by the Jeunesse Ouvrière Chrétienne (JOC) to starting an unusual experiment with Kinshasa's Bills. The Jocist movement had taken root in Kinshasa starting in 1931, under the aegis of another Scheutist missionary, Father Frédéric Gangler. Targeting mostly young urban workers and vocational school students, the organization tried to help students transition into professional life by instilling Catholic values in them. Once they embarked on their careers, JOC cadres continued to guide their steps into professional, family, and civic life through regular meetings and activities. But as Charles Tshimanga (2001) has shown, from Gangler's death in 1944 to the mid-1950s, the JOC languished for lack of trained African personnel and suffered from the competition of more popular and robust organizations such as the Boy Scouts.

With the advent of a left-leaning government in Belgium and the appointment of Auguste Buisseret as minister of colonies in 1954,[32] the JOC focused its attention on training an African lay cadre. This coincided with a shift in its activities, which now included helping its African members find employment and negotiate rents (Tshimanga 2001: 209 and 212). Most importantly, Jocist leaders mediated on behalf of their members in all of their dealings with the colonial authorities, and in the process they developed a close-knit community in the townships, with many of the white JOC missionaries living in the heart of the African quartiers. Not surprisingly, these congregants responded in kind during the January 1959 riots by providing protection and shelter to the white missionaries who found themselves in the crosshairs of popular discontent. Had it not been for the role played by courageous African Jocists who stood their ground and deflected the angry mob away from missionary targets, European casualties would certainly have been greater.

In late 1959, when Père Buffalo set up his JOC headquarters on Movenda Avenue in Ngiri-Ngiri's Quartier Dynamique, he rode the crest of a resurging organization that he would soon turn on its head. Rather than cater to working-class youths, he decided to minister to the désoeuvrés. In Ngiri-Ngiri, he gradually wooed Grands Bills Billy, Ross Samson, Kroutchev, Langliza, and Néron, quickly learned Indoubill, compiled a rudimentary thesaurus, and, at one point, even mused about translating the Bible into Indoubill. The sight of this young Scheutist missionary clad in a white robe, breaking bread, dancing, and frolicking with black youngsters in one of the roughest African townships did not sit too well with the European establishment because it breached the strict Belgian color bar. Yet it was not until he had tasted weed, surreptitiously stuffed into his pipe by one of his protégés, that Père Buffalo was inducted into the Bill brotherhood (Gondola 2009: 94).

The "Château JOC" on Movenda Avenue had a restaurant where for 10 francs Bills could daily enjoy a copious lunch. Having finally buried the hatchet, Bills from the two erstwhile rival quartiers of Mofewana and Dynamique would mingle there at any time of day to catch the latest Indoubill sermon Père Buffalo delivered every Tuesday evening; play checkers, Ping Pong, and marbles; listen to Néron's guitar tunes; lift weights; and occasionally smoke weed (see figure 7.4). Néron's song *Zambele Kingo* was a particular hit—so much so that it became the Bills' anthem. Néron had been profoundly inspired by the theme song of Brazilian filmmaker Limo Barreto's much-acclaimed 1953 spaghetti Western *O'Cangaceiro*. The movie's theme song, "Mulher Rendeira," with its searing melody and soothing guitar, served as a template for Néron's musical ad-libbing on what it meant to be a Bill.[33]

Figure 7.4 Former Bills of Quartier Mofewana in Ngiri-Ngiri. On the far left is Vieux Néron, Mofewana's legendary sheriff and the author of *Zambele Kingo*, the Bills' anthem; in the back with a checkered shirt is Petit Moloch, July 2005. Photo by the author.

With money raised from various sources—most notably the Belgian embassy in Kinshasa, the new Congolese government, and local businesses—Père Buffalo steered Bills toward several trades. Some specialized in car repair, masonry, and woodworking, while others took on tailoring and shoemaking and shoe repair. The Château had its own bakery that supplied bread to Ngiri-Ngiri and other townships. The Bill's metallic steeds—their bicycles—long used to emulate the peripatetic cowboy's jaunts, now served to peddle bread all over the city. Père Buffalo would hire experienced tradesmen to teach Bills the rudiments of the different trades. Once the youth became sufficiently practiced, they would work in small crews in the different workshops at the Château and go out to external sites to repair cars, private homes, and so forth.[34] Part of the earnings accumulated helped keep the restaurant, which generated virtually no profit, and other JOC programs operating in full mode. Bills for their part gained valuable working experience and earned enough income to be tempted to turn their backs on street gang life and embrace a respectable career. Père Buffalo, it seemed, had led them, where others had failed, to a place of self-realization and self-empowerment. In fact, before Père Buffalo's intervention, Bills would have had great difficulties envisioning themselves as anything but "rebels without a cause," partly because being labeled "jeune délinquants" (young offenders) became a self-fulfilling prophecy in and of itself. Père Buffalo helped them create new scripts and parlay old scripts into some palatable achievements.

Esprit de la Jeunesse

Two years into Père Buffalo's ministry, Bills found an outlet for expressing themselves in the makeshift magazine *Esprit de la Jeunesse,* which touted itself as the first and foremost "Journal des jeunes, pour les jeunes et par les jeunes" (see figures 7.5 and 7.6). Its inaugural issue appeared in 1962 as a six-page roneotyped publication, with short entries in French, Lingala, and Indoubill. Right off the bat, the magazine allowed Bills from different quartiers to manufacture a number of colloquialisms that until then had rarely percolated beyond the confines of their own townships. Many quaint idioms managed to reach ecumenical status once they appeared in the magazine and caught the keen eyes of its readers. The canonical technique adopted by authors consisted of presenting these idioms followed by a parenthetical translation, just as scholars would do. For example, the term *micause* was immediately appended by its French equivalent (*causerie*); *Masta Kepi* meant police, *linzaka lia soso* (*écriture*),[35] *nkekele* (*cravate*), *batchicoulier* (*étudiant*), and so forth.

The magazine also mitigated the "dialectization" that Indoubill had experienced over the years as a result of gangs' close-knit identity and competition. This was done not by standardizing Indoubill, something that Père Buffalo could only contemplate, but by allowing *Esprit de la Jeunesse* to serve as a forum and a crucible where all could experiment with new styles and coin neologisms through mix-and-match association.

At its peak, *Esprit de la Jeunesse* was twelve pages long, with an editorial and columns devoted to issues pertaining to the parishes and quartiers ("A travers les paroisses et les quartiers"), local news ("Actualités"), and girls ("Se mpo ya banzele," Indoubill for "For Girls Only"). *Esprit de la Jeunesse* appeared sporadically at first, but as it caught on with a wider audience (including other parishes and JOC centers), it became a monthly magazine boasting, according to one source, a circulation of more than 10,000 copies,[36] a figure that should be taken with a grain of salt.[37] At any rate, circulation was wide enough to reach many parishes and townships, even though most copies were sold downtown to readers eager to peer into Kinshasa's gangland. Congolese politicians especially, who kept close tabs on Père Buffalo's experiment, took the pulse of large segments of Kinshasa's populace through the quirky and vintage Bill stories distilled in the magazine.

The ultimate success of this magazine can be measured by its influence in spawning a cottage industry of Bill magazines across the townships. In Kintambo,

Le quartier de ce mois : MO..FE..WA..NA.

QU'EST-CE QUI SE PASSE DANS LE QUARTIER FAR-WEST ?

Mofewana est un simple nom de jeunes. Il ne signifie rien de spécial, mais veut seulement exprimer le sentiment d'entente, l' 'esprit des jeunes qui habitent ce quartier-là. Le quartier Far West ou Mofewana est situé dans la commune de Ngiri-ngiri, et est limité par les avenues Assosa, Joséphine Charlotte, et le Prince Baudouin.

Notre quartier a un atmosphère spécial, quoique nous formons de petits groupes d'amitié, nous avons quand-même le même sentiment d' unité, parce que nous appartenons au quartier Far West, parce que nous vivons dans le rythme du Far West. Nous avons notre cri commun : Mo....fewana ; nous avons des chants communs composés par des Mofewana comme, p.ex. Nzambe yeye, Santa Maria...

z.G. des dorseaux...

Djavolo, Roy, Samson, Cladiateur, Ross, Langlia, Napoléon. Une petite exhortation de notre "Buffalo" nous a fait plaisir et nous espérons que beaucoup d'entre nous soient convaincus, comme a dit notre Buffalo, que la formation de notre esprit est nécessaire. L'orchestre "Amigos – mambo" du Far West nous a réjoui avec ses chants et musique : notons : le dirigeant, Matondo (Doudou), Biccoro, Scoty, Tino, King Mario, Randolf, Gary, Opalon. Les gâteaux

Nous avons nos "durs des durs", qui nous unissent et qui forment notre gouvernement, comme notre Vieux-Ross, le grand maître de la force physique, notre Langlisa, notre Carrol, notre John, notre Néron, le prêtre de la puissance... etc...

Ce qui nous attire dans notre quartier, c'est nos équipes de football, notre club de culture physique, nos orchestres de tous genres et de toutes inventions, nos réunions de quartier, notre château JOC, etc...

Et ce qu'on voit maintenant : il y a un bon esprit qui influence les Mofewana et qui nous pousse à notre formation complète pour devenir un homme complet. Et comme ça dans nos réunions de quartier on parle maintenant de choses sérieuses, on prie et on tâche de s'entr'aider. Plusieurs se sont affiliés dans un mouvement de jeunesse, des autres veulent se donner complètement à leur formation et à leurs camarades et sont devenus militants jocistes, qui tâchent maintenant dans les réunions de quartier de communiquer leur formation, qu' ils recçoivent dans les réunions d'équipe et par leurs efforts personnels, pourque tous les jeunes de notre quartier Far West aient un esprit fort et une vie fructueuse.

Voilà ce qu'il y a de spécial dans notre quartier et avec quoi nous devançons leurs autres quartiers.

Dimanche passé, le 3 juin 1962, nous avons eu une Rencontre de tous les jeunes du F.W. dans notre château JOC. C'était formidable ! Dans une ambiance à la Far West, nous avons admiré ce que Far West peut prester : nous avons vu Vieux-Ross au travail avec son équipe des Apollo's : des biceps, des paquets, somo '. Ont "claqué" devant nous : Accident, offerts par le restaurant JOC étaient délicieux. Proficiat, cuistot Rocky !

Et le mois prchain : grand rencontre de nouveau : notre Journée Internationale de la Jeunesse.

Nous attendons des nouvelles des autres quartiers des jeunes de tout Lipopo, chacun aura son tour pour nous raconter des nouvelles de son quartier.

EMERY.

Figure 7.5 *Esprit de la Jeunesse*, inaugural issue, 1962.

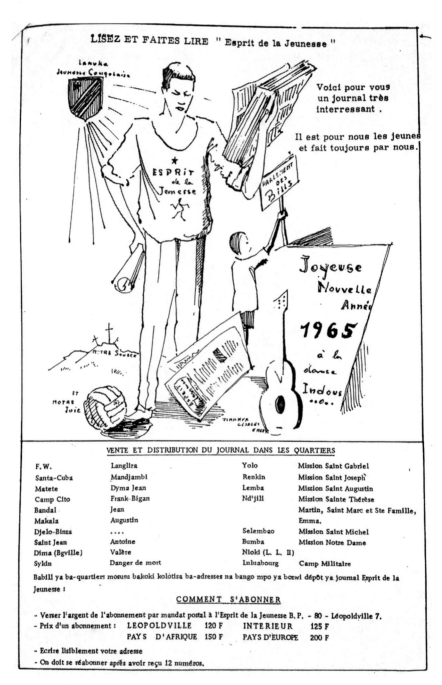

Figure 7.6 Back cover of *Esprit de la Jeunesse*, issue 14, January 1965, with subscription instructions and names of newspaper carriers, listed by quartier and mission post.

another Belgian Scheutist, Père Alexandre, took his cue from Père Buffalo and launched *La Voix de Mangembo*. Other magazines, *Allô Mangembo, Jeunes pour Jeunes, Gento Oyée,* and *Likembe,* followed suit quickly but never reached the popularity of *Esprit de la Jeunesse.*[38]

How the magazine sold in the different quartiers suggests that by 1963–1964 other Bills outside of Ngiri-Ngiri had taken notice of Père Buffalo's ministry and many recognized him as one of them, an avuncular figure of some sort. A designated salesperson covered each quartier: Bill John in Dynamique, Langliza in Fewe, Danger de mort in Sykin, Frank Bigan in Camp Cito, Degazin in Saint-Jean, Cassans in Ruwet, Fantôme in Fort King, and so forth. Roitelet, a musician and a Bill, sold the magazine to fellow musicians, who found the Bills' stories inspirational and even recycled many of the Bills' tropes and idioms into their own lyrics. An example is Franco's song "Ngai Rideau ya Ndako" (I am a house curtain), released in late 1964, in which Franco (aka Luambo Makiadi; see figure 7.7) lends his voice to the laments of a married woman. While her husband stays out all night and fools around with other women, she remains confined in

Figure 7.7 François Luambo (aka Luambo Makiadi), Congo's rumba icon and a Bill in his own right. He wears the obligatory checkered shirt with a raised collar, or modega. © Photo Jean Depara, Kinshasa ca. 1950–65. Courtesy of Revue Noire.

a male-dominated domestic space where she is as much chattel and as decorative as a house curtain.

Franco's song may have been inspired by a story that appeared in *Esprit de la Jeunesse* months before the release of his song. The story begins with the writer, an anonymous Bill, recounting a spirited conversation he overheard in the street between "bilenge babali babale" (two young men). We take up the story midway, when one protagonist berates his buddy for manhandling his own girlfriend:

Q: Bongo mista olingi mpenza nini po na nzele yango, libala to te?

R: Olobi boni nabala ye?

Q: Te, nalobi obala ye te, mais ezali seulement kaka kotuna.

R: Ah! Bon mista, kolobaka bipoki ya ndenge wana te; nalingi tout simplement na wuyaka ye.

Q: Bongo suka na yango wapi?

R: Oh! Tomelanaki makila; tolobaki suka se liwa.

Q: Comment suka se liwa; olobi okobala ye te, bongo ndenge nini mpenza wana?

R: Ndenge kaka ko.

Q: Bongo si par hazard otondisi ye?

R: Oh! Bongo wana mpe epaka dur. Jamais.

Q: Nakotuna mpo nayeba ndenge okosala?

R: Soki atondi . . . ngai naloba na ye . . . Oyebi yo moko, navandaka na ngai te, ngai mbembe jamais nazala prisonnier. Yo banda lelo ozali se Rideau.

Q: Azali Rideau ndenge nini?

R: C'est-à-dire asekamaka libela na chambal, akengelaka palais.[39]

Q: So, buddy, what is it that you really want with that girl?

A: What do you say? Should I marry her?

Q: No, I didn't say you should marry her. I am just asking.

A: Yeah, don't say things like that. All I want is to nail her.

Q: Yes, but where are you going with this?

A: Look, we drank each other's blood in a pact; we swore to be together until death.

Q: I don't get it. Until death? But you said you won't marry her. What's goin' on?

A: That's the way it is.

Q: What if you knock her up?

A: Oh! That's no big deal. Never.

Q: I am just wondering what you gonna do.

A: If she gets knocked up . . . I'll simply tell her . . . "You know I don't stick around, a guy like me can't be a prisoner. Starting today, you'll be just a curtain."

Q: A curtain? What's that?

A: That means she never goes out, she stays in the crib for good to take care of it.

The conversation goes on, with the philanderer finally coughing up his plan to send the girl back to her village in the event she becomes pregnant, only to be interrupted by the sight of the girl approaching. The moral of the story borrows from the way Jesus closed his parables: "bilengi basi botirer conclusion, oyo azali na miso, atangaka, mpe oyo azali na moto, abombaka" (Young women, draw your own conclusion: who has eyes to read, let her read; and who has understanding, let her hold onto this story).

Aside from such parables about girls and other stories written by Bills (and occasionally by banzele themselves) for consumption by "girls only" (an indication that the magazine aggressively courted female readers), *Esprit de la Jeunesse* crusaded against all sorts of social and moral ills, adopting a deferential stance that buttressed the civic and social order. A new spirit now, wrote a certain Emery, "is holding sway in Mofewana and influencing us to train hard to become a complete man (*un homme complet*). And now in our township meetings we talk about serious stuff, we pray, and do our best to help one another."[40]

Using the Christian parable as a didactic foil, Bills advised their readers about courtship and marriage; cautioned against the use of charms to attract girls; admonished those who performed éboulement, abortion, billing (fighting) over banzele (girls), wall tagging, and muggings at checkpoints between quartiers; and vilified *nualairs* (drug addicts), "Je le connais" (smartasses), and fathers who put undue financial burdens on their daughters' suitors. Usually a moral coda brought these somewhat murky stories to a startling epiphany. For example, one éboulement story that occurred in Ndjili "Britannique" concluded with a repudiation of amour forcé (see chapter 6):

Totika époque ya PREVENUE, ki amoureux basalaka yango na makasi te, mpe mikolo yonso mizali eyenga te.[41]

Let's leave the era of the prévenue. Love is not performed by force, and every day shouldn't be a party.

Another story that appeared in the "A travers les paroisses et quartiers" (Across parishes and quartiers) section recounts the vagaries of an inveterate éboulementaire in Quartier Canada in the township of Saint-Jean (now Lingwala). After abducting a *tétaire* (young girl) one evening and forcing her to have sex, only to release her in the wee hours of the morning, the *mbembe* (dude) ran into trouble. The girl's father would not have any of it and got rather hot under the collar. He alerted the police, after being tipped off by a Bill. Despite lying low and eluding the police for a fortnight, the law finally caught up with the miscreant. Comeuppance: he was sentenced to serve two months in the *nganda ya lolendo* (literally, "cabaret for haughty people," one of the many ways Bills referred to Kinshasa's newly built prison of Makala). Next follows the obligatory moral of this crime-and-punishment parable:

> Vrai bill, soko amoni nzela ya ye ebongi, akoluka nzele moko mpo balingana, mpe babongisa nzela ya libala. Mista oyo akamati tetard lokola eloko ya kosakana, ezali mivais nde mivais na misu ya Tata Nzambe.[42]

> When he succeeds in life, a true Bill looks for a girl so that the two can love one another and prepare themselves for marriage. A guy who uses a girl like a plaything is doing an awful, really awful thing before God.

From this story and others, we can surmise an iterative pattern in which the notion of the *vrai Bill* (true Bill), *Bill ya sérieux* (trustworthy Bill), and *Bill civilisé* (civilized Bill) reoccurs in a palimpsest of contrapuntal narratives intended to downgrade the faux Bill and conjure up a reformed, postcolonial image of the Bill. That this palimpsestic construct emerged in the post-independence moment suggests at least two further remarks.

First, Père Buffalo's ministry was successful, all things considered, in helping Bills put aside some of their wayward inclinations without completely abandoning their initial quest for manhood. By transfiguring Jesus into the über Bill and distilling a gospel in which manliness was next to godliness, Père Buffalo enabled Bills to hold onto their most colorful performances (language, music, and insouciance), which would later suffuse succeeding interstitial youth groups.

His was not a Jesus in travails and in agony, tortured and humiliated, undeified and emasculated, a martyred figure to whom previous missionaries had attempted to endear young people. Nor was he the iconic and salvific *"Enfant Jésus."* Instead, it was a muscular and masculine Jesus that Père Buffalo preached to the Bills. Père Buffalo's muscular Christianity did not just cast Jesus as a "religious Rambo, always ready to fight," to borrow Kimmel's (1996: 178) celluloid analogy, but also a working-class hero who, although living in a Roman world dominated by class and ethnicity—the parallel with colonial society is startling—took pride in his craft and used his métier as a ministry to advance social justice and empower the community.

Several pieces in *Esprit de la Jeunesse* echoed and rhapsodized about this muscular Christian version of Billism, including an offbeat editorial signed

"J. Victor Hugo dit Ecrivain." Mixing French, Lingala, and Indoubill, its author delivered a Bill version of Paul's poetics on love:

> Vrai Bill il faut azala na bolingo . . . azali na lolendo te, akoluka esengo ya ye moko te . . . Le sacrifice du Christ sur la croix est la plus haute et la plus irrécusable preuve de l'amour du grand-bill (J[ésus].C[hrist].) pour nous.[43]

> A true Bill must have love . . . he must not be arrogant, and must not seek his own happiness . . . Christ's sacrifice on the cross is the highest and most irrefutable proof of the love of the Grand Bill (J[esus].C[hrist].) for us.

Second, the emergence of the vrai Bill as one version of hegemonic masculinity in Kinshasa's townships signaled deep-seated aspirations, especially among older Bills, for a *sortie en beauté* at a time when the country was hurtling down the path of a botched and disorderly independence. Mobutu's coup, the third *Billesque* act in postcolonial politics—if we consider Lumumba's June 30, 1960 speech to have been the first and Mobutu's "neutralizing" both the president and the prime minister in a bold political maneuvering the second (Gondola 2002: 125)—provided just such an opportunity for older Bills to part with the movement.

Fin de Partie

In the postcolonial years, the Bills' overall relationship with violence, as well as the standards of masculinity they strove to enforce in their quartiers, continued to borrow from the cowboy lexicon. As discussed above, they also naturalized Biblical elements and infused the movement with a muscular Christian ethos under the aegis of Père Buffalo. Yet they tended to mimic new patterns of state and international violence that ushered in Congo's independence as well. Nothing better demonstrates this than the names gangs adopted, names that could sometimes be used interchangeably to designate the gang itself or the area of township under its control.[44] Examining some of them—for instance, ONU, URSS, Ambassade des Juifs, Okinawa, and Fédérés—one cannot help but emphasize how international involvement in the "Congo Crisis" shaped social and cultural behaviors.

The Cold War did not just affect political developments in Congo; it deeply altered popular attitudes toward everyday violence and served as a catalyst for reshaping existing manliness norms. For example, recrudescence in drug consumption among the Bills should be linked to the same phenomenon among the soldiers of the new Armée Nationale Congolaise (ANC), while the Bills' enforcement of the "curfew" in their "republics" and their creation of "township governments" and "local militias" reflected the influence of political events in their lives (Raymaekers 1963).

Similarly, the fact that the abduction and rape of teenage girls became rampant among the Bills in the first two years of independence cannot be attributed solely to the influence of cowboy movies. Nor can it be blamed solely on the wide circulation of pornographic magazines among gang members. The fact that ANC soldiers could routinely rape and terrorize females without being held accountable banalized rape even within civilian society. Although colonial authorities had sometimes gone after rapists and got notorious éboulementaires off the streets, the postcolonial debacle and its climate of impunity led to the proliferation of "detention centers" where girls suffered the worst kind of sexual abuses at the hands of faux Bills and éboulementaires. One of the most infamous of these centers, dubbed "Shanghai City," saw a constant traffic of girls and young hoodlums, sometimes in broad daylight. Some crassly pimped while others paid for sex and still others, too young to be admitted, peeped through holes, sometimes in exchange for a 5-franc coin.

In 1963, when Billy (aka Tshibumdu Madimba), the Grand Bill in Quartier Dynamique, returned from a trip to Belgium funded by Père Buffalo, he decided to carry out a raid against Shanghai City. He later teamed up with juvenile judge Renaud Coppieters and accomplished his goal of dismantling Shanghai City (Kolonga Molei 1977: 32). Billy went on to become a leader in the CVR (Corps des Volontaires de la République, discussed below) and in President Mobutu's youth party.

In June 1964, as Congo's civil unrest gradually abated, Camp Luka's splinter gangs, Mottawana and Santa-Feu, which had been at each other's throats for several months (see chapter 5), finally decided to smoke the peace pipe. The changing political climate, coupled with Père Buffalo's ministry and perhaps with plain common sense, prompted the Bills to strip their movement of its belligerent features. One Bill, Fanfan le Seigneur, made a strong case for the end of billing by arguing that "kibill etikali lisusu ya billing te . . . sik'oyo tokoma ba citoyen" (Billing should no longer be part of Billism. Let's now become citizens). Fanfan's argument appealed to many older Bills because it captured the mood that had befallen a great majority of Congolese in 1964. The silent majority had grown so weary of endless fighting, civil unrest, political mayhem, and their harmful impact on an already fragile economy that it was willing to throw itself into the arms of a brutal dictatorship if this was the price to be paid for a restoration of law and order.

Most importantly, the early 1960s witnessed a volatile situation that afforded sundry opportunities for quick social promotion. Indeed, rags-to-riches stories abounded in a political environment where heightened ethnic clientelism and nepotism became commonplace. This made Fanfan's case for ending street violence and embracing mainstream citizenry all the more palatable and earned him some accolades from other gang leaders, including Cosmos Pilatu, Grand

Bill Massacre, and Massacre's minion Samy-Ngunza (whom Massacre called his "secretary"). They all touted Fanfan's proposal and agreed to downgrade billing to an affair for the neophytes (*petits*). Samy-Ngunza even went so far as to extol drug consumption as a bonding ritual and the mark of toughness and masculinity, beseeching Bills to walk away from billing and embrace zoumbel instead: "Todié kokanga zumbele [zoumbel] na biso, billing etikala epaka moko ya ba petit" (Let's go smoke some dope and leave billing to the novices).

Thus, by 1965, when Congo was still reeling from the devastation caused by the rebellions and was poised to become one of the most Orwellian postcolonial regimes in Africa, street gangs had already been written off by some pundits as relics of a turbulent past.[45] This observation had some merit. In Ngiri-Ngiri, for instance, most of the gang members had retired from the streets as a great many of them became Jocists.[46] Père Buffalo had contributed directly to that exit from gang life through his "craft-and-trade" program. For example, Mobarona (aka Mamena Nu Ntima) went through the program and with JOC support opened up a restaurant in Kinshasa that he christened "Koseka moninga te" (Don't laugh at your neighbor). Several other Bills left the movement to tap into the ethnic networks and clientelism that flourished in Kinshasa, while still others just outgrew the Bills' juvenile lifestyle and decided it was time to seek more gratifying opportunities in the "adult" world.

The rise of the Mobutu regime was indeed a major turning point, especially in its determination to curtail the autonomy of all political, religious, and cultural groups. Mobutu also understood that the battle to rein in the political chaos that presided over independence—and to win Kinshasa, the seat of power—hinged on dealing with the Bills. To this end, he enlisted the help of Gaston N'Sengi Biembe and Paul-Henri Kabaidi. On January 9, 1966, the two men issued a communiqué announcing the creation of a vanguard movement called CVR (Corps des Volontaires de la République).[47] Yet it was not until its first national seminar in December 1966 that its promoters defined the CVR's main tenets. With a slogan ("Conscience, Vigilance, Reconstruction") that matched its acronym, the CVR endeavored to organize the masses and foster a sense of nationalism in order to revitalize the country's flagging economy (Kueno 1992: 234). In reality, under the guise of promoting nationalism, the CVR served an increasingly authoritarian regime as a trial balloon for charting its course into a single-party system.

Laying the groundwork for the single-party state, the CVR cajoled, co-opted, and at times coerced youth, students, and trade organizations, aiming to mobilize them behind the regime. Kabaidi used his bona fide reputation as a Bill and his familiarity with many gang members to make the rounds of Kinshasa's quartiers to recruit Bills into the CVR. In Kintambo, he picked up Bingema, Nala, Botomba, and others and trained them as recruiting agents. His biggest prizes, however, were DeSoto (see chapter 6) and Billy, both of whom honed their militant skills in the CVR before exercising them in Mobutu's single-party youth wing. Paurret, too, was enrolled after serving his time in deportation. His and other informants' recollections point to a seamless transition between the CVR and the JMPR (Jeunesse du Mouvement Populaire de la Révolution), Mobutu's youth party, on the one hand, and the role Bills played in winning the quartiers for the new regime, on the other:

> We all enlisted into the CVR. The CVR was just like the MPR [Mouvement Populaire de la Révolution]. There was this Yankee, Botomba, burgomaster of Limété, who came looking for me. When we left the CVR we all got into the MPR.[48]

> Then, Kabaidi appointed [De]Soto head of unit within the JMPR to catch thieves in the Grand Market. Soto lived next to the Grand Market on Itaga. When we created the JMPR in the quartiers and townships, we took Bills and appointed them heads of quartiers. Thugs became leaders in the quartiers. That's why there were no more troubles in the quartiers.[49]

> He [Kabaidi] enlisted gangsters to stop gangsterism in the quartiers.[50]

Perhaps what won unanimity at the December 1966 CVR seminar was the decision to elevate Mobutu as Congo's "second national hero," next to Lumumba. This spurred a cult of personality that saw Mobutu's effigy being printed on pagnes (cloth) worn by both men and women, and later on banknotes and pins, and his praises laced into countless rumba lyrics. In fact, Bob W. White (2008: 74) is correct in dating *animation*—that is, Mobutu's political pageantry, parades, and self-aggrandizing propaganda machine—back to the CVR rather than to 1974, after Mobutu's much-heralded trip to China and North Korea.

Although short-lived, the CVR did not fizzle out but formed the backbone of Mobutu's newly created single party, the MPR (Mouvement Populaire de la Révolution), and especially its youth wing, the JMPR (Jeunesse du Mouvement Populaire de la Révolution). Formers Bills staffed all the ranks in both the JMPR and the MPR. N'Sengi Biembe and Kabaidi became members of the national committee of the MPR (Young and Turner 1985: 190). Some, like Lémi (aka Capitaine Lisika), joined Mobutu's security detail. General Mahele, whose demise is described in the introduction to this book, rose through the ranks to become Mobutu's army chief and one of the most decorated generals in the armed forces. Others, such as Nimy Mayidika, Paul-Henri Kabaidi, Hugor Bomina Nsoni, Jacques Atenda Mongebe Omwango,[51] and Jean-Jacques Kande, who in their youth had lived according to the Bills' modus vivendi, shorn of its hard knocks and dire straits, formed Mobutu's political inner circle.

Not all Bills were enthusiastic about the new regime and sought opportunities within its ranks. Many parlayed their rebellious ethos into music careers, to such an extent that one can hardly discuss 1960s and 1970s Congolese rumba without mentioning the role played by the Bills. In fact, one would be hard-pressed to name a single Congolese musician of any note who either did not come from the Bill movement or was not heavily influenced by it. From the 1960s well into the 1980s and beyond, popular musicians often vindicated their kinicité (the quality of being Kinois) by flaunting their Bill pedigree. For example, in 1983, wanting to settle score with Prime Minister Léon Kengo wa Dondo, who may have had a hand in his fall from presidential grace and his brief stint in jail,[52] Luambo Makiadi (aka Franco) shot back with a scathing song in which he sought to portray himself as a true-blue Kinois. He invoked a constellation of Bill demigods, locales, and apocrypha to vouch for his kinicité and demonstrate his toughness:

> Nga nakima Kinshasa?
> Kinshasa mboka na koli?
> Kinshasa ya Kin Malebo?
> Kinshasa oyo ekomisa nga boye nakima bino?
> Nayekolaki guitare na nga na wenze ya bayaka na quartier Farwest nani abungi ngai ah?
> Luambo ayebi Okure Keke
> Luambo ayebi Kukulu Elombe
> Luambo ayebi Paka Djuma
> Luambo ayebaki Moruma na Debaron
> Luambo ayebaki Vieux Eboma
> Nakataka kamô epayi ya Vieux Eboma
> Nabetaki moto na nzete, nzete ekawukaki
> Botika ko tumola nga
> Luambo ayebaki Mbele Kete, eh
> Luambo ayebaki William Bot [Booth]
> Luambo ayebaki Trace Esange
> Luambo ayebaki Zando ya Imbwa
> Luambo ayebaki Zamba ya Avocat epayi tozalaka kolokota bimpiatu ya mfwe
> Botika kombo na nga
>
> (Franco [aka Luambo Makiadi], "Lettre à Monsieur le Directeur, Suite Lettre no 2," 1983)

> Did I flee Kinshasa?
> Kinshasa where I grew up?
> Kinshasa, that is Kin Malebo?
> Kinshasa that made me who I am, could I leave it?
> I learned to play the guitar in the Wenze ya Bayaka market in Quartier Farwest, who doesn't remember me there, ah?
> Luambo knows Okure Keke
> Luambo knows Kukulu Elombe
> Luambo knows Paka Djuma
> Luambo knew Moruma and Debaron

Luambo knew Vieux Eboma
I had my kamô cut by Vieux Eboma
I head-butted a tree, and the tree dried up
Stop getting under my skin
Luambo knew Mbele Kete, eh
Luambo knew William Bot [Booth]
Luambo knew Trace Esange
Luambo knew Zando ya Imbwa
Luambo knew Zamba ya Avocat, where we used to pick up caterpillars
Leave my name alone.

Behind Franco's biting lyrics lies an important truth: nearly two decades removed from the time Mobutu stopped the Bills' rebellious ride in its track, Yankees and Kinois had become two sides of the same coin and had the same values, in terms of grit and guts, and a blend of resourcefulness and insouciance.

8 Avatars

Tosala na Kisasa proverbe ya masangu:
"Moto nionso mandefu na mandefu
Okoyeba te nani moke"

We came up in Kinshasa with a proverb about corn:
"Everybody is full of beard,[1]
You wouldn't know who's a kid."

Franco and le T. P. OK Jazz, "Où est le sérieux?" 1973

In early 1965, the Bill could be seen strolling nonchalantly in Kinshasa's main streets, unmistakably sporting a leather jacket, a checkered shirt knotted at the waist, its collar raised, a kerchief loosely tied around his neck, tight pants, and pointed shoes. In 1970, T. K. Biaya wrote, "the *ambianceur*[2] speaks the language of the Bill, who himself has discarded his blue jeans to don the most elegant attire" (Biaya 1997: 99). By this time the Bill no longer elicited fear from residents and was more preoccupied with seducing girls with his debonair look and suave demeanor than with mugging passersby at makeshift checkpoints. A 1964 article in a Kinshasa daily newspaper described him as the "fervent défenseur des droits et des libertés de la personne humaine" (fervent defender of the rights and liberties of the human being). Whereas his colonial counterpart had conceived of rape as "a natural attribute of masculinity" (un attribut naturel de la masculinité), the article went on, "the Bill prides himself on not crossing the line beyond flirting."[3]

By 1965, "Bill" had become a byword for youthful elegance and insouciance, while his performing body and quick-witted vernacular had become subversive sites of self-realization and resistance at a time when other sites had been gutted by postcolonial dictatorship. This, however, was only a brief moment of respite between the quagmire of the early 1960s and Mobutu's long reign of terror, a moment when Congolese wrestled with the ideas of modernity, self-representation, and, of course, freedom. Here, again, young people led the way, just as in later years they would spearhead the struggle against Mobutu's dictatorial regime before succumbing to its hubris.

Perhaps one way to conclude this book is to examine the impact the Bills have left on Kinshasa's urbanscape, not only through, for example, the cultural debris that has littered Kinshasa's nightlife but by examining the brood of avatars they have spawned. All interstitial juvenile groups that followed in the Bills' footsteps, including those who became "Parisiens" and "Belgicains," or more generally "Mikilistes" and "sapeurs,"[4] had to engage and contend one way or the other with the legacy the Bills left behind.

Street Culture

According to Congolese historian Tshikala Biaya, much of the exuberance, delinquency, and counterhegemonic creativity that Kinshasa's youths have exhibited since the heyday of the Bills can be explained by the nature of Kinshasa's street (*la rue kinoise*). Using la rue kinoise as a heuristic device, Biaya (1997: 100) argues that street culture in Kinshasa has become a crucible where young people resort to a thousand and one schemes (*mille et une ruses*) to eke out a living and participate in Kinshasa's legendary ambiance.

Biaya's analysis contains the perfunctory demographic statistics that preface any discussion of Kinshasa's youth culture. As Kinshasa's youth population soared at a dizzying rate in the postindependence years, so did youth unemployment and homelessness. With fewer opportunities for work in the formal sector and heightened competition for jobs in the informal sector, the street was no longer a temporary playground. It became a permanent shelter where tens of thousands of disenfranchised youths lived hand to mouth and sought respite from the burden of their crushed lives. La rue kinoise then morphed into a stage for what situationist thinkers such as Henri Lefebvre and Guy Debord have called the "spectacularization" of everyday life (see Debord 1983). Spectacularization is used here not as a top-down hegemonic bourgeois scheme intended to lull and distract the masses from their plight, but as a conscious, subversive grassroots performance that challenges the social and political status quo on a daily basis. Spectacularization also means that the street becomes a site of social conflict and a space teeming with infrapolitics, counterhegemonic discourses, and deviant infracultures.

One work that reflects on this postcolonial metamorphosis is Filip De Boeck and Marie-Françoise Plissart's *Kinshasa: Tales of the Invisible City* (2005), a tantalizing cultural urbanography that looks at how Kinshasa has reinvented itself in the postcolonial years. What seems to set this "new" Kinshasa apart from its former self—its colonial mirror, as it were—is not just the contrast between *Kin-la-belle* (Kinshasa the beautiful) and *Kin-la-poubelle* (Kinshasa the trash bin). Rather, the new Kinshasa has "moved away from the mimetic reproduction of an alienating model of colonialist modernity, imposed by the colonial and the Mobutist state upon the city's population through a wide ranging arsenal of physical and symbolic forms of violence," a process De Boeck and Plissart (2005: 34) define as "post-urbanism" or "villagization" (see also Devisch 1995: 602).

Here again we witness what to situationist thinkers amounts to a détourne-ment (see Debord and Wolman 1956). Kinois have gone beyond appropriation. They have diverted and subverted a dysfunctional urban space that is no longer the preserve of the predatory state. By the same token, street occupation and détournement also suggest the creation and quotidian defense of a "democratic space" (Jewsiewicki 2004: 263; see Geenen 2009). Once barred from the "European city" by an arsenal of prophylactic and legal barriers, Kinois reclaimed and invested what then became downtown Kinshasa (*centre-ville*) with new meanings.

Kinois have also gone beyond the survival economy (*la débrouille*) to cope with a litany of sacrifices and deprivation: "people do without food, they do without fuelwood, they do without primary health services and they do without safe drinking water. They also do without political participation, security, leisure or the ability to organize their time as they would like" (Trefon 2004: 4). At the heart of this duplicitous if orchestrated disorder and dystopia, Theodore Trefon discerns the contour of a tenuous yet resilient order "of the people and by the people," which often bypasses, circumvents, and, when no other options are left, stands up to the state. This disorder, or chaos, should also be attributed to the sheer hubris of a city that French sociologist Georges Balandier first described back in the late 1950s as *une ville en devenir,* perpetually in flux, in motion, and reinventing itself over and over. Yet what happened in Kinshasa starting in the 1990s indicates that this city of ten million inhabitants (the third most populous city in Africa) has also become *une ville théâtre* (a city on stage) where everyday life is a matter not just of survival but also of performance. Kinshasa has become a sort of tropical Far West where acts of bravado and derring-do are performed in broad daylight and where people air their dirty laundry in the streets, seeking to enlist neighbors and passersby's assistance.

Another contribution to this discussion comes from Koffi Olomide, one of Congo's reigning musical icons, who set the tone for his 1996 theme song "Wake Up" with the following spoken aphorism: "Tozali ko vivre na system ya lifelo, veut dire, moto ezali kopela kasi tozali kozika te" (We're living in the scheme of hell, I mean, fire is blazing, yet we do not get burned). Olomide's jarring rendition offers a shorthand take on Kinois' wonted resourcefulness and ingenuity in the face of dereliction.

As the epigraph of this chapter also suggests, the struggle to stay alive in Kinshasa and to dodge the pangs of hunger and sickness knows no generational boundaries. Children, too, especially when despondent parents expect them to fend for themselves, have "grown a full beard" in order to survive in Kinshasa, adopting all manner of tactics, street smarts, and tough talk to tame the city's mean streets.

Interstitiality, the street culture of détournement, and spectacularization continue to act as grains of sand—so fine they seem at times to be invisible—that threaten to bring the oppressive machine of life in Kinshasa grinding to a halt. This was particularly the case in the 1990s, when recurring popular uprisings sent the Mobutu regime reeling from bouts of fury and looting that echoed the January 1959 riots. In fact, in Kinshasa everything starts in the street and ends in the street. Much of this has to do, of course, with the sheer number of people crowding the streets at any given time of the day or night,[5] people who become participants and interlocutors and who are brought into the drama as witnesses, experts, judges, and even as executioners when events take on a sordid twist or turn into a matter of life or death, as they often do in Kinshasa.

Kinshasa's streets bustle with vendors: women setting their goods on the sidewalks, currency traders handling thick stashes of banknotes in the open without fear of being robbed, phone-card vendors, and shoeshiners peddling their goods and services using the noise of two metallic castanet-like devices to get the attention of potential clients. They make the rounds up and down the streets, loudly alerting residents to their offerings: *mapa!* (bread), *pétrole!*[6] *eau pire!*[7] *kombo!* (broom), *pondu!* (cassava leaves), and so forth. Other vendors peddle an assortment of manufactured goods Kinois have come to christen "Guangzhou." Guangzhou, they believe, is the devil's workshop, where cheap, half-baked, low-cost, and shoddy goods are spewed out by the ton and dumped into the cesspool that their city has become thanks to globalization. Then there is the proverbial *radio trottoir* (pavement radio), continuously buzzing with news and rumors. And even nowadays, passersby congregate in front of newspaper pages hung up with clothespins to catch the latest headlines and printed news.

Kinshasa would not be Kinshasa if it were not for its doomsday-and-prosperity Christian preachers, who preach their gospel in buses, on street corners, in markets, and in stadiums in exchange for *mabonza* (offerings). And on Sunday mornings, as local congregations (*assemblées*) vie to outdo each other in a contest of decibels that spill out of the private compounds where these services are usually held, Kinshasa drapes itself in sackcloth and ashes. Life then, as Pype (2012: 38) argues, is construed as a spiritual battle between good and evil while signs of an imminent apocalypse are spotted everywhere.

Last but not least, the city is now "shared by the living and the dead," as De Boeck and Plissart (2005: 82) have noted. The economy of death, from the *matanga* (wake ceremony) to the procession and burial, has been commandeered by the youth, who now exercise a liminal power once held by the elders. Devisch, who observed these processions in the late 1980s, vividly describes their Rabelaisian topsy-turviness:

> The crowd escorting the corpse to the cemetery violates the social domains and their regulations: it takes up the whole street, adopts shocking behavior, assails passing pedestrians and cars, intrudes into nearby properties and

market stands, and carries on with other aggressive behavior, whose purpose is to circumvent and undo the evil curse. (Devisch 1995: 611)

In addition to being ubiquitous in the city, owing to their sheer numbers and energy, young people now stand betwixt and between; they straddle Kinshasa's physical and mystical universes and give the city its pulse and rhythm. More recently, as Katrien Pype (2012) has shown in her exploration of Kinshasa's Pentecostal teleserials (*maboke*), spectacularization has come full circle using not only the street but also the screen (where, as suggested in chapter 3, everything started, back in the late 1940s) to reenact and perform the drama of masculinity. For Pype, teleserials function as didactic devices aimed at reorganizing and resignifying Kinshasa's urban reality of misfortune, infertility, illness, sudden enrichment, and so on, through carefully scripted plots enacted by young Kinois[8] actors and packaged for what she calls an "imagined Christian community." These teleserials have become the new medium where essentialized, heteronormative values are negotiated and receive new currencies. Although Pype is not explicit about it, one can easily imagine that these teleserials are serving as a platform for the promotion of a millennial version of the muscular Christianity that the Bills embraced in the early 1960s under the aegis of Père Buffalo.

The Next Generations

As discussed in previous chapters, Bills were by no means the first generation of interstitial youths who took center stage in the postwar vortex that has shaped the urban experiences of many young Kinois. Before they appeared on Kinshasa's scene, several groups of juvenile delinquents had come and gone. Yet Bills were the first to display the kind of hybridity and Janus-facedness that the contributors to Alcinda Honwana and Filip De Boeck's (2005) edited volume *Makers and Breakers: Children and Youth in Postcolonial Africa* have stressed. As Honwana and De Boeck remind us, African youths display an uncanny ability to mediate, to cross geographic and symbolic boundaries, and to use their mobility and liminality to carve out agency. They also and always act as makers and breakers, ever walking the tightrope between the "ludic" and the "lethal," "affection and affliction," hope and nihilism (Honwana and De Boeck 2005: 10).

Kompani Kitunga

As the Bills left the scene, Kompani Kitunga briefly resurfaced as a result of the new social and political environment. Whereas their colonial counterparts had preyed on market women and commuters, using familiar tactics and tricks, and often operated in transient youth bands, the new Kompani Kitunga involved intricate family networks. They took to dwelling in Citas's sewers and under the Kasa-Vubu bridge, from where young men would emerge at sundown to mug passersby (Shana 1984: 40). Some of them, known as "Bana ya US" or "US Air Force," broke into people's homes not only to snatch whatever they could lay their hands on but to abduct females they would take to Synkin (Kintambo), where a large patch of forest concealed their criminal business.[9]

Breaking into people's private residences signaled shifting social patterns in the postcolonial years. The flight of Belgian civil servants, business owners, and army officers allowed some Congolese to move into those vacant posts, a total of "5,900 upper-level positions in the administration, 3,681 in the middle level, and 1,000 officer positions in the army" (Kisangani 2012: 77). This overnight social mobility, with its sundry rags-to-riches trajectories, took place against a backdrop of massive unemployment and salary arrears affecting mostly lower-rank functionaries and teachers. In fact, the income gap between a few rich and a mass of poor widened to such an extent that it accounted for the economic doldrums in Kinshasa and the culture of *la débrouille* (hustling). The new regime of banditry to which Kompani Kitunga subjected Kinshasa's residents was also a reaction to the ostentatious consumption and hedonistic lifestyle that had become the hallmark of Congolese nouveaux riches. Mobutu's underlings and the regime's cronies flaunted their newfound wealth with luxurious villas and their extravagant tastes for expensive Western imports. Despoiling them of their ill-gotten wealth played out as a revolutionary act, following the pattern of redistributive justice that White (1981) uncovered in his study of postbellum American social banditry.

In addition to the emergence of a new class of wealthy entrepreneurs and political ruling elite, independence witnessed a breakdown of social networks and, conversely, a rise in ethnic sentiments. With rebellions fueled by foreign powers engulfing a large swath of the country and oftentimes spiraling into cycles of ethnic violence, Kinshasa became a haven for ever-increasing numbers of young migrants and refugees. Many looked for opportunities to find work and shed their provincial ways. Other migrants joined the ranks of delinquent youths and oftentimes conceived of violence, especially when it targeted the elite class, as a way to settle scores triggered by ethnic feuds in war-torn provinces.

Ballados

Then came the Ballados, arguably the most brazen interstitial youth group to claim the Bills' mantle. The term "Ballado," a corruption of the French *se balader* (to stroll or amble along), was used in print for the first time in a November 1977 article in the Kinshasa newspaper *Salongo*. In the late 1970s, *Salongo* devoted its "Kinshasa et ses problèmes" column to issues about "delinquency" and "deviance," and each column lay the blame for Kinshasa's woes squarely at the feet of the Ballados.

The Bills, as we have seen in previous chapters, used violence mainly to police territorial and gender boundaries. They rarely targeted township residents precisely because they had strong township affiliations and cultivated the fiction of social banditry. Ballados, in contrast, were misfits and drifters. Some came from broken families, having run away from home situations they described as unbearable. Oftentimes, as Shana's study (1984: 52) clearly indicates, children turned to a life in the streets after their parents repeatedly goaded them to manage on their own (*se débrouiller*) in order to supplement the household's meager income. Others were left to fend for themselves after their parents divorced or died—a pattern that became fairly common in the postcolonial years. Young migrants who came to join an uncle or an elder brother in the city and then found themselves stranded, without family or an ethnic support network, could hardly resist the temptation to mingle with Ballados and learn from them how to survive on the edge.

One cannot separate the Ballados from broader economic changes that swept the country, wreaking havoc where the most vulnerable people already lived on the brink of famine. Ill-conceived policy decisions created a particularly severe economic downturn from which the country never recovered. Among Mobutu's many ill-fated policies, the one that nearly bankrupted the country, the so-called Zairianization, actually came about not as an economic policy as such but as a scheme to buttress the regime's patrimonialism.[10] Launched in 1973, the policy called for the seizure of foreign-owned small- and large-scale businesses and property-holding companies in all sectors, including commerce, transportation, construction firms, agribusiness, and manufacturing. Most of these economic ventures had remained firmly in the hands of Belgians (who held the lion's share), Portuguese, Italians, Greeks, Jews, and Pakistanis. They were handed over to handpicked Congolese *acquéreurs* (beneficiaries), many of whom had no business background.

Under the guise of exercising greater control over its economy—a legitimate case of "economic nationalism" that was not unheard of in other newly independent African countries—the regime essentially created "a new reserve of prebends to be used for the manipulation and control of the political bourgeoisie" (Young and Turner 1985: 328). The calamitous consequences of Zairianization included "dislocation of commercial circuits, shortages, layoffs in Zairianized enterprises, pay arrearages, inflation, tax evasion by *acquéreurs,* [and] abandonment of businesses" (343). By 1977, Zaire's economic growth rate plunged into the negative for the first time (325).

Largely unforeseen even when the policy had all but failed was the rapid expansion of the informal sector to compensate for layoffs and the collapse of huge swaths of the formal economy. Ballados joined the informal sector, as most downtrodden Kinois did, as a way to keep famine at bay and weather the *conjoncture* (economic recession) that no one at the time knew would become synonymous with life in Kinshasa. Filling the oddest and lowliest *petits métiers* (odd jobs), such as the positions of watchmen, street vendors, porters, dishwashers, car washers, *chargeurs*,[11] shoeshiners, and sweepers, they became indispensable to the operation of formal businesses while also providing a host of low-cost services to residents who would not otherwise have been able to afford them.

They also used street jobs as a front to hatch various schemes. Working in cahoots with his accomplices, a Ballado would, for example, infiltrate a quartier as a domestic worker (*boy*) or a security guard (*sentinelle*), a perfect cover for surveying the vicinity and spotting residences to loot. Then, at night, he would return to the quartier and lead his buddies to break into houses he had slated for looting. Younger Ballados carved out a niche in busy parking lots in downtown Kinshasa by offering to watch cars while their owners ran errands. Rather than wait for the small tip they would receive, these urchins would steal items left in the car and make off with auto parts that they became experts at removing in a matter of seconds. Stolen items included side-view mirrors, hubcaps, headlights, gas caps, antennas, and car radios and speakers. They would all end up in make-shift roadside markets known as "Kuwaits" where receivers sold them off at *prix mangondo* (slashed prices), sometimes to the robbery victims themselves.

Thus, starting in the late 1970s, Ballados introduced an important element to Kinois culture by inserting themselves as a critical link in the transactional chain of commodities. They contributed to the democratizing of consumption by helping goods once flaunted only by the regime's nouveaux riches to trickle down to the populace. Whether removed by dark of night, snatched in broad daylight, or stolen at knifepoint, goods that transited through "Kuwait" markets and other fly-by-night selling spots gave an illusion of modernity to millions of disadvantaged Kinois.

Bindomania and the Economy of Pillage

Until the late 1990s, several interstitial groups jockeyed for the control of Kinshasa's lucrative streets, some using hard-core violence (including drug trafficking, petty crime, and prostitution), others mainly interested in sartorial performances, still others barely surviving Kinshasa's mean streets. Their ages varied from little ones (four to seven years old) known as *moineaux* (French for "sparrows"), living hand to mouth mostly by begging and rummaging through the city's ubiquitous trash heaps, to oldsters (over thirty years old) known as *Kraneurs* (derived from the French *crâner,* "to show off"). According to Tshikala Biaya, Kraneurs were former Yankees who had quit the billing business in the 1960s to settle down. Some had even mustered enough resources to become family men. Then, with the economy of la débrouille rearing its ugly head in the 1970s, they relapsed into a life of the street, this time as fraudsters and mobsters, masterminding all sorts of illicit tricks. With connections in high places based on mutual profit, they found a niche in drug and mineral-ore trafficking. Kraneurs could always count on the loyalty and chutzpah of a close-knit posse of Ballados to conjure up and execute the most sophisticated scams (Biaya 2000: 14).

By the early 1990s, the political context had deteriorated significantly, with a botched National Sovereign Conference[12] and a desperate regime clinging to power only by fanning the flames of chaos and disorder. On the economic front, Zaire exemplified perhaps more than any other country the "paradox of plenty," being a rich country where people starved, a cornucopia of precious mineral ores where the majority of the populace lived on less than a dollar a day. In 1988, at a time when the country was not yet engulfed in the bloodiest conflict since World War II, its GDP per capita ($170) ranked it among the poorest countries in the world. Inflation, a mere 3 percent in 1970, had skyrocketed to 3,642 percent by 1991. That same year, the budget deficit exceeded the government's forecast by such a large margin (20 times more than what economists had predicted) that the government resorted to increasing the supply of money both in volume and in larger denominations, leading to hyperinflation. Prices of basic commodities, such as cassava, rice, and coal, rose daily, while salaries paid to public servants remained unchanged. While pauperization afflicted an increasing mass of Kinois, a small group within the regime's inner circle, including a certain number of expatriates, thrived with impunity.

Yet this was also a time when, to most Kinois, money "appeared to be a mysterious and fantastic entity, retaining no relation to either labor or production" (Devisch 1995: 605). It was within this context that a young man by the name of Michel Bindo started a modest Ponzi scheme that later mushroomed into an elaborate and intricate swindle that actually dwarfs Bernie Madoff's $65 billion investment fraud. To attract "small investors," Bindo made an offer that few could resist. For a deposit of 40,000 zaires (the equivalent of eight dollars in early 1991), Bindo promised a return of 200,000 zaires (that is, forty dollars) within just forty-five days! At its height, "Bindomania" saw "investors" come all the way from the interior of the country and members of the Zairian diaspora flock back to the capital city to pump large sums of money into this gigantic pyramid scheme (see Gondola 1997b). In Kinshasa, Bindo installed branches all over the city's townships, main markets, university campuses, military camps, and police headquarters. By May 1991, the swindle had metastasized to such an alarming extent that conservative estimates suggest that at least one-third of the monetary mass in circulation in Zaire had been siphoned off.

More importantly, Bindomania created a pernicious system in Kinshasa whereby *l'argent facile* (easy money), through gambling, swindling, and other ways of obtaining ill-gotten gains, became a substitute for any meaningful economic activity. Young people especially, who worked in Bindo's branches as cashiers, further eroded the pyramid by running their own private pyramids within the system. As the reign of l'argent facile spread, rags-to-riches stories became common even in the seediest parts of the city. Young people, who were the backbone of Zaire's informal economy, had deserted their jobs for the elusive quick gains of Bindo's scheme. But in the end, only a very few "investors" struck it rich, while the vast majority sulked amid the colossal loss of investments.

The collapse of Bindo's pyramid scheme in May 1991 brought down an economy already teetering on the brink of chaos due to decades of corruption and mismanagement. On August 21, against a backdrop of public unrest and volatile prices of basic commodities, the government sent the economy reeling by devaluating the national currency by 100 percent. While students at the Unikin (Université de Kinshasa) and other tertiary institutes clashed with the Garde Civile (Police Force) on their respective campuses, rioting for the government to reimburse the sums invested, small bands of Ballados took matters into their own hands by holding passersby for ransom and shoplifting in the markets. More generally, the notion took hold that Kinshasa was a free-for-all place, a sort of tropical Far West where people were entitled to take what they needed by any means necessary in order to survive. And this was true not only for young people in the townships but also for civil servants, the police, and the military. It seemed, as Gauthier de Villers and Jean Omasombo Tshonga (2004) have argued, that the economy of Kinshasa took a nosedive from the informal economy to the economy of pillage.

It was against this volatile background of unrest and lawlessness, with the state in command of virtually nothing and unable to curb hyperinflation, that the 31st Brigade of the Air Force mutinied on the night of September 22, 1991. Soldiers marched from the airport of Ndjili to downtown Kinshasa, cheered by throngs of onlookers once they made it known that they were bent on looting. The following day, they were joined by civilians in a looting frenzy that has perhaps not been seen elsewhere in modern times. Men, women, and children targeted stores, warehouses, and the private homes of the regime's dignitaries. After clearing the rooms of electrical appliances and equipment, furniture, and wall coverings, they removed bathtubs, bath fixtures, sinks, faucets, electrical wiring and outlets, light bulbs, ceiling and floor tiles, timberwork and roofing, windows, and doors. If paint could have been removed, it would have suffered the same fate. All this booty was hauled away on people's heads, sometimes over incredible distances. The language that looters used to qualify their actions operated within a sort of Hobbesian state of nature. Rather than acknowledge that what they did was looting (*koyiba* in Lingala), they referred to their exploits as *kotombola* (to lift), *kobomber* (to carry), and *kodéplacer* (to move).

Just as they had made their livings in the informal economy, so young people sustained themselves and their families within the economy of pillage, which spread throughout the country and reared its head again in Kinshasa in late 1992 and early 1993.[13] Looting then came to define survival in an urban context of total dereliction and disorder. Indeed, looting became a way to subvert disorder, reestablish order, and redistribute wealth.

The War Generations

Mayhem and terror unleashed by youth gangs in Kinshasa climaxed as a result of the momentous regime change that occurred in 1997, after a beleaguered Mobutu relinquished power under the threat of Laurent-Désiré Kabila's AFDL (Alliance des Forces Démocratiques pour la Libération du Congo) troops. Starting from the city of Goma, in eastern Congo, Kabila's ragtag forces trekked across the country and marched triumphantly into Kinshasa on May 17, 1997. Although the battle of Kinshasa was averted after General Donat Mahele, who reappears later in this chapter, convinced troops loyal to Mobutu to step aside, the city became a contested generational battleground.

Kadogos

As Kabila's forces swept across the country, they elicited huge popular enthusiasm that resulted in the recruitment of child-soldiers known as Kadogos (Swahili slang for "child combatants"). Kadogos were among the first foot soldiers to breach the suburbs of Kinshasa and make their triumphant way into the heart of the city.

During Kabila's first year in power, Kadogos exercised their influence by providing security in and around Kabila's palace. Kinshasa's population initially welcomed them but later came to fear them. Kadogos spoke Swahili and not Lingala, Kinshasa's vernacular; they were young, oftentimes high on drugs, and always toting weapons that they never hesitated to use. They could be seen patrolling the city on foot, enforcing order that many Kinois came to resent. People who were caught misbehaving or flouting the rules that the new regime had imposed could bear the brunt of the Kadogos' ire. For instance, taxi drivers could be asked to get out of their cars if they were caught transporting two people in the passenger's seat. They were usually flogged with a chicote, lying on the ground in a posture reminiscent of the most humiliating form of punishment under Belgian colonial rule. According to a scripted public performance, a Kadogo would first ask the driver his age and then proceed to give him the appropriate number of strokes (e.g., a forty-year-old driver would be given forty strokes; the older he was, the more strokes he would receive). The same retribution was meted out to women, especially those who dressed "inappropriately" (tight pants, low-cut tops, etc.), and to anyone the Kadogos thought was acting in a disorderly fashion. Kadogos were given such broad license to police urban behavior that most of them ended up abusing their authority and came to be loathed by Kinois.

Nothing incensed Kinshasa's population more than the shift from geron-tocracy to youthocracy that Kadogo power represented in a society that had long revered seniority. The daily sight of these young soldiers, toting guns that some-times dwarfed their small frames and lording it over old men and women, jarred a society that had chafed under thirty-two years of Mobutu's dystopic regime and initially welcomed AFDL troops as liberators.

In June 1997, less than a month after taking over, Kabila deported many sol-diers and officers of the former Forces Armées Zaïroises (ex-FAZ) to a military base in Kitona (located in the town of Moanda, 350 kilometers southwest of Kin-shasa), where they were to undergo reeducation. The press in Kinshasa reported stories of their ill treatment by AFDL troops there. Former high-ranking ex-FAZ officers bore the brunt of AFDL troops' retribution through routine humiliation and abuses, sometimes at the hands of Kadogos. At least 40,000 ex-FAZ soldiers were forcibly sent to the Kitona army base and detained in facilities meant to ac-commodate roughly 10,000 people. Lack of food, hygiene, and access to medical care, coupled with degrading treatment, including torture and wanton execu-tion, claimed the lives of at least 4,000 troops (an average of five to ten deaths every day during the first few months).

In Kinshasa Kadogos were feared not just for their cold-blooded hubris—people said that they showed no mercy or remorse in killing—but also because they ushered into an already chaotic and bruised city the figure of the Pro-methean youth who has usurped the power to mete out violence, within a cul-tural context that had traditionally bestowed authority and visibility in the public space to older men. This generational permutation climaxed in the assassination of President Laurent-Désiré Kabila on January 16, 2001. Accounts that surfaced following Kabila's death point to a Kadogo named Rachidi Kasereka as the trig-german (Prunier 2009: 249; Ngolet 2011: 181; Stearns 2011: 280). The narrative that unfolded in the local and international press interpreted Kabila's assassination through notions of "parricide" and "betrayal." Kasereka (who was eighteen at the time of Kabila's assassination) had been with Kabila since the beginning of the rebellion in Kivu. Like some of his comrades, he served as a member of Kabila's bodyguard but harbored deep resentment against him.

The bone of contention between Kabila and the Kadogos went back to the beginning of the rebellion, when Kabila had shared leadership of the AFDL with André Kisase Ngandu, head of an opposition group, the National Council of Re-sistance for Democracy, which attracted many Kadogos. Vying for the backing of Rwanda and in an effort to position himself as the sole and unquestioned head of the AFDL, Kabila had Kisase Ngandu physically eliminated. On November 27, 2000, he had another Kadogo benefactor, Masasu Nindaga, executed near Pweto, in Katanga, on suspicion of conniving with the Tutsi enemy to overthrow his regime. Nindaga, a Banyamulenge like many Kadogos, had been Kabila's first chief of staff and the head of the Revolutionary Movement for the Liberation of the Congo, one of the four original parties that formed the AFDL (Prunier 2009: 130 and 252–53; Stearns 2011: 238 and 278).

Kabila also never attempted to secure the loyalty of Kadogos through the payment of regular salaries but kept them in wretched conditions. Kadogos were seldom fed or paid, lacked adequate military equipment, and received no military training of any sort. Kabila nonetheless used them as cannon fodder to contain the Rwandan-backed rebellions that erupted on the eastern frontier. Even after they had disappeared from Kinshasa's scene in the days following Kabila's assassination, Kadogos left their mark on the urban social landscape by contributing to the emergence of a "youth power" culture that came to define the urban experience in Kinshasa.

Bashegue

Kadogos had thus fulfilled Franco's "corn" proverb (see epigraph to this chapter) by upending a gerontocratic system that had withstood several generations of youth interstitiality. One has only to think of the 1950s Bill, dressed in cowboy gear with a fake pistol in his holster, policing the township with his bare knuckles and a sharp, quick-witted tongue, to realize how youth violence in Kinshasa had now strayed from its somehow ludic and performative beginning. Behind this remark lies a painful truth: the urban economy of la débrouille had flattened an age hierarchy that had traditionally bestowed privilege on seniority, replacing it with an urban bedlam replete with men still living under the paternal roof and children serving their households as breadwinners. In doing so, it had also exposed the fault lines of a deeper "crisis of masculinity" that found its roots in the colonial period.

Before the Kadogos appeared on the scene, the urban space in Kinshasa was also occupied by the Bashegue, the street children. Filip De Boeck and Marie-Françoise Plissart have pieced together the figure of the Shegue (urchin) through a complex urban archaeology that excavates fragments of an invisible city. Lurking in the interstices of this city is the figure of the "witch-child" who, according to De Boeck and Plissart, harnessed the imaginary and symbolic power of the occult, straddling the visible and the invisible city. Here, too, the mystical power to channel occult forces and harm the living, which had previously been the prerogative of adults (especially older men and women), was now seized by children and youth. Never before, write De Boeck and Plissart (2005: 159), have children and young adolescents occupied "a more central position in the public spaces of urban life, whether in the popular urban music culture, the media, the churches, the army, the street, or the bed." As a result of this ubiquity of "children in the streets," a growing number of "children of the streets" (those who have nowhere to go, lack family networks, or have been torn from kith and kin) emerged in the city.[14]

The connection between witchcraft and homelessness appears when accusations of witchcraft leveled at children leave them with no choice but to seek refuge in the streets of the capital. Preteens and teens "are being accused of causing misfortunes and mishaps, as well as the illness or death of other children and adults in their family and neighborhood environment" (De Boeck and Plissart 2005: 168). Each township and each neighborhood in Kinshasa have their version of common narratives: stories of children commuting between the daytime world and the nocturnal (invisible) world to "eat" their victims; young girls transforming themselves into beautiful women or, sometimes, into *mami wata* (mermaids) to lure men into bed, only to spirit away their penises (170); or children signing evil blood pacts requiring that they "hand over" one of their relatives (mother, brother or sister, etc.) to guarantee success in any given venture. They become key players in the "nocturnal economy of power and desire" (160) and, for better or for worse, use their alleged power to eat people.

Stories of nightly sorties by "witch-children" pervade Kinshasa—especially redemptive narratives, which have become the best selling points of evangelical churches. De Boeck and Plissart (2005: 163) have collected a number of those redemptive narratives, including the following one, which speaks volumes about the symbolic and imaginary agency invested in young people in Kinshasa:

> My name is Mamuya. I am fourteen years old. I became a witch because of a boyfriend of mine, Komazulu. One day he gave me a mango. During the following night he came to visit me in my parents' house and threatened that he would kill me if I didn't offer him human meat in return for the mango he had given me earlier. From that moment I became his nocturnal companion and entered his group of witches. I didn't tell my mother. In our group we are three. At night we fly with our "airplane," which we make from the bark of a mango tree, to the houses of our victims. When we fly out at night, I transform myself into a cockroach. Komazulu is the pilot of our airplane. He is the one who kills. He gives me some meat and some blood and then I eat and drink.

The narrative goes on to explain how Mamuya came out of the "world of shadows thanks to the preacher who treats [her] in church" (163) but had to fend off powerful spiritual attacks from former nocturnal companions who felt she had betrayed the secrets of their occult activities and therefore deserved to be "eaten."

Although not all Bashegue claim to possess mystical power (*kindoki*) or to partake in these nocturnal rituals of mystical death and cannibalism, Kinois recoil at the sight of these urchins and have come to fear them as *ndoki* (witches or those with other extraordinary powers).[15] Yet, for most Kinois, it is not a matter of these jarring narratives registering as prima facie evidence of witchcraft, in the sense that many Western scholars have theorized and articulated.[16] Rather, what qualifies Bashegue as ndoki in the eyes of Kinois is their ability to survive in

Kinshasa's mean streets, especially at night, without parental, governmental, or NGO support. This alone baffles Kinois and gives Bashegue a Promethean aura of invincibility. Their presence night and day at all the intersections of Kinshasa's sprawling urban milieu has added to their "youth power" to such an extent that even the government considers them a force to reckon with.[17] During Mobutu's and especially Kabila's regime, whenever the opposition decided to stage ghost-town campaigns (*opérations ville morte*) or demonstrations, the government secretly bought Bashegue's neutrality for fear of what their active participation might entail.

Kuluna

The latest and most fearsome youth gang movement today is known as Kuluna.[18] It is responsible for a large number of the petty crimes, larcenies, and even murders committed daily in Kinshasa. Kuluna has become a byword for insecurity, crime, and havoc that even trumps references to armed soldiers or the police force. As the latest avatar in this long pedigree of youth culture, Kuluna is as much the result of Kinshasa's deep-rooted "crisis of masculinity" as it is linked to "Africa's first world war" that has wreaked havoc in Congo since 1997. The same patterns of sexual violence, violence against defenseless civilians, and looting that have become the hallmark of the Congolese ragtag lumpen militariat and their Rwandan acolytes and foes are now exhibited by Kuluneurs.

Like the Bashegue, Kuluneurs make up a fair proportion of Kinshasa's interstitial peer groups. They share a number of features with the Bashegue, including the age group to which they belong, their ubiquity in Kinshasa's streets, and their gang culture. Their delinquent activities—which run the gamut from shoplifting to drug consumption—also make the two groups nearly indistinguishable. Yet Bashegue and Kuluneurs could not be more different. Whereas the Bashegue belong to the streets and have developed an entrenched street culture, Kuluneurs enjoy a family safety net. And whereas Bashegue account for a sizable segment of Congo's informal sector and can be seen transporting heavy loads at the quays of Kinshasa's harbor (Beach Ngobila), washing cars, roaming the streets with their makeshift shoeshine equipment, and peddling assortments of Guangzhou items, Kuluneurs have veered off into criminal activities that in many ways reflect Kinshasa's urban trajectory from Kin-la-belle to Kin-la-poubelle.

In his study of Kuluna, Crispin Kabasa Yambeng (2006) provides the example of the Bofala gang, which cropped up in Kinshasa's commune of Ngaba in 2002. Among the many factors that drove these young people out of their homes and brought them together in the streets, addiction to martial arts figured prominently. In addition to judo and karate, they practice a hybrid wrestling form they dubbed *mukumbusu* (Lingala for "gorilla"), which Pype (2007: 261) has wittily described as a ruleless discipline reminiscent of the Bills' *bikumu* (discussed at the end of chapter 5). Whether through esoteric formulas and prayers that the leader of the gang, Cédric Makasi, had learned from his stint as an altar boy at the Saint-Laurent Parish (Kabasa Yambeng 2006: 25), through nkisi (power objects) worn on several parts of the body, or through the perennial kamô (Pype 2007: 261; see also chapter 5), the Kuluneurs' use of magic follows the same pattern found among Bills. And as with the Bills and movies of the American Far West, cinematic images from Arnold Schwarzenegger's *Terminator* movies and Jackie Chan's action-packed martial-arts stunts serve as "imaginary spaces" in Kuluneurs' quest for both modernity and masculinity (264).

Kuluneurs vie for territorial supremacy within tight-knit *écuries* (French for "stables") sporting names that are drawn from the global kaleidoscopic lexicon, including Zoulous (Zulus), Armée Rouge (Red Army), Brigades Rouges (Red Brigades), Moudjahidine (Mujahedeen) Soweto, Jamaïque (Jamaica), Dragons Forces, Anglais (English), Bana Chicago, or names that underscore their nihilism, such as Mbeli Mbeli (Knife), Boa ya Mayi (Water Boa), Moto Epela (Light Up the Fire), and Congo Ebeba (Let Congo Fall Apart). They operate in many of Kinshasa's communes, such as Kalamu,[19] Ngaba, Makala, Limété, Masina, Barumbu, Kasa-Vubu, Matété, and Kintambo, where they square off day and night over the control of strategic locales—busy street intersections, thoroughfares, university campuses, stadiums, market grounds, and bus stops. Armed with stones, broken bottles, and machetes that they sharpen on the street pavement as they advance in platoon formation, Kuluna écuries clash while residents cower in their homes and the police look the other way.

The bad reputation heaped upon Kuluna stems not just from what some have characterized as a "low-intensity urban insurgency."[20] After all, turf wars have been part of Kinois gangland culture since the time of the Bills. As long as gangs did not inflict collateral damage, residents and authorities tended to turn a blind eye. Enter Kuluna gangs, armed with machetes and knifes and targeting passersby and residents in orchestrated plundering raids. Consumption of a volatile mix of *supu na tolo* (a locally brewed hard liquor) and marijuana inures them to bloodshed. The pattern of some of their raids clearly shows a resurgence of the "economy of pillage" that the late Kabila had by and large managed to stamp out.

Yet the pattern also indicates a widening of the colonial gap between schooled and out-of-school youth. For example, in 2008, when Kuluna's weaponized violence reached a high watermark, many of their attacks targeted students. On Monday, November 24, 2008, they stormed the ISC (Institut Supérieur de Commerce) in the plush neighborhood of Gombe, ransacked the place, assaulted several students, and got away with some loot.[21] In Yolo and other places, they singled out graduation parties with the objective of terrorizing revelers and seizing cash, cell phones, cameras, watches, jewels, and other valuables in the panic that generally ensued. When ambushing an individual or small group of students, Kuluneurs often warn their victims with the formulaic menace, "Tosa obika, pamba te Kuluna" (Obey and live, or else Kuluna). Victims usually relinquish their valuables under the threat of a posse of scar-faced Kuluneurs high on drugs and itching to use their machetes and clubs. But sometimes Kuluneurs deliberately choose *nzela mukuse* (shortcut) and waste no time getting what they want. Without warning they strike devastating machete blows before proceeding to rob their helpless victims.[22]

Kinois students being notoriously impecunious, assaulting them may exact vengeance and vent Kuluna rage, but it hardly yields much booty. This may explain why street and market vendors have suffered from the Kuluna looting frenzy more than any other group. For example, in the commune of Ngaba, Kuluna violence accounted for nearly 80 percent of the 240 violent acts the police recorded there in July 2005. The majority of these acts fell under the rubric of robbery, pillage, and assault and battery and targeted a huge number of vendors (Kabasa Yambeng 2006: 30).

There is even evidence that points to female involvement in Kuluna, not only as ancillaries, lookouts, and receivers of stolen goods, but also as active participants in crimes hitherto committed only by males. In Selembao and in Kasa-Vubu, where an abandoned cemetery served as their bivouac, female Kuluneurs routinely raped men after abducting them at knifepoint with the help of male accomplices.[23] In Matété, the Bana Murah *écurie,* an exclusively female Kuluna gang, made headlines in September 2009 after some of its members went on a rampage and seriously wounded their opponents with machetes.

Kuluna's violent outbursts have also spilled over into the musical scene. Young Kuluneurs orbit around musical performances of major artists like flying termites swarming around a lit streetlight. They advertise their favorite artists' concerts by word of mouth, spreading the buzz across their respective townships. During concerts, they circle the scene in their self-appointed functions as bodyguards and gatekeepers, especially when those performances take place in their township.

In 1997, as Kabila's ragtag troops stormed into Kinshasa after a thousand-mile trek from the country's eastern border, the band Wenge Musica, which had stood throughout the decade as "the flagship of the fourth generation of Congolese popular dance music" (White 2008: 5), was beset by feuding that reached the boiling point by year's end. They finally split into two rival groups, Wenge Musica BCBG, led by J. B. M'Piana, and Werrason's Wenge Musica Maison Mère. The breakup also exposed ethnic fault lines as fans sided either with J. B. M'Piana (a Muluba from Kasai) or Werrason (a Mukongo). To retain their followings, the two band leaders tried to outdo each other not just within the realm of musical composition and performance but by enlisting the help of Kuluna gangs in Kinshasa's townships. Werrason, for example, called his retinue of Kuluneurs "Mazanka ya Nkoy" (Leopard's Claws), not only as a throwback to Mobutu's regime but as a way to signal the ferocity of his personal security detail (Pype 2007: 259).

The concerts of both artists then served as a dress rehearsal for the violence that Kuluneurs would later unleash in Kinshasa's streets. Bent on derailing the performance of a reviled artist, Kuluneurs would suddenly breach the concert venue and start pelting spectators with stones and bottles until the organizers had no choice but to interrupt the performance lest all hell break loose.

In a metonymic process that speaks volume about "youth power," the word Kuluna seems now to connote evil itself and is applied to a host of different actors to denote predatory and criminal activities. For instance, corrupt politicians and officials are commonly vilified as *Kuluna en cravatte* (white-collar Kuluna), as opposed to *Kuluna à machette* (machete-wielding Kuluna). Kinois have also heaped scorn on the state itself, which, they maintain, has mutated into *l'état-Kuluna* (the Kuluna state) or *l'état-voyou* (the thug state). In November 2011, after evidence built up that Joseph Kabila had rigged the presidential election to remain in power, both he and his supporters, on one hand, and the opposition at home and abroad, on the other, traded barbs using Kuluna as a (dis)qualifier. While the opposition denounced a *Kuluna électoral* (electoral hold-up), Kabila's surrogates branded Belgium's *Bana Congo*[24] the *diaspora Kuluna*.[25]

Just as the unclean or evil spirit that Jesus casts out (Matthew 12:43) comes back to haunt their hosts with a vengeance, so has Kuluna gained strength with every crackdown. In November 2013, reacting to popular pressure, the government tasked Attorney General Luzolo Bambi Lessa with the implementation of several "Likofi" (Iron Fist) and "Tolérance Zéro Kuluna" operations that dispatched dozens of Kuluneurs to Makala prison in Kinshasa and to Buluwo, Angenga, Muzenze, Osio, and Ekafela detention centers in far-flung rural areas.[26] Yet Kuluna remains as endemic and as alarming as ever, because of the authorities' inability to address the factors that underlie their reign of terror. Extreme poverty, educational neglect, and police collusion contribute to the violence Kuluna unleashes in the streets of Kinshasa.

Though they have not formed vigilante groups, Kinois have nonetheless taken matters into their own hands. In January 2011, in Quartier Barumbu, they zeroed in on a Kuluneur who had hit a vendor on the head with a bottle, robbing him and leaving him for dead before escaping to Brazzaville, across the Congo River. After returning to his stomping grounds in Barumbu, he was immediately spotted and grabbed around the waist by the victim himself. Congo Mikili, an amateur, investigative web-based network that has earned accolades from the Congolese digital diaspora for its *journalisme de proximité* (street reporting) and staunch opposition to Kabila's regime, caught the scene on camera. In its usual hands-off journalistic style, the network provided an open-mike platform for residents to vent their frustration with what they perceive as the authorities' apathy:

> [MOLOBI YA LIBOSO AZALI KOLOBA PO MIKONZI BA YOKA YE]: Biso toza ba jeunes. Tozo tanga, tozo luka na pasi. Bana boye, ake prison azongi, ake prison azongi. Tobandaka koboma bango biso moko.

> [BALOBI EBELE NA ELONGO]: Tokoboma ye mpenza!

> [MOLOBI YA LIBOSO]: Faut bazwaka bango, bamema bango na terrain moko, baboma bango en public. Po biloko oyo esila, toza 'susu na banzela ya koleka te.

> [MOLOBI YA MIBALE]: To kangi ndoki, to bandaka kotumba ye. Kuruneur aza pe lokola ndoki. Biso pe tolembi. Kaka ba Kuluna, Kuluna. Tolembi. Sikoyo ekomi système. Oza Kuruneur, tokangi yo, to tie yo pine, to tumbi yo, tokati kaka ata kokata yo.

> [FIRST WITNESS ADDRESSING THE AUTHORITIES]: We are the youth. We go to school; we're struggling to make ends meet. Kids like that: he goes to jail, he gets out; he goes to jail, he comes back. Let's start killing them ourselves.

> [SEVERAL WITNESSES IN UNISON]: We'll kill him for real!

> [SAME WITNESS]: They should take them to the stadium and execute them there in public. That's the only way it'll stop; we can't walk in the streets anymore.

> [ANOTHER WITNESS]: When we catch a witch, we set them alight. Kuluneur is just like a witch. We're sick and tired. Kuluna, Kuluna, always Kuluna. We're fed up. A new system is in place now. You are a Kuluneur, we catch you, we put a tire around you, we set you on fire, we chop you into pieces.

> (www.congomikili.org, "Qui vivra verra," reporting from Quartier Barumbu, January 2011)

One is left to wonder whether Kuluna, the last avatar of Kinois youth interstitiality, can be viewed as a quest for masculinity gone awry. How did the Bills' performativity and ritualization of violence beget such unadulterated and wanton violence? Is Degazin's filiation between Bills and Kuluneurs (see introduction) a mere flight of fancy or is it borne out in reality? "Like father, like son," Degazin's daughter wailed when she gathered that her father never disclosed that his own son was a Kuluna.[27]

Vrai Yankee?

In Kinshasa, one is always being lured down the path one has trod before. Degazin's son had followed in his father's footsteps, in a way. Did he know the extent of his father's rebel past or feel that his father had passed the torch to him? We have to wonder whether Degazin's failure to mention his own son when he came out in defense of the Kuluna was a way to vicariously relive the bygone era of his own youth through a youth movement that has strayed far from the roots of Billism.

Maybe Degazin is right. Maybe Billism is still alive and kicking in Kinshasa's streets. Still, the image of a cold-blooded, machete-wielding Kuluneur does not seem to qualify as one of the Bills' putative avatars. Although, as Degazin has hinted, the two movements share some common features and represent successive iterations of youth power, they could not be more different. Kuluneurs may have borrowed some tricks from the Bills' playbook, but they remain anti-Bills or faux Bills par excellence. The Kuluneurs are an offshoot in the long line of misfits who since the time of the Bills have walked the tightrope between culture and crime and forked off, down the road to perdition.

Billism or Yankeeism (kiyankee) resonates in postcolonial Kinois life and culture as a soundtrack, a beating pulse that echoes from the heart of the tropics through the wintry frost of northern cities. Recycled through its many avatars, kiyankee itself has morphed into a new paradigm that has become a yardstick against which all men in Kinshasa are measured. From the street kid to the popular artist and soccer player, to the journalist, entrepreneur, and politician, to the traffic police and uniformed soldier, and even to the gospel preacher (*pasteur*), all men in Kinshasa have claimed the mantle of the Yankee. One of them, now familiar to us, was General Mahele. Telling his story at the end of this book, a story largely undocumented, illustrates how Billism continues to suffuse Kinshasa with a make-or-break masculinity that may have become a one-fits-all category, cutting across even gender lines.

On May 16, 1997, as Laurent-Désiré Kabila's ADFL[28] troops and its Kadogo (child-soldier) frontliners breached the outskirts of Kinshasa after a thousand-mile trek across the country, a tragedy was unfolding in Camp Tshatshi, where the last of Mobutu's diehard presidential guard was holed up. The battle for Kinshasa was exactly what the Clinton administration feared. Hoping to avoid a bloodbath, Washington made a deal with General Mahele, Mobutu's army chief and defense minister: if Mahele would convince his troops not to put up a last-ditch struggle, then he would be guaranteed a major role in the post-Mobutu regime. Mahele ordered his troops to step aside.

As night quickly fell in the city and people hid in their homes, bracing for the showdown, gunshots could be heard in downtown streets. Rumors spread like wildfire that Camp Tshatshi's soldiers would not go quietly without putting up a fight. Their leader, Mobutu's own son "Saddam Hussein" (aka Kongolo Mobutu), had vowed to fight until the end, even though the "Leopard" (Mobutu) himself had precipitously left the city. By then, Mahele's secret dealing with the Americans and Kabila had become fodder for Kinshasa's radio trottoir, leading to rumors that Mahele had sided with the enemy and betrayed his own "father," as Bobi Ladawa, Mobutu's wife, is rumored to have exclaimed (Stearns 2011: 161).

General Donat Lieko Mahele stood six feet tall; proud and fearless, he belonged to a bygone era where to earn the ultimate badge of manhood boys singlehandedly tracked and killed wild beasts. After more than thirty years of an outstanding army career, he unapologetically adhered to the Congolese army's rallying cry of "Oyo ekoya eya!" (Whatever comes, let it come!). General Marcel Bopeya, whose student Mahele had been in Kitona in 1965 and with whom Mahele had developed a fond relationship over the years, remembered him as a *baroudeur,* a swashbuckler who relished combat and displayed uncanny sangfroid in the face of danger.

Mahele was born in 1941 in Leopoldville (today Kinshasa) and raised by an uncle. During his youth, he hustled as a street vendor, peddling peanuts in Kinshasa's bars (especially Kongo Bar). He grew up in the streets, Bopeya said, and he quickly learned *la débrouille* (how to fend for oneself), *la bagarre* (how to fight), and *la triche* (how to cheat; even how to cheat death). In Quartier Farwest (aka Mofewana), where Mahele came of age, people remember him not as one of the toughest guys, but as someone who had true grit. According to Bopeya, Mahele was no saint; nor was he the villain that some have portrayed him to be. He achieved great military feats throughout his career, especially during the Second Shaba War in March 1978, when, leading the 31st Brigade, he parachuted into Kolwezi and held the airport in spite of enemy fire until the arrival of French and Moroccan troops. In 1990, commanding the same brigade, he came to the aid of Hutu president Juvénal Habyarimana's regime and routed the Rwandan Patriotic Front troops. During the looting frenzy (*pillages*) that erupted in Kinshasa in 1991 and, again, in 1993, Mahele put an end to the havoc by patrolling the streets on foot and personally shooting soldiers caught looting. Yet, while reining in uniformed hotheads that wreaked havoc in Kinshasa's streets, he directed his own men to loot banks and car dealer lots, a scheme that partly contributed to his wealth.[29]

When word that Mobutu's last redoubt had mutinied reached Mahele at his residence, he was conducting meetings and readying the city for the "soft landing" the Americans had called for. Without hesitation, he hopped into his personal Jeep with only a small posse and rushed toward the eye of the storm. The gates of Camp Tshatshi had been flung open. Unhinged presidential guards, high on drugs, were shooting into the air. They motioned the vehicle to stop. Mahele ordered his driver to park the car outside the compound. He got out alone and walked straight into the lions' den.

Surely he could talk it out with the officers in charge and bring them back to reason, he must have thought. His cocksure act and sheriff-like swagger had paid off so many times in the past and gotten him out of peril. This time, however, he was met with a do-or-die mood that matched his own. He had but an ice cube's chance in hell of getting out of there alive. Camp Tshatshi soldiers were completely unnerved by what appeared to be the imminent end of a long regime during which they had ruled the roost throughout the country. Still more unyielding was "Saddam Hussein's" hatred of the man he believed had betrayed his father.

Shouts of "You have betrayed us!" preceded a shootout from which Mahele first emerged miraculously unscathed. One of his bodyguards who had returned fire was shot dead. Others escaped and hid in the nearby bushes while Mahele himself jumped back into the Jeep. Mutineers quickly cornered the vehicle and sprayed it with bullets. They looked inside, but Mahele was nowhere to be seen. They finally spotted him underneath the car, lying motionless. They manhandled him out of his hiding place and took him back inside the compound where, according to radio trottoir, "Saddam Hussein" shot him twice in the back of the head, execution style.

To be a Yankee has become coterminous with being an authentic, hard-boiled Kinois, a man who oozes confidence as he negotiates the treacherous maze of life in Kinshasa, proves his mettle without batting an eye, always finds ways to make things happen and ends meet, and talks his way out of trouble. Indeed, as Papa Wemba, Congo's musical icon and the king of *la sape* (high fashion; see Gondola 2010), reminded his listeners, kiyankee is not all brawn, but brains as well:

> Omeli, olangwe, obundisi bato okanisi okomi Yankee
> Yankee ezali te azala monene to muke
> Yankee ezali te azala molayi to mokuse
> Kasi ezali oyo ayebi komaitriser mokili
> vrai yankee azali eeh oyo azali na boule eeh
> vrai yankee azali eeh oyo azali mayele eeh
> vrai yankee azali eeh oyo azali responsable eeh
>
> You drink, get drunk, get in a fight and you think you're a Yankee
> Yankee doesn't mean you're big or small
> Yankee doesn't mean you're tall or short
> But it's the one knows how to handle the world
> A true Yankee is the sharp one
> A true Yankee is the smart one
> A true Yankee is the responsible one
>   ("Ba Yankee," Viva La Musica Nouvelle Écriture & Papa
>   Wemba, *Dans L* CD/album, 1998)

It would be remiss not to mention that on several occasions Kinois have been heard to marvel at a female money-changer or a market woman's resolve and resourcefulness by quipping, "Mère oyo aza Yankee" (This woman is a Yankee).

As we retrace the twists and turns it took for Yankee—a term that stemmed from Hollywood's romanticization of the American West—to be thrust into a one-size-fits-all category in the heart of the tropics, we are left to wonder whether this reflects the hypnotic power of the cowboy's silhouette, or Kinshasa's hubris, or its youth power, or all three at once. Nowhere but in Kinshasa has the liminal figure of the most famous (and wanted) of the West's denizens—the horse-riding, drifting gunslinger—registered such a visceral and enduring fascination. Bereft of the gear, the mount, the Colt 45, the breathtaking landscape, young Kinois nevertheless scout the streets of their tropical frontier, and, just like the legendary cowboy, they have it all—the slang, the swagger, and the sangfroid. They may not look the part, but at heart they remain committed to their own tropicalized ideal of the cowboy.

Glossary

Apollons: Bills who practice bodybuilding and martial arts
Bafakwa: Thieves
Bikumu: Ruleless soccer game
Bilayi: Head-butts
Billesse: Female Bill
Billing: Fight
Biyalo: Authority, power
Dur des durs: Toughest of the tough
Éboulement: Abducting or taking female hostages for the purpose of rape
Éboulementaire: Bill or Yankee who engages in éboulement
Ekila (pl. bikila): Dietary prohibitions and other prohibitions given by the kamô master
Epaka: Activity or event
Goza (Godias): Short for "Godzilla"; tough guy
Indiana: New gang recruit, usually very young
Indoubill: Bills' slang
Kamô: Magical rituals intended to increase physical strength
Kibill: Bill behavior and culture
Kintulu: Bodybuilding
Kiyankee: Yankee behavior and culture
Kolúka: To wander; term applied to girls who display a "rebellious" or "flirtatious" behavior
Masta (mista): From the English "mister"; friend or buddy
Mbembe: Dude
Modega: Shirt collar; Bills would raise their modega to mimic their cowboy heroes and indicate their rebellion to adult strictures
Mofewana (Fewe): Bills' stronghold in the Ngiri-Ngiri district of Kinshasa
Momie: Girl
Moselebende (moserebende): Charm designed to attract female attention and love
Mpomba: Originally used in precolonial Congo among Bobangi traders and ivory makers for "elder" as in mpombe e mboka (village elder), this term is currently used in Kinshasa's argot to mean "strong man"
Nkisi: Mixture applied to nzoloko during a kamô ritual
Nua: Marijuana
Nualair: Drug addict
Nzele (pl. banzele): Girl
Nzoloko: Scarifications performed on a subject as part of kamô
Petit mbongo: Young, sometimes prepubescent girl
Pomba: Strong man (*see* Mpomba)
Prévenue: Girl abducted and held by gang members

Sheriff: Older, charismatic Bill who exhibits both strength and sangfroid and usually intervenes to disrupt bad behaviors

Tétaire: Young girl

Te-terre: To coerce a girl to have sex; rape

Tournoi: Gang rape and sexual activities (similar to the *tournante* practiced in French gangland)

Yuma: Dupe or sucker

Zoumbel: Marijuana

Notes

Introduction

1. Kamô consisted of several bodily and mystical rituals which were intended to endow extraordinary physical abilities to Bills who underwent such ritual (see chapter 5).

2. Degazin (aka Jean Sumbuka Bigonda), personal interview, Kinshasa (Kauka), July 29, 2009.

3. There is some evidence to suggest that the Bill movement was not uniquely urban but spread from Kinshasa to its rural hinterland; see MacGaffey (1971: 223), who witnessed this fact in the Bas-Congo region.

4. Oliviero Dossio, "Le Gouvernement Muzito s'attaque au phénomène 'Kuluna' par de sévères sanctions contre les délinquants en cause," *Le Potentiel*, March 25, 2009.

5. To be sure, the explosion of feminist literature on gender, labor, and leisure in the 1980s made it virtually impossible for African historians writing in that period to sidestep the roles African women played in the late colonial period. Yet, the same spotlight that shone on women's roles also cast a pale of suspicion on scholars who struggled to establish what would materialize later as the field of men's studies. With no space yet, and certainly no theoretical framework at their disposal to think in terms of masculinity, many historians concerned themselves with disentangling and restoring women's agency and roles.

6. Let us not forget that when Connell and others first introduced and theorized the notion of hegemonic masculinity in the early 1980s, they listed heterosexuality as its most salient and important feature (see Whitehead 2002: 89).

7. In the realm of infrapolitics and in the popular imagination of the 1950s, évolués were handily dismissed as *mindele ndombe* (whites with black skins), which when used derogatorily conveyed the notion of inauthentic, inadequate, and histrionic masculinity.

8. It is hardly an accident that the bulk of the literature on African masculinities originates in South Africa (Nixon 1994; Fenwick 1996; Glaser 1998, 2000; Morrell 1998, 2001; Waetjen 2004), a country where similar strategies of dehumanization and emasculation were meted out to African men during apartheid.

9. Just as he came to represent for Kinshasa's youth the embodiment of manliness, Buffalo Bill—the Bills' eponymous hero—carved out for himself a place in American popular culture as the "paragon of American manhood" at a time when sweeping economic and social changes "converged to usher what historians now term a 'crisis of masculinity'"; see Martin (1996: 100).

1. "Big Men"

1. According to Congolese scholar Michel Lusamba Kibayu, the toponym Nshasa derives from the Teke verb *tsaya*, which conveys the idea of exchanging and trading; quoted in Piette (2011: 607); see also Tchebwa (2012: 28).

2. Vansina provides a much lower estimate of about 10,000 Tio around the Pool and fewer than 5,000 Bobangi, of which only half lived permanently there (Vansina 1973: 256). According to Stanley (1885: 369), Kintambo alone may have numbered at least 5,000 residents in 1882.

3. Already in the 1880s, even before the construction of the Matadi–Leopoldville Railroad, when loads from Europe still had to be carried by African porters, secondhand clothes were quickly overtaking other imports from Europe. Worn by chiefs and their retinues, they tended to draw sumptuary lines between the elite and the commoners (see Liebrechts 1889: 28; for neighboring Brazzaville, see Gondola 2010: 158).

4. One high-grade fermented beverage, known as *pombe,* was particularly sought after in Malebo Pool. It took expert and dedicated hands to concoct it from mixing some or all of the fermented alcohols from cassava, sugarcane, maize, millet, pineapple, and banana (Liebrechts 1889: 22).

5. This seems to have been a favored and lucrative way for polygamous headmen and lords to acquire more slaves, by falsely accusing some of their subjects or enticing one of their wives to sleep with whomever they wanted to trick into slavery.

6. Vansina (1973: 357) discusses an open conflict that erupted in the 1880s between two headmen, Opontaba and Ngandzio, the embers of which were still smoldering when he visited the area in 1963!

7. This must have happened fairly frequently because Tio traders were middlemen and would deliver to people on the coast (namely, Kongo and Zombo traders) ivory received from their upstream creditors. In effect, ivory represented a loan that the Tio had to repay in slaves, cloth, ironware, and European goods once the transaction took place with downstream partners. Given the multiplicity of actors involved (ivory hunters, wholesalers, porters, and buyers, among others), there were bound to be recurring disagreements and conflicts, not only over the methods of payment but also over the weight, number, nature, and quality of goods exchanged.

8. For example, in his analysis of Congolese urban music, Bob W. White (2008: 114) ties the splintering of popular bands to African lineage-based societies and so-called traditional segmentation.

9. Among the Tio residing in the Malebo Pool, Vansina (1973: 70–75) reports a similar division of bigger villages into quasi-autonomous wards, which could give the appearance of a collection of small villages.

10. Indoubill, the argot the Bills created in the 1950s, drew most of its vocabulary and syntax from Lingala, a lingua franca currently spoken in both Congos as well as some areas of Angola and the Central African Republic. Lingala derived from the nineteenth-century version of Bobangi, which came to be known as Mangala or Lingala ya Makanza and supplanted Swahili after World War I as Bobangi recruits joined the Force Publique (Public Force, the combined police and military force) in ever-increasing numbers (Sesep 1986).

11. For example, Theodore Roosevelt, who despised the Chinese for falling victims to Western imperialism, singled them out as a decadent and effeminate race and used their example to call on American young men to display their manliness and bear the burden of war on behalf of America's "virile vision of empire" (Bederman 1995: 193). The same racial emasculation was leveled at Africans as the French strove, in the aftermath of Algeria's takeover, to justify further expansion into the heart of the continent. One French colonial observer wrote in 1839, "Le noir me paraît être la *race femme* dans la famille humaine, comme le blanc est la race male. De même que la femme, le noir est privé des facultés politiques et scientifiques; il n'a jamais créé un grand état, il n'est point astronome, mathématicien, naturaliste. [. . .] Comme la femme il aime aussi avec passion la parure, la danse, le chant" (quoted in Hoffman 1973: 203). ("Blacks, it seems, are part of the female race in the human family just as whites are part of the male race. Just as women, Blacks lack scientific and political faculties. They have never created a large state; no astronomer, mathematician, and naturalist are to be found amongst them. [. . .] Just as women they love adornment, dancing, and singing.")

12. Gender partition, when it came to socioeconomic activities, could not be mistaken in most Congo Basin societies. Men and women were first defined by the kind of socioeconomic activities they undertook, with agriculture, for example, falling to women while men were responsible for hunting, trade, and some crafts, such as iron smelting.

2. A Colonial Cronos

1. "The dream of my life is to raise the populations under my custody. I eliminated tribal wars, ended invasions, expelled slave traders, put an end to the slave trade, prevented alcohol from poisoning the heart of Africa, went to war against cannibalism, against trials by ordeal, and against all customs which dishonor humanity. Now that pacification is over, and that initial impediments have been removed, I would like to attempt to raise my blacks, to raise them gradually to the level of our civilization, if at all possible."

2. Daye would later join Léon Degrelle's Rexist movement, notorious for its extreme nationalist, Catholic, and anti-Semitic ideology, to become one of its most vocal propagandists and a staunch collaborationist during World War II. Shortly before the end of the war, he fled to Spain, and then to Argentina, where he died in 1960. Both Degrelle and Daye may have influenced the work of their friend and fellow Rexist Hergé (the pen name of Georges Prosper Remi), the author of the now controversial *Tintin au Congo*.

3. Ivory from Congo was particularly prized and sought after because of its density, weight (there were reports of tusks weighing over 150 pounds!), and finer grain compared to Asian elephant tusks. After Leopold II took control of the ivory trade in what he considered his private domain, and accumulated substantial profits, the port of Antwerp in Belgium overtook London as the leading ivory market in the world, handling over half a million pounds of ivory (30,000 tusks) in 1897.

4. Some authors favor "Kinshasan" as an English equivalent for the French term "Kinois" (a resident of Kinshasa). Kinois is used throughout this book, rather than the vapid Kinshasan, both because Kinois has crossed over into virtually all the languages of Congo and because it remains loaded with meanings that go beyond just a sense of place or belonging.

5. Boma (or Mboma), wrote Stanley (1885: 97), "has a history, a cruel blood-curdling history, fraught with horror, and woe, and suffering. Inhumanity of man to man has been exemplified here for over two centuries by the pitiless persecution of black men, by sordid whites."

6. Translated and quoted in Gondola (1997a: 82).

7. The same hill was later used by Mobutu as the site of a monumental presidential palace, Mont-Ngaliema, that came to be associated with his regime.

8. In 1928, Kinshasa's main camp of workers (Leopoldville I) had a population of 21,500 men and only 5,000 women, among whom 358 were legally married; the majority had been illegally introduced into the city.

9. The term "employer" is used here euphemistically, since in the Belgian Congo the language and practice of work contracts between an African worker and a European employer defined the two parties as *indigène et maître civilisé* (native and civilized master), respectively; see Gondola (1997a: 85).

10. The French term *race*, a versatile word, is the equivalent of the same term in English. Yet it can also mean "tribe" or "tribal affiliation," as in the instance above.

11. The Force Publique was both a police and a military force in Congo from 1885 until independence in 1960.

12. From an estimated 37,054 legal residents in 1929, Leopoldville's population had dwindled to only 22,184 inhabitants by the end of 1933 (Gondola 1997a: 103).

13. In 1938, the "cordon sanitaire" ran in a long corridor of about 2,500 meters long and 300 meters wide between the two residential areas, covering roughly 80 hectares of thick bushes and small garden plots as far as the eye could see.

14. The cordon sanitaire did not originate with the Depression but surfaced with the creation of the European settlement itself. However, with the growth of the European urban complex, it had all but disappeared in many areas by the late 1920s, sending shivers down European residents' spines. Their lobbying efforts to have African workers' camps pushed farther back resulted in official debates in the late 1920s, as echoed in the 1928 *Rapport annuel sur l'activité de la colonie du Congo belge* (Annual activity report of the Belgian Congo), but no real decision would be implemented until the demographic hemorrhage of the 1930s.

15. The impetus to use the cordon sanitaire for gardening actually came from the municipal authorities themselves as early as 1920 as a way to boost the supply of fruit and vegetables for Kinshasa's growing population. Yet as a colonial report bemoaned (see Gondola 1997a: 63), African men claimed they were too exhausted after work and on Sundays to garden. Though this may well have been true, given their grueling work conditions and schedules, it hardly conceals the fact that they also perceived gardening as women's work.

16. "Comme quoi le cabaret est le parlement du peuple" (which goes to show that the cabaret is the people's parliament), Honoré de Balzac wrote in *Les Paysans* (quoted in Gondola 1999c: 39).

17. Within just a few years, the number of mixed-race children nearly doubled in Kinshasa, reaching 191 in 1934 (from 108 in 1932). Until World War II, the unwritten policy favored putting those children, whom one writer described as "nés d'une nuit de fièvre" (born out of a night of fever), in the care of missionary institutions, since the sight of a mixed-race child being reared by an African mother and their likely return to the rural community disquieted white residents' conscience; see Jadot (1927) and Vindevoghel (1938).

18. These buvettes also provided a space for interracial sexual encounters between white residents and Congolese free women (see Lauro 2009: 466).

19. The term *filles publiques* (public girls), a demeaning label attached to single women who saw in the city new opportunities to escape the burden of gender expectations, fell into disrepute by the late 1940s, to be replaced by *femmes libres* (free women), a testament to the power that women had gained in Kinshasa.

20. In Greek mythology, Cronos was the youngest of the Titans and the father of the gods and goddesses of Mount Olympus. He castrated his father with a sickle and later swallowed his own children to ward off the prophecy that he, too, would be deposed by one of his sons.

21. Before voicing their complaints about Congolese women in the popular music lyrics of the 1950s and 1960s (see Gondola 2003), Congolese men aired their grievances through formal letters sent to colonial administrators, starting in the 1930s. Therein lies not just *une crise du mariage* but also *une crise des masculinités*, as recently uncovered by Lauro (2011a).

22. Made out of an adult hippopotamus hide, the chicote (from the Portuguese word for whip) or *fimbo* (in Lingala) became shorthand for the brutal oppression under the rule of the Belgian colonizer. Its presence and use were so intertwined with Belgian colonization that one cannot think of a time when the chicote was not employed. Coquilhat mentioned its use as early as 1882, a few years before the Berlin Conference, and railed against the danger and absurdity of abolishing corporal punishment. Just as, in the expansion of the American West, gun apologists promoted the gun as an instrument of civilization, so did Belgian colonizers with the chicote. Banning the chicote, wrote Coquilhat, would "delay the elevation of Negroes toward civilization" (Coquilhat 1888: 101).

23. Colonial reports list Africans deserting their jobs as the most serious impediment to economic expansion. In 1929, for instance, employers reported 1,315 cases of desertion to the

municipal authorities, resulting in 1,054 fugitive workers being apprehended and tried in court (Gondola 1997a: 101).

24. Now almost extinct, at least in the Kinshasa area, the malebo is a type of palm tree that once proliferated in the area.

25. When traveling by boat, Congolese not only chafed under suffocating segregation rules (they had to find accommodation in the hold) but remained subject to the curfew. Journalist Camille Mwissa-Camus recounts a business journey he made up the Congo River in 1951: "at 6 pm, even on the boat, the curfew was enforced. Blacks had to go back to the hold and sleep while white people remained on the ship's deck, sipping a glass of wine, or beer, dancing" (quoted in Ryckmans 2010: 54). In Belgium, at the Brussels Expo 58 (also known as the Brussels 1958 World's Fair), the Congolese delegation took up its quarters at the CAPA (Centre d'Accueil du Personnel Africain), next to the Tervuren Museum. To their dismay, they were greeted by a curfew similar to the one that regimented their lives in the colonial townships. Assigned to the quarters was a Belgian officer who monitored their whereabouts day and night and enforced a strict curfew (Ryckmans 2010: 150).

26. Known in Congolese parlance under the Fanonian category of *mindele ndombe* (whites with black skins), évolués emerged as a vocal group of the African urban elite (clerks, medical assistants, male nurses, shopkeepers, accountants, teachers, and clergymen) who clamored for basic civil rights during and after World War II. Their fight gained a sounding board in the monthly magazine *La Voix du Congolais,* launched in January 1945.

27. Alphonse Marie Filip, "Relation entre Mulâtres et Noirs," *La Voix du Congolais,* January 1948, 76.

28. Belgian writer and anticolonial activist Oscar-Paul Gilbert coined *l'empire du silence* (the empire of silence) as the title of his scathing 1947 book on Belgian colonial society.

29. Jean Labrique, "Le Congo belge: Un exemple de paternalisme sans mauvaise conscience," *Le Monde,* January 7, 1959, 2. Labrique served as press secretary to Governor General Pétillon in the late 1950s. At the behest of the colonial government, he spearheaded the creation of several news outlets, including *Agence Belgo-Congolaise de Presse, Actualités Africaines,* and the controversial and ephemeral *Quinze,* which published several reports, including a long investigative report on the Bills' underworld in Kinshasa. As a result, *Quinze* was banned, and Labrique and his family were expelled from Congo.

30. "They thought of us as children," reminisced one informant. "When we went to the hospital, we were always given just one dosage to take home, never the whole prescription, 'because you never know, those Negroes (*nègres*) will take the whole prescription all at once, and that's too dangerous.' So, they had to guide our steps: 'come back tomorrow to get your next tablespoon.' Every morning we had to go to the clinic to get another tablespoon of cough syrup" (André Bailama, quoted in Ryckmans 2010: 53).

31. J. Vanhove, Ministère des Colonies, Première Direction Générale, Note pour Monsieur le Ministre, Bruxelles, February 25, 1948, AA AI (4743) II T. 4, Carte du Mérite Civique.

32. This number of 50,000 évolués in 1957 would double by the end of 1959 (Mutamba Makombo Kitatshima 1998: 53).

33. Applicants to the immatriculation status had to submit to a battery of intrusive investigations of their homes, had to secure recommendations from employers, friends, neighbors, and acquaintances, and had to sit through condescending if not downright sardonic interviews. "People came to your home," recalls Joseph Mabolia, "to see if you had chairs, if you had a bed, if you knew how to hold a fork, if your children wore shorts and shoes. . . . It was revolting" (quoted in Ryckmans 2010: 30).

34. Francis Monheim, who would later become Mobutu's confidante and biographer, collected several examples of European residents' sovereign contempt for the évolués, including

the following: "A Congolese decked out in his Sunday best sits down in a café and orders a cup of coffee and some croissants. The waitress brings the croissants in a plastic bag. 'You [*tu*] will get your coffee when you [*tu*] bring back an [empty] bottle'" (Monheim 1959: 36). During a visit in Thysville in 1946, Antoine-Roger Bolamba met a group of évolués who could no longer bear the sad plight of their incipient status. Many Europeans, they complained, uttered the term "évolués" with contempt and derision (Bolamba 2009: 46).

35. "Nous ne sommes plus vos macaques!" (We are no longer your monkeys!) Lumumba is reported to have ad-libbed in closing his fiery independence speech.

36. Évolués, who strove to comport themselves according to the European standard, were particularly aggrieved by the invective "Sale macaque!" (Filthy monkey!), for it not only suggested that they could only grotesquely ape Europeans but also obliterated any possibility of assimilation. Even when a white person simply wanted to get a black person's attention, recalls Damas Tshiautwa, he would yell "Macaque! Hé! Macaque! Viens un peu ici [Come over here]" (quoted in Ryckmans 2010: 84). "Sale macaque" was indeed the verbal equivalent of the dehumanizing chicote.

37. Excerpt from Monsignor Roelens's 1941 speech in Baudoinville for the fiftieth anniversary of his arrival in Congo; quoted in Mutamba Makombo Kitatshima (1998: 43).

3. Missionary Interventions

1. The reliance on Belgian missionaries to carry out the civilizing mission in Congo served several purposes, as Masandi has convincingly argued. Leopold II, it should be recalled, had embarked on the colonial venture amidst the indifference if not outright suspicion and opposition from a large segment of the Belgian populace. To mollify the public, he tapped into a religious (Catholic) vein, or what Masandi calls *enthousiasme religieux,* that ran deep in nineteenth-century Belgium (Masandi 1982: 36). Leopold II also used the strong missionary presence in the Congo Free State to shroud his colonial oeuvre in a philanthropic veil, so as to allay opposition from Britain and other European colonial powers.

2. In fact, "Protestant" and "foreign" were used interchangeably in Belgian colonial parlance, and crystallized fears of a fifth column working on behalf of foreign forces to infiltrate and ultimately wrest the Belgian Congo from its rightful proprietor. In 1934, for instance, colonial authorities wailed about rumors of an imminent arrival of Americans to take over the colony running amok in the colony, vaunting the American control as the end of taxation and forced labor; Service des Renseignements à Monsieur le Commissaire de Province, Léopoldville, April 11, 1934, AM GG 6965/208. Supposedly spread by perfidious and envious Protestant missionaries, these rumors came to a head during World War II (Markowitz 1973: 39). Belgians were particularly concerned with the Protestant missionaries' tendency to allow more freedom to their Congolese pupils and to promote local, independent churches. This, the Belgians objected, could spur nationalism and xenophobic sentiments among the natives.

3. The impetus for such policy came directly from Belgium, where twenty-three of the twenty-nine successive ministers of colonies, starting with Jules Renkin in 1908, belonged to the Parti Social Chrétien, which essentially served as the political wing of the Belgian Catholic church. This was also true for governors general, of which only three (out the ten governors who ruled the colony from 1908 to 1960) were not affiliated with the Catholic party; see tables provided by Markowitz (1973: 24 and 27).

4. One area where the alliance between church and state tore at the seam involved immatriculation (see chapter 2). Catholic missionaries defiantly resisted the colonial government's

injunction to have newly trained African priests, who qualified as de facto évolués, apply for the status of immatriculés.

5. Born in 1890, de la Kethulle was, next to Joseph Van Wing and Victor Roelens, the longest-serving Catholic prelate in colonial Kinshasa and certainly the one who had the most significant impact on the capital. He carried out his missionary work there from 1917 until 1954. Still fondly remembered in Congo as "Tata Raphaël" (Father Raphael), de la Kethulle singlehandedly promoted sports and educational activities and facilities in Kinshasa. When he died in Belgium in June 1956, before Congo gained its independence, Kinois clamored to have his body interred in Kinshasa the following month.

6. Stuart Hall (1997: 128) notes in a reprinted article that blacks have often used their bodies as cultural capital and "canvasses of representations." (This notion should be interpreted as a "defense mechanism," given that the black body has served both as a locale and a metaphor to demote Africans and define them as "primitive," without a body politic; see Spurr (1993).)

7. The creation of the Apostolic Vicariate of Congo, and the fact that it fell under the purview of the CICM, was the direct result of intense diplomatic negotiations between Leopold II's agents and the Vatican; see Tshimanga (2001: 81). By 1960, 16 of Leopoldville's 20 parishes were headed by Scheutists, and of the 130 priests active in the city, 88 belonged to the CICM; see *Léopoldville dans la tourmente* (Brussels: Procure des Pères de Scheut, 1959), 4–5.

8. On May 26, 1906, Leopold II signed a Concordat with the Vatican, which scholars consider to have greatly expanded Catholic missionary activities in the Congo and prompted new Catholic orders to settle in the colony. Among other things, the Concordat called for grants of land (up to 200 hectares per mission station) to be held in perpetuity and school subsidies to be awarded only to Belgian Catholic missions. Despite relentless petitioning, Protestant missions had to wait until 1948 to enjoy public monies for schooling. By then, Catholic missions owned seventeen times more land than did their Protestant counterparts.

9. One is reminded of Hergé's *Tintin au Congo* (see chapter 2), perhaps the most iconic propaganda tool of this approach, and a book that lulled generations into complacency and a sense of grandeur as to what little Belgium had accomplished in the heart of Africa. Hergé (the pen name of Georges Prosper Remi) credited missionaries with all the progress that unfolded in the colony. Whenever a school, hospital, or stone building appears in *Tintin au Congo,* a white-bearded missionary dressed in a cassock stands in the foreground, proudly displaying the wonders of modernity.

10. Most big corporations, even the powerful British firm HCB (Huileries du Congo Belge), granted Catholic missionaries exclusive control of education within their compounds. In 1931, the Protestants appealed to the Lever Brothers board in London to give them access to their compound, only to be told that "the directors were satisfied with the situation" and did not wish to be troubled any further about the matter (Markowitz 1973: 45).

11. As recently as the late 1980s, a noted Belgian historian could not refrain from resorting to the ignominious metaphor of blacks being like children in attempting to distinguish the history of Congo from that of Belgium: "Even when a child is weak, his history is indeed his own and not that of his parents who may have guided him. . . . For a long time, Congolese were reduced to obedience. Yet they have their own history, which is distinct from that of Belgium" (Stengers 2007: 193).

12. At home as well abroad, these theories trickled down and became popular through journalistic and literary condensations. In a widely quoted interview, Hergé eventually sought to exculpate himself for his most infamous work, *Tintin au Congo:* "All I knew about that country was what people told me at the time: 'Negroes are big children. It's a good thing we are there, etc.'" (Sadoul 1989: 74).

13. As Convents (2006: 65) rightly notes, propagandist objectives trumped commercial goals in the colonial authorities' reliance on Catholic missionaries and lack of interest in the development of a thriving private film industry. Private film entrepreneurs could not be fully trusted to carry out the colonial state's propagandist agenda. Indeed, whereas private entrepreneurs' paramount concern was entertainment and profit, missionaries never lost sight of the larger picture.

14. No other missionary film production rivals colonial missionary film production in the Belgian Congo. One of the reasons for this supremacy is the predominant role played by Catholic film organizations in Belgium. One Belgian missionary, Father Abel Brohée (1880–1947), had set the tone by describing cinema as "a school of paganism" and "immorality"; a "promoter of adultery," "greed," "evil passions," and "free love"; and an "auxiliary to socialism" (Biltereyst et al. 2012: 189). To counter the criminogenic influence of cinema, Brohée took command of the Office Catholique International du Cinéma (OCIC) and made Belgium the "international command-and-control center" of Catholic cinema (Trumpbour 2002: 213).

15. The general government also decided, in 1947, to fashion its film unit after the successful British Colonial Film Unit but still enlisted the assistance of Catholic missionaries who had created, a year earlier, a Centre Congolais d'Action Cinématographique Catholique and who ended up taking the lead on film production and projection for the "natives" (Ramirez and Rolot 1985: 24)

16. Abbé Cornil, who passed away in 2011 at the age of seventy-seven, arrived in Congo in 1949 as a secular priest, claiming to have spent nearly two years (1947–1948) studying film in Hollywood (Convents 2006: 89). Cornil churned out nearly eighty films within an eleven-year span, more than any of his competitors.

17. The film *L'Utilité de la couverture* found a favorable echo in *La Voix du Congolais,* with a prophylactic editorial penned by Antoine-Roger Bolamba urging the indigène (native) to use the blanket and providing a vade mecum detailing when it should be used, by whom, and why; see Antoine-Roger Bolamba, "Nécessité de la couverture," *La Voix du Congolais,* December 1947, 920–21.

18. Odile Goerg (2015: 71) has documented this predominant opinion in French and British West Africa as well.

19. Van Bever's depiction of addled African viewers bears a startling resemblance with the ways in which, in *Tintin au Congo,* Hergé describes a film projection in a makeshift village theater. Incensed by a scene in which the village's medicine man plots with a white miscreant, the audience goes berserk and starts to throw spears at the screen.

20. In remote villages, missionaries may have used Africans in this capacity, but in large urban areas, including Leopoldville (see Capelle 1947: 80), Europeans performed the task.

21. Disillusioned with missionaries' paternalistic attitudes, one Congolese évolué, speaking for many, commented that "Europeans, including the missionaries, put us all in the same sack. To them we are all ignorant children. When we dare to offer our opinion to a European, they say we are arrogant. Sometimes we ask ourselves, what good is the training that the missionaries have given us; has it totally failed?" (quoted in Markowitz 1973: 107).

22. As missionaries introduced African audiences to Western films, to palliate a growing lack of interest in educational films, there was certainly the idea that these films could deflect attention from the growing problems associated with the expansion of postwar Kinshasa. Although there were other pacifying outlets (sports, church choirs, social and leisure clubs), film, as Jean Renoir once claimed, was the future—and that future in the Belgian Congo, as in other places, included Westerns.

23. André Scohy, a major film producer who championed the production of cartoons for Africans, organized film projections in Leopoldville's townships to nearly 6,000 African

spectators, "standing up squeezed next to each other, huddled at street intersections, spilling over alleys, backed up inside private courtyards, crammed in front and behind the screen, sometimes even sitting on rooftops" (Convents 2006: 72).

24. By the late 1950s, township moviegoers had all but weaned themselves of watching the missionaries' educational movies and the Service de l'Information's vapid films. Documentaries such as *Le Cuir* (Leather), *La Houille* (Coal), *Aspects d'Andalousie* (Glimpses of Andalusia), *La Suisse en ski* (Skiing in Switzerland), and *La Culture des pommes de terre aux États-Unis* (Potato farming in the United States) left a sour taste in the mouths of avid cinephiles. As a result, they started to boycott such film projections. An informant, Nimy Mayidika Ngimbi, recounted how as a young boy he would get permission from his parents to go watch Cornil's educational films, accompanied by older cousins. Then, en route, the young boys would beg their older relatives to take them instead to a Western show. On their way home, after watching the documentary *La Chasse en AEF* (*Hunting in AEF*) in the township of Ngiri-Ngiri, some young viewers were overheard by the local administrator who had attended the projection: "Ezali malamu te!" (It's no good!) the youths complained (Lettre du Chef de zone A Croonenborghs à l'Administrateur de Territoire J. Cordy, AA GG 19175). Some angry moviegoers, as reported in Kintambo in 1957, even threw stones at the screen during one of Cornil's open-air shows (Convents 2006: 100).

25. As early as 1938, the publishers of the American *Film Daily Year Book* saw in Belgium's open and "quasi-unregulated" film market an opportunity to encourage more American distributors to stake their claims there. "There is no compulsory censorship in Belgium," wrote the authors. "When pictures are released, the distributor is not obliged by the law to submit his films to any institution for censorship" (quoted in Biltereyst et al. 2012: 187).

26. In a 1952 report sent to the governor general, Abbé Cornil railed against commercial cinema as "anti-educational" and called for "adapting, reorganizing, and keeping this powerful education tool [cinema] in safe hands" (Ramirez and Rolot 1985: 265). Yet despite relentless lobbying to push colonial policymakers to regulate the movie market and tip the playing field against commercial film promoters, missionaries could never maintain the kind of monopoly in film that they held in other areas.

27. Bent on recouping their losses, film entrepreneurs could always lobby the Censorship Commission to allow "unsuitable" films to proceed to theaters bereft of the incriminated scenes. Since the same movies were shown to the European audiences as well, and therefore could not be literally "cut," the projectionist would just cover the projector to prevent African spectators from viewing the censored scenes (personal conversation with Guido Convents). Scenes in which white male characters behaved improperly or scenes in which hapless white females fell prey to lewd and unknowable Indians or other non-whites were invariably expunged.

28. Lettre du Gouverneur Général du Congo Belge au Gouverneur de la Province de Léopoldville, October 19, 1954, AA GG 19175. Such was, for instance, the case of two documentaries, *Nurse Ademola* and *Private Officer Peter Thomas, R.A.F.*, produced by the British Colonial Film Unit in 1943 and shown to an African audience, in December 1944, at the Baptist Missionary Society temple in Leopoldville. One film shows the training of Nigerian nurse Ademola while the second features Sierra Leonean Peter Thomas, the first African pilot officer to join the RAF. After watching the movies in a room packed with up to 130 British West Africans, a Belgian officer deemed them unsuitable to a Congolese audience because they were likely to tarnish the prestige of Europeans ("porter atteinte au prestige de l'Européen"); "Lettre du Commissaire de District du Moyen Congo Robert le Bussy au Gouverneur de la Province de Léopoldville," December 18, 1944, AA GG 6965/208.

29. Paul Raymaekers, personal interview, Rhode Saint-Genèse (Belgium), May 11, 2012.

30. Instead of the 5 francs admission fee immatriculés would normally pay in their townships, they paid 15 francs, and sometimes 25 francs for special nights, to be admitted in European movie theaters.

31. Yet, until the mid-1930 when the first movie theater opened its door in Brazzaville, its denizens had to cross the river to neighboring Kinshasa to enjoy the new media (see Goerg 2015: 118).

32. Already in 1955, an obscure Patrice Lumumba had written a piece in *La Voix du Congolais* in which he alluded to the "deep wounds" (*blessures profondes*) and "lingering hatreds" (*haines vivaces*) caused by colonial color bar; see Patrice Lumumba, "A propos de l'accès des Congolais dans les établissements publics pour Européens," *La Voix du Congolais,* October 1955, 805.

33. Mobile projectors operated in Leopoldville as early as the beginning of the century, catering first to the European population. In 1916, Georges Fabre et Cie installed a mobile theater on Avenue Militaire and charged admission fees of 3 francs for Europeans, 1 franc for indigènes, and 50 centimes for children (Georges Fabre, Lettre à Monsieur le Gouverneur Général, Léopoldville, July 2, 1916, AA GG 16339). The following year, the year de la Kethulle arrived in Kinshasa, Mamadou Zane, a Sierra Leonean tailor with an established business in the cité indigène, obtained a license to operate a mobile projector "Pathé Kok," that he had ordered directly from Europe. He also acquired twenty-two films, including *Le Sacre de Napoléon, Les Chutes du Niagara, Match de boxe,* and *La Vie du mineur.* A two-man ad hoc censorship commission looked at the movies and granted him the license; see Octave Collet, Lettre à Monsieur le Gouverneur Général, Léopoldville, May 25, 1918, AA GG 19737.

34. In addition to full-length movies, some Greek and Lebanese private entrepreneurs would show a potpourri of trailers, usually for a smaller fee; email exchange with Paul Raymaekers, December 10, 2012.

35. Named after Belgian monarchs (Cinéforum Baudoin, Cinéforum Albert Ier, etc.), these film clubs were also patronized by white missionaries, colonial administrators, and other officials and had by far the most avant-garde film selection. For example, on November 13, 1958, Cinéforum Albert Ier screened in Kalina (European city) Kurosawa's *Rashomon,* winner of the 1950 Venice Biennale. In 1958, évolués created two other cinéforums, this time in Matété and Bandalungwa quartiers of the cité indigène.

36. According to Convents, the three main private film promoters—Van Heffen, Hourdebise, and Jacober—joined hands to cut costs. Together, they purchased 300 feature-length films and 700 short films and bonus materials in 1954. Films would make the rounds from one promoter to another, usually starting in Leopoldville (where they arrived from Europe in trunks) and then circulating to Elisabethville and other locales, with Europeans watching them first before they trickled down to the évolués and then to the less lucrative movie venues. It usually took a whole year for a film to cycle through this cinematic circuit; see A. Van Heffen, Lettre à Mr. Le Gouverneur Général P. Ryckmans, Léopoldville, May 13, 1938, AA GG 16339.

37. With a few exceptions, such as the popular *Tarzan's Secret Treasure* (1941), in which an African "tribe" kidnaps and manhandles a group of greedy white miscreants hell-bent on plundering the jungle's resources, Tarzan movies always cleared the Censorship Commission (see Convents 2006: 183).

38. In the Belgian Congo, colonial authorities never believed that film projections could give way to uprising and acts of insubordination, so they were less concerned with crowd and space control than Ambler (2001: 90) and Burns (2002a: 113) observed in northern Rhodesia, where African constables were sometimes called in to restore order after shows turned violent.

39. *Rapport sur l'administration du Congo belge 1953,* 154.

40. Joseph Davier, "La Compagnie Kitunga," *La Voix du Congolais,* August 1955, 676.

41. For colonial Zambia and Zimbabwe, see Ambler (2001) and Burns (2002a, 2002b).

42. "Tonto," which in Spanish stands for "stupid" or "fool," functions as one of the many elements in *The Lone Ranger* that emasculates and dehumanizes the Indian character.

43. Interestingly, several authors, including Art T. Burton, have identified Black Marshall Bass Reeves, who was born a slave in Arkansas, as the prototype that may have inspired the creators of *The Lone Ranger.* Bass Reeves, Burton (2006: 14) wrote, "is the closest real person to resemble the fictional Lone Ranger on the American western frontier of the nineteenth century."

44. Brennan (2005: 492) has shown that colonial Tanzania exhibited a similar pattern. In the 1930s, as educated Africans struggled to gain full access to film, just as educated Indians and Arabs did, they lobbied the colonial government to enforce censorship "by level of education instead of race" and requested that "educated natives of good character be granted special permits to see films passed for Non-natives only."

45. Michel Colin, "La Jeunesse et le cinéma," *La Voix du Congolais,* March 1959, 17.

46. As much as the Censorship Commission strove to police African cinematic experience, it also carefully weighed morality against profitability, knowing all too well that the future of colonial cinema hinged on the latter. As a result, it tried to accommodate film entrepreneurs who paid hefty rental fees, insurance, shipping, and reshipping and who could never recoup these expenses if projections of a particular film incurred a ban. Hence, in 1955, for instance, the Commission met eighty-four times to examine 881 films. It allowed 823 films to be shown in their entirety, cut 35, and banned only 23, including Jerry Hopper's *Pony Express* (*Le Triomphe de Buffalo Bill*), Gordon Douglass's *The Charge at Feather River* (*L'Attaque de la rivière rouge*), and Budd Boetticher's *Seminole* (see Convents 2006: 184).

47. Paul Kabaidi, personal interview, Brussels, April 4, 2006.

48. By 1944, the consumption of beer—which was selling in Kinshasa at the rate of 300,000 bottles of the "Primus" alone per month—increased to such an extent that alarmed Catholic missionaries lobbied the government to curb its production and reduce the number of licenses awarded to prospective buvette owners in Kinshasa (Comhaire-Sylvain 1950: 49).

49. A cinematic cultic dyad, invariably mentioned as contributing to the rise of the blousons noirs (who derived their names from wearing black leather jackets) and blamed for providing crime scripts to these interstitial youths, included 1953's *L'Équipée sauvage* (*The Wild One,* starring Marlon Brando) and 1955's *La Fureur de vivre* (*Rebel without a Cause,* which hit American theaters just a few weeks after James Dean's fatal car crash).

50. Stanley Corkin (2004) has shown that the rise of the film genre of Westerns corresponds in American history to a period of heightened imperial aspirations from the end of World War II to the Vietnam War. Given its cultural influence, this genre turned hegemonic and chauvinistic ideas into palatable concepts that resonated with the American public.

4. Tropical Cowboys

1. "Je viens!" is the caption on a poster used to advertise Buffalo Bill's Wild West show in France. Americanist Jane Tompkins (1992: 197) vividly captures its salvific air in the following description: "The poster consists of a huge buffalo galloping across the plains, and against the buffalo's hump, in the center of his hump, is a cutout circle that shows the head of Buffalo Bill, white-mustachioed and bearded now, in his famous hat, and beneath, in large red letters, are the words '*Je viens*' [I am coming]."

2. Youth the world over have taken the Western movie from the screen to the street. Several studies (Hair 2001, on Nigeria; Leslie 1963, on Dar es Salaam; Nixon 1994, on South Africa; Moorman 2001, on Angola) have briefly discussed the impact and legacy these movies had on youth cultures in colonial Africa. In comparison, what happened in Kinshasa starting in the 1950s defined culture, including masculinities, for several generations and decades to come.

3. Cowboys in the Southwest's cattle industry, known initially by the Spanish term *vaqueros,* then the English words "drovers" and "cowhands," did include a significant number of unsung black frontiersmen. For that reason, several historians believe that the word "cowboy" itself "derives from the fact that so many were African Americans—and whites would not dignify them with the term 'men'" (Katz 2005: 137). As late as 1865 "Africans whose livestock responsibilities were with cattle were referred to as 'cowboys' in plantations records. After 1865, whites associated with cattle industry referred to themselves as 'cattlemen' and "cowpunchers" to distinguish themselves from 'cowboys'" (Holloway 2005: 95).

4. One incident that has caused historians to dispute some of the events in "Buffalo Bill" Cody's frontier life was the killing of the Cheyenne warrior Yellow Hand in 1876 to avenge the death of General Custer at the Little Big Horn River. Not only did Cody claim to have killed Yellow Hand in retaliation for the death of Custer but he retrieved some evidence, including the obligatory scalp, and rushed to Fort Laramie to publicize the feat, even persuading a correspondent from the *New York Herald* to immediately file a press dispatch to appear in the newspaper of his hunting friend, James Gordon Bennett (the same man who, in 1869, had financed the famous Stanley Congo expedition to find Dr. Livingstone). A letter Cody wrote to his wife the day after the event describes the fight in self-aggrandizing fashion, alerting her that he plans to send Yellow Hand's war bonnet, shield, bridle, whip, weapons, and scalp to a family friend in Rochester to display in his store window (Carter 2000: 200). The *New York Herald* described the scene as follows: "The Indians turned savage . . . on Buffalo Bill and the little party at the outpost. The latter sprang from their horses and met the daring charge with a volley. Yellow Hand, a young Cheyenne brave, came foremost, singling Bill as a foeman worthy of his steel. Cody coolly knelt, and, taking deliberate aim, sent his bullet through the chief's leg and into his horse's head. Down went the two, and before his friends could reach him, a second shot from Bill's rifle laid the redskin low" (Carter 2000: 201).

5. "It is safe to say," writes Robert Carter, "that the western movie would not have been the same without Buffalo Bill." He is portrayed in at least twenty-seven movies, both silent and with sound, starting with the 1923 Universal Pictures serial *In the Days of Buffalo Bill* and John Ford's 1924 *The Iron Horse* (Carter 2000: 454). These films even include a French production, the 1974 *Touche pas à la femme blanche* (Don't touch the white woman). Shot in Les Halles, once described by Zola as *le ventre de Paris* (the belly of Paris), the movie boasts an impressive Franco-Italian cast, including actor Michel Piccoli (starring as Cody), Catherine Deneuve as *la femme blanche,* Philippe Noiret, Marcello Mastroianni, and Ugo Tognazzi.

6. The popularity of Edgar Rice Burroughs's *Tarzan of the Apes* (first published in 1912 and filmed in 1918) came about largely as a rejection of bourgeois civilization and a reappraisal of the "noble savage" trope that runs deeply through the literary tradition of the American West.

7. Out West, Cody's show gave birth to rodeo, another American spectacle concerned with the West, patriotism, and masculinity.

8. This is where we got the tradition of playing and singing national anthems at the beginning of entertainment events and ceremonies, from school graduations to the Super Bowl.

9. One of Cody's managers, Nate Salsbury, described Buffalo Bill's Wild West as "the grandest and most cosmopolitan Object Teacher ever projected by the exceptional experience and executive genius of man," a truthful and authentic representation of the battle between "civilization" and "savagery" (Kasson 2000: 252).

10. In his celebrated piece, "The Significance of the Frontier in American History," American historian Frederick Jackson Turner credited America's westward expansion for the American democratic spirit, which he claimed, "gained new strength each time it touched a new frontier" (Turner 1925).

11. Cody wrote to a friend: "I will have a hard time to get away from the show—but if I don't go—I will be forever damned by all—I must go—or lose my reputation. . . . America is in for it, and although my heart is not in this war—I must stand by America" (Carter 2000: 386).

12. E. Alexander Powell, "All Aboard for Cape Town!" *Outlook 99,* November 25, 1911, 728 (quoted in McCarthy 1977: 192).

13. Art Buchwald, "P.S. from Paris: It Happened in Brussels," *Sarasota Herald-Tribune,* August 6, 1958, 13. The show had to battle not just other attractions at the World's Fair, such as the popular Bolshoi Theater and the Moscow Circus, but Brussels's deplorable weather after their big tent had collapsed; see also Reineke (2009: 97–98).

14. As both amateur historian and U.S. president, Theodore Roosevelt contributed to the construction of a mythic West as much as his fellow mythologizers William F. Cody, Frederick Jackson Turner, Owen Wister, and Frederick Remington. In his writing, Roosevelt touted European expansion over the world's "waste space" as the "most striking feature" of the history of humanity (quoted in McVeigh 2007: 20).

15. KADOC–Scheut, Personal Files 643, de la Kethulle. Nicknamed by his pupils "Tata Raphaël," the Scheutist priest would later endear himself to many Congolese youths thanks to his indefatigable work to promote sports and other youth activities (including boy scouting) in Leopoldville.

16. The personal files given in note 15 acknowledge de la Kethulle's zeal for sporting activities and apathy for the ministry ("Beaucoup de zèle pour les oeuvres sportives, mais guère pour le ministère," September 1932).

17. The character Gavroche in Victor Hugo's *Les Misérables* is an urchin who speaks the slang of the streets and has even had to choose his name himself, having been cast into the streets by his unfeeling parents.

18. De la Kethulle's personal files at the KADOC contain a draft of this article (i.e., de la Kethulle 1922). The draft is dated April 17, 1920, and includes an appendix containing the names of twenty-four "bandits" grouped in five different bands; "Le Vagabondage à Kinshasa" (six pages), KADOC–Scheut, Personal Files 643, de la Kethulle.

19. A 1922 missionary report derided these young workers' sartorial fixation, attributing their labor instability to a desire to purchase a *costume blanc* (white suit). Once they had acquired the attire, they returned to their villages to dazzle their peers; *Rapport sur l'Ecole primaire de la Mission de Kinshasa,* KADOC–Scheut, O/II/a/9/5.

20. In Dar es Salaam, Andrew Burton describes a similar pattern in which youngsters were leaving school after Standard VI (age eleven). Too young to jockey for jobs, a police report noted, they found themselves "thrown on the streets . . . and for three or four years they are at a loose end with nothing to do but learn the 'tricks of the trade'" (Burton 2001: 213).

21. "Lettre de l'Administrateur de Territoire, Chef du Service de la Population Noire à Monsieur le Commissaire de District du Moyen-Congo," Léopoldville, January 28, 1949, AA GG 19137.

22. Antoine-Roger Bolamba, "La Situation scolaire à Léopoldville," *La Voix du Congolais,* June 1952, 329. In Dar es Salaam where gang activities (including "cowboy" gangs) proliferated in the postwar period, Burton (2005: 198) found for the same year that three-quarters of children received no education.

23. G. L., "Un An à Léopoldville: Le Problème de la jeunesse," *Essor du Congo,* February 10, 1956, 1.

24. Burton (2005: 176) identified in Dar es Salaam, as early as 1931, youth gangs known in Swahili as *kompania ya sinzia*, a name that refers to their methods of operation: they stole, snatched, and pickpocketed while some of their accomplices distracted or harassed the victim.

25. *Kitunga* is a Swahili term for "basket," the kind that women carry, oftentimes on the head, for shopping and other errands, pointing to markets as the initial sites where Kompani Kitunga first operated and gained notoriety.

26. Nganga nkisi is a polysemic Lingala term that usually connotes an ability to heal both body and mind. Hence "tradi-practitioner" or "traditional healer" would be the most common translations. Yet the term can also mean "magician" or "occultist," and it was in these capacities that KK youths consulted them.

27. The years of World War II had witnessed the proliferation in Leopoldville of love potions (*filtres d'amour*) and charms (some called *ndoki*) meant to protect the natives against, and neutralize the authority and actions of, colonial officials. A time of deep-seated anxiety and weariness from an "invisible" war that nonetheless exacted increasing amounts of labor and resources from the native population, the war was also fraught with rumors, fears, and hopes. One particular rumor, spread by some Leopoldville Senegalese residents, predicted the end of the world in 1942, with the arrival of a new "Bula Matari" (Breaker of Rocks) in the Congo—none other than Adolf Hitler; AA GG 18167.

28. Joseph Davier, "La Compagnie Kitunga," *La Voix du Congolais*, August 1955, 677.

29. In fact, Eugène N'Djoku investigated Kompani Kitunga in 1951, relying mostly on information provided to him by a certain "Boileau," and submitted a piece to *La Voix du Congolais* in 1951. The article, however, did not come out in print until 1953, at a time when KK activities had abated somewhat; lettre de J. Cordy, l'Administrateur de Territoire, Chef du Service de la Population Noire au Directeur du Service des AIMO, Léopoldville, April 10, 1954, AA GG 17665.

30. The source of the list is Archives de la Province de Léopoldville, quoted in Babillon (1957: 126–27). The development of quartiers is described in some detail in the text.

31. Just as Marcel Mauss articulated, in his influential study of gift giving, the gift as a "total prestation" intended to create reciprocity and a social bond, so KK youths used their ability to mobilize gifts to establish a form of clientelism across townships (see Mauss 1924).

32. Sesep (1986) has published the most exhaustive study of Indoubill to date. Derived from Lingala, Kinshasa's lingua franca, Indoubill appropriated and diverted several French, Kikongo, and English words to create a hybrid, protean, and esoteric vernacular that Kinshasa's mainstream population long regarded as the "Lingala ya bayankee" (Sesep 1986; Nicolaï 2000: 194; Kießling and Mous 2004). As of late, however, Lingala and Indoubill form a popular diglossic pair in Kinshasa as well as in the Congolese diaspora. Goyvaerts (1988: 232) has even uncovered in Bukavu (eastern Congo) a variant of Indoubill that uses Swahili (not Lingala) as its linguistic substrate.

33. G. L., "Un An à Léopoldville," 1.

34. This concurrent use of the "customary" name and the "cowboy" moniker is taken as an indication that the early 1950s served as an incubation period for the Bills. Starting in the late 1950s, no Bill worth his salt would ever have allowed any name but his moniker to be known and used.

35. *Rapport sur l'administration de la colonie du Congo belge*, 1953, 154. These groups seemed to have been short-lived, since the following year's report noted their gradual eradication as a result of a two-pronged action that combined police monitoring, on the one hand, and fewer screenings of cowboy movies, on the other; *Rapport*, 1954, 154.

36. Although the focus here is on "colonial" cowboys, it might be worth mentioning that the 1960s so-called Spaghetti Westerns, especially Eastwood's universally celebrated trilogy

(*A Fistful of Dollars,* 1964; *For a Few Dollars More,* 1965; and *The Good, the Bad and the Ugly,* 1966), spawned their own "cowboy youths." In early 1970s Antananarivo, for example, a youth organization called Zwam (Zatovo Western Amical Malagasy), which recruited its members among descendants of slaves, dressed for duress in cowboy style to champion justice and fight state discrimination (Sharp 2002).

37. African American troops disembarked in Matadi in 1942 but had to be immediately reassigned after white residents and the Belgian government vehemently objected to their being stationed there. Captain James V. Harding, who was white but nonetheless empathized with his aggrieved men, wrote complainingly, "There are no places where our [colored] troops may go to be served food, or drink, in contrast to the freedom which is enjoyed by our white troops" (quoted in McGuire 1993: 228).

38. See Camille Mwissa-Camus and Claude Maféma, "La Grande Plaie de tous les temps: Incursion au fief des 'K.K.,'" *Croix du Congo* 44, November 3, 1957, 5.

39. When Western films finally saturated Leopoldville's makeshift screens in the late 1940s, so did a host of other American commodities inundate the city, including secondhand clothes, some of which came from U.S. army surplus suppliers. Referring to the role Congo played as a regional hub and entrepôt for secondhand clothes imported from the United States and Europe, then smuggled across the border to northern Rhodesia, a British district commissioner wrote, "A journey down the Luapula Valley is like paying a visit to a camp of American Armed forces" (Hansen 2000: 61 and 66).

40. The presence of the American troops in Leopoldville may also have dispelled widespread rumors of an imminent *fin du monde* (end of the world) with the arrival of Hitler and the Germans in Congo (see note 27).

41. Père Buffalo (aka Jozef de Laet), personal interview, Sint Pieters-Leeuw, Belgium, April 3, 2006.

42. Chege (aka Makenge Baudoin), personal interview, Kinshasa (Kintambo-Chicago), July 10, 2005.

43. Zanga Zanga (aka Zanga Mabueta Honoré), personal interview, Kinshasa (Kintambo), April 1, 2009.

44. The process by which Yankees or Bills abducted and raped girls was encapsulated in the untranslatable term "éboulement"; someone who engaged in these activities was an éboulementaire. See chapter 6 for more detail.

45. Papa Fantomas, personal interview, Kinshasa (Kasa-Vubu), July 10, 2005.

46. For more on Néron and Petit Moloch, see chapter 6.

47. Vieux Néron (aka Katshaya Kopombo Joseph) and Petit Moloch (aka Abraham Koko Yawadio), personal interview, Kinshasa (Ngiri-Ngiri-Mofewana), July 9, 2005.

48. Vieux Caïman (aka Kibakila Zamuani Pierre), personal interview, Kinshasa (Lingwala-Paka Zuma), April 16, 2009.

49. Paul Kabaidi, personal interview, Brussels, Belgium, April 4, 2006.

50. In a section devoted to "le phénomène Bill," Congolese musicologist Manda Tchebwa makes no attempt to distinguish between Yankees and Bills. His dichotomy contrasts two types of Bills: "Bill agressif (bandit) et Bill moderé (évolué) [*sic*]," the former group including a few éboulementaires. He actually never uses the term "Yankee" in his narrative (Tchebwa 1996: 128). Neither does historian Kolonga Molei in his well-documented article (see Kolonga Molei 1977). Graeme Ewens (Franco's biographer), however, does differentiate between the two but makes several gross anachronisms. Dating the movement to the 1950s, he describes Yankees as youths who "affected the 1940s gangster fashions of pegged trousers and crisp shirt," following cowboy fashion, while Bills (combining the influence of cowboys and Indians and popular Asian movies) "posed around on their mopeds and scooters, riding recklessly and pulling all

kind of tricks" (Ewens 1994: 50–51). Ewens is right, however, in defining the Yankee dandies (whom he wrongly places in the 1950s) as the early forerunners of the Sapeurs (see chapter 8) of the 1980s and onwards.

51. Burlan (aka Nseki Kiubi Philippe), personal interview, Kinshasa (Ngiri-Ngiri-Mofewana), July 16, 2007.

52. Roitelet (aka Moniania Augustin), personal interview, Brazzaville (Centre Culturel Français), August 7, 2006.

53. *Goza* is short for Godzilla, implying brute force and invincibility. A Goza often reigned supreme in his township, unchallenged and universally respected and feared.

54. We owe to Jane Tompkins the most tantalizing evocation of manhood and silence in Western movies. In her analysis, silence seals the male's body, renders it hermetic, and allows it "to attain the solidity and self-containment of an object," whereas speech implies vulnerability, breach of its integrity, openness, and the risk of exposing the male's interiority (Tompkins 1992: 56). Although verbal shenanigans and contests of verbal wit remained central to Billism and even gave way to a new vernacular, Indoubill, Bills seem to have also taken their cue from the laconic heroes of Western movies and their fetishization of masculine restraint and apparent detachment.

55. "Vrai premier Yankee, nani," *Esprit de la Jeunesse* 14, 1964, 4.

5. Performing Masculinities

1. In the face of mounting local and international pressure to recognize impunity as the most significant factor contributing to rape, the Congolese parliament passed a far-reaching law on July 20, 2006, that defines rape as a crime against humanity. According to the new law, rape is no longer restricted to vaginal penetration with a sexual organ but results from the forced use of any object to penetrate, even superficially, any part of a female or male body. In addition, the law defines sex with a minor (under age eighteen) as statutory rape even when mutual consent could be established. The penalty can also double when the perpetrator is a public official, it is a case of gang rape, the act involves a weapon, or the victim is held captive. Yet the low number of convictions limits the law's impact in curbing rape. For example, in 2008 only 27 soldiers faced prosecution for rape in the Kivu provinces even though the UN registered 7,703 new cases of rape there in the same year (Human Rights Watch 2009: 6).

2. In addition to countless press articles and media reports, two projects have had a particular impact: Lisa Jackson's documentary *The Greatest Silence: Rape in the Congo,* which premiered in Kinshasa's National Assembly on December 12, 2008, under the title *Un Silence pesant: Le Viol en République Démocratique du Congo,* and the 2009 Pulitzer Prize drama winner *Ruined,* by African American playwright Lynn Nottage.

3. All informants had a clear idea of what rape meant back then, although, as suggested earlier, their understanding of rape may also have been refracted through media treatment of the ongoing sexual violence in eastern Congo. In any case, the use of Indoubill terms such as *éboulement* and *te-terre* (see chapter 6) points to local knowledge about rape.

4. Because rape (and sex for that matter) still remains a taboo in Congolese culture, the topic was not broached with most informants. For instance, Roy, the main female informant, felt so squeamish about dredging up her "sinful" past (she had become a born-again Christian), that questions about éboulement (rape) were met with an awkward silence.

5. Roitelet (aka Augustin Moniania), personal interview, Brazzaville (Centre Culturel Français), August 7, 2006.

6. Paul Kabaidi, personal interview, Brussels, Belgium, April 4, 2006.

7. Emery, "Qu'est-ce qui se passe dans le quartier Far-West?" *Esprit de la Jeunesse* 1, 1962, 4.

8. Jean Depara was born in Kbokiolo, Angola, in 1928. In 1951, he moved to Leopoldville where he first opened a makeshift shop as a shoe, watch, camera, and bicycle repair. He then picked up the profitable business of photography and set up a studio on Rue Kato, in the commune of Kinshasa. In addition to his interest in the city's nightlife—which made him the favored photograph of musicians such as Franco—he also captured several Bills on still black-and-white pictures (Martin Saint Leon and Pivin 2010).

9. In contrast to the recent Hollywood-driven trends, femininity in 1950s Kinshasa was defined by extra layers and standards of modesty rather than by low-cut blouses and bold statements.

10. The word *kamô* may have originated from the French *canon* (gun, cannon), which the Belgians fired in Kinshasa every July 21 in celebration of their national day. Another term for kamô was bilayi, which, depending on the context, could also mean head-butt.

11. On July 23, 1932, the general government passed a decree authorizing Congolese natives to consume alcohol sold in bars operated by "colored people" (*personnes de couleur*). However, unless they were immatriculés (registered) or holders of the Carte du Mérite Civique, they were not allowed to drink wine until the April 18, 1955, decree. Congolese across the river, in neighboring French Congo, faced no such restrictions (Gondola 1997a: 256).

12. Fantômas (aka Mayoyo Gracia), personal interview, Kinshasa (Kasa-Vubu), July 10, 2005.

13. Poison (aka Jean-Christian Matabul), personal interview, Kinshasa (Lemba), July 23, 2009.

14. Degazin claimed that close to fifty "clients" would visit his practice in Saint-Jean (now Lingwala) on any given day; Degazin (aka Jean Sumbuka Bigonda), personal interview, Kinshasa (Kauka), February 29, 2009.

15. Degazin (aka Jean Sumbuka Bigonda), personal interview, Kinshasa (Kauka), February 29, 2009.

16. Jean-Jacques Kande started a career as a journalist in 1950, and it was in that capacity that he befriended Mobutu, who was an aspiring journalist before joining the army and politics. Kande made a name for himself by writing a controversial article on the Bills after a thorough investigation in their underworld. He went on to become Mobutu's trusted collaborator and his first minister of information in 1968.

17. Bomina Nsoni served as Congo's ambassador to Gabon and the Organization of African Unity (OAU). He ended his diplomatic career after a short-lived appointment as Congo's ambassador to the UN in 1997.

18. Paul Kabaidi served as governor of Kinshasa for most of the 1970s. An important figure in Kinshasa's political scene, he singlehandedly brought many Bills into Mobutu regime through the CVR (Corps des Volontaires de la République) that he helped establish in 1967.

19. All cut kamô except Vieux Caïman (aka Kibakila Zamuani Pierre), Lingwala's caïd (tough guy).

20. Hugor Bomina Nsoni, personal interview, Kinshasa, August 2, 2009.

21. The few Billesses or cowgirls, who made up some of the gangs also rely on kamô for the same reasons as boys. Roy (aka Thérèse Muyaka) was strong, she told me, to the point of delivering lethal head-butts (bilayi) even to male opponents. Jane Russell was Sans Loi's hired gun and could kick anybody's ass thanks to her powerful kamô (Bissot 2009 [1958]: 13).

22. The term "Aufheben" was used by Hegel to explain his dialectic, the process by which a thesis and antithesis are at once negated and preserved, cancelled and transcended within a synthesis.

23. Chege (aka Baudoin Makenge), personal interview, Kinshasa (Kintambo-Chicago), July 10, 2005.

24. Fantômas (aka Mayoyo Gracia), personal interview, Kinshasa (Kasa-Vubu), July 10, 2005; see also Tchebwa (1996: 124). Of course, biblical narratives had sufficiently suffused the Bills' community to lead some to such borrowing (see, e.g., Matthew 21:19). After all, it was under the auspices of Belgian missionaries that young people were first exposed to the films that largely contributed to the emergence of the Bill movement.

25. Bourdieu (1998: 78) argues that some forms of "courage" found among youth gangs, but also typical bravados, acts of derring-do that lead boys and men to "defy danger," are paradoxically rooted in fear. Because manhood operates within a context of homosociality, Bourdieu contends, more than anything else men fear to *perdre la face* (lose face) before "buddies" or "peers" and to be relegated to the category of *faibles* (feeble-minded) in the company of wimps, sissies, and fags.

26. Poison (aka Jean-Christian Matabul), personal interview, Kinshasa (Lemba), July 23, 2009.

27. Sylvain Eboma (Kutino Sylvain Miranda), personal interview, Kinshasa (Barumbu), June 3, 2009.

28. A few informants denied any power to kamô. Atenda, for instance, went to great lengths to explain that kamô had purely psychological effects, much like the effect that a placebo would have on some patients, and also that many just faked it; Jacques Atenda Mongebe Omwango, personal interview, Kinshasa (Gombe), May 27, 2009.

29. "Les Problèmes de jeunesse" (1960: 11).

30. I am grateful to Paul Raymaekers for allowing me to purchase a copy of the Bissot Report, which along with other rare documents are sold at his foundation in Rhode-Saint-Genèse, outside of Brussels.

31. Such was the fear of incurring the wrath of the colonial administration that, after undertaking a similar investigation, Paul Raymaekers published in 1959 a series of articles on juvenile drug use in Kinshasa under a Congolese pseudonym (see Edouard Motuli, "Une Partie de la jeunesse congolaise est-elle vraiment condamnée?," *Présence Congolaise*, April 27, 1959). According to his conclusions, half of all young male people (whether they were schooled or on the streets) smoked marijuana.

32. By 1956, colonial repression had eradicated Les Cowboys du Farwest. Some were deported back to their villages, while others were whisked away into the newly created juvenile detention wards of Madimba in the Lower Congo.

33. Like marijuana consumers in the United States, Bills had to be "creative" to conceal their use of zoumbel. The American Office of National Drug Control Policy has compiled a lexicon of terms for marijuana that includes hundreds of variations, from "Acapulco Red" to "Zacatecas Purple." "Are you anywhere?" is a code phrase for "Do you smoke marijuana?" with variants such as to "blow a stick," "blow one's roof," "blast a joint," "fire it up," and "get the wind." Similarly, Bills created a slew of new terms to conceal drug activities from adults and authorities. Raymaekers (1963: 299) has identified at least 75 such terms—for example, *zoumbel, nua, boul, likeke,* and *lititi.* This creative process could come about as follows: "Sometimes, we just sat together and discussed how people started to understand what *nua* meant. Let's make it *diato* from now on. Then we all adopted *diato.* We constantly changed those terms"; Petit Moloch (aka Abraham Koko Yawadio), personal interview, Kinshasa (Ngiri Ngiri / Mofewana), July 16, 2007.

34. Jean-Jacques Kande, personal interview, Kinshasa (Matongé), June 4, 2009. Colonial authorities arrested Kande in his office and banned *Quinze*. After his release from the Ndolo prison, Kande recidivated with an article exposing drug use among prisoners.

35. *Cannabis indica* was smuggled into Kinshasa in fishermen's canoes from Brazzaville and the Upper Congo region. The market for marijuana seems to have increased around 1959, prompting some local farmers to grow it in cassava (or manioc) plots (Raymaekers 1960: 18; 1963: 300). Marijuana consumption in the precolonial period remained negligible, from what anecdotal evidence suggests. For example, Baptist Missionary Society missionary John S. Weeks (1909: 123), who lived fifteen years among the Bangala, noted the marginal use of hemp (called *mungulu*), the Bangala preferring to smoke tobacco (*makaya*).

36. See chapter 4, note 34, on the early concurrent use of the "customary" name and the "cowboy" moniker. On the other side of the Atlantic, one young American vindicated Kinshasa's claim to cosmopolitanism: an active gang member who grew up in Harlem watching the Bills' favorite show, *The Lone Ranger,* he took on the name Kwando Kinshasa. A former Black Panther, Kinshasa went on to earn a doctoral degree in sociology from New York University and now chairs the African American Studies Department at a City University of New York campus.

37. *Mivais* or *mivé* comes from the French *mauvais* (bad).

38. Buck-John le Grand, "Camp Luka Leo II," *La Voix de Mangembo,* July 12–13, 1964, 4.

39. The term "Yuma" originated from Delmer Daves's 1957 movie *3:10 to Yuma* (starring Glenn Ford and Van Heflin), which depicts a battle of wills between a vicious outlaw, Ben Wade, and a struggling yet plucky rancher, Dan Evans. After Wade and his outfit rob a stagecoach and kill one of its drivers, Evans leads the marshal to his capture and accepts a secret mission to escort Wade to Contention City to await the 3:10 train to Yuma. Although the movie never shows the city of Yuma, it alludes to it as a forlorn place, a place where Wade will meet his fate in court and in jail. Young viewers may have associated Yuma with being naïve and cowardly for several reasons, including the presence of a slew of craven characters throughout the movie. Wade's last line, as Evans wonders why he has deliberately jumped into the baggage car bound for Yuma, may have solidified the notion of the city of Yuma as an emblem of naïveté, weakness, and effeminacy in moviegoers' minds. "Why did you do it?" presses Evans. "I broke out of Yuma before," replies Wade coolly.

40. Bills created their own informal geography of Kinshasa's townships. Kintambo, for example, was divided in three different sectors, named Assassin, Chicago, and Lumière.

41. Durango (aka François Matouéni), personal interview, Kinshasa (Kintambo), April 7, 2009.

42. Sylvain Eboma (Kutino Sylvain Miranda), personal interview, Kinshasa (Barumbu), June 3, 2009.

43. Most games that pitted Bill teams against each other ended in what they dubbed bikumu. On Sunday morning, while other children went to church, Bills converged on their usual makeshift fields to play soccer, sometimes for more than four hours straight. Shortly before noon, the referee would leave the field, which was the boys' cue for an all-out, ruleless match in which street fighting skills mattered as much as (if not more than) soccer techniques. Bikumu allowed Bills to settle scores while honing their fighting skills.

44. Jacques Atenda Mongebe Omwango, personal interview, Kinshasa (Gombe), May 27, 2009.

45. See chapter 4, the section "Yankee versus Bill: The Battle That Was Never Fought," for the wide range of opinion on the distinction between or congruence of the terms Yankee and Bill.

46. Jean-François Muteba Kalombo, personal interview, Kinshasa (Lemba), July 23, 2009.

6. Protectors and Predators

1. I am grateful to Jan Vansina for his willingness to discuss this topic and for suggesting that different modalities of rape could be identified in precolonial Central Africa.

2. In the French Ancien Régime, notes Vigarello (1998: 61), popular usage merged *vol* (robbery) and *viol* (rape) in a deliberate semantic confusion through the single word *rapt*. To "rapt" a woman (that is, to carry her away by force) and to rape her were one and the same.

3. According to 2009 estimates, more than 200,000 women and girls had been raped, and sometimes sexually mutilated, since the beginning of the war in 1997. Many of these women contracted HIV/AIDS, prompting several observers and human rights activists to frame the war in Congo in terms not only of genocide but of gendercide as well (see Kristof and WuDunn 2009: 85).

4. Amandine Lauro points to a whole genre of hygienic compendia and travelogues that endeavored to link colonists' sexual incontinence to factors ranging from Congo's tropical climate to their proverbial loneliness to sheer boredom. At the end of the nineteenth century, *congolite* (Congolitis) came to designate the physiological and psychosomatic disorder that gripped most white men who ventured out to Congo (Lauro 2005: 58). In keeping with the Victorian ideology of the time, some Belgian doctors cautioned against abstinence (perceived as a health hazard) and recommended regular sexual intercourse as a healthy antidote to tropical hypochondria (68–69).

5. Interracial rape involving a white woman, arguably the greatest of all colonial taboos a black man could violate, was extremely rare in the Belgian Congo. Colonizers branded such rape not simply a breach of property but the most radical, subversive, and profane act a black man could carry out. One way to explain the raping spree that targeted European women during the independence debacle of 1960 is to reference Eldridge Cleaver's defense of the rape of white women, in his prison essays *Soul on Ice,* as an "insurrectional act" against "white oppression."

6. The first case of rape mentioned in colonial jurisprudence dates back to 1929, and Lauro (2009: 298) surmises that it may not have been rape per se that brought infamy to the case but the resulting death of the young victim.

7. The first colonial legislation criminalizing indecent assault (*attentat à la pudeur*) and the rape of a minor was in 1897 and prescribed a prison sentence of up to ten years (articles 71 and 72 of the Belgian Congo Penal Code). However, the minority age in the colony was set at ten years and under, whereas in Belgium it stood at fourteen and under. With the growing number of white children in the colony, the law was amended in 1931 to make a distinction between two categories: "la personne d'un enfant européen agé de moins de 16 ans" (European child under sixteen), on the one hand, and "un enfant de race non-européenne qui n'a pas atteint l'âge de puberté" (prepubescent non-European child) on the other. As Lauro (2009: 296) notes, the deliberate omission of age for the latter category recycled century-old racist tropes about the black female body and its supposed precocious sexuality.

8. Vigarello's (1998: 40) apt rendering is worth quoting here: "la victime est enfermée dans l'impudeur qu'elle voudrait dénoncer" (the victim is trapped in the very shamelessness she would like to denounce).

9. For a discussion of how popular narratives about sexual violence may contribute to the occurrence of sexual aggression, see Bourke (2007: 141).

10. Camille Mwissa-Camus, personal interview, Kinshasa (Matongé), June 4, 2009.

11. In Indoubill the term *momie* (mummy, from the French) implied, paradoxically, that a girl had a fresh, neat, and clean body.

12. The term *mifidé* refers to mangoes so ripe that one could just poke a small hole and suck on them rather than peel them off and slice them. Mifidé were so prized that access to Kintambo's mango trees at the peak of the rainy season prompted constant billings with out-of-township gangs. When Tex Bill (aka Mantane Rémy) took over after Paurret had been deported (see later in this chapter), he renamed all three territories of Kintambo (Assassin,

Chicago, and Lumière) Mangembo, both to stamp his authority on his *quartier* and as a symbol of Kintambo's most coveted resource; "Mangembo" is actually a combination of the word *mangolo* (mangoes) and the name of their other natural fans, *ngembo* (bats).

13. *Popi* is from the French *poupée* (doll).

14. Lingala being a tonal language, while *kolúka* connotes "to wander," *koluka* means to "look for" and to "search."

15. Though some Congolese female victims felt that the war was being fought on their bodies, the weapon-of-war model hardly fits the Congolese situation because the single largest group that commits rape there is the FARDC, Congo's ragtag armed forces, and their targets are defenseless Congolese girls and women (Human Rights Watch 2009: 25).

16. In some cases, rape as a weapon of war remains undeniable. For example, when Congolese activist Justine Masika confronted a CNDP representative in 2008 and asked him point-blank why CNDP troops rape women, his answer unabashedly fit the weapon-of-war model: "Today, our [strong] position vis-à-vis the [Congolese] government is largely due to rape. By humiliating women, mothers, we're perceived as being powerful. That's why the government was forced to negotiate with us" (quoted in Guinamard 2010: 37).

17. Eriksson Baaz and Stern turn to this model of "failed masculinity" only after recognizing that although martial rape existed during the Mobutu regime, the intervention of neighboring armies with established records of systemic and massive rape contributed to the widespread "culture" of rape among all belligerent forces in eastern Congo.

18. In his rendition of the story, especially its denouement, Bingema surprisingly put such a high premium on kamô ("our kamô had started to act up and Degazin got scared") that one is left to wonder whether, for many of these youngsters, kamô was not thought to be a substitute for physical strength; Bingema, personal interview, Kinshasa (Kintambo), March 29, 2009.

19. Degazin (aka Jean Sumbuka Bigonda), personal interview, Kinshasa (Kauka), July 29, 2009.

20. Sylvain Eboma, personal interview, Kinshasa (Barumbu), June 3, 2009.

21. Poison (aka Jean-Christian Matabul), who was born in 1932, referred to William Booth not only as his master but also as a father figure, leading to the conjecture that William Booth may have been well into his thirties, perhaps in his early forties, when he engaged in Yankee-ism in the early 1950s.

22. William Booth was eventually apprehended in 1954 by detective Maurice Derungs (a métis Belgian police officer the Bills nicknamed "Nkoyi Mobali" [Lion Man]) and detained in Luzumbu in the Lower Congo. Booth went blind and fell ill while in detention. He was transferred to Kinshasa, where he died around 1960; Degazin (aka Jean Sumbuka Bigonda), personal interview, Kinshasa (Kauka), July 29, 2009.

23. "Note sur la coutume des Ngobo," Brussels, Archives Africaines du Ministère des Affaires Etrangères (AAMAE), March 9, 1935, Aimo, Léopoldville Kwango.

24. "Lettre du Procureur Général Guido Tinel à Monsieur le Gouverneur Général," Léopoldville, January 22, 1936, Brussels, AAMAE.

25. In 2008–2009, during my stay in Kinshasa, 500 francs congolais were the equivalent of slightly less than $1 U.S.

26. The nickname was given to him as a kid because his sickly condition required weekly visits to the doctor (*monganga*). Paurret came to embrace it in his adult life, especially when he started to cut kamô.

27. Paurret (aka Iyoma Bayaka), personal interview, Kinshasa (Bandal), February 20, 2009.

28. Ibid.

29. DeSoto borrowed his moniker from the new De Soto automobile that Walter Chrysler introduced in 1929, named after the Spanish explorer Hernando de Soto.

30. Parc de Boeck, known today as Kinshasa's Botanical Garden, was located between the zoo and the central market. What once symbolized the city's charm is now a forlorn and derelict space unknown to most Kinois.

31. *Maputa* and *pagne* are Lingala and French, respectively, for the brightly colored wax-print wrapper and top universally worn by Congolese women both in the colonial period and under the Mobutu regime.

32. Monstre (aka Diana Pierre Ryckmans), personal interview, Kinshasa (Barumbu), May 28, 2009.

33. Ibid.

34. According to Meda Chesney-Lind and John M. Hagedorn's edited volume, *Female Gangs in America*, the 1970s women's movement served as a watershed in both the emergence and the independence of female gangs vis-à-vis their male counterparts. Studying Chicana gangs in East Los Angeles, John C. Quicker wrote in 1974, "I have not encountered any instance of a girls' gang existing independently of a boy's gang" (reprinted in Chesney-Lind and Hagedorn 1999: 49). Traditionally, girls were less likely to become involved in gang activities because of close adult supervision and their incorporation within the family, the church, and other social structures (see Frederic M. Thrasher, "Sex in the Gang," 1927, reprinted in Chesney-Lind and Hagedorn 1999: 15).

35. To my knowledge, no one besides Father Jozef de Laet (aka Père Buffalo; see chapter 7) employed the term "Billesse" to describe female Bills.

36. Thérèse Muyaka, led by Andrada and his bunch, recalled how, to complete their resemblance to Hollywood's cowboys, they even planned to steal horses from a European equestrian center and parade them through the streets of their quartier, Ruwet; Thérèse Muyaka, personal interview, Kinshasa (Limété), July 29, 2009.

37. Andrada worked for Constantine Pipinis, a Greek entrepreneur who established the first privately owned public transportation company in Kinshasa, in 1947, using retrofitted trucks with bench seating along each side.

38. Zanga Zanga (aka Honoré Zanga Zanga Mabueta), personal interview, Kinshasa (Kintambo), April 1, 2009.

39. Although horseless Westerns—the so-called town Westerns—abound, and some, such as *High Noon*, garnered huge box-office success, most Westerns could not do without horses, just as they could not do without the obligatory pistols and rifles. This, of course, had to do with what Westerns should be about: manliness. Indeed, as Calder (1974: 103) notes, "If the hero is on a horse he is half way towards convincing the reader of an irresistible manliness."

40. Bicycling was the most popular way for Kinois to move around the city, so even though only a few thoroughfares had been paved, bicycles remained a common sight in Leopoldville. In 1954, the city boasted 47,000 registered bicycles. As a result, bike theft also increased significantly, doubling from 371 stolen bicycles in 1952 to 792 in 1954; see Daubresse (1955: 37 and 71).

41. Paurret (aka Iyoma Bayaka), personal interview, Kinshasa (Bandal), February 20, 2009.

42. Petit Moloch (aka Abraham Koko Yawadio), personal interview, Kinshasa (Ngiri Ngiri / Mofewana), July 16, 2007.

43. Ibid.

44. Ralph Austin's (1986: 89) insistence that Hobsbawm's social bandit archetype "ultimately does not fit very much African historical experience" cannot go unchallenged because focusing, as he does, on the redistribution of goods (see also Crummey 1986) creates an artificial distinction between Africa and the West. If, however, we emphasize the subversion of social order, the détournement of dominant social norms, and the creation of alternative standards as forms of redistributive justice à la Robin Hood, perhaps we can place the Bills within the long and universal line of "populist redistributors" (92).

7. Père Buffalo

1. Colonel Zack Miller wrote this eulogy for Bill Picket, an African American cowhand who is credited with having invented bulldogging, one of the eight rodeo sports. Pickett toured the United States and Europe with the Miller brothers' 101 Ranch Wild West Show as its main box-office attraction.

2. I am grateful to Dom Pedro for sharing the synopsis of his documentary with me. Due to funding setbacks, the film, *Père Buffalo: Ambassadeur de la paix au Congo*, remains in gestation.

3. In a 1969 interview published in *Zaïre*, Père Buffalo admitted to having a few puffs of marijuana with Grands Bills in order to fit in; "but I refrained from making a habit of it. I just wanted to reassure my new friends and show them they could count on me. They used to come to my place and we would talk like buddies (*d'égal à égal*), stories about their girls and all that"; see "L'Aventure fantastique du Père 'Buffalo' et de ses 'Bills,'" *Zaïre*, March 24, 1969, 38.

4. "Oyée!" probably originated from the Spanish *oye* (listen up) but came to mean *vive* (French for "long live," as in "Long live the king!"). Initially coined by the Bills, the term found its way into Mobutu's *animation* and self-aggrandizing pageantry (see White 2008), thanks to former Bills turned political caciques, such as Paul-Henri Kabaidi and Nimy Mayidika, who parlayed many of the Bills' antics into cogs of Mobutu's propaganda machine.

5. "Buffalo Awadié" [Buffalo moved on], *La Voix de Mangembo*, July 12–13, 1964 (in collaboration with *Esprit de la Jeunesse*), 1.

6. *Godias* is short for Godzilla in Indoubill and conveys the idea of sheer force and invincibility.

7. Catholics ordained the first Congolese priest in 1917. By the end of colonization, Congo had more than one-third of all African priests and prelates combined; see Young (1965: 199).

8. A staunch anticolonial militant and co-founder of Abako, the main ethnic organization and political party that catered to the Bakongo people, Joseph Kasa-Vubu became Congo's first president in 1960 before being deposed by Mobutu in 1965.

9. Bissot (1952) offers some clues to his deep interest in African culture.

10. Paul Raymaekers, who made the report available, vehemently disputed Bissot's claims of homosexual sex in Kinshasa. According to him, Bissot may have concocted the stories about homosexual behavior out of a desire to sensationalize, and thus voyeurize, Kinshasa's youth underworld.

11. The report, he wrote, was the result of "stories and confessions" he collected from delinquent youths and gathered from hundreds of cases he witnessed in person (Bissot 2009 [1958]: 30).

12. Bissot made his report available in a single copy to each of several administrative sections, including the governor of Leopoldville Province and all sections and agencies that dealt with childhood and education issues. The report also went to the governor general of the penitentiary affairs section, the Crown Prosecutor (Procureur du Roi), and the colonial security office (la Sûreté).

13. These children, Bissot pleaded with his readers, crave affection and must be loved. And then he added, "I am able to write without pretension that I offered affection to these wretched children. In so doing, I was moved (which is no merit on my part) by feeling pity for their immense distress" (Bissot 2009 [1958]: 30).

14. See Trouillot (1995).

15. Marres and De Vos (1960) provide an account of events from the standpoint of European residents and at times liken these events to the situation that prevailed in Algiers.

16. Congo's independence occurred in 1960, defying colonial pronouncements. As late as 1956, hardly anyone in the colony or in the *métropole* entertained the idea of Congo's

independence in the foreseeable future, even though all over Africa, in French and British colonies, independence had become both imminent and ineluctable.

17. The Abako, Congo's foremost political party, drew most of its constituencies from the Bakongo people. However, the MNC (Congolese National Movement) attempted to cast a wider net to muster the support of the motley of ethnic groups that dwelled in Kinshasa. Led by Patrice Lumumba, the MNC provided a unified, political space with one overarching goal: to curtail Abako's political influence and thwart its separatist agenda.

18. Antoine Lumenga Neso Kiobe, personal interview, Kinshasa (Gombe), June 9, 2009.

19. For an inventory of the destruction, see A.-R. Bolamba, "Léopoldville a été le théâtre de tristes incidents," *La Voix du Congolais* 155, February 1959, 63–67.

20. *Léopoldville dans la tourmente* (Brussels: Procure des Pères de Scheut, 1959).

21. "Les Problèmes de jeunesse" (1960).

22. According to the law, urban residents could be stripped of their temporary residence permits if they failed to show proof of unemployment for a period of thirty days.

23. "Les Problèmes de la jeunesse" (1960: IX).

24. In fact, some of the Europeans who supervised these youth camps, including Paul Raymaekers, had been previously involved with Boy Scout activities and recruited trainers among Boy Scouts.

25. In fact, any time an experiment attempted to displace young Kinois and acclimate them to a new rural working environment, it was bound to fail. Even Père Buffalo, so successful in mentoring and turning around the lives of young délinquants in Kinshasa, headed for fiasco when, in 1979, at the behest of Mobutu's regime, he created in Lokandu a youth camp to help rehabilitate youth délinquants from Kinshasa's Ndolo prison.

26. Juvenile inmates woke up daily at 5:30 a.m. and performed a number of set tasks until the curfew at 8 p.m. They wore a uniform similar to that of common law detainees, were allowed visitation for two and half hours the first Thursday of each month, could end up in solitary confinement for breaking rules, and had to attend religious counseling every Saturday evening and mass on Sunday (Lafontaine 1957).

27. Many youths could see their sentences reduced and get early release for good behavior and after successfully completing their training.

28. Le Gouverneur de Province à Monsieur le Gouverneur Général, Léopoldville, June 23, 1953, AA GG 18363.

29. Le Secrétaire Provincial à Monsieur le Commissaire de District du Moyen-Congo, Léopoldville, December 24, 1953, AA GG 18363.

30. Le Commissaire de District du Moyen-Congo à Monsieur le Gouverneur de la Province de Léopoldville, Léopoldville, October 2, 1954, AA GG 18363.

31. The list of African délégués, as they were called, reads like a *Who's Who* of Congo's political establishment. It includes people such as Daniel Kanza, Abako's vice-president and Kinshasa's first burgomaster; Antoine-Roger Bolamba, *La Voix du Congolais* editor-in-chief and Congo's minister of information in Lumumba's cabinet; and Jean Bolikango, Bolamba's successor after Lumumba's demise, to name just a few.

32. Auguste Buisseret is remembered for his pivotal role in ushering in the era of secular schooling in the Belgian Congo, against entrenched Catholic resistance to his reforms.

33. Néron's song contained a one-line refrain or chorus, "Nzambe na likolo, ba Yankee na se" (God on high, Yankees on earth), around which Néron would improvise lyrics depending on his mood of the moment and inspiration. When I asked him to sing *Zambele Kingo* for me, Néron admitted half-jokingly that he performed this particular song better when he was high on zoumbel (marijuana) but a few bottles of beer could also do the trick. He then proceeded to

churn out a few verses: "Nzambe na likolo, ba Yankee na se / Nzambe mfumu a ntoto / Nzambe ya wele kingo / masta akimi combat / pona epaka ya ba momi / masta abundaka te / batindi John na Makala" (God on high, Yankees below / God, Lord of earth / God is King indeed / Buddy chickened out of a fight / Because of a girl / Buddy never fights / They locked John up in Makala). Vieux Néron (aka Katshaya Kopombo Joseph), personal interview, Kinshasa (Ngiri-Ngiri-Mofewana), July 9, 2005.

34. Père Buffalo (aka Jozef de Laet), personal interview, Sint Pieters-Leeuw, Belgium, April 3, 2006; see also Dieudonné Nzuzi Mayela, "Le Père Buffalo Bill parle de la jeunesse congolaise," *Renaître* 20, October 31, 2004, 27.

35. The expression *linzaka lia soso* (écriture) could be translated literally as "the traces left by chickens as they forage for food by pecking and scratching the ground with their claws."

36. "L'Aventure fantastique du Père 'Buffalo,'" 40.

37. Père Buffalo himself put the figure at 5,000 copies that came out of a printing house located in Quartier Limété.

38. Intensive search and research over the years have turned up only a few issues of *Esprit de la Jeunesse* (obtained through Père Buffalo), one issue of *La Voix de Mangembo,* and nothing else.

39. "Soki aboti, nasundoli ye" [If she has the baby, I'd get rid of her], *Esprit de la Jeunesse* 10, 1964, 3.

40. Emery, "Qu'est-ce qui se passe dans le quartier Far-West?" *Esprit de la Jeunesse* 1, 1962, 4.

41. Alph[onse] Daudet, "Djili Britanique [*sic*]," *Esprit de la Jeunesse* 14, 1964, 6.

42. Lepe Napoleon, "Peuple Canada," *Esprit de la Jeunesse* 13, 1964, 5.

43. J. Victor Hugo dit Ecrivain, "Tolingana" [Let's love one another], *Esprit de la Jeunesse* 14, 1964, 1.

44. Glaser (1998) argues convincingly that the construction of masculinity among Soweto's gangs was largely mediated through the preoccupation with territory, which in turn forged a strong sense of local identity.

45. See, for example, L. L., "Pour une définition du 'Bill,'" *Courrier d'Afrique,* August 20, 1964, 3.

46. Augustin R. Verbeck, "La Vie du Grand Bill Buffalo," *La Voix de Mangembo,* July 12–13, 1964, 2–3.

47. The name Corps des Volontaires de la République (CVR) apparently derived from the Corps de Volontaires Européens (CVE), used sporadically as a white police force throughout the colony (Lauro 2011b: 107). Yet, according to an informant, it was modeled after the (American) Peace Corps and was brewed in a bar, Café Rio (located in Quartier Matongé), owned by Jean-Pierre Dericoyard (a wealthy Congolese businessman) and operated by Paul-Henri Kabaidi. A group of intellectuals met there, including Bomina Nsoni, Mundabi, Pierre Kongolo, Léon Mbuyi, and Kabaidi himself. When Mobutu staged his second coup in November 1965, he dispatched his right-hand man Gaston Sengi Biembe to make contact with the group; Jean-François Muteba Kalombo, personal interview, Kinshasa (Lemba), July 23, 2009.

48. Paurret, personal interview, February 20, 2009.

49. Bingema, personal interview, March 29, 2009.

50. Monstre, personal interview, April 4, 2006.

51. Jacques Atenda Mongebe Omwango served as head of Congo's internal security agency (Centre National de Recherches et d'Investigations) before joining the diplomatic corps as Congo's ambassador to Zambia and then to Kenya, a post he held until Mobutu's demise in 1997.

52. Léon Kengo wa Dondo, then attorney general, had Franco and some of his band members prosecuted over two profanity-laced songs, "Hélène" and "Jackie," that shockingly verged on pornography. Adding insult to injury, the court ordered Franco to hand back his Order of the Leopard medal, the country's highest civilian honor; see Ewens (1994: 166).

8. Avatars

1. One has to think of the corn silk to fully grasp Franco's analogy.

2. The term *ambianceur,* for which I have found no adequate English equivalent, refers to a person who gaily provokes, participates, and performs in any given event where food, music, alcohol, and fashion play a role.

3. L. L. "Pour une définition du 'Bill,'" *Courrier d'Afrique,* August 20, 1964, 3.

4. These terms refer to the diasporic identities claimed by groups of young Congolese migrants in Paris, Belgium, and several other European locales and have been thoroughly investigated by Gandoulou (1989), Devisch (1995), Gondola (1999b, 1999c, 2010), MacGaffey and Bazenguissa-Ganga (2000), Thomas (2003), and Hanneken (2008), among others.

5. According to De Boeck and Plissart's (2005: 33) findings, the city incurs a yearly shortage of about 200,000 houses.

6. Kerosene vendors usually start swarming the streets at night, following Kinshasa's chronic *délestage* (power outage).

7. Street vendors, mostly young boys, carry on their heads dozens of 600-milliliter plastic bags of cold water, which they sell for 50 Congolese francs a bag (the equivalent of a little more than a nickel) to weary and thirsty commuters and pedestrians. In a twist of irony, *eau pure* (pure water) has become *eau pire* (worst water), since those young, uneducated boys cannot pronounce the "*u*" in *pure*" Pandemonium ensued in Kinshasa in February 2010 following the vendors' concerted decision to double the price of *eau pure* to offset the cost of refrigeration.

8. Pype (2012: 276) is right in emphasizing how much these young actors' urban identity (kinicité) supersedes their religious affiliation when she writes, "Christian TV actors are first of all Kinois and only secondarily Christian."

9. Bingema, personal interview, Kinshasa (Kintambo), March 29, 2009.

10. What had been the Belgian Congo and is now the Democratic Republic of Congo was the Republic of Zaire from 1971 to 1997.

11. Ballados made taxi drivers an offer they could not easily turn down. Drivers were allowed to transport up to six passengers (with two of them seated in the passenger's seat), whom they would drop along the way. Rather than drive around to look for passengers, they would park their cars along busy intersections and let the Ballados, as *chargeurs,* do the locating and herding of passengers in exchange for a tip.

12. In the 1990s many African countries underwent a democratization process triggered by external as well as internal factors. Starting first in Benin, National Sovereign conferences were convened to chart a constitutional path toward a multiparty, democratic system. Zaire's Conférence Nationale Souveraine (CNS) opened in August 1991 and adjourned in December 1992 after establishing a provisional legislature, the High Council of the Republic, to continue its work (Gondola 2002: 157).

13. Between 1988 and 1993, the highest denomination of the national currency went from 5,000 zaires to 5,000,000 zaires, a startling testament to the country's unbridled hyperinflation. When in January 1993 Mobutu's beleaguered regime attempted to break the boycott of the new 5,000,000-zaire denomination (the equivalent of two dollars) by the population, matters came to a head, climaxing in widespread lootings in Kinshasa.

14. According to a UNICEF census widely echoed by local media outlets, the number of homeless children in Kinshasa's streets went from 5,000 in 2005 to 24,000 in 2011; see Modwa (2011).

15. In Kinshasa's culture, the notion of ndoki refers to witches (imbued with harmful power) but also to individuals who exhibit unsurpassed abilities or accomplish extraordinary exploits. The latter laudatory connotation may be used, for instance, to characterize a skillful soccer player, a successful businesswoman, or a gifted student.

16. For a review of the literature on African witchcraft, see Pype (2012: 45–49).

17. Sites occupied day and night by Bashegue include the central market pavilions, military camps, stadiums, major traffic intersections (such as Rond-Point Cabu, Place de la Victoire, and Boulevard du 30 Juin), and other public spaces that tend to draw crowds of pedestrians and commuters. It is precisely because of the children's presence in these strategic locales, whence rumors can spread like wildfire, that the government keeps tab on their whereabouts and activities.

18. The term "Kuluna" originated from the Portuguese *coluna,* which translates as "infantry column on foot patrol." The return from Angola of young Congolese diamond diggers (known as *Bana Lunda*) in the late 1990s may have introduced this term in Kinshasa. Kuluneurs are also called *Batu ya makasi* (strong people) and *délinquants sportifs,* a reference to their martial-arts regimen.

19. According to blogger Alex Engwete and Radio Okapi, Kuluna first surfaced in Quartier Yolo, in the Kalamu commune, before spreading like spokes on a wheel to surrounding communes.

20. Alex Engwete, blog, "Kuluna and Kuluneurs in Kinshasa: A Low-Intensity Urban Insurgency?" February 2, 2010.

21. "Des 'Kuluna' ont frappé à l'ISC," *Le Phare,* November 29, 2008.

22. "Bandalungwa: Des bandes des [sic] Kuluna se préparent à une guerre à la machette," *Le Phare,* August 26, 2010.

23. Engwete, blog, "Kuluna and Kuluneurs in Kinshasa."

24. Bana Congo, also called "Les Patriotes" and "Les Combattants," have spearheaded the anti-Kabila front in Belgium. They have embraced a more radical and violent agenda since the death of their comrade Armand Tungulu, detained and murdered by Kabila's security forces in October 2010, after he threw a stone at the presidential convoy in Kinshasa; see Bodeux (2011: 33).

25. "La Sûreté belge traque les durs de Bana Congo, ces 'Kuluna' de la diaspora congolaise en Belgique," *Soft International,* February 4, 2012.

26. "On doit aller jusqu'au bout dans l'éradication du phénomène 'Kuluna!'" *Le Potentiel,* November 23, 2013.

27. Another example of filiation comes from Paurret, who called me on September 24, 2013, asking for financial help. His young nephew, a Kuluna gang member in Bandal, had been arrested in the "Opération Likofi" and Paurret was determined to bail him out. The family, he said, had given up on the young misfit, but Paurret had plans for his nephew to join the army.

28. Consisting of various groups united by fierce determination to overthrow Mobutu's regime, the Alliance of Democratic Forces for the Liberation of Congo (ADFL) fell under the command of Laurent-Désiré Kabila, a longtime rebel turned diamond smuggler on the eastern border.

29. General Marcel Bopeya, personal interview, Springfield, IL, July 17, 2012.

Bibliography

Ambler, Charles. 2001. "Popular Films and Colonial Audiences: The Movies in Northern Rhodesia." *American Historical Review* 1 (106): 81–105.

Anstey, Roger. 1966. *King Leopold's Legacy: The Congo under Belgian Rule, 1908–1960.* New York: Oxford University Press.

Asencio, Marysol W. 1999. "Machos and Sluts: Gender, Sexuality, and Violence among a Cohort of Puerto Rican Adolescents." *Medical Anthropology Quarterly* 13 (1): 107–26.

Austin, Ralph. 1986. "Social Bandits and Other Heroic Criminals: Western Models of Resistance and Their Relevance for Africa." In *Banditry, Rebellion, and Social Protest in Africa,* edited by Donald Crummey, 89–108. London: Heinemann.

Babillon, Jacques. 1957. "Léopoldville: Étude générale du problème de la jeunesse autochtone." Master's thesis, Catholic University of Louvain.

Barker, Gary T. 2005. *Dying to Be Men: Youth, Masculinity and Social Exclusion.* London: Routledge.

Bederman, Gail. 1995. *Manliness and Civilization: A Cultural History of Gender and Race in the United States, 1880–1917.* Chicago: University of Chicago Press.

Bentley, W. Holman. 1900. *Pioneering on the Congo.* Vols. 1 and 2. London: Religious Tract Society.

Beti, Mongo [Eza Boto]. 1971 [1954]. *Ville cruelle.* Paris: Présence Africaine.

Biaya, Tshikala K. 1997. "Les Paradoxes de la masculinité africaine moderne: Une Histoire de violences, d'immigration et de crises." *Canada Folklore* 19:89–112.

——. 2000. *Les Jeunes, la violence et la rue à Kinshasa: Entendre, comprendre, décrire.* Dakar, Senegal: CODESRIA.

Biltereyst, Daniël, Philippe Meers, Kathleen Lotze, and Liesbeth Van de Vijver. 2012. "Negotiating Cinema's Modernity: Strategies of Control and Audience Experiences of Cinema in Belgium, 1930s–1960s." In *Cinema, Audiences and Modernity: New Perspectives on European Cinema History,* edited by Daniël Biltereyst, Richard Maltby, and Philippe Meers, 186–201. London: Routledge.

Bissot, Louis. 1952. "A propos du théâtre indigène." *Zaïre* 1 (6): 624–30.

——. 2009 [1958]. *Étude qualitative sur la délinquance juvénile à Léopoldville (ca. 1957).* Rhode-Saint-Genèse, Belgium: Paul Raymaekers Foundation.

Bodeux, Leila. 2011. "The Political Opposition to the Congolese Government within the Belgian Congolese Diaspora." Master's thesis, Oxford University.

Bolamba, Antoine-Roger. 2009. *Carnets de voyage (Congo-Belgique 1945–1959).* Paris: L'Harmattan.

Bouchard, Vincent. 2010. "Commentary and Orality in African Film Reception." In *Viewing African Cinema in the Twenty-First Century: Art Films and the Nollywood Video Revolution,* edited by Mahir Şaul and Ralph A. Austen, 95–107. Athens: Ohio University Press.

Bourdieu, Pierre. 1998. *La Domination masculine.* Paris: Seuil.

Bourke, Joanna. 2007. *Rape: Sex, Violence, History.* Emeryville, CA: Shoemaker and Hoard.

Brennan, James. 2005. "Democratizing Cinema and Censorship in Tanzania, 1920–1980." *International Journal of African Historical Studies* 38 (3): 481–511.

Brownmiller, Susan. 1975. *Against Our Will: Men, Women, and Rape.* New York: Simon and Schuster.

Bucholtz, Mary. 2002. "Youth and Cultural Practice." *Annual Review of Anthropology* 31:525–52.

Burns, James. 2002a. "John Wayne on the Zambezi: Cinema, Empire, and the American Western in British Central Africa." *International Journal of African Historical Studies* 35 (1): 103–17.

——. 2002b. *Flickering Shadows: Cinema and Identity in Colonial Zimbabwe.* Athens: Ohio University Press.

——. 2006. "The African Bioscope? Movie House Culture in British Colonial Africa." *Afrique et Histoire* 1 (19): 65–80.

Burton, Andrew. 2001. "Urchins, Loafers and the Cult of the Cowboy: Urbanization and Delinquency in Dar es Salaam, 1919–61." *Journal of African History* 42 (2): 199–216.

——. 2005. *African Underclass: Urbanisation, Crime and Colonial Order in Dar es Salaam.* Athens: Ohio University Press.

Burton, Art T. 2006. *Black Gun, Silver Star: The Life and Legend of Frontier Marshal Bass Reeves.* Lincoln: University of Nebraska Press.

Butler, Judith. 1993. *Bodies That Matter: On the Discursive Limits of Sex.* London: Routledge.

Calder, Jenni. 1974. *There Must Be a Lone Ranger: The American West in Film and Reality.* New York: Taplinger.

Campbell, Anne. 1984. *The Girls in the Gang.* Oxford: Basil Blackwell.

Capelle, Emmanuel. 1947. *La Cité indigène de Léopoldville.* Élisabethville, Belgian Congo: Centre d'Études des Problèmes Sociaux Indigènes.

Carter, Robert A. 2000. *Buffalo Bill Cody: The Man behind the Legend.* New York: Wiley.

Chalux. 1925. *Un An au Congo belge.* Brussels: Albert Dewit.

Chesney-Lind, Meda, and John M. Hagedorn, eds. 1999. *Female Gangs in America: Essays on Girls, Gangs, and Gender.* Chicago: Lake View.

Chin, Christine B. N. 1998. *In Service and Servitude: Foreign Female Domestic Workers and the Malaysian "Modernity" Project.* New York: Columbia University Press.

Cody, William Frederick. 1978 [1879]. *The Life of Hon. William F. Cody, Known as Buffalo Bill, the Famous Hunter, Scout, and Guide.* Lincoln: University of Nebraska Press.

Comhaire-Sylvain, Suzanne. 1950. *Food and Leisure among the African Youth of Léopoldville (Belgian Congo).* Communications from the School of African Studies, n.s., 25. Cape Town: University of Cape Town.

——. 1968. *Femmes de Kinshasa: Hier et aujourd'hui.* Paris: Mouton.

Connell R. W. 1995. *Masculinities.* Berkeley: University of California Press.

Connell, R. W., and James Messerschmidt. 2005. "Hegemonic Masculinities: Rethinking the Concept." *Gender and Society* 19 (6): 829–59.

Convents, Guido. 2006. *Images et démocratie: Les Congolais face au cinéma et à l'audiovisuel. Une Histoire politico-culturelle du Congo des Belges jusqu'à la République démocratique du Congo (1896–2006).* Kessel-Lo, Belgium: Afrika Filmfestival.

Coquilhat, Camille-Aimé. 1888. *Sur le Haut Congo.* Paris: J. Lebègue.

Corkin, Stanley. 2004. *Cowboys as Cold Warriors: The Western and U.S. History.* Philadelphia: Temple University Press.

Cornwall, Andrea, and Nancy Lindisfarne. 1994. "Dislocating Masculinity: Gender, Power, and Anthropology." In *Dislocating Masculinities: Comparative Ethnographies,* edited by Andrea Cornwall and Nancy Lindisfarne, 11–47. London: Routledge.

Crummey, Donald. 1986. "Introduction: 'The Great Beast.'" In *Banditry, Rebellion, and Social Protest in Africa,* edited by Donald Crummey, 1–31. London: Heinemann.

Curtin, Philip. 1964. *The Image of Africa: British Ideas and Action, 1750–1850.* Madison: University of Wisconsin Press.

Daubresse, Henri. 1955. "La Cité indigène de Léopoldville." Master's thesis, Catholic University of Louvain.

Daye, Pierre. 1923. *L'Empire colonial belge.* Paris: Berger-Levrault.

De Boeck, Filip, and Marie-Françoise Plissart. 2005. *Kinshasa: Tales of the Invisible City.* Tervuren, Belgium: Ludion.

De Certeau, Michel. 1990 [1980]. *L'Invention du quotidien.* Vol. 1, *Arts de faire.* Paris: Gallimard.

De la Kethulle, Raphaël. 1922. "Le Vagabondage à Kinshasa." *Congo,* 727–30.

De Villers, Gauthier, Bogumil Jewsiewicki, and Laurent Monnier, eds. 2002. *Manières de vivre: Économie de la "débrouille" dans les villes du Congo/Zaïre.* Tervuren, Belgium: Institut Africain / Centre d'Étude et de Documentation Africaines.

De Villers, Gauthier, and Jean Omasombo Tshonga. 2004. "When Kinois Take to the Streets." In *Reinventing Order in the Congo: How People Respond to State Failure in Kinshasa,* edited by Theodore Trefon, 137–54. London: Zed Books.

Debord, Guy. 1983. *The Society of the Spectacle.* Detroit: Black and Red.

Debord, Guy-Ernest, and Gil J. Wolman. 1956. "Mode d'emploi du détournement." *Les Lèvres nues* 8, May (translated in Ken Knabb, ed., *Situationist International Anthology,* 8–14. Berkeley, CA: Bureau of Public Secrets, 1981, as "Methods of Detournement").

Demetriou, Demetrakis Z. 2001. "Connell's Concept of Hegemonic Masculinity: A Critique." *Theory and Society* 30 (3): 337–61.

Devisch, René. 1995. "Frenzy, Violence, and Ethical Renewal in Kinshasa." *Public Culture* 7 (3): 593–629.

Diamond, Andrew J. 2009. *Mean Streets: Chicago Youths and the Everyday Struggle for Empowerment in the Multiracial City, 1908–1969.* Berkeley: University of California Press.

Dupré, Marie-Claude. 1982. "Pour une histoire des productions: La Métallurgie du fer chez les Téké (Rép. du Congo)." *Cahiers ORSTOM, Série Sciences Humaines* 18 (2): 195–223.

Ebiatsa, Hopiel. 2010. *Conquêtes européennes et pouvoir royal Teke: Fin XVe–milieu XIXe siècle.* Paris: Edilivre.

Emecheta, Buchi. 1979. *The Joys of Motherhood.* London: Allison and Busby.

Eriksson Baaz, Maria, and Maria Stern. 2008. "Making Sense of Violence: Voices of Soldiers in the Congo." *Journal of Modern African Studies* 46 (1): 57–86.

——. 2009. "Why Do Soldiers Rape? Masculinity, Violence, and Sexuality in the Armed Forces in the Congo (DRC)." *International Studies Quarterly* 53 (2): 495–518.

———. 2010. *The Complexity of Violence: A Critical Analysis of Sexual Violence in the Democratic Republic of Congo (DRC)*. Uppsala: Nordiska Afrikainstitutet / Swedish International Development Cooperation Agency.

Ewens, Graeme. 1994. *Congo Colossus: The Life and Legacy of Franco and OK Jazz*. North Walsham, UK: Buku.

Fabian, Johannes. 1996. *Remembering the Present: Painting and Popular History in Zaire*. Berkeley: University of California Press.

Fenwick, Mac. 1996. "'Tough Guy, Eh?': The Gangster-Figure in *Drum*." *Journal of Southern African Studies* 22 (4): 615–32.

Fieldhouse, David Kenneth. 1978. *Unilever Overseas: The Anatomy of a Multinational, 1895–1965*. Stanford, CA: Hoover Institution Press.

Fumunzanza Muketa, Jacques. 2008. *Kinshasa d'un quartier à l'autre*. Paris: L'Harmattan.

Gandoulou, Jean-Daniel. 1989. *Au coeur de la sape: Moeurs et aventures des Congolais à Paris*. Paris: L'Harmattan.

Geary, Christraud. 2002. *In and Out of Focus: Images from Central Africa, 1885–1960*. Washington, DC: National Museum of African Art, Smithsonian Institution.

Geenen, Kristien. 2009. "'Sleep Occupies No Space': The Use of Public Space by Street Gangs in Kinshasa." *Africa* 79 (3): 347–68.

Gilbert, Oscar-Paul. 1947. *L'Empire du silence: Congo 1946*. Brussels: Peuple.

Gilmore, David D. 1990. *Manhood in the Making: Cultural Concepts of Masculinity*. New Haven, CT: Yale University Press.

Glaser, Clive. 1998. "Swines, Hazels and the Dirty Dozen: Masculinity, Territoriality and the Youth Gangs of Soweto, 1960–1976." *Journal of Southern African Studies* 24 (4): 719–36.

———. 2000. *Bo-Tsotsi: The Youth Gangs of Soweto, 1935–1976*. Portsmouth, NH: Heinemann.

Goerg, Odile. 2015. *Fantômas sous les tropiques: Aller au cinéma en Afrique coloniale*. Paris: Vendémiaire.

Gondola, Ch. Didier. 1996. "Popular Music, Urban Society, and Changing Gender Relations in Kinshasa, Zaire." In *Gendered Encounters: Challenging Cultural Boundaries and Social Hierarchies in Africa*, edited by Maria Grosz-Ngaté and Omari H. Kokole, 65–84. London: Routledge.

———. 1997a. *Villes miroirs: Migrations et identités à Kinshasa et Brazzaville, 1930–1970*. Paris: L'Harmattan.

———. 1997b. "Jeux d'argent, jeux de vilains: Rien ne va plus au Zaïre." *Politique Africaine* 65 (March): 96–111.

———. 1999a. "La Contestation politique des jeunes à Kinshasa à travers l'exemple du mouvement 'Kindoubill' (1950–1959)." *Brood en Rozen: Tijdschrift voor de Geschiedenis van Sociale Bewegingen* 2 (January): 171–83.

———. 1999b. "Dream and Drama: The Search for Elegance among Congolese Youth." *African Studies Review* 42 (1): 23–48.

———. 1999c. "La Sape des *mikilistes*: Théâtre de l'artifice et représentation onirique." *Cahiers d'Études Africaines* 39 (1): 13–47.

———. 2002. *The History of Congo*. Westport, CT: Greenwood.

———. 2003. "*Ô, Kisasa Makambo!* Métamorphoses et représentations urbaines de Kinshasa à travers le discours musical des années 1950–1960." *Mouvement Social* 204 (July–September): 109–29.

——. 2009. "Tropical Cowboys: Westerns, Violence, and Masculinity among the Young Bills of Kinshasa." *Afrique et Histoire* 7 (1): 75–98.

——. 2010. "La Sape Exposed! High Fashion among Lower Class Congolese Youth: From Colonial Modernity to Global Cosmopolitanism." In *Contemporary African Fashion,* edited by Suzanne Gott and Kristyne Loughran, 157–75. Bloomington: Indiana University Press.

——. 2013. "Le Culte du cowboy et les figures du masculin à Kinshasa dans les années 1950." *Cahiers d'Études Africaines* 52 (1–2): 173–99.

Goyvaerts, Didier L. 1988. "Indoubill: A Swahili Hybrid in Bukavu." *Language in Society* 17 (2): 231–42.

Guinamard, Louis. 2010. *Survivantes: Femmes violées dans la guerre en République Démocratique du Congo.* Paris: Ouvrières.

Guiral, Léon. 1889. *Le Congo français: Cu Gabon à Brazzaville.* Paris: Plon.

Hair, P. E. H. 2001. "The Cowboys: A Nigerian Acculturative Institution (ca. 1950)." *History in Africa* 28:83–93.

Hall, Stuart. 1997. "What Is This 'Black' in Black Popular Culture?" In *Representing Blackness: Issues in Film and Video,* edited by Valerie Smith, 123–34. New Brunswick, NJ: Rutgers University Press.

Hall, Stuart, and Tony Jefferson, eds. 1993. *Resistance through Rituals: Youth Subcultures in Post-war Britain.* London: Routledge.

Hanneken, Jaime. 2008. "*Mikilistes* and *Modernistas*: Taking Paris to the 'Second Degree.'" *Comparative Literature* 60 (4): 370–88.

Hansen, Karen Tranberg. 2000. *Salaula: The World of Secondhand Clothing and Zambia.* Chicago: University of Chicago Press.

Harms, Robert. 1981. *River of Wealth, River of Sorrow: The Central Zaire Basin in the Era of the Slave and Ivory Trade, 1500–1891.* New Haven, CT: Yale University Press.

Hearn, Jeff. 2004. "From Hegemonic Masculinity to the Hegemony of Men." *Feminist Theory* 5 (1): 49–72.

Hegel, Georg Wilhelm Friedrich. 1902 [1837]. *The Philosophy of History.* New York: American Home Library.

Herzfeld, Michael. 1985. *The Poetics of Manhood: Contest and Identity in a Cretan Mountain Village.* Princeton, NJ: Princeton University Press.

Hobsbawm, Eric. 1959. *Social Bandits and Primitive Rebels: Studies in Archaic Forms of Social Movement in the 19th and 20th Centuries.* Glencoe, IL: Free Press.

Hochschild, Adam. 1998. *King Leopold's Ghost: A Story of Greed, Terror, and Heroism in Colonial Africa.* Boston: Houghton Mifflin.

Hodgson, Dorothy L. 2001. "'Once Intrepid Warriors': Modernity and the Production of Maasai Masculinities." In *Gendered Modernities: Ethnographic Perspectives,* edited by Dorothy L. Hodgson, 105–45. New York: Palgrave.

Hoffmann, Léon-François. 1973. *Le Nègre romantique: Personnage littéraire et obsession collective.* Paris: Payot.

Holloway, Joseph E. 2005. "Africanisms in African American Names in the United States." In *Africanisms in American Culture,* edited by Joseph E. Holloway, 82–110. Bloomington: Indiana University Press.

Honwana, Alcinda, and Filip De Boeck, eds. 2005. *Makers and Breakers: Children and Youth in Postcolonial Africa.* Trenton, NJ: Africa World.

Hottot, Robert, and Frank Willett. 1956. "Teke Fetishes." *Journal of the Royal Anthropological Institute of Great Britain and Ireland* 86 (1): 25–36.

Howson, Richard. 2006. *Challenging Hegemonic Masculinity.* London: Routledge.

Human Rights Watch. 2009. *Soldiers Who Rape, Commanders Who Condone: Sexual Violence and Military Reform in the Democratic Republic of Congo.* New York: Human Rights Watch.

Hunt, Nancy. 2008. "An Acoustic Register, Tenacious Images, and Congolese Scenes of Rape and Ruination." In "Scarred Landscapes and Imperial Debris," edited by Ann Laura Stoler. Special issue, *Cultural Anthropology* 23:220–53.

Ivaska, Andrew. 2011. *Cultured States: Youth, Gender and Modern Style in 1960s Dar es Salaam.* Durham, NC: Duke University Press.

Jadot, Jean-Marie. 1927. "La Question des mûlatres." *Essor Colonial et Maritime* 276 (17): 1–2.

Jewsiewicki, Bogumil. 2003. *Mami Wata: La Peinture urbaine au Congo.* Paris: Gallimard.

———. 2004. "Kinshasa: (Auto)représentation d'une société 'moderne' en (dé)construction. De la modernisation coloniale à la globalisation." In *La Nouvelle Histoire du Congo: Mélanges eurafricains offerts à Frans Bontinck,* edited by Pamphile M. Mantuba-Ngoma, 251–66. Paris: L'Harmattan.

Johnston, H. H. 1895. *The River Congo: From Its Mouth to Bolobo.* London: Sampson Low, Marston.

Kabasa Yambeng, Crispin. 2006. "Gangs et insécurité dans le "district" de Mont-Amba / Ville de Kinshasa." Master's thesis, University of Kinshasa.

Kandolo, Emmanuel. 2009. "La Saga des 'Bills' et des 'Yankees' kinois." http://www .mbokamosika.com/article-36439261.html.

Kasson, Joy S. 2000. *Buffalo Bill's Wild West: Celebrity, Memory, and Popular History.* New York: Hill and Wang.

Katz, William Loren. 2005. *The Black West: A Documentary and Pictorial History of the African American Role in the Westward Expansion of the United States.* New York: Harlem Moon.

Kelley, D. G. Robin. 1994. *Race Rebels: Culture, Politics, and the Black Working Class.* New York: Free Press.

Kießling, Roland, and Maarten Mous. 2004. "Urban Youth Languages in Africa." *Anthropological Linguistics* 46 (3): 303–41.

Kimmel, Michael. 1996. *Manhood in America: A Cultural History.* New York: Free Press.

Kisangani, Emizet François. 2012. *Civil Wars in the Democratic Republic of Congo, 1960–2010.* Boulder, CO: Lynne Rienner.

Kolonga Molei. 1977. "Kinshasa Révolutionnaire." *Zaïre* 448 (7): 23–33.

———. 1979. *Kinshasa, ce village d'hier.* Kinshasa: Sodimca.

Kristof, Nicholas D., and Sheryl WuDunn. 2009. *Half the Sky: Turning Oppression into Opportunity for Women Worldwide.* New York: Knopf.

Kueno, Tshingi. 1992. "La Jeunesse et le parti unique au Zaïre." In *Les Jeunes en Afrique: La Politique et la ville,* edited by Hélène Almeida-Topor, Catherine Coquery-Vidrovitch, and Odile Goerg, 2:226–46. Paris: L'Harmattan.

La Fontaine, Jean S. 1969. "Two Types of Youth Group in Kinshasa (Léopoldville)." In *Socialization: The Approach from Social Anthropology,* edited by Philip Mayer, 191–213. London: Tavistock.

——. 1970. *City Politics: A Study of Leopoldville, 1962–63.* Cambridge: Cambridge University Press.

Lafontaine, Georges. 1957. *La Législation sur l'enfance délinquante au Congo belge et son application.* Brussels: Ferdinand Larcier.

Lauro, Amandine. 2005. *Coloniaux, ménagères et prostituées au Congo belge (1885–1930).* Loverval, Belgium: Labor.

——. 2009. "Les Politiques du mariage et de la sexualité au Congo belge (1908–1945): Genre, race, sexualité et pouvoir colonial." Ph.D. diss., Free University of Brussels.

——. 2011a. "'J'ai l'honneur de porter plainte contre ma femme': Litiges conjugaux et administration coloniale au Congo belge (1930–1960)." *Clio* 33:65–84.

——. 2011b. "Maintenir l'ordre dans la colonie-modèle. Notes sur les désordres urbains et la police des frontières raciales au Congo belge (1918–1945)." *Crime, History and Society* 15 (2): 97–121.

Le Pajolec, Sébastien. 2007. "Le Cinéma des blousons noirs." In *Les Bandes de jeunes: Des "blousons noirs" à nos jours,* edited by Marwan Mohammed and Laurent Mucchielli, 61–81. Paris: La Découverte.

Lemarchand, René. 1964. *Political Awakening in the Belgian Congo.* Berkeley: University of California Press.

"Les Problèmes de jeunesse." 1960. *Courrier hebdomadaire du CRISP* 22 (68): 1–22.

Leslie, J. A. K. 1963. *A Survey of Dar es Salaam.* London: Oxford University Press.

Liebrechts, Charles. 1889. "Léopoldville." *Bulletin de la Société Belge (Royale) de Géographie,* 501–36.

Likaka, Osumaka. 2009. *Naming Colonialism: History and Collective Memory in the Congo, 1870–1960.* Madison: University of Wisconsin Press.

Lindsay, Lisa A., and Stephan F. Miescher, eds. 2003. *Men and Masculinities in Modern Africa.* Portsmouth, NH: Heinemann.

MacGaffey, Janet, and Rémy Bazenguissa-Ganga. 2000. *Congo-Paris: Transnational Traders on the Margins of the Law.* Oxford: James Currey.

MacGaffey, Wyatt. 1971. *Custom and Government in the Lower Congo.* Berkeley: University of California Press.

Madzou, Lamence. 2008. *J'étais un chef de gang.* Paris: La Découverte.

Magnuson, Eric. 2007. *Changing Men, Transforming Culture: Inside the Men's Movement.* Boulder, CO: Paradigm.

Maistriaux, Robert. 1957. *L'Intelligence noire et son destin.* Brussels: Éditions de Problèmes d'Afrique Centrale.

Mansfield, Harvey C. 2006. *Manliness.* New Haven, CT: Yale University Press.

Markowitz, Marvin. 1973. *Cross and Sword: The Political Role of Christian Missions in the Belgian Congo.* Stanford, CA: Hoover Institution Press.

Marks, Laura. 2000. *The Skin of the Film: Intercultural Cinema, Embodiment, and Senses.* Durham, NC: Duke University Press.

Marres, Jacques, and Pierre De Vos. 1960. *L'Équinoxe de janvier: Les Émeutes de Léopoldville.* Brussels: Euraforient.

Martin, Jonathan D. 1996. "'The Grandest and Most Cosmopolitan Object Teacher': Buffalo Bill's Wild West and the Politics of American Identity, 1883–1899." *Radical History Review* 66 (Fall): 92–123.

Martin Saint Leon, Pascal, and Jean Loup Pivin. 2010. *Jean Depara. Kinshasa—Night and Day, 1951–1975.* Paris: Revue Noire.

Masandi, Kita Kyankenge. 1982. *Colonisation et enseignement: Cas du Zaïre avant 1960.* Bukavu, Zaire: Ceruki.

Mauss, Marcel. 1925. "Essai sur le don: Forme et raison de l'échange dans les sociétés archaïques." *Année Sociologique* 1 (1923–1924): 30–186.

Maximy, René de. 1984. *Kinshasa ville en suspens.* Paris: ORSTOM.

McCarthy, Michael. 1977. "Africa and the American West." *Journal of American Studies* 11 (2): 187–201.

McGuire, Phillip, ed. 1993. *Taps for a Jim Crow Army: Letters from Black Soldiers in World War II.* Lexington: University Press of Kentucky.

McVeigh, Stephen. 2007. *The American Western.* Edinburgh: Edinburgh University Press.

Meillassoux, Claude. 1992. *The Anthropology of Slavery: The Womb of Iron and Gold.* Chicago: University of Chicago Press.

Merlier, Michel. 1962. *Le Congo de la colonisation belge à l'indépendance.* Paris: Maspero.

Messner, Michael A. 1992. *Power at Play: Sports and the Problem of Masculinity.* Boston: Beacon.

Miescher, Stephan F. 2005. *Making Men in Ghana.* Bloomington: Indiana University Press.

Mille, Pierre. 1913. *Les Baluba (Congo belge).* Brussels: Albert Dewit.

Mitchell, Lee Clark. 1996. *Westerns: Making the Man in Fiction and Film.* Chicago: University of Chicago Press.

Modwa, Michel. 2011. *Enfants de la rue: Libre prisonnier.* Kinshasa: Éditions Universitaires Africaines.

Monheim, Francis. 1959. "Léopoldville en juin 1959." *Revue Générale Belge* (July): 29–46.

Moorman, Marissa. 2001. "Of Westerns, Women, and War: Re-situating Angolan Cinema and the Nation." *Research in African Literatures* 32 (3): 103–22.

Morrell, Robert. 1998. "Of Boys and Men: Masculinity and Gender in Southern African Studies." *Journal of Southern African Studies* 24 (4): 605–30.

———. 2001. *From Boys to Men: Settler Masculinity in Colonial Natal, 1880–1920.* Pretoria: University of South Africa Press.

Mosley, Philip. 2001. *Belgian Cinema and Cultural Identity.* Albany: State University of New York Press.

Mudimbe, V. Y. 1994. *The Idea of Africa.* Bloomington: Indiana University Press.

Mulambu-Mvuluya, Faustin. 1971. *Contribution à l'étude de la révolte des Bapende (mai-septembre 1931).* Brussels: Centre d'Étude et de Documentation Africaines.

Mutamba Makombo Kitatshima, Jean-Marie. 1998. *Du Congo belge au Congo indépendant 1940–1960: Émergence des "Évolués" et genèse du nationalisme.* Kinshasa: Institut de Formation et d'Études Politiques.

Muteba Kalombo, Jean-François. n.d. "Mémoires de Léopoldville." Unpublished manuscript.

Namputu-Zi-Ndongala. 1972. "Sur la trace des homosexuels." *Elima*, November 23, 2, 5.

Ndaywel è Nziem, Isidore. 1998. *Histoire générale du Congo: De l'héritage ancien à la République Démocratique.* Brussels: Duculot.

N'Djoku, Eugène. 1953. "Compagnie Kitunga." *La Voix du Congolais* (November): 719–21.

Ngolet, François. 2011. *Crisis in the Congo: The Rise and Fall of Laurent Kabila.* New York: Palgrave Macmillan.

Ngongo, Enika. 2012. "La Délinquance juvénile au Congo belge (1908–1960): Construction du problème et réponses judiciaires des autorités coloniales. Autour du décret du 6 décembre 1950 sur l'Enfance délinquante." Master's thesis, Catholic University of Louvain.

Nicolaï, Robert. 2000. *La Traversée de l'empirique: Essai d'épistémologie sur la construction des représentations de l'évolution des langues.* Paris: Ophrys.

Nixon, Rob. 1994. *Homelands, Harlem and Hollywood: South African Culture and the World Beyond.* New York: Routledge.

Obenga, Théophile. 1976. *La Cuvette congolaise: Les Hommes et les structures.* Paris: Présence Africaine.

Ombredane, André. 1949. "Principes pour une étude psychologique des Noirs du Congo belge." *Année Psychologique* 50:521–47.

Otten, Rik. 1984. *Le Cinéma au Zaïre, au Rwanda et au Burundi.* Brussels: OCIC.

Ouzgane, Lahoucine, and Robert Morrell, eds. 2005. *African Masculinities: Men in Africa from the Late Nineteenth Century to the Present.* New York: Palgrave.

Pain, Marc. 1984. *Kinshasa, la ville et la cité.* Paris: ORSTOM.

Peck, Joseph H. 1981. *The Myth of Masculinity.* Cambridge, MA: MIT Press.

Piette, Valérie. 2011. "La Belgique au Congo ou la volonté d'imposer sa ville? L'Exemple de Léopoldville." *Revue Belge de Philologie et d'Histoire* 89:605–18.

Posel, Deborah. 2005. "The Scandal of Manhood: 'Baby Rape' and the Politicization of Sexual Violence in Post-Apartheid South Africa." *Culture, Health and Sexuality* 7 (3): 239–52.

Prunier, Gérard. 2009. *Africa's World War: Congo, the Rwandan Genocide, and the Making of a Continental Catastrophe.* New York: Oxford University Press.

Pype, Katrien. 2007. "Fighting Boys, Strong Men and Gorillas: Notes on the Imagination of Masculinities in Kinshasa." *Africa* 77 (2): 250–71.

——. 2012. *The Making of the Pentecostal Melodrama: Religion, Media, and Gender in Kinshasa.* New York: Berghahn.

Ramirez, Francis, and Christian Rolot. 1985. *Histoire du cinéma colonial au Zaïre, au Rwanda et au Burundi.* Tervuren, Belgium: Musée Royal de l'Afrique Centrale.

Ranger, T. O. 1968. "Connexions between 'Primary Resistance' Movements and Modern Mass Nationalism in East and Central Africa: I." *Journal of African History* 9 (3): 437–53.

——. 1975. *Dance and Society in Eastern Africa, 1890–1970: The Beni Ngoma.* Berkeley: University of California Press.

Raphael, Ray. 1988. *The Men from the Boys: Rites of Passage in Male America.* Lincoln: University of Nebraska Press.

Raymaekers, Paul. 1960. "Matériaux pour une étude sociologique de la jeunesse africaine du milieu extra-coutumier de Léopoldville." *Notes et Documents* 1 (5): 1–20. Institut de Recherches Économiques et Sociaux, Université Lovanium, Leopoldville.

——. 1963. "Pre-delinquency and Juvenile Delinquency in Leopoldville." *Bulletin de l'Institut Inter-Africain du Travail* 10 (3): 329–57.

——. 1993. *Nzala: Autobiographie d'un coopérant en Afrique Centrale.* Rhode-Saint-Genèse, Belgium: J. M. Collet.

———. 2010 [1961]. *Prédélinquance et délinquance juvénile à Léopoldville (1960–1961): Cliché sociologique*. Rhode-Saint-Genèse, Belgium: Paul Raymaekers Foundation.

Reineke, Hank. 2009. *Ramblin' Jack Elliott: The Never-Ending Highway*. Lanham, MD: Scarecrow.

Reynolds, Glenn. 2015. *Colonial Cinema in Africa: Origins, Images, Audiences*. Jefferson, NC: McFarland.

Roach, Joyce Gibson. 1990. *The Cowgirls*. Denton: University of North Texas Press.

Rotundo, E. Anthony. 1993. *American Manhood: Transformations in Masculinity from the Revolution to the Modern Era*. New York: Basic Books.

Rubi, Stéphanie. 2005. *Les Crapuleuses: Délinquance et déviance des filles des quartiers populaires*. Paris: Presses Universitaires de France.

Ryckmans, François. 2010. *Mémoires noires: Les Congolais racontent les Congo belge, 1940–1960*. Brussels: Racine.

Rydell, Robert W., and Rob Kroes. 2005. *Buffalo Bill in Bologna: The Americanization of the World, 1869–1922*. Chicago: University of Chicago Press.

Sadoul, Numa. 1989. *Entretiens avec Hergé, édition définitive*. Paris: Casterman.

Saint-Moulin, Léon de. 1976. "Contribution à l'histoire de Kinshasa." *Zaïre-Afrique* 108–109 (October–November): 461–73 and 527–38.

Schneider, Eric C. 1999. *Vampires, Dragons, and Egyptian Kings: Youth Gangs in Postwar New York*. Princeton, NJ: Princeton University Press.

Schrevel, Michel de. 1970. *Les Forces politiques de la décolonisation congolaise jusqu'à la veille de l'indépendance*. Louvain, Belgium: Symons.

Scott, James. 1990. *Domination and the Arts of Resistance: Hidden Transcripts*. New Haven, CT: Yale University Press.

Seidler, Victor J. 2006. *Young Men and Masculinities: Global Cultures and Intimate Lives*. London: Zed Books.

Sesep, N'sial Bal-Nsien. 1986. "L'Expansion du lingala." *Linguistique et Sciences Humaines* 27 (1): 19–48.

———. 1990. *Langage, normes et répertoire en milieu urbain africain: L'Indoubil*. Quebec City: Centre International de Recherche sur le Bilinguisme.

Shana, Wunga Loomani. 1984. "Le Phénomène ballados à Kinshasa." Master's thesis, Free University of Brussels.

Sharp, Lesley A. 2002. *The Sacrificed Generation: Youth, History, and the Colonized Mind in Madagascar*. Berkeley: University of California Press.

Slade, Ruth. 1960. *The Belgian Congo*. London: Oxford University Press.

Sohier, Jean. 1958. *Essai sur la criminalité dans la Province de Léopoldville: Meurtres et infractions apparentées*. Brussels: Académie Royale des Sciences Coloniales.

Spurr, David. 1993. *The Rhetoric of Empire*. Durham, NC: Duke University Press.

Stanley, Henry Morton. 1879. *A travers le continent mystérieux*. Paris: Hachette.

———. 1885. *The Congo and the Founding of Its Free State: A Story of Work and Exploration*. New York: Harper and Brothers.

Stearns, Jason. 2011. *Dancing in the Glory of Monsters: The Collapse of the Congo and the Great War of Africa*. New York: PublicAffairs.

Stengers, Jean. 2007 [1989]. *Congo, Mythes et réalités*. Brussels: Racine.

Stoler, Ann Laura. 2002. *Carnal Knowledge and Imperial Power: Race and the Intimate in Colonial Rule*. Berkeley: University of California Press.

——, ed. 2013. *Imperial Debris: On Ruins and Ruination*. Durham, NC: Duke University Press.

Tchebwa, Antoine Manda. 2012. *Sur les berges du Congo . . . On danse la rumba: Ambiance d'une ville et sa jumelle: Kinshasa/Brazzaville des années 50–60*. Paris: L'Harmattan.

Tchebwa, Manda. 1996. *Terre de la chanson: La Musique zaïroise hier et aujourd'hui*. Louvain-la-Neuve, Belgium: Duculot.

Thomas, Dominic. 2003. "Fashion Matters: La Sape and Vestimentary Codes in Transnational Contexts and Urban Diasporas." *Modern Languages Notes* 118:947–73.

Tompkins, Jane. 1992. *West of Everything: The Inner Life of Westerns*. New York: Oxford University Press.

Trefon, Theodore, ed. 2004. *Reinventing Order in Congo: How People Respond to State Failure in Kinshasa*. London: Zed Books.

Trouillot, Michel-Rolph. 1995. *Silencing the Past: Power and the Production of History*. Boston: Beacon.

Trumpbour, John. 2002. *Selling Hollywood to the World: U.S. and European Struggles for Mastery of the Global Film Industry, 1920–1950*. Cambridge: Cambridge University Press.

Tshimanga, Charles. 2001. *Jeunesse, formation et société au Congo/Kinshasa, 1890–1960*. Paris: L'Harmattan.

Turner, Frederick Jackson. 1925 [1893]. "The Significance of the Frontier in American History." *Wisconsin Magazine of History* 8 (3): 255–80.

Turner, Victor. 1967. *The Forest of Symbols: Aspects of Ndembu Ritual*. Ithaca, NY: Cornell University Press.

Uchendu, Egodi. 2008. "Introduction: Are African Males Men? Sketching African Masculinities." In *Masculinities in Contemporary Africa*, edited by Egodi Uchendu, 1–17. Dakar, Senegal: CODESRIA.

Vale de Almeida, Manuel. 1996. *The Hegemonic Male: Masculinity in a Portuguese Town*. Providence, RI: Berghahn.

Van Bever, L. 1952. *Le Cinéma pour Africains*. Brussels: G. Van Campenhout.

Vansina, Jan. 1965. *Les Anciens royaumes de la savane*. Leopoldville, Democratic Republic of Congo: Institut de Recherches Économiques et Sociales.

——. 1973. *The Tio Kingdom of the Middle Congo, 1880–1892*. London: Oxford University Press.

——. 1990. *Paths in the Rainforests: Toward a History of Political Tradition in Equatorial Africa*. Madison: University of Wisconsin Press.

Vigarello, Georges. 1998. *Histoire du viol: XVIe–XXe siècle*. Paris: Seuil.

Vindevoghel, Jean. 1938. *La Question métis au Congo belge*. Brussels: Imprimeries Cock.

Waetjen, Thembisa. 2004. *Workers and Warriors: Masculinity and the Struggle for Nation in South Africa*. Urbana: University of Illinois Press.

Weeks, John H. 1909. "Anthropological Notes on the Bangala of the Upper Congo River." *Journal of the Royal Anthropological Institute of Great Britain and Ireland* 39 (January–June): 97–136.

White, Bob W. 2008. *Rumba Rules: The Politics of Dance Music in Mobutu's Zaire*. Durham, NC: Duke University Press.

White, Richard. 1981. "Outlaw Gangs of the Middle Border: American Social Bandits." *Western Historical Quarterly* 12 (4): 387–408.

———. 1994. "Frederick Jackson Turner and Buffalo Bill." In *The Frontier in American History,* edited by James Grossman, 7–66. Berkeley: University of California Press.

Whitehead, Stephen M. 2002. *Men and Masculinities: Key Themes and New Directions.* London: Polity.

Wright, Richard. 1954. *Black Power: A Record of Reactions in a Land of Pathos.* New York: Harper.

Young, Crawford. 1965. *Politics in the Congo: Decolonization and Independence.* Princeton, NJ: Princeton University Press.

Young, Crawford, and Thomas Turner. 1985. *The Rise and Decline of the Zairian State.* Madison: University of Wisconsin Press.

Index

Page numbers in italics refer to figures and tables.

African embodied masculinities, 10–12
Afro-Victorian ideology, 122
Against Our Will (Brownmiller), 116–17
agency, 5, 14, 40, 58–60, 63, 151, 183, 192; transgressions as, 11–12
Air Force, 31st Brigade, 188
Alliance des Forces Démocratiques pour la Libération du Congo (AFDL), 189–90, 198
Ambler, Charles, 67
American outlaws, 2–4, 144. *See also* cowboys, U.S.
American servicemen, 87–88, 219n37
Amharas (Ethiopia), 104
Amin, Samir, 5
amour forcé (forced love), 135, 171
Andrada (Bill), 130, 135–40, *136*, 226nn36–37
animal-man, Hegelian, 18
Apollons, 97–98, *98, 99, 100, 101*, 112
apprenticeship system, 27
Armée Nationale Congolaise (ANC), 173–74
Association des Bakongo (ABAKO), 63, 97
Athénée Officiel Interracial, 159
Aufheben, 6–7, 103, 221n22
Austin, J. L., 11
Austin, Ralph, 226n44
avatars, 3, 14, 179–201; Ballados, 184–86; Bashegue, 191–93; Bindomania, 186–89; Kuluna, 4, 193–97; next generations, 183–86; war generations, 189–97

Balandier, Georges, 5, 181
Baldwin, James, 41
Ballados, 184–86, 187, 188, 230n11
Bambuna youth, 127–28
bana (term for women), 131–32
Bana Murah écurie, 195
"Bana ya US" ("US Air Force"), 184
Bandal quartier, 131
bandeko (relatives in corporate group), 28–29
Bangala youth, 33, 79, 223n35
Bapende Revolt of 1931, 160
Bapende youth, 127–28

Barker, Gary, 94–95
Barreto, Limo, 164
bars, 131–32, 138, 199
Bashegue (street children), 191–93
Bateke (Teke, Tio), 20, 23–24, 32–33
Belgian Congo (1908–1960), 78; anxieties over culture, 9–10; French-occupied, 20; urbanization, 32; war since 1996, 14. *See also* colonial project; Mobutu, Sese Seko
belonging, 27–30, 87, 96
Bentley, W. Holman, 22
Benveniste, Émile, 25
Beti, Mongo, 41–42
Bhabha, Homi, 9
Biaya, Tshikala K., 179, 180, 186
bicycles, 82, 143, 165, 226n40
Biembe, Gaston N'Sengi, 175
"big men," 20–23, 25, 33, 91
bikila (taboos and prohibitions), 103
bikumu (ruleless soccer game), 114, 194, 223n43
Bill John (Bill), 169
Billesses, 135–41
billings (fights), 29–30, 99, 174; head-butts (bilayi), 29, 100, 103, 105, 125; kamô ritual, 98–105; "Mama alobaki" (Mother said) proverb, 71, 115; over names, 110; as performances, 112–13
Bills: as Cold War warriors, 92; decline of, 1–2, 14, 173–78; as emancipatory figures, 160–61; faux, 14, 89, 94, 96, 172, 198; as good Samaritans, 96; January 1959 riots and, 159–60; Kompani Kitunga and, 80–81; legacy of, 6, 179–80; Ngiri-Ngiri commune, 85; Yankees vs., 87–93. *See also* Grands Bills; Yankees
Billy (aka Tshibumdu Madimba; Bill), 164, 174, 175–76
Bindo, Michel, 187–89
Bindomania, 186–89
Bissot, Louis, 105–6, 155, 227n13
Bissot Report, 106, 130–31, 155–58, 227n12
Black Power: A Record of Reactions in a Land of Pathos (Wright), 65–66

blousons noirs, 66–67, 215n49
Boali (Ekolongo woman), 145–46
Bobangi, 19, 25, 26–28
body: pendulum process, 7; performance of, 3, 11, 179; as site of corporeal agency, 14; as site of masculinity, 76, 103–4; as subversive site, 107; women's, sexual violence and, 116–20, 124, 133–34, 142, 145–46
Bofala gang, 193–94
Bois Dur quartier, 156
Bolamba, Antoine-Roger, 81, 210n34, 212n17
Boma, Congo, 33–34
Boma garrison rebellion (1900), 160
Bondroit, André, 54
Booth, William (Bill), 125–30, 142, 225nn21–22
Bopeya, Marcel, 199
Bouchard, Vincent, 64
bourgmestres (burgomasters), 84
Bourke, Joanna, 116, 124, 141
Bourse du Travail Indigène (Labor Exchange for Natives), 39
Boy Scouts, 86, 91, 163–64
Brasseries Limonaderies Malteries (BRALIMA), 37
Brazza, Savorgnan de, 21, 35
Brazzaville, 20, 31, 35, 48, 59, 79, 81, 83, 99, 106, 125, 131, 159, 196, 214n31, 223n35
brevets de civilisation (certificates of civilization), 44–45
Brohée, Abel, 212n14
Brownmiller, Susan, 116–17, 118, 119, 125, 141
Bucholtz, Mary, 94
Buck-Danny (Bill), 112
Buck-John (Bill), 112
Buffalo Bill: contestants for name, 108–9; Leopoldville, influence on, 76–78. See also Cody, William Frederick
Buffalo Bill Memorial Association, 72
Buisseret, Auguste, 164
Bulu/Windy (Bill), 83, 106, 131
Burlan (Burt Lancaster; Bill), 89
Burns, James, 66
buvettes (beer halls), 41, 66

Caïman (Bill), 89
Calder, Jenni, 71, 73, *111*, 120, 226n39
Camp Luka (territory), 112, 174
Capelle, Emmanuel, 59, 79–80
capital cities, 33–35
carte de contrôle (control card), 58
Carte du Mérite Civique, 44, 118, 163

Cassans (Bill), 169
Catholic missionaries, 13, 34, 43, 47–48, 210n3; attempt to redeem youth, 48–51; clash with youths, 78–80; educational programs, 79; exposure to Wild West shows, 77; January 1959 riots and, 159; manhood, remaking of, 51; use of Jesus as foremost Yankee, 93, 172–73. See also Père Buffalo
Censorship Commission, 58–59, 63–64, 213n27, 215n46
Cercle Hippique de Léopoldville (Leopoldville Equestrian Circle), 77
Certeau, Michel de, 160
Chan, Jackie, 194
chantiers de jeunesse (youth camps), 162, 228nn24–25
Chaplin, Charlie, 61
Chege, Vieux (Bill), 88, 103
Chemin de Fer Matadi–Léopoldville (CFML) Railroad, 34, 36
chicote, 42, 189, 208n22
child protection committees, 162–63
Citas (Casamar), 97, 104, 126
cité africaine, 84
cité indigène, 40, 59–60, 84, 106
Cody, William Frederick (Buffalo Bill), 2, 13–14, 18, 216n4; European tours, 77; as man and legend, 72–76; naming and, 108; patriotism, 74–75; "quick-firing expeditions," 86; sense of theatricality, 76; Spanish-American War and, 75; Wild West show, 73–75, 216n9
Cold War, 92, 107, 151, 173
Colin, Michel, 64
colloquialisms, 166
Colonial Cinematographic Office, 55
colonial project: African cultures vilified, 35–36; as battle between civilization and savagery, 76–78; capital cities, 33–35; Congolese as "big child," 12–13, 18, 37, 42–43, 51–53, 161, 209n30, 211nn11–12, 212n21; culture as source of anxiety, 10; emasculation of Congolese man, 5, 12–13, 18, 37, 39–45; guilt banned from, 157–58; infrapolitics, 4–6; January 1959 riots, 151, 154, 158–61; as othering process, 51; planting wedges between villages, 23–24; rape as tool of, 118–19; sexual boundaries, 37–38; social Darwinism, 13, 18, 30; triune essence, 43, 50–51, 159, 162–63, 211n10; weaponry owned by lords and "big men," 22–23
colonial situation, 5, 57
color bar, 38, 164

Commission of Inquiry (1905–1906), 146
communes, 84–85, 120
Compagnie Industrielle et de Transports au Stanley Pool (CITAS), 32, 36
Comstock, William (Billy "Medicine Bill"), 109
Congo Free State (1885–1908), 33, 44, 78
Congo Mikili, 196–97
Congo Reform Movement, 47
Congo River, 17, 34–35
Congo ruffians (écumeurs du Congo), 19
"Congo ya Sika" (new Congo), 51, 53
Congolese army ethos, 6
Congolese National Movement (MNC), 228n17
congolite (Congolitis), 224n4
Congregatio Immaculati Cordis Mariae (CICM), 50, 152, 153
Connell, R. W., 8–9, 10, 11, 145
Convents, Guido, 59, 212n13, 214n36
Coppieters, Renaud, 174
Coquilhat, Camille-Aimé, 20, 22
cordon sanitaire, 40–41, 42, 208nn13–15
Cornil, André, 54–55, 57, 64, 212n16, 213n24, 213n26
Cornwall, Andrea, 93
corporations, 32, 36–39, 50–51, 162–63, 211n10
Corps des Volontaires de la République (CVR), 174, 175–76, 229n47
Cosmos Pilatu (Bill), 174
counterhegemony, 5
courage, 104
Courageous Company of Cowboys, 86, 87
courtship, 135
cowboys, U.S., 73–74. *See also* American outlaws; tropical cowboys
crime, public fears about, 47, 67, 80
Cronos, colonial, 41–42
cultural studies, 11–12
Cummings, E. E., 73
curfew, 42–43, 173, 209n25
Curtin, Philip, 51
Cyprien (Bill), 143

Danger de mort (Bill), 169
Dangwa, Vieux (Grand Bill), 104–5, *110*, 110, 126
Daniel Deronda (Eliot), 5
Dar es Salaam, 86
"Dark Continent" myth, 12–13, 76
Darwinism, social and civilizational, 13, 18, 30
Daubresse, Henri, 59
Davier, Joseph, 81

Daye, Pierre, 31, 35, 37, 207n2
De Boeck, Filip, 14, 107, 160, 180, 182, 183, 191
death, economy of, 182–83
Debord, Guy, 3, 13, 180
Debosard (aka Abosa Philippe), 156
debris, imperial, 145
debt collecting, 26–27
decolonization process, 14
Degazin, Vieux (Grand Bill), 1, 3, 99–101, 116, 124–25, 169, 197–98
Degrelle, Léon, 207n2
Demetriou, Demetrakis, 9
democratic space, 181
Depara, Jean, 97–98, 136–37, 221n8
Depp, Johnny, 63
désoeuvrement, 159, 161–63
DeSoto (Bill), 130, 131–35, *134*, 142, 175–76, 225n29
"detention centers," 174
détournement, 3, 12, 181
détribalisés (detribalized) migrants, 36
Devisch, René, 182–83
discourse, 7
domestication, 49
Durango (Bill), 113
Dying to Be Men (Barker), 95
Dynamique quartier, 154, 164

Ebe (village), 86, 87
Eboma, Sylvain, 104–5, 113, 126
Eboma, Vieux (Bill), 101, 103, 128, 177
éboulement/éboulementaires, 88, 90, 121–25; Andrada, 135–40, *136*; definition, 125; DeSoto, 130, 131–35, *134*; Paurret, 128–31, *129*; vilified in *Esprit de la Jeunesse*, 171–72; William Booth, 125–30
Écumeurs du Texas (Texas Raiders), 159
écuries (stables), 194
education, 113–14, 141; of girls, 122; Grands Bills interest in, 114, 142–43; youths banned from, 79–80, 159
Eliot, George, 5
Elisabethville, 61, 85
emasculation, 5; brevets de civilisation, 44–45; colonial Cronos, 41–42; Congolese man as "big child," 12–13, 18, 37, 42–43; workplace as location of, 39–40, 42
embodiment, 10–12
Emecheta, Buchi, 39–40
empire du silence, 43, 63, 209n28
end of empire (fin d'empire), 82, 96, 152

enfants de rue (street children), 79
Eriksson Baaz, Maria, 122–24
Esprit de la Jeunesse (magazine), 97, 166–73, *167–68*; Indoubill in, 166; muscular Christianity in, 172–73; parables about girls, 169–71; salespersons, *168*, 169. *See also* Jeunesse Ouvrière Chrétienne
ethnicity, 29, 97
Étude qualitative sur la délinquance juvénile à Léopoldville (Bissot Report), 106, 130–31, 155–58
European masculinities, 9–10
évolués, 9–10, 13, 205n7, 209n26, 209n32, 209–10n34, 210n36; Bills snatch girlfriends from, 133; *brevets de civilisation*, 44–45; on Censorship Commission, 63–64; publications, 81; as threat, 45

family networks, 183–84, 231n27
Fanfan le Seigneur (Bill), 174–75
Fanon, Frantz, 5
Fantômas, Vieux (Bill), 88, 99, 169
Far West Dima (gang), 130–31
Farwest (Fewe) territory, 112, 144
Fataki, Michel, 79
female gangs, 135–41, 226n34
feudal structure, 20–21
feuds, 26
filles publiques (public girls), 41, 208n19
film, 13, 47–67, 212n14; African traditional myths in, 57; agency of audience, 57–58; audience behaviors, 58–59, 64–67; censorship, 57–59, 63–64, 213n25; cinematic monikers, 110; colonial, 53–56; genres shown, 60–61; Gold Coast audiences, 65–66; intramural movie theaters, 59; in Johannesburg, 86; Leopold II as mythic figure, 77–78; on- and off-screen schemes for, 56–59; optical visuality privileged, 64; privately owned theaters, 60; public fears about, 47, 67; racist images, 54–55; segregated theaters, 58; subtitles, 55, 57; Tarzan movies, 60, 214n37; theater types, 59–60; translations, 55–56, 57. *See also* Westerns
film clubs (cinéforums), 59, 214n35
film projectors, *60*, 214n33
Force Publique, 39, 42, 59
Forces Armées de la République Démocratique du Congo (FARDC), 6
Forces Armées Zaïroises (FAZ), 6
former Forces Armées Zaïroises (ex-FAZ), 190
Fowler, Gene, 72

Franco (François Luambo Makiadi), 89, 132, *169*, 169, 177–78
Frank Bigan (Bill), 169
French Equatorial Africa, 35

Gamankono (big man), 21
Gangler, Frédéric, 163
gangs: 1920s bands, 78–79; female, 135–41; urban context as impetus, 71–72. *See also* Bills; Yankees
gardening businesses, 40–41, 208n15
gavroches (youths), 79
Geary, Christraud, 55
gender, 9; female gang members, 135–41, 226n34; policing of, 3, 140–41, 145; social construction, 7; women as absolute other, 51
gender identity, 10–11, 17
gender relations, 7, 38–41
gerontocratic system, 190, 191
gift economy, 82, 87, 218n31
Gilbert, Oscar-Paul, 43, 209n28
Gilmore, David D., 104
Glaser, Clive, 135
globalization, 182
Goffman, Erving, 8
Gold Coast, 65–66
Gouvernement Général du Congo Français, 35
Gramsci, Antonio, 5, 8, 9
Grands Bills, 14, 85, 99; avuncular roles, 1, 91, 97, 126–27, 143; billings and, 110; education, view of, 114, 142–43; Père Buffalo, 164
Great Congo Commerce, 19–20, 33
Great Depression, 39
"Guangzhou" goods, 182
guilt, colonial, 157–58
Guiral, Léon, 19, 23
Gusii (Kenya), 116

Habyarimana, Juvénal, 199
Hair, P. E. H., 86
Harms, Robert, 25, 28
head-butts (bilayi), 29, 100, 103, 105, 125
Hegel, G. W. F., 6–7, 221n22
hegemonic masculinity, 8–10
Hergé (Georges Prosper Remi), 31, 207n2, 211n9, 211n12
Herzfeld, Michael, 92
Heston, Charlton, 61, *62*
"hidden transcripts" (Scott), 160
Hobsbawm, Eric, 2, 144, 226n44
Hochschild, Adam, 118

Hollywood cowboy genre. *See* Westerns
homosexuality, 9, 155–57, 227n10
homosociality, 9, 41
honor, 83, 110
Honwana, Alcinda, 107, 183
Hottot, Robert, 23
housing credit (fonds d'avance), 153
Huileries du Congo Belge (HCB), 37
humanity of Africans questioned, 51–53
Hunt, Nancy, 145, 146
hybridity, 9
hypermasculinity, 29, 105, 141–45

identity: gender, 10–11, 17; naming and, 110; violence as productive of, 2, 5, 7
Igbo youths, 86
imagined Christian community, 183
immatriculation (registration) status, 44–45, 49, 118, 209n33
immatriculés, 44–45, 59
incrementalist politics, 45, 158–59
independence, 96–97, 227n16; reluctance to grant, 49–50
Indians, in films and shows, 75, *111*
Indoubill argot, 83, 90–91, 97, 107, 112, 206n10, 218n32; Père Buffalo's use of, 149–50, 164; rejection of, 114; terms for girls, 122
infantilization, 12–13, 18, 37, 42–43, 51–53, 161, 209n30, 211nn11–12, 212n21; in missionary films, 54–55
infrapolitics, 4–6
inkooru (magical charm), 29
Inongo, Sakombi, 128
Institut Supérieur de Commerce (ISC), 194
intelligence of the black man, 51–53
interstitial youth, 4, 13–14, 63, 83, 172, 181
ivory business, 33

Jadotville, 61, 85
January 1959 riots, 151, 154, 158–61, 164, 182
Janus-faced behavior, 3, 4, 14
Jesus, as manly, 93, 172–73
Jeune Cowboy (Yankee), 125
Jeunesse du Mouvement Populaire de la Révolution (JMPR), 176
Jeunesse Ouvrière Chrétienne (JOC), 93, 96, 153, 163–66, 175. See also *Esprit de la Jeunesse*
Jocists, 163–64, 175
Johannesburg, 86
Johnston, Harry Hamilton, 34
Joys of Motherhood, The (Emecheta), 39–40

Kabaidi, Paul-Henri, 89–90, 96, 175, 221n18
Kabila, Joseph, 196
Kabila, Laurent-Désiré, 189–91, 193, 195, 198
Kadogos (child combatants), 189–91, 198
Kalambaye, Paul, 64
kamô (magical protection), 1, 14, 98–105, 128–29, 221n21
Kande, Jean-Jacques, 107, 114–15, 221n16, 222n34
Kandolo, Emmanuel, 91–92
Kanza, Philippe, 64
Kanza, Thomas, 49
Kasa-Vubu, Joseph, 63, 155, 227n8
Kasereka, Rachidi, 190
Kasson, Joy, 75–76
Katz, Jack, 10
Kengo wa Dondo, Léon, 177
Kethulle, Raphaël de la, 13, 48–49, 78–79, 155, 211n5, 217n15
Kimmel, Michael, 8, 17, 74, 161, 172
kinicité (spirit of Kinshasa), 5–6, 33, 72, 177, 230n8
Kin-la-belle (Kinshasa the beautiful), 180
Kin-la-poubelle (Kinshasa the trash bin), 180
Kinois (Kinshasan), 6, 33, 177
Kinshasa, Congo: 1923–1929 boom, 35–37; as capital, 34–35, 96–97; communes, 84–85, 120; cordon sanitaire, 40–41, 42; demographic boom, 37–39; demographic gender imbalance, 39, 120–22, *121*; deportations, 1929–1933, 39; early youth bands, 48–51; European population, 36–39; fragmentation, 83; growth of, 31–32; as Leo I, 36–37; location, 19; male migrants to, 37–38; map, *85*; new townships added, 83–84; nightspots, 42; precolonial village, 32; residential segregation, 37–39; securitarian order, 78; street names, 40. *See also* Leopoldville
Kinshasa, Kwando, 223n36
Kinshasa commune, 84
Kinshasa: Tales of the Invisible City (De Boeck), 180
Kintambo-Assassin, 113
Kintambo-Chicago, 103, 135
Kintambo quartier, 20, 22, 25, 36, 84
kintulu (bodybuilding), 97–98
Kiobe, Antoine Lumenga Neso, 158
kiyankee (Yankeeism), 91, 92
kolúka (to wander), 122, 138, 141, 142
Kompani Kitunga (KK), 80–82, 145, 183–84, 218n25
Kraneurs (oldsters), 186–87

Kriegel, Leonard, 17
Kroes, Rob, 77
Kroutchev (Bill), 164
Kuluna gangs, 2, 4, 14, 145, 193–97, 231n18; female involvement, 195
Kunguniko, Hubert, 137
"Kuwaits" (roadside markets), 186
Kwango District, 127

la débrouille (hustling) culture, 184
La Fontaine, Jean, 80
La Voix de Mangembo (magazine), 169
La Voix du Congolais (magazine), 81
Labrique, Jean, 43, 209n29
Ladawa, Bobi, 199
Laet, Jozef de. *See* Père Buffalo
Lagos, 40
Lamu (Kenya), 85–86
Langliza (Bill), 164, 169
l'argent facile (easy money), 187–88
Lauro, Amandine, 119, 224n4
Le Dernier des fédérés (*The Lone Ranger*), 142–43
Le Pajolec, Sébastien, 66–67
Le Rêve d'un grand roi: Léopoldville capitale du Congo belge (film), 77
Le Triomphe de Buffalo Bill (*Pony Express*), 61, 62
Lefebvre, Henri, 3, 180
Lemba (village), 20, 33
Leo I (Kinshasa), 36–37
Leopold II, 13, 20, 31, 33, 207n3, 210n1; Catholic missionaries and, 47; as mythic figure, 77–78; view of Africans, 46
Leopoldville, Congo, 26, 36; Buffalo Bill's influence on, 76–78; cité indigène, 59; map, *84*; population growth, 1923–1955, *154*; Wild West shows, 77. *See also* Kinshasa
Leopoldville commune, 84
Les Amoureux, 133
Les Cowboys du Farwest, 83, 106–7
Leslie, J. A. K., 86
Lessa, Luzolo Bambi, 196
L'Essor du Congo, 83
Lever Brothers, 37, 211n10
LeVine, Robert, 116
Likaka, Osumaka, 108
Limété commune, 84
liminality, 3, 94–95
Lindisfarne, Nancy, 93
Lingala language, 1, 87, 152, 206n10
lingomba (mangomba, corporate group), 28–29

Lone Ranger, The, 61, 63, 215nn42–43
looting, September 1991, 188, 199
lords, 20–23; clash of, 23–27
Lower-Congo Bakongo, 33
low-intensity urban insurgency, 194
Loya, Abbé Jean, 154
Luluabourg Revolt (1895), 160
Lumumba, Patrice, 45, 96, 173, 214n32; independence speech, 45, 59, 161, 173
L'Utilité de la couverture (film), 54, 212n17

M23 rebels, 5
Madimba juvenile detention and reeducation center, 162
Madoff, Bernie, 187
Madzou, Lamence, 135
magazines, Bill, 167–69
magic, 1, 14, 29, 81; kamô ritual, 98–105
magic wallet, 81
Mahele, General Donat Lieko, 6–7, 189, 198–200
Maistriaux, Robert, 52–53
Makabi (lord), 21
Makasi, Cédric, 194
Makers and Breakers: Children and Youth in Postcolonial Africa (Honwana and De Boeck), 183
Makoko (chief), 21–22, 35
male erotics, 124
Malebo Pool, 17–18; belonging and, 27–30; frontier war in, 32–33; location, 19–20
"Mama alobaki" (Mother said) proverb, 71, 115
manhood: defined, 7–8; ethnicity and, 29; performances of, 18, 92; quest for, 17; rites of, 51; slavery and, 25; workplace as location of attacks on, 39–40, 42
manhood entitlement, 95
Manifest Destiny, 64, 76
Manifeste de Conscience Africaine, 161
manioc cultivation, 19
manliness, 28; Christian, 172–73; defined, 7–8; as performative, 8, 28
Mansfield, Harvey, 8, 104
Marie Cowboy, 144
Marks, Laura, 64
martial arts, 193–94
Masandi, Kita Kyankenge, 48, 51–52
Masculinities (Connell), 8
masculinity, 2; African embodied, 10–12; American crisis of, 74; in colonial milieu, 4; as commodity, 9; criteria, 29; defined, 7–8; hegemonic, 8–10; as ongoing construct, 103; pre-

colonial standards, 30; rape as performance, 124; as relational, 7, 94; subordinate, 9–10
Massacre (Grand Bill), 174–75
Matadi, port of, 34
matanga (wake ceremony), 182
Matété, Congo, 152–53
Mathewson, William C., 108–9
Matongé quartier, 131
Mayidika, Nimy (former Bill), 102, 103
mboka (villages), 27–28
McCarthy, Michael, 76
"Mémoires de Léopoldville" (Muteba Kalombo), 91
men's studies, 8, 11
mermaid (mamba mutu, mami wata), 119–20, 192
Messerschmidt, James, 11
Meta (Billess), *137*, 137, *139*
Middle Passage, 34
Mitchell, Lee Clark, 66
Mivais John (Bad John), 112, 143–44
mixed-race children, 38, 41, 208n17
mobanda (rape victim), 127
Mobarona (aka Mamena Nu Ntima; Bill), 175
Mobutu, Sese Seko, 4, 6, 102, 173; cabinet, 113–14, 128; fall of regime, 198–99; and Père Buffalo, 228n25; rise to power, 14, 151; single-party youth wing, 175–76; Zairianization, 185
modernity, 2–3, 5, 11, 32, 50, 67, 78, 118, 122, 160
Mofewana territory, 112, 143–44
moineaux (street children), 186
mokonzi (chief), 27, 28
Molokai territory, 112, 144
Monganga. *See* Paurret, Vieux
Monheim, Francis, 209n34
moselebende charm, 81
Mosley, Philip, 56–57, 59
Mottawana gang, 112, 174
Moulaert, Georges, 34
Mount Khonzo Ikulu (Mount Leopold), 36
Mouvement Populaire de la Révolution (MPR), 176
Moye group, 27
mpombe e mboka (village elder), 27–28
Mudimbe, V. Y., 49, 50, 53
mungulu (hemp), 30
musicians, 86, 89, 131–32, 176–78; Kuluna and, 195–96
Muteba Kalombo, Jean-François, 90–92, 115
Muyaka, Thérèse (Roy; Billess), 136–39, *139*, 220n4
mwasi-mandefu (bearded women), 10

Mwissa-Camus, Camille, 113–14, 209n25
mythe du héros, 57

naming, 108–13, 194; cinematic monikers, 110; names by quartier, *110, 111;* territories and, 112
Naming Colonialism (Likaka), 108
National Council of Resistance for Democracy, 190
National Sovereign Conference, 187, 230n12
Nchuvila, Chief, 21, 24
ndeko (relative), 28
N'Djoku, Eugène, 81, 82
ndoki (witches), 191–92, 231n15
Ndolo prison, 142, 162
Néron, Vieux (Bill), 85, 88–89, 112, 142, 143–44, 164, *165*, 228n33
next generations, 183–86
"Ngai Rideau ya Ndako" (Franco), 169–71
Ngako (lord), 21
Ngaliema (Teke chief), 20, 21–23, 27; rivalries between villages and, 24–25
Ngaliema commune, 84
Ngandu, André Kisase, 190
nganga nkisi (healers or magicians), 81, 218n26
Ngiri-Ngiri commune, 85, 93, 112, 159; parish, 154
ngobo rape, 127–28
Nigeria, 86
nightspots, 42
Nindaga, Masasu, 190–91
Nixon, Rob, 67
nkira spirit, 23
nkisi (mystical power, power objects), 12, 23, 128, 194
"No elite, no problem" policy, 44
Nsoni, Bomina, 103, 107
ntambi (public woman), 127
Ntamo (Kintamo/Kintambo) village, 20, 33
Numéro ya Kinshasa (Franco), 132
nzele/banzele (girls), 115, 122. *See also* women
nzoloko incisions, 99–100

O'Cangaceiro (film), 164
Oedipal complex, 94
"offender" (délinquant), 4
Office des Cités Africaines (OCA), 152, 153
OK Bar, 131
OK Jazz, 131
Olomide, Koffi, 181
Ombredane, André, 52, 53
oral tradition, 87
Otten, Rik, 59

Parc de Boeck, 131, 226n30
paternalism, 18, 35, 43, 49, 56
Paurret, Vieux (Yankee), 102, 106, 124, 126, 128–31, 129, 142–43, 176, 225n26
pendulum process, 7
Pentecostal teleserials (maboke), 183
Père Alexandre, 169
Père Buffalo (aka Jozef de Laet), 14, 85, 87, 93, 96, 107, 149–78; background, 152; "Château" JOC, 163–66; photographs of, 150, 153. See also Catholic missionaries
performance: billings as, 112–13; of manhood, 18, 92; rape as, 124, 126–27
performative excellence, 92
performativity, 5, 8, 11, 82
Pétillon, Léon, 43
Petit Moloch (aka Abraham Koko Yawadio; Bill), 88, 143–44, 164
pillage, economy of, 186–89, 194
Plissart, Marie-Françoise, 14, 180, 182, 191
poaching, 33
Poison (Jean-Christian Matabul), 90–91, 99, 225n21
popular cultures, 2–3, 6
pornography, 174
Portuguese, 19
Powdermaker, Hortense, 65, 87
precolonial societies, 12, 17–20, 18, 30, 32; rape in, 116–17, 127
primitive mind, theories of, 52
protectors and predators, 3, 14, 87, 98, 116–46
"protest masculinity," 145
Protestant missionaries, 53, 210n2
protests, 151, 154, 158–61
"psychology of the black man," 51–53
Pype, Katrien, 182, 183, 193–94, 230n8

Quartier Saint-Jean (today Lingwala), 1
quartiers, 81–85
quotidian oppression, 4, 5

radio trottoir (pavement radio), 182, 198–99
rags-to-riches stories, 186–89
Ramirez, Francis, 59
Ranger, T. O., 85–86, 160
rape, 90, 220n1; as amour forcé, 135, 171; colonial debris and, 145–46; at "detention centers," 174; dismissed by informants, 95–96; evil, 124; gang rape, 125; interracial, 224n5; martial, 117, 122–24, 174, 225nn15–16; ngobo, 127–28; parental views of, 142; as performance, 124, 126–27; police collusion, 126; as policing of gender boundaries, 117; precolonial practices, 116–17, 127; prévenues (defendants, or accused), 126–27; as property crime, 119; as punishment, 117, 127; as tool of colonial project, 118–19; weapon-of-war narrative, 124. See also sexual violence

Raphael, Ray, 9
Raymaekers, Paul, 80, 157, 162, 227n10
rehabilitation, 163
Renkin (Matongé), 81
residence permits, 161
residential segregation, 37–39
Revolutionary Movement for the Liberation of the Congo, 191
Rexist movement, 207n2
Reynolds, Glenn, 86–87
Rift Valley, 76
rites of passage, 94–95, 104, 105; rape as, 127
Roaring Twenties, 38–39
Roelens, Victor, 45, 50
Roitelet (Kinglet; Bill), 89–90, 96, 169
Roitelets (Kinglets) soccer team, 114
Rolot, Christian, 59
Roosevelt, Franklin Delano, 87
Roosevelt, Theodore, 72, 74–76, 206n10, 217n14
Ross (Bill), 110, 112
Rossignol (aka José-Philippe Lando; Bill), 138
Rossy Ross (Bill), 111, 143, 144
Rouch, Jean, 65
Routiers de la Croix du Sud, 163
Rubbens, Antoine, 38
rural life, 42
Ruwet quartier, 131–32
Rwandan Patriotic Front, 199
Ryckmans, Pierre, 49
Rydell, Robert W., 77

"Saddam Hussein" (aka Kongolo Mobutu), 198, 200
Saint-Jean commune, 84
Saint-Jean quartier, 1, 103
Saint-Moulin, Léon de, 19
Salongo (newspaper), 184
Salvation Army, 126
Samson, Ross (Bill), 164
Samy-Ngunza (Bill), 175
sans peur et sans reproche (fearless and blameless), 7
Santa-Feu gang, 112, 174
Sapeurs, 180, 220n50

sartorial ostentation, 12, 22, 86, 186
schadenfreude, 82
Schneider, Eric, 10
Schwarzenegger, Arnold, 194
Scohy, André, 212n23
Scott, James C., 5, 11, 82, 160
Searle, John, 11
Second Shaba War, 199
Seidler, Victor, 133–34
self-defense ethos, 115
Service de la Population Noire (Black Population Office), 155
Service de l'Information du Congo Belge, 56, 59–60
Sesep, N'sial, 90
sexual awkwardness, 133–35
sexual boundaries, 37–38
sexual excesses, myth of, 51–53
sexual taboos, 103
sexual violence, 14, 116–46; "zero-tolerance" policy, 95. *See also* rape
Shana, Wunga Loomani, 185
"Shanghai City," 174
sharp objects, internal absorption of, 103–4
Shegue (urchin), 2, 191
sheriffs (Bills), 90, 112, 144
Sikitu, le boy au coeur pur (film), 54–55
Simarro Lutumba (Bill), 89
Sita, Alphonse, 63–64
situationist thinkers, 3, 180, 181
Six, Georges, 162
slavery, 25, 28–29, 34
soccer, 114, 158, 223n43
social bandits, 2–4, 144, 185, 226n44
social embodiment, 11
social mobility, 174–75, 184
Société Anonyme des Savonneries Congolaises (SAVCO), 37
Société de Textile Africaine (TEXAF), 37
Société d'Entreprises Commerciales au Congo (SEDEC), 37
Société Nationale des Transports Fluviaux au Congo (SONATRA), 37
sociétés d'élégance, 131
soldiers' narratives, 122–23
Somba Zikida market, 131–32
Sophiatown, 67
sous-évolution, 52–53, 71
South Africa, 106
Spanish-American War, 75
spectacularization of everyday life, 180–83

speech, sexuality and, 133–34
Stade Reine Astrid theater, 64
Stanley, Henry Morton, 19–20, 21, 25, 33; Leopoldville settlement, 36; negotiations with chiefs, 22–23
state violence, 2, 10
status symbols, 22
Stengers, Jean, 44
Stern, Maria, 122–24
Stoler, Ann Laura, 37–38
strategies, 160
street culture, 180–83
street jobs, 185–86
street names, 40
strikes, 42, 160
students, 113–14, 194–95
subalternity, 5
succession, 117
survival economy (la débrouille), 181

tactics, 160 (de Certeau)
Tanganyika African National Union (TANU), 86
Tanzania, 86
Tarzan, Vieux (Bill), 143
Ten-Year Plan (1949–1959), 161
Terminator movies, 194
Tétard, Françoise, 66
Tex Bill (Grand Bill), 124–25, 130
Thatcher, Margaret, 8
Thérèse d'amour (song), 138
Thirty-Year Plan for the Political Emancipation of Belgian Africa, 161
Tintin au Congo (Hergé), 31, 207n2, 211n9, 211n12
Tio (or Teke) traders, 19–22, 26; ivory business, 33
Tompkins, Jane, 66, 73, 74, 215n1, 220n54
Torday, Emil, 127
"toughest of the tough" (*dur des durs*), 90, 97, 112
tournoi (sexual exploitation), 130–31
trade, 19, 25–27, 206n7
transportation networks, 34–35, 36
Trefon, Theodore, 181
trinity, colonial, 43, 50–51, 159, 162–63
tropical cowboys, 2, 7; appearance, 86–88; international violence and, 92; musical, 86; vs. other cowboys, 83–87; in other locales, 85–87. *See also* cowboys, U.S.
Trouillot, Michel-Rolph, 158
Tshibangu, Alexis, 138
Tshimanga, Charles, 163

Tshonga, Jean Omasombo, 188
Turner, Victor, 94
Turnerian frontier thesis, 75
Twain, Mark, 76

unemployment, 78, 105, 155; désoeuvrement and, 161–63; Père Buffalo's programs to combat, 163–64, 175
Union Nationale des Transporteurs Fluviaux (UNATRA), 37
urban revolution, 39
urbanization, 31–33
U.S. Declaration of Independence, 161

Vale de Almeida, Manuel, 157
Van Bever, L., 55–56, 212n19
Van Bilsen, A. J., 161
Van den Heuvel, Alexander, 59
Van Eetvelde, Edmond, 47
van Gennep, Arnold, 95
Van Wing, Father, 38–39
Vansina, Jan, 19, 27
viewing practices, 64
Ville cruelle (Beti), 41–42
Villers, Gauthier de, 188
Vilvoorde, Belgium, 152
violence, 2; "black-on-black" not addressed, 106; grammar of, 28; international, 92, 103, 107; Oedipal complex and, 94; performative, 5, 7; as productive of youth identity, 2, 5, 7; state, 2, 10; vicious circle of, 94–95; weaponized, 14
Vivi, Congo, 33

"Wake Up" (Olomide), 181
Walker, Bruno (Bill), 112–13
Wallerstein, Immanuel, 5
war captives, 25, 29
war generations, 189–97
war in Congo, 14
Wauters, A. J., 34
Wayne, John, 8, 71
weapon-of-war narrative, 124
Webb, Walter Prescott, 120

Wemba, Papa, 200
Wendo, Kolossoy, 104
Wenge Musica, 195
Werrason, 195–96
West, idea of, 2, 76
Westerns, 3, 12–13; B Westerns, 61; "rape scripts," 120; silence and action, 66, 220n54; spaghetti, 164, 218n36; tropicalized, 72; youth banditry linked to, 61–62
White, Richard, 2, 4, 75, 144, 184
Wild West shows, 13, 73–75, 77, 216n9
witchcraft, 191–92
women: abduction stories, 124–25; as absolute other, 51; African urban views of, 122; Bill names, 110, 111; bodies sexualized, 118–19; girlfriends of youth bands, 81, 83; performance of masculinity, 135–40; power objects not owned by, 23; as property, 117, 119; reduced to their bodies, 118–19; shortage of as factor in violence, 121; socialized as rape victims, 116; as sous-évoluées, 71; white, as "colonial virgin," 119–20
women's studies, 11
World War II, 59, 87–88, 218n27
World's Fair, Brussels (1958), 77, 217n13
Wright, Richard, 65–66

Yambeng, Crispin Kabasa, 193–94
Yankees, 7, 219n50; 1950s geneaology of, 72; American servicemen, influence of, 87–88; as "big men," 91; Bills vs., 87–93; discursive practices, 10; legacy of, 200–201. *See also* Bills
Young, Crawford, 48
Yuma (wimp or half-wit), 7, 113–15, 141, 223n39

Zabara (Moloch, Mpindi David), 144
Zaire, 4, 185–88
Zairianization, 185
Zambele Kingo (Bills' anthem), 88–89, 142, 164, 228n33
Zanga, Vieux, 88
zoumbel (marijuana), 105–7, 138, 142, 175, 222n33, 223n35

CH. DIDIER GONDOLA is Professor of History and Chair of the History Department at Indiana University–Purdue University Indianapolis. He is author of *Villes miroirs: Migrations et identités urbaines à Brazzaville et Kinshasa, 1930–1970* (1997); *The History of Congo* (2002); *Africanisme: La Crise d'une illusion* (2007); and co-editor of *Frenchness and the African Diaspora: Identity and Uprising in Contemporary France* (2009).